OFFICERS

LIEUT. COLONEL (SILVER)   MAJOR (GOLD)   CAPTAIN   1ST LIEUTENANT (SILVER)   2ND LIEUTENANT (GOLD)

NON-COMMISSIONED OFFICERS

SERGEANT (4TH GRADE)   TECHNICIAN (4TH GRADE)   CORPORAL (5TH GRADE)   TECHNICIAN (5TH GRADE)   PRIVATE 1ST CLASS (6TH GRADE)

OFFICERS' COLLAR INSIGNIA

ADJUTANT GENERAL'S DEPARTMENT   AIDS TO GENERAL   AIDS TO LIEUT. GENERAL

COAST ARTILLERY CORPS   CORPS OF ENGINEERS   FIELD ARTILLERY   FINANCE DEPARTMENT   OFFICERS NOT MEMBERS OF A BRANCH

MEDICAL CORPS   DENTAL CORPS   VETERINARY CORPS   MEDICAL ADMINISTRATIVE CORPS   U.S. ARMY BAND

MILITARY POLICE   NATIONAL GUARD BUREAU   ORDNANCE DEPARTMENT   QUARTERMASTER CORPS   AIR CORPS AND FLYING CADETS

School of the Citizen Soldier

An Officer of the 6th Division, Fort Leonard Wood, Missouri, Instructing a Class in Geography. This is a typical scene in administration of the Second Army Educational Program.

SCHOOL OF THE CITIZEN SOLDIER

Adapted from the Educational Program
of the Second Army

Lieutenant General Ben Lear, Commanding

EDITOR
Robert A. Griffin, Lieutenant Colonel, General Staff Corps

ASSISTANT EDITOR
Ronald M. Shaw, Lieutenant Colonel, Cavalry

Civilian Defense Edition

D. APPLETON-CENTURY COMPANY
INCORPORATED

New York   London

To

General Douglas MacArthur

and

the American and Filipino soldiers of Bataan

¡ Recuerda Bataan!

The genius of this people is that one must first explain—and then give the order.

VON STEUBEN, *1778*.

One who knows what he fights for and loves what he knows.
CROMWELL'S *definition of the citizen soldier in 1653*.

PREFACE

The material in this volume comprises the educational program prepared for the Second Army at the direction of the Army Commander, Lieutenant General Ben Lear. His decision, several months before the United States was at war, resulted from observation and analysis of a general lack of comprehension among many soldiers—similar to that among much of the civilian population—of the stakes of the war in which the United States had not yet entered and of the necessity for diligent and arduous training in preparation for our probable entry in the war.

It was, moreover, discovered that there were gaps in the education of the youth of the country in world geography and trade and even in the fundamentals of American history and constitutional government. Among some, this lack of understanding resulted in lack of appreciation of the advantages they had enjoyed. This affected the *esprit* of an Army, the training of which was directed to arrive at the goal—"fit to fight."

It was the Army Commander's conviction that an improvement of the intellectual background of the Army personnel would widen the mental and spiritual horizons of many men, would introduce new vistas of understanding for many others, would increase the soldier's interest in current events.

In July, 1941, General Lear ordered studies to be made of this problem and the plan for a course of lectures to be prepared. A balanced schedule was formulated to carry out the Army Commander's objective and was adopted in October, 1941, in the form, arrangement, and proportion indicated in this volume. The assistance of civilian educators of high standing was solicited and generously offered to prepare a substantial number of the lectures. A small board of Second Army officers was named to assemble and prepare the balance of the program. Machinery was put into motion to secure the best available talent for instructors in all units. Maps and charts were prepared at Army Headquarters by the Army Engineers.

Throughout the Second Army, the administration of the pro-

gram began on January 12, 1942. The excellently prepared War
Department Orientation Course, which covered other ground and
did not duplicate the Second Army program, has been given concurrently.

Reports from Second Army Divisions and separate units in the
field have provided conclusive evidence that this course of lectures
has filled a need, has challenged the attention of the personnel, has
stimulated discussion, made for greater interest in and study of
maps, and increased the extent of "outside reading." As a by-
product it has developed new instructor talent that will be useful
in other training activities.

Much ingenuity has been shown by many instructors, some of
whom have been selected from the enlisted strength. Their enterprise in the coloring and improvement of maps and charts and in
methods of presentation have been welcomed. Where polls have
been conducted among enlisted men by their commands, nearly
90 per cent have indicated that they have benefited by this instruction, understand better *what* they are fighting for.

The program has had its difficulties in administration. Uniform
excellence in delivery and much simpler administration would be
effected if the program could be given in motion pictures, with
accompanying lecturer's discourse, animated maps, and other advantages that the combination of this visual-auditory method makes
possible.

The Second Army is especially indebted to Professor Ralph H.
Gabriel of Yale University, author of the lectures on American
History and the Constitution; to Dr. William G. Fletcher, also of
Yale University, for the lectures on Geography and World Trade;
to other civilian educators who contributed advice, counsel and
materials for the program; and to Lieutenant Colonel Robert Allen
Griffin for his initiative and constant efforts in arranging and super-
vising the preparation and execution of the program.

R. B. PATTERSON,
Colonel, A.G.D.,
Adjutant General.

CONTENTS

CONTENTS

CONTENTS

ILLUSTRATIONS AND MAPS

Introduction

CHAPTER I

INTRODUCTION *

Today (January 12, 1942) marks the beginning of the Second Army Educational Program for all personnel of the Second Army, officers, and enlisted men.

The program, which is unlike any previously undertaken on a large scale among the armed forces, needs only the briefest introduction.

Its purpose is not to tell you *why* to fight. You have known why since December 7, 1941. You remember Pearl Harbor. You remember the declarations of war by Germany and Italy that closely followed the attack Japan prepared to launch while Japanese "peace emissaries" were conferring with our statesmen in Washington and the blows that were delivered while "peace" was still being discussed. You know *who* your enemies are and what your mission is.

Nor is the purpose of this program to explain to you why you must devote your keenest attention and efforts to your training, to your self-improvement as soldiers and citizens, to close attention to details, initiative in carrying out orders, a model disciplined behavior at all times. Months ago the Army Commander told you he expected the most of you. "Never the least, always the most," he said.

We don't intend to give you any pep talks. The purpose of this program is to assist you to attain a better and clearer understanding of the world affairs at stake in this world war that traverses all the seas and has placed its heavy hand upon all the continents. It is to make clear to you *not why* you are fighting, but *for what you are fighting*—in material things and in the things of the spirit. It is the Army Commander's hope that this course will assist you in understanding current events and in following them with keener interest, in developing your mental background, in adding to your capacity to think for yourselves, clearly and honestly.

*The following instructions to lecturers accompanied this Introduction: "These introductory remarks or similar remarks by the lecturer will be delivered preceding Lecture No. 1 and will be immediately followed by the first lecture on Geography and World Trade."

3

The material for this program has been in course of preparation for several months. Civilian educators have assisted us in preparing more than half of the lectures. They are authorities of high standing; and they gave us their services and hard work for this purpose out of a spirit of patriotism and because they felt the need for this work. A board of especially selected Army officers of scholastic attainments has prepared the other lectures.

The program is divided into two parts. One comprises the general educational course, which will cover lectures on world geography and trade, American history, and the events that led up to the second World War. This will be a background that will assist you in the understanding of current events.

The other part comprises lectures on the armed forces of the United States, including the Navy and the Marine Corps. You will be instructed in the duties and operations of the Arms and the Services, how staffs operate and what staff duties are, the composition of task forces for their specific objectives, and many other matters that will assist you in a general comprehension of the bigness and complexity of the team of land, sea, and air forces. You will be instructed also in the methods of propaganda and psychological warfare—the methods our enemies have employed against other nations, the methods they have endeavored to use and will continue to try to use against us.

What you will get out of this course of lectures will largely be measured by your attention, your keenness, your desire for self-improvement.

In reference to this program, the Army Commander, Lieutenant General Ben Lear, recently stated: "The uniform should not be an insulation against mental activity that isn't directly military. The soldier who understands what is going on in the world and where it is taking place, who knows in his mind as well as in his heart what America means, what America will continue to mean, and what is his responsibility to preserve and carry on the traditions of the Republic, will be a soldier who will undertake the rest of his military work with greater zeal to perfect himself as a soldier, to make himself fit to fight for the country that is the greatest beacon of hope for the preservation of the institutions of free men in this war that has challenged freedom."

PART I

Geography and World Trade

by

William G. Fletcher

Yale University

CHAPTER II

THE GEOGRAPHIC FOUNDATION OF WORLD TRADE

One of the greatest soldiers of history, Napoleon Bonaparte, once observed that the "policies of all States are to be found in their geography." Whether he made this remark bitterly, when the vast distances, bitter cold, and deep snows of Russia were forcing his once-great army back in retreat or not, is unknown; whatever the circumstances in which Napoleon said it, however, he stated a basic truth. Every man who shares in the service of his country—whether he be an official in Washington making a treaty with some other state, or a naval man plotting the course of his ship, or a soldier in a tank—is immediately confronted with facts of geography. His decision as to what he is going to do will be influenced and often determined by some of these facts: whether the other country produces something which we want and cannot produce ourselves; what are the winds and storm conditions on an ocean; or whether a certain river is too deep to be forded.

In the normal everyday life of the millions of people who make up a nation, geography influences nearly every action they take during a day. The housewife buys bread in New York or Boston made out of wheat grown in South Dakota or in Canada, for the climate and soil of the northeastern United States do not favor wheat cultivation. Every automobile which runs in this country is manufactured from materials which have come, in the raw state, from many different parts of the world. Every telephone is manufactured from over fifty different materials, many of which are not to be found in the United States. Without going further into detail, then, it is easy to see that certain factors of geography obtrude themselves into every aspect of the life both of individuals and of nations.

We are rather concerned here, however, with the meaning of geography for nations. Before raising this question, we must be clear as to what geography really *is*. Many ask whether geography is a valid field of study for college students or adults. The answer is simple; there are many kinds of "geography," and that which most people study in grade school is not the most valuable kind. That kind of geography requires one to memorize the names of the capitals of the countries of the world or the States of the United States, and to know the names of the countries through which some river such as the Danube flows. This is information, but it is not understanding. We are seeking not only to *know* but to *understand*. Why is the United States interested in an obscure, far-away island in the Pacific called New Caledonia? Why must we be concerned about a port in West Africa called Dakar? How do different types of soil and varying weather conditions affect the defense and power of a country? What significance for us lies in the fact that there are vast differences between the climate of the Dutch East Indies and the climate of all the United States? The answer to these questions is largely to be found in a study of *differences of environment*. Geography, as we must study it, is a study of differences in environment and their effect on men's lives.

The briefest of looks around the world will demonstrate easily that differences in environment are all-important. In the last 150 years great changes and improvements have come about in the standards and ways of living of the people of the United States and much of Western Europe; the development of industry, coupled with and to some degree making possible the high intelligence of the majority of the people, have brought us the best living conditions in the whole world. Not so, however, in the Andes Mountains of South America—in Peru or Bolivia, for example—where Indians live at altitudes of 12,000 feet and more and carry on their daily lives in a manner hardly changed from the time approximately 400 years ago when the Spanish conquerors found them. Not so in the deep rain forests and jungles of central Africa or in Tibet on the high Himalayan plateau, or in certain parts of China or India. It is sometimes hard for Americans to realize that on many parts of the earth's surface people are living, working, and thinking— or failing to think—in about the same fashion as their forebears of many centuries ago. A few examples will illustrate the influence of geographic environment in determining these differences. The

Eskimo in northern Canada, Greenland, or Alaska surely has wants which are remarkably different from those of people in more temperate regions; he will be very happy indeed if he can secure a small amount of blubber in a good catch of walrus or whale; if he can obtain a good dog team and if he has the physical ability to build a fairly sturdy igloo for the winter. The Indian living somewhere in the Amazon basin of South America, on the other hand, is not so concerned with shelter—palm leaves which are on every hand will be enough for a house, along with some sturdy poles to keep it high off the ground, safe from snakes and wild animals; his food abounds about him, in such wildly uncontrolled quantity that the plants and trees must constantly be cut down lest they choke off his small clearing in the jungle. The former, then, fights against scarcity and cold; the latter fears only wild life and the excessive heat and humidity which make work difficult and disease common. There exist entire countries whose economy and way of life have been chiefly influenced by geographic location or the nature of the prevailing climate or topography. Norway, for example, a nation which is partly in a temperate climate somewhat similar to the northeastern part of our own country but which extends well within the Arctic Circle, consists chiefly of a barren mountainous terrain which is not suitable for raising many crops; further, it possesses no minerals which could be used in developing industry. As a result, Norwegians have always faced to the sea, and in immediately adjoining waters they have found the basic item of their food supply—fish. Fish and fish products have formed, as well, the most important item exported by Norway to other nations of the world. Before Nazi aggression enslaved the country, hardly any British breakfast table was complete without some kind of fish imported from Norway. Norway also developed one of the greatest merchant marines of the world, and Norwegian ships and sailors could be met in the far corners of the world's seven seas.

In our own country, finally, one may see hundreds of thousands of illustrations of the far-reaching effect of environmental differences; we have a land of many and varied environments, and to no small degree that is the key to our greatness. Because of variation in climate conditions between New England and Florida,

Kansas and Montana, because of differences in soil and the mineral wealth which lies under the soil in the form of iron, coal, and oil, we have been able to build up a national economy which is both agricultural and industrial; there are few, if any, countries which compare with us in this way. The daily occupations and conversations of men and women all over the United States illustrate this influence of varying environment—a man on Cape Cod can tell you everything you need to know about fish and the sea, but probably knows little about life and duties on a farm in Kansas or Iowa; Wall Street talk about "bulls" and "bears" would mean something quite different in the stockyards of Chicago or the mountains of Idaho.

There is one world-embracing, fundamental importance of environmental difference which remains to be mentioned. It is the basis of all of our present discussion. Why is there world trade, exchange of products between the nations of the world? The answer is very simple: because nature has dictated that certain areas and countries of the world can raise certain crops which others cannot raise at all, or not so cheaply; because minerals, which are the basis of industry, are found in abundance in some countries and hardly at all in others. The basic fact about international trade is that it functions on a basis of specialization; countries specialize in the production of those raw materials or manufactured products for which they are best fitted and ship them to other countries which are not so well fitted to produce them and which produce or manufacture other products which are needed by the first country. How does one decide what a country is "best fitted" to produce? There are, of course, several matters to be considered, but certainly first and foremost is the geography of the country. Whether a nation can produce wheat in great quantities, as do the United States, Canada, Argentina, and Australia, will be pretty completely determined by the nature of the soil, by climate which must give a long enough growing season, and by topography. Wheat, to be grown profitably, must be grown in quantity; therefore, one looks for great expanses of plains where the proper soils and climatic conditions are to be found. There are few areas in the world where all of the necessary elements are to be found. Production of other materials, such as coffee, tea, sugar, and wine, is likewise determined by these factors.

Whether a country will manufacture cotton or woolen goods will in part at least be determined by asking whether soils and climate within the country can produce cotton, and whether there is territory suitable for the grazing of sheep. One must have supplies of iron, coal, and many other minerals in order to develop great steel or automobile industries. Other factors, such as the availability of water or electric power, and the availability of labor, must also be present, of course, but the fundamental elements in determining production for export in any nation must be these geographic factors. Thus, Britain exports woolen goods of all kinds, and products of steel, based on her good supplies of coal and iron; Brazil exports coffee, France exported wine and perfume, and so on. World trade consists of the exchange of specialized products between countries.

ELEMENTS OF GEOGRAPHY

Several different geographic elements which are important to any nation have been mentioned in discussing the differences in environment in the world. Let us examine them briefly in somewhat more detail, for they provide a kind of framework upon which one may try to estimate the power of any country. One of the simplest questions which may be asked about any country is, "How big is it?" Size should be some indication of the country's power—if certain other geographic elements are present. For example, if a vast country is broken up by topographic features which are difficult to cross and overcome, it will probably be difficult to unify the country so that the central government can exert power over all of the various sections. Further, topographic barriers within a vast country, such as high mountain ranges or great river basins and jungles, will almost certainly slow up or even make impossible the settlement and the development of regions beyond those barriers. For example, Brazil is one of the largest countries of the world, actually having more square miles of territory than continental United States, but it contains a population of only about 42,000,000 compared with our 130,000,000. Tremendous expanses of territory, such as the Amazon Valley and areas in the

central part of the country, are either totally uninhabited or populated only by savage Indians. These facts are the direct result of the
nature of the terrain and the difficulties of developing transportation facilities. One of the greatest problems of the Soviet Union
in the past twenty years, to give another example, has been that
of developing railroads and highways which would link the central
parts of the country around Moscow and Leningrad with the
Ural Mountains, where a new industrial center has been built up.
In other words, without taking space for more illustrations, size
alone does not necessarily mean that a country will be great and
powerful, for topographic features may impede its development.

On the other hand, great size will usually mean that within the
country different types of climate will be found, and this is a very
favorable factor. The notable development of our own country,
for example, is to a large degree the result of the fact that within it
there is a great range of climate. Much of the country is in the
temperate zone, which is known to be the best climate for the
energy and efficiency of most of the inhabitants. Recall that the
centers of power in the world today—the United States, Western
Europe, and East Asia—are within this zone. Further, differences
of climate within the country will almost inevitably mean that
it will be possible to develop the cultivation and production of
many different crops and raw materials—to develop an economy,
in other words, which will not be wholly dependent on the outside
world for most of the goods consumed by the people.

Another fundamentally important geographic element, besides
size, topography, and climate, to be noted with regard to any
country in the world is its *location*. No matter if your position
were that of President deciding American foreign policy, citizen
or soldier trying to understand that policy and to carry it out, or
enemy plotting an attack, the location of the country is surely
consideration No. 1. Naturally, one must first consider the position of his country with regard to those other nations which may
immediately surround it. For example, surely it can be demonstrated that the foreign policy of Belgium ever since it achieved
independence has been fundamentally motivated by the fact that
she was surrounded by three large powers, Germany, France, and
Britain, the first being always a potential and sometimes an actual

enemy of the latter two. Belgium, then, has always been a weak and only semi-independent buffer between these larger, more powerful states. The United States, on the other hand, is not immediately flanked by any possible enemies on her land borders and has rather been concerned with the safeguarding of her tremendous ocean frontiers.

Mention of this fact requires a final word about the significance of location for any country. The facts of location obviously do not change, but the *meaning* changes with the times. For more than 150 years Americans believed that the two great oceans, the Atlantic and the Pacific, physically separated them from possible attack. But science has changed the meaning of our world location; the airplane has shown us, and has shown the British in terrible fashion, that there are no islands in the twentieth century which are safe behind ocean walls. Finally, location on the oceans of the world shifts in meaning as the interest of great nations in the routes across oceans changes. Across the Atlantic Ocean, in normal times, pass about two-thirds of all the exported products of the world; in wartime this figure becomes doubly important to the United States and Britain. Across the Pacific pass many of the materials which the United States vitally needs. Thus the great countries of the world are interested, as we shall see in detail later, in ocean routes, which are sometimes called "lifelines." To protect those routes, bases are essential *on* the routes; because of new threats to our routes, from the airplane as just mentioned, Iceland and her location in the Atlantic assume wholly new importance in the world of 1942. To the details of the importance of these routes to the United States we shall come in the next chapter.

One final geographic element to be taken into account at all times remains to be mentioned, namely, economic resources, or raw materials. This is a term which embraces a multitude of different articles and products, from wool to wheat to tin to quinine. For the housewife who must have bread and meat for her family, for the manufacturer who must have copper, iron, coal, tin, and chromium for his factory and its products, for the Army which must have all of these and many more for its tools, the all-important question always is: *Which of these materials do we have within our country?* Better to have them within your country

in time of peace, because, in all probability, you can thus get them
cheaply; better to have them in time of war, for the "lifelines" of
which we just spoke may be threatened. If they cannot be found
or produced within one's country, the natural second question is:
How near-by can they be found or produced? Thus, the American in search of tin naturally first looks to Latin America, and
happily in one of our neighbors to the south, Bolivia, his search
is rewarded.

In the next chapters, then, we will raise specific questions for
the United States which arise from these fundamental facts. How
have environmental differences between our country and others
of the world affected the nature of our trade with the rest of the
world? What raw materials do we have and what do we lack?
Where are our lifelines?

CONCLUSION

A final observation about the geography of the world in general must be constantly kept in mind while thinking about these
questions. In the past, differences in the environment *plus* geographic distances kept the world apart, and separated it into many
little units, physically and mentally worlds apart. To the ordinary
American, Java, Malaya, Persia were strange lands, beyond his
knowledge and interest. People in Chile knew little and cared
less about people and rulers in Germany or Japan. Yet today, the
regions sharply different in environment from others become
fewer all the time; Americans can travel to Europe in less time
than it took to go from Boston to New York in 1776; a trip from
San Francisco to Manila takes less time than the journey which
Washington took from Mount Vernon to New York for his first
inauguration in 1789. In time and space relations the world has
become smaller. Science, in its influence on the development of
industry and the resulting high standards of living, has brought
the world into a smaller compass as well. On the American breakfast table are coffee from Brazil or Java, tea from Ceylon; the man
at the table may wear a suit made from Canadian or British wool;
his wife wears silk from Europe or the Far East; the twine which
wrapped the bundles in which food was brought home from the

corner grocery came from the Philippines or Mexico. The American soldier uses weapons the materials for which come from every continent in the world. While becoming smaller, each part of the world has become more dependent on some other part. No nation can live alone.

CHAPTER III

THE MINERAL PROBLEM OF THE UNITED STATES

In the last chapter raw materials were mentioned as one of the most important geographic elements to be considered by the officials and citizens of any country. At the time the United States achieved its independence this was not true in anything like the sense that it is today. Before the so-called Industrial Revolution began late in the eighteenth century, raw materials meant either the crops which farmers raised for their own families or those rare and valuable materials such as gold, silver, spices, and diamonds, found in Asia and the Americas, far distant from the centers of civilization in Europe. The early battles for the world between the empires of Spain, France, and England were largely fought over the question as to which nations would control those remote areas of the globe where great riches could be discovered and exploited.

It was the Industrial Revolution, particularly in its more recent development of great industries such as the manufacture of steel and automobiles, which enormously complicated the problem of raw materials in the world. To any country such as Britain or the United States, a great many kinds of raw materials are absolutely necessary to feed both the machines and the mouths of the working people. One reason for the World War today is the desire on the part of Germany, Japan, and Italy to control raw material resources and thus dominate the trade and the politics of the world. It is very necessary, therefore, for Americans to know about raw materials, both in the world as a whole and for ourselves in particular. We must know what materials we need for our industries and for our national life; we must know what materials we can produce within our borders, and what we cannot; and finally, we must know where we can get those materials which we do not and cannot produce ourselves. In the answer to these questions we shall see the truth of the statement that no nation can live alone.

Every American knows that in many of the materials which are vital to our life nature has been generous. The iron mines of Alabama and Minnesota, the coal mines of Pennsylvania and West Virginia, the oil wells of Texas, the wheat fields of the prairies, and so on through a long list of materials and places are so huge that we need not fear any lack for hundreds if not thousands of years. But there are a considerable number of materials, both minerals and non-minerals, which cannot be found or produced within this country; many of them are extremely important to normal industry and vitally important to war industry. It is essential that we concentrate upon obtaining a knowledge of those materials which we lack. This knowledge will make the interest of the United States in many somewhat remote corners of the earth clear beyond any doubt.

MINERALS WHICH WE LACK

Let us consider first the minerals we must import. First on the list is one which is not very well known, but which nearly everyone has used at one time or another in his life. It is *antimony*. Antimony has a variety of uses; perhaps its most important is in the manufacture of storage-battery plates and bearing materials; further, with other materials, it is extremely useful in hardening bullet and shrapnel cores. We are normally one of the largest users of antimony in the whole world, and as a nation at war we must use even greater quantities than before. Yet we produce within this country a little *less* than 1 per cent of all the production in the world. Where have we obtained antimony in the past, and where can we get it today? One of the greatest producers in the world is China, and from that country we obtained most of our supply until the Japanese attacked her in 1937. The mines are in the western part of the country and are still controlled by the Chinese, but the roads and rivers by which the antimony must be brought out to the sea have been under the military control of the Japanese for several years. As a result, we have not been able to get the mineral from this former source since 1937. We have found an answer in a part of the world which we in the United States realize now is highly important—Latin America. It will become more and more clear as we go on with this discussion how important all of Latin America is to us, just as we are important to them; the wisdom of the "Good Neighbor Policy" begun by President Roosevelt in 1933 is obvious. As in the case of several other raw materials, antimony is to be found in sufficient quantity to take care of all of our needs in two countries of Latin America. New supplies have been opened up in both Mexico and Bolivia which are flowing from the mines to the factories of the United States in ever-increasing amounts. There is more of the mineral in Mexico than in Bolivia, and the former country in the last four years has been our largest supplier. Therefore there need be little worry in this country about antimony; supplies are near at hand, and in countries which are the best of neighbors of the United States.

A more serious situation exists in the next mineral which we must study, namely, *chromium*. Every automobile in the United States has chromium in it, for this metal is necessary for the manufacture of stainless steel, which is of course used for many other purposes as well. Chromium is very widely used in the construction of ships for our Navy, and like antimony it is employed to harden and toughen various kinds of projectiles. We know of no material which can be substituted for it. Very little chromium is produced within this country. What we do produce comes chiefly from California; most of the ore, however, is of poor grade and not the type which both industry and the Army need. In the past we have imported chromium ore chiefly from two regions of the world, areas which are widely separated geographically. One is the southern and central part of Africa, in the Union of South Africa, one of the British Dominions, and the British colony of Rhodesia; the other is the Philippine Islands and the little island called New Caledonia, far in the southwest Pacific. This latter island belongs to France. Cause for rejoicing in this country has been the fact that the governor of the island refused to join the Vichy government in its collaboration with Hitler, and has joined the forces of Free France under General de Gaulle. It is easy to see that here are two of America's lifelines—through the South Atlantic Ocean to South Africa and across the Pacific to New Caledonia. Our stake in keeping those lines open against the attacks now being launched against them is more apparent still when we note that there is only one possible present source of chromium in the Americas, and that is a very small one in Cuba. This island produces normally about 8 per cent of total world production, and output can be somewhat increased. Some chromium has been found in Brazil, but development of production would take some time, since the source is far in the interior of the country. We must concentrate on helping Cuba to develop her supply; we must insist, as we are doing already, that the use of chromium by civilians be cut off; we must try to keep the sea routes open.

The mineral *manganese* is one of the most important to the United States today. It is absolutely necessary in the manufacture of steel, both for hardening and for purifying the metal. The United States is one of the smallest producers of the mineral in the world. In various parts of the country, notably in the Rocky Mountain States and in Arkansas, there are manganese deposits, but they are generally of a low grade which is not the kind demanded for steel manufacture. Domestic production can be and is being expanded, but we must rely on imports from other countries. In the past we, like most of the other nations in the world, have obtained our supplies of manganese from the two most important world producers, India and Soviet Russia. Anyone can see today that the Russians will need all of their own production for steel in the war against the invading German armies; further, it must be noted that the best Russian mines are in territory which the Nazis took, at least temporarily, in the autumn of 1941. Likewise, it is obvious that for a time at least the import of manganese from India will be difficult because of the threats to our Pacific and South Atlantic lifelines. Here is one more reason which makes that lifeline—the trade route across the Pacific—of direct importance to every citizen of the United States. The significance of Latin America is again emphasized with regard to this mineral. Again two "good neighbor" republics are producers of a commodity which America needs. Cuba and Brazil are both endowed with rather large reserves of manganese mines. They were developed especially during the last World War and are ready to serve our demands again. Especially in Brazil much more can be produced than formerly, if better railroad and highway facilities are developed; these facilities our government is aiding the Brazilians to develop today. Thus, help from our Latin American friends, development of our own production, use of large existing stores which steel manufacturers have, and defense of our Pacific lifeline can insure us this mineral, without which the all-important steel cannot be made.

Let us mention together two minerals which are not very well known, which are needed only in small quantities by this country, but which nevertheless are important—*mercury* and *mica*. Mercury is probably most familiar because of its uses by doctors and dentists. It is thus important from the point of view of maintaining a healthy military and civilian population. It is used also in making detonating caps for high explosives. Fortunately, we are the third largest world producer, having good mines in California and in Oregon; yet world production is so small that this does not mean that we have enough for all of our needs. Former sources of supply in Spain and Italy are shut off today, and again we turn to Latin America to find an answer to our problem—in Mexico, Bolivia, Peru, and Venezuela. Their supplies, in each case, are small, but together with our production in this country will supply needs both for the Army, Navy, and Air Force and for the men and women behind the lines.

Mica, in the special form in which industry demands it, is one of the rarest minerals in the world. It is considered essential for radio condensers and for spark-plugs, which we obviously have to be able to make. The greatest world producer of the type of mica which is required for these purposes is India, and she has sent us most of our supplies in the past. We have very little ourselves and again one sees how real and strong the chain of friendship is among the nations of North and South America, for other supplies are being opened to us in Canada, Brazil, and Bolivia. Until the Pacific lifeline once more is safe and open, these countries will help to keep radios and automobiles and trucks going in the United States.

The tin can, tinfoil, and tinplate are all articles which are used directly or indirectly every day by nearly every American; *tin* appears as one of the materials used in the manufacture of bearings, solders, and gun-metal. Yet the United States produces practically no tin itself. Here, then, is one of our most important lacks. Where have we obtained tin in the past? The theater of war in southeast Asia provides the answer—in British Malaya, in the Dutch East Indies—from this area which is now overrun by the Japanese aggressor we have in the past obtained about 85 per cent of all our tin. One other source which is also far overseas, Nigeria—a British colony on the western coast of Africa—also has yielded much tin for our factories and can today give us much more. Finally, it is with this mineral that Latin America makes perhaps her most dramatic contribution to the defense of all the Americas. High in the central part of the South American continent is Bolivia, with no part of her territory touching the sea, hemmed in from the outside world on three sides by some of the most magnificent mountain ranges in the world, shut off from communication on the eastern side by the vast, nearly impenetrable jungles of the Amazon River Basin extending into Brazil. Here on the Bolivian plateau, at an altitude of more than 13,000 feet above sea-level, are some of the best tin mines in the world. In the past, Bolivia has not produced and exported as much tin as those regions of southeast Asia which we have mentioned, because she did not seem to be "best fitted" to produce it. The cost of transporting the tin ore from the mines over the great mountain ranges of the Andes to ports in Peru or Chile is tremendous; then it would have to be shipped to Great Britain to be smelted, and then finally reshipped to the United States. Now, however, we have built and are already using our own smelter in Texas, and the little freight-cars which grind their way slowly over great grades and along the cliffs and mountain walls are loaded with tin for the United States. Despite Nazi efforts to prevent it, we signed a contract with Bolivia in June, 1941, by which for the next three years practically all of the tin produced in that country will come to us. This is President Roosevelt's "Good Neighbor Policy" in action! Mention of this world situation in tin emphasizes especially well the three important facts which we can deduce from this survey: (1) in several different materials we have been heavily dependent on the Far East in the past; our lifeline across the Pacific must be defended and the areas taken by the Land of the Rising Sun must be regained eventually; (2) in several materials sources of supply can be made available in Africa; our lifeline in the South Atlantic must be defended; (3) in most of those materials in which we ourselves are lacking, Latin America can provide us with quantities which will go far towards satisfying our needs; our "good neighbors" are good in the most practical sense of the word; they are extending to us a needed helping hand.

CRITICAL MINERALS

These minerals which have just been discussed are considered by the United States to be "strategic"; that is, the problem of supply is particularly difficult, not only because we need them all badly for one or another type of industrial or war effort, but because we have such small quantities within our own country. There is one final list of a few minerals which are considered to be not "strategic" but "critical"; that is, the problem of obtaining them is not so great because we produce more ourselves. Yet many of them must cross the mountains and plains of other countries en route to the ports and the trade routes of the oceans on the way to the United States, and it is important that we know about them.

The first which may be considered in this group is the rather little-known mineral, *tungsten*. It is one of the most important in the manufacture of munitions, for it must be used, along with others, in the production of high-speed tool steel and in armor-piercing projectiles. Further, every electric light filament contains some tungsten. We are more happily situated with regard to tungsten than the others which have been mentioned, for we are able to produce at least two-thirds and probably more of our needs; these American mines are in California, Utah, and Nevada. Yet, especially today, it is necessary to have other sources of supply available. In the past, as in the case of antimony, as we have already seen, the United States obtained most of her imported tungsten from China and from the British Far Eastern colony of Burma. Again, the four and one-half-year-old war between Japan and China has shut off that source, and now the lifeline to Burma is severed. Once more the hitherto unimportant Latin American country of Bolivia comes to our aid. Besides tin and antimony, Bolivia possesses rich deposits of tungsten; American mining experts are working today high on the Bolivian plateau helping the people of that country to develop those mines. Besides the contracts for tin and antimony which we have signed with the Bolivian government, our diplomats have been successful in obtaining a three-year contract which is also giving us most of her tungsten production. Once more the Nazis failed and our good-neighbor policy succeeded.

Every American is certainly familiar with the metal called *aluminum*—almost every kitchen in the land has at least a few cooking utensils made of it, it is used in all kinds of tools, and it is very essential in the production of airplanes. The characteristics of the metal—lightness, hardness, and strength—are so superior to those of any other that it can be considered practically indispensable. But while all know aluminum, perhaps few realize that the ore from which it is obtained—*bauxite*—is not commonly found. We have always known that the United States possessed some bauxite mines, but in the last few years new mines have been developed which make our problem easier, and our dependence on foreign supplies has been lessened. Bauxite is to be found, in small quantities, in many parts of the world, both in Africa and in Europe; most fortunately for us, however, large and good deposits exist in this hemisphere in the Dutch colony of Surinam (also called Dutch Guiana) and in smaller quantities in British Guiana, which is directly northwest of Surinam. There can be little doubt that the Axis Powers know the value of the bauxite mines of Surinam to the United States, that they see the direct connection between those mines, airplane production in the United States, and their eventual defeat. Sabotage in the form of blowing up some of these mines, which are deep in the jungle, could do much damage to the defense production of the United States. Here, then, in the form of the world geography of raw materials, is the reason for the presence of United States Army forces in Surinam today: to guard those mines against marauders.

Only four more minerals remain to be mentioned. Two may be considered together, if for no other reason than the fact that they are not needed by us in such great quantities as some of those which have been mentioned—*asbestos* and *graphite*. The former is probably not thought of usually as a mineral and of course is not similar to those which we have been discussing. It is a mineral *fiber*. The fact that it is non-inflammable, reacts only slightly to acids, and is largely weatherproof has made it a very necessary item in modern industrial life. It is used especially in roofing and in brake linings in all kinds of motor vehicles. While we as a nation use more asbestos than any other country in the world, we produce only an extremely small percentage of what we consume. Fortunately our ally, Canada, is the world's largest producer and can supply all of our possible needs.

Much the same situation is to be found in the case of graphite, which is, of course, the so-called "black lead" used in pencils; as the softest mineral in the world, it has a tremendous number of important uses in factories—in making crucibles and linings for example. Though some graphite is mined in nearly every country of the world, our own supply is small, but again Canada can produce all and more than we need.

Finally, there must be noted two rare and precious minerals which we rarely actually see but which are very important behind the lines in the factories of the nation which make it possible for the wheels to roll, the ships to sail, and the guns to speak. *Platinum* is one. Used in the dental and jewelry trades, it is even more important in the laboratories of the country, where it is necessary in the making of both nitric and sulphuric acids. A small amount of the total production of the world comes from this country, but far from enough to supply our needs. One of our Pacific outposts, Alaska, possesses some of the largest and richest deposits in the world. We have been developing those mines in the last few years, foreseeing the need; those supplies must be guarded and the route down the coast which the ships loaded with platinum follow will have to be kept open. Colombia is also an important producer.

The last mineral, *vanadium*, is known by few. Like manganese and antimony, it is demanded by the steel industry because it helps to harden and toughen steel. We are the largest world producer of this mineral, but we are also the greatest consumer and need to import some of it every year to fill our tremendous needs. A Latin American nation, Peru, possesses, high in the Andes Mountains, the biggest single deposit of vanadium in the whole world; it is owned by a United States company, and all of its production is coming to us today.

MINERALS

Percentage scale: 0% 10% 20% 30% 40% 50% 60% 70% 80% 90% 100%

Material	Sources (left to right by share)
ANTIMONY	MEXICO · BOLIVIA · CHINA · OTHERS
CHROMIUM	RHODESIA · SO. AFRICA · NEW CALEDONIA · PHILIPPINES · TURKEY · GREECE · INDIA
MANGANESE	U.S.S.R. · GOLD COAST · INDIA · SO. AFRICA · BRAZIL · CUBA · PHILIP. · OTHERS
MERCURY	ITALY · SPAIN · MEXICO · OTHERS
MICA	INDIA · MADAGASCAR · OTHERS · GR. BR. · CANADA · FRANCE
TUNGSTEN	CHINA · AUSTRALIA · OTHERS · MEX · BOLIVIA · JAPAN · ARGENTINA · PERU
TIN	MALAYA · GR. BRITAIN · CHINA · NETH-E. INDIES · OTH-NETH. · BOLIVIA · AUSTRALIA

U.S. production compared to total U.S. imports is shown by black bars above.
No U.S. production of non-minerals below except for wool, U.S. production of which equals 11.4% of imports.

NON-MINERALS

Percentage scale: 0% 10% 20% 30% 40% 50% 60% 70% 80% 90% 100%

Material	Sources (left to right by share)
COCOANUT SHELL CHAR	PHILIPPINES · BR. OCEAN · OTHERS · NETH. E. IND.
ABACA (Manila Hemp)	PHILIPPINES · NETH. E. IND.
QUININE	NETHERLAND E. INDIES · COLOMBIA · ECUADOR · GUAT.
RUBBER	MALAYA · NETHERLAND E. INDIES · CEYLON · FR. INDO-CHINA · NICARAGUA · BRAZIL · OTHERS
SILK	JAPAN · CHINA · ITALY · OTHERS
CORK	PORTUGAL · ALGERIA · SPAIN · MOROCCO · SWITZERLAND · OTHERS
KAPOK	NETHERLAND E. INDIES · ECUADOR · INDIA · PHIL. · OTH. ASIA · DOM. REP.
OPIUM	YUGOSLAVIA · TURKEY · BULGARIA
TANNING MATERIAL (Quebracho)	ARGENTINA · PARAGUAY
CATTLE HIDES (Wet-Salted)	ARGENTINA · CANADA · BRAZIL · OTHERS
WOOL (Apparel-Type)	ARGENTINA · URUGUAY · AUSTRALIA · SO. AFRICA · OTHERS

SOURCES OF U. S. IMPORTS OF STRATEGIC AND CRITICAL RAW MATERIALS AND U. S. PRODUCTION OF THESE MATERIALS
(From a chart prepared for Second Army Educational Program by U. S. Army Engineers)

CONCLUSIONS

What general conclusions can be reached after this survey? In the first place, the warning made at the beginning must be repeated. In most of the minerals and raw materials needed by a country today, the United States is rich and strong. But, in time of crisis, we have to ask ourselves, what do we lack? In terms of minerals here is the picture. Two main facts emerge: the lifeline to East Asia, and the lifeline to West and South Africa are important; as far as the period of emergency is concerned, we had very real and practical interests in southeast Asia; we needed their products and we needed safety on the routes to them. The loss of this area to Japan is serious, a hard blow.

Secondly, the all-important value of Latin America, Canada, and Alaska is easy to see. In time of crisis these countries can do much to tide the United States over. It should also be noted that, since Latin America is a region rich in minerals and, as we shall see, in other raw materials, surely we are not alone in our interest in the area. Nazi Germany, Italy, and Japan are lacking in most of these raw materials which we have been discussing; their wars of conquest are partly fought for the purpose of obtaining them. Latin America is thus a prize which they would like to win. Every measure which powerful America can take must be used to protect this region from their attack.

CHAPTER IV

THE RAW MATERIAL PROBLEM OF THE UNITED STATES

The fact has been noted that the words *raw materials* cover a great variety of articles and commodities; we have considered the situation of the United States with regard to the minerals and have put special emphasis on those minerals which we badly need today and which we must secure from sources outside the United States. The same series of questions arises with regard to another type of raw materials—the type which we may call the *vegetable and animal* raw materials. For a full survey of this type of raw materials in any country, it will be necessary to study its agricultural situation. Can the country produce enough food to provide the necessities for its own people? Does it perhaps produce enough of such products as corn, wheat, beef, eggs, and so on to have some to spare which can be shipped abroad to other nations? Certainly we do not need to state in detail here what every American knows —that the United States is one of the greatest farming countries in the world; that in nearly every one of those articles which are common items in the food supply of our people we not only produce enough for ourselves but have always exported a surplus to other countries, such as Great Britain. Today the United States is not only supplying food enough to keep our people and our armed forces well-fed and healthy, but is able to provide the people of Britain with those kinds of food which the British cannot produce in any quantity on their small island. The ships which cross the Atlantic to England today are carrying, in always-increasing quantity, not only weapons of war in the form of guns, tanks, and airplanes, but weapons in the form of eggs, milk, beef, and wheat which can keep the people of England, who are in the front line in the war, alive and healthy.

Likewise, in regard to many other vegetable raw materials, such as cotton, tobacco, flax, and so on, the soils and climate of the

United States are great providers both for our own people and for those of other lands. These are, of course, facts which are well known to all; they are not those with which we must deal here.

As in the case of the minerals, complete understanding of the position of the United States in the world and knowledge of our interest in many areas of the world are aided by a study of those raw materials which we do not have ourselves. Also, as in the case of minerals, there are several different materials of vegetable or animal origin, vital to one or another phase of industrial or military activity, which we use all of the time, hardly ever think about, and cannot produce ourselves. Especially is this true of certain materials which demand very special conditions of soil and climate for growth. There are a few areas of the United States which fall into the geographical category of "sub-tropical" areas, such as the coast of the Gulf of Mexico and Florida. Yet even here the conditions of temperature and rainfall are not entirely suitable for the cultivation of some materials which are very important. Let us examine certain of these materials and our sources of supply, past and present, in some detail.

One material which up until recently has been of great concern to the United States and which illustrates the problem is a form of charcoal which is obtained from the shells of cocoanuts. If the shells are burned for a certain length of time in a confined space, the charcoal which results is considered to be one of the best fillings for the canisters of gas masks. Of course, supply of this material comes only from those regions of the world which are tropical, and, further, from regions which are surrounded by the sea, for the combination of atmosphere resulting from salt water, tropical temperatures, and rainfall conditions are necessary to produce the trees. The region of the world which produces the largest amount of cocoanut trees is the south Pacific and especially the region of southeast Asia, in the Dutch East Indies group above all. However, our dependence on this area for this somewhat unusual article has been lessened in the last few years by the development of a substitute charcoal made from our own sources; this seems to be satisfactory, and we no longer have to concern ourselves with foreign sources of supply. We mention this article, however, because it is typical of the nature of the problem with which the

United States is faced in terms of several of these raw materials which for the simple reason of absence of favorable geographic conditions we cannot grow ourselves. In the case of all of them we are today faced with the necessity of keeping trade routes across the oceans open and as safe as possible, of developing new sources of supply close at hand if this can be done, or of finding substitutes which will perform the same job for us. In cocoanut-shell charcoal we see an example of the success of our government in solving the problem. It is clear also that the government must have been concerned with these questions for some time.

The next material to be considered, however, is a very different story. *Manila hemp*, as one might guess from the name, is a product which is to be found almost entirely in the Philippine Islands. About 99 per cent of all of this particular kind of hemp is produced there, and in only one province at that. Despite attempts and experiments by many men in many countries, no known satisfactory substitute has been developed for manila hemp in making the rope which is absolutely necessary for use in ship rigging, in cables on oil wells, and in various types of construction work. In the last few years several attempts have been made to develop the cultivation of this fiber in the little countries of El Salvador, Honduras, Guatemala, Nicaragua, and Costa Rica, but they have not been very successful. Though the climatic and soil conditions in this region of Latin America probably are favorable, another difficulty which we will see arising in connection with several of these materials has held up the development. Fibers such as manila hemp must be stripped from the trees of which they are a part; this demands hand labor. It is a slow and laborious process. The fiber can be cultivated profitably only if there is a large number of laborers who will work for very low wages. Even though the laborers' wages in many parts of Central America are rock-bottom as compared with any of our own, they are not as cheap as in parts of southeast Asia, like the Philippines and the Dutch East Indies. Here the native worker, called a "coolie," is perfectly content to work for wages of from five to ten cents a day; this will provide food, clothing, and shelter for him and his family, and he asks no more. In this way, East Asia is "best fitted" both by geography and the nature of the workers, to produce many of these materials.

Quinine is another raw material which is not frequently thought about but which is certainly one of the most important in the world. It is an extract made from the bark of a rare tree called cinchona; its use is entirely medical, as a preventive of and a cure for the dread tropical disease malaria. All kinds of other medicines have been tried in the fight against malaria which the doctors and the governments of the world have been waging for many years, but none has proved so effective as quinine. Before 1942 the production of quinine in the world was controlled almost 100 per cent by a few individuals in the Dutch East Indies. This was a development of fairly recent times. Like some other articles which will be mentioned, quinine at first was produced in Latin America; it was first discovered there. According to the story as we have it today, the wife of one of the Spanish nobles who governed Peru in the period when Latin America was a part of the Spanish Empire was near death from malaria; an old woman, an Indian, who was one of the servants in the palace of the governor, came in bringing a drug which she said would cure the lady. All of the doctors had stated that there was no hope for her life, and so, in desperation, her husband allowed the Indian woman to give her the drug. The sick woman began to recover immediately, and within a few days she was out of danger. The drug, of course, was quinine, which had been used by the Indians in the jungles of South America for an unknown number of years to cure malaria. After some time the tree was transplanted to the Dutch East Indies, where the same climatic conditions were to be found which made it possible for the tree to grow and where the cheap labor which has been mentioned made possible more profitable cultivation than in Latin America where the tree originated. The United States is today making great efforts to develop its cultivation again in Brazil, Peru, and other countries of the Amazon basin. For the health of the Army and the general health of the people of the tropical part of the western hemisphere this is necessary, yet it is probable that production can never be developed in our hemisphere on the large scale of production in Asia. One more reason for the inevitable interest of the United States in both Asia and Latin America is clear.

Shortly after war broke out, newspapers all over the United

States announced that rubber tires would be rationed in this country. Today the lack of tires is a favorite dinner table topic all over the United States. Here is one of our greatest raw material problems. It is estimated that rubber is absolutely essential in the manufacture in this country of twenty-one different articles; it is used in the manufacture of over 100 other articles for which it is not absolutely necessary. On a basis of value, we find that rubber is the single most important article imported into this country; we have the largest rubber-manufacturing industry in the world. Where is rubber produced in the world? The answer is simple— over 97 per cent of all that is produced in the world comes from southeast Asia, from British Malaya and the Dutch East Indies, from the British colony of Burma, and from Indo-China, which are now under the domination of the Japanese. Other areas where rubber can be produced and where very small amounts are raised today are the Philippine Islands, Liberia on the west coast of Africa, Panama, Costa Rica, Mexico, and the Latin American nations through which the Amazon River and its tributaries flow. Like quinine, rubber originated in South America, in the Amazon basin in Brazil. Here the wild rubber tree was discovered over 150 years ago, and for some years the cultivation of the tree flourished. However, some British business men realized that the tree could be grown in the Far East, and they knew as well that the cheap labor of that region would make it possible to carry on the business with great profit. A few seeds were transplanted, and the fate of rubber-growing in Brazil was sealed. Today the whole region of Latin America produces less than 2 per cent of the world's rubber. For the past few years private business companies in this country with the help of the government have been trying to develop rubber again in various parts of Latin America, and especially in Brazil. Hundreds of thousands of trees have been set out, but there are great difficulties to be overcome. In the first place, it must be noted that a rubber tree requires five years from the time that it is planted until it begins to produce. Secondly, in South America there is a plant disease which affects the leaves of the tree and finally kills it off. The experts of the United States government are trying every possible means to stop the spread of the disease but have not been fully successful to date. The fact that labor is not so plentiful and not so cheap will make whatever rubber is produced in Latin America more expensive than that of Asia. Further, it is difficult and expensive to transport the rubber from the deep jungles of interior Brazil or Peru or Bolivia. The product will have to be shifted from one river boat to another and finally reshipped on ocean-going vessels from the port of Pará at the mouth of the Amazon in Brazil.

The United States is forced today by these facts of geography to take steps of several different kinds in the attempt to secure enough rubber to keep the vehicles of the Army and the industries of the nation moving. Every possible region of Latin America which has been mentioned must be developed; "soldiers" in the form of experts on this problem are in all of those regions working on it today. Every possible effort must be made to produce rubber synthetically; every year for the past several years we have produced more in this way, but the amount is still very small as compared with our great demands. In the past three years we have bought unusually large amounts of rubber and put the surplus into stock-piles upon which we can now draw. Finally, no rubber can be thrown away and wasted. From old tires and other material it is possible to reclaim several hundreds of thousands of tons a year. Even with success of all of these measures, the strictest kind of civilian rationing and sacrifice is inevitable.

Only a few more materials remain to be mentioned. Some such as *silk* are for obvious reasons not available to the United States today. Silk is raised only in Japan, some parts of China which are occupied by Japan, Italy, and unoccupied France. The military uses of silk are being largely supplied today by substitutes, and there are still large stock-piles available in this country. This is one of the materials which will call for sacrifices on the part of the women of America.

One final material in our long list is not at all well known and is not basically important but should be mentioned for the sake of completeness. *Kapok* is a fiber which is derived from a type of tropical tree grown only in southeast Asia. Nations are interested in kapok because it is the best material to use in the manufacture of life-preservers. We have a huge supply of kapok on hand in this country, and a large reserve of life-preservers as well; thus there is little reason for concern over the problem of obtaining more at this time.

Let us raise some general questions regarding the world importance of these raw materials which we have discussed in detail and the thousands of others which we have not discussed because the United States possesses them in abundance. In the first place the simple listing of these materials brings to light the great importance of the region of southeast Asia to many of the nations of the world. Here is one of the great reservoirs of riches in terms of raw materials of the whole world. Besides the tin, rubber, quinine, and other materials which have been mentioned, the Dutch East Indies possess very rich oil wells, great reserves of gold which have hardly been tapped, and many other valuable minerals as well. Japan's objective, both in foreign policy and in her attack on the United States, Britain, and the Netherlands, is to obtain the military and political domination of this entire region. The area is the key to the power of the East. Japanese domination of this region is part of a huge plan based on economic and political geography which the Germans have formulated under which the whole world will be divided into great regions all under the domination of one big "master" country. To the details of that plan we will come later.

Further, Latin America emerges from a survey such as the one we have just made as a region which is of great importance, both to the United States today as a provider of materials which we badly need, and in the future as an area which will remain one of the great raw material-producing regions of the world. In past times Latin America's raw materials were mostly left for development in the future. After the original development of some kinds of mineral wealth by the Spaniards, who looked on Latin America simply as a treasure-house from which they could obtain silver and gold in almost unlimited quantities, much of the wealth of the area was not developed. The rubber of Brazil and the tin of Bolivia, for example, were not exploited to any great degree until recently, chiefly because transportation and labor difficulties made these products more expensive than similar products from other regions. Certainly in the present and the future these supplies and the many others which have been mentioned are going to be increased in output to a greater degree than ever before. Both during and after the war, then, the region of Latin America will acquire new importance in the world in general. Naturally, not only the United States will have an interest in the area; throughout the war we will have to be always on guard against attempts to sabotage the mines or to break down the few railroads which bring the products to the sea. Only recently it was reported that Germans had been trying to wreck the railroads which go from Bolivia over the mountains to Chile. We will have to be on guard constantly, on land, on sea, and in the air, against any attack on any part of the hemisphere. These countries must be defended with as much determination as would be used in defending the soil of the United States.

This problem of raw materials is basic and fundamental today, for much of the reasoning behind the Nazi, Fascist, and Japanese aggression against the world can be traced to the nature of the geographic distribution of raw materials. Mussolini has screamed for years that Italy is a "have-not nation"—since she does not have raw materials within her own boundaries, she must obtain them by force, he has stated. Hitler has looked with lust at southeastern Europe, the Ukraine area of Russia, and the far-flung areas of Africa and Latin America. The Japanese have never concealed their desire to take control of the Indies and southeast Asia. Why is it necessary that a nation *control* supplies of raw materials? Cannot Germans, Japanese, and Italians buy raw materials in the markets of the world and sell their own manufactured products in return? Certainly, if they were not preparing an economy based upon the intention to wage war and to control these various regions of the world! In order to be sure of the supplies, in order to be able to fight future wars, they make war today. Frequently, furthermore, these so-called "have-not" countries have stated that they desire only colonies, that if they possess colonies their raw-materials problem will be solved. A simple examination of geographic fact proves the falseness of this claim, and proves that if they are determined to possess the sources of raw materials many independent countries must be conquered. For of all the raw materials produced in the world, colonies yield only 3 per cent! The independent countries of Brazil, Bolivia, Russia, Turkey, Iran, and

Iraq and many others are greater producers of raw materials than all of the colonies in the world put together. It is certain that the aggressor nations know these facts and that independent countries are on their timetable of conquest.

Raw materials, then, are a key to victory in war, and a key also to the kind of world which we will have in the future. Loss of the areas of raw-material production such as southeast Asia and Latin America to the countries which have attacked our kind of world would mean that another kind of world, in the Hitler manner, would be imposed. Further, we fight our war on many fronts, and not only in the sense of actual combat. Men growing rubber in Brazil, extracting quinine from the cinchona trees in Ecuador, or mining tin in Bolivia and antimony in Mexico are fighting the war. To reach our people and our factories, however, these materials must pass over many leagues of water, on the lifelines of our Western world. To a consideration of the problem of those lines and routes we shall next turn.

CHAPTER V

THE STRATEGIC GEOGRAPHY OF "LIFELINES"

The last pages have been chiefly concerned with phenomena and problems which fall under the heading of what is generally called "economic geography"—the raw materials, minerals, and foodstuffs which are the life-blood of our people, our factories, and our war effort. The fact has been especially emphasized that the United States, though more favored by nature than any other single country in the world, is nevertheless dependent on many different foreign areas and countries for many very important supplies. Both in time of war and in time of peace, then, the areas which produce those materials are of interest to this country. It is highly desirable in peacetime that domination of those regions should not rest with those states such as Germany and Japan which would control the products of those areas, using them as instruments to bring pressure upon the economies of other countries. In time of war, every effort must be bent to keep these vital raw-material producing regions out of the hands of the enemy, or to retake them expeditiously if they have already fallen to him.

Mention of these problems suggests the many-sided nature of war today. The phenomenon of "total war" which first burst upon the consciousness of the world in the spring of 1940, when the Nazis attacked Denmark, Norway, the Low Countries, and France in turn, is both complicated and far-reaching. It embraces all kinds of activity within the State which is forced to wage it. Total war is much more than the roar and smoke of battle, the movement of ships and planes and men. It is fought equally as hard behind the lines, and indeed, if it is to be waged successfully, is fought, long before the actual combat begins, by the men who plan its tactics and grand strategy.

In a classification of the categories of total war it is possible, by a process of some oversimplification, to enumerate four types of "battles." In the first place, there is the Battle of Production, fought in the factories and mines of the nation and of its allies and friends, in the wheat-fields, in the office which allocates priorities. There is the Battle of Morale, fought in the minds and hearts of every individual within the nation, fought by its leaders who tell the people the truth rather than propaganda, fought by those who seek to reach the people in other countries with the truth by means of radio, to overcome the lies and distorted statements of their leaders. There is the Battle of Transportation—and finally, only after all of these forms of total war are being waged successfully, can the actual "Battle of Combat" in all of its myriad forms be fought.

In the light of the problems which have been discussed in preceding chapters, it should be easily seen that the third category, the Battle of Transportation, is fundamental. Certainly if you cannot obtain the supplies for your factories, if you cannot move men and supplies to them, the chances of victory are slim indeed. Fairly obviously, there are two major phases in this battle which girdles the world. We must bring the raw materials which have been discussed to the ports of continental United States. When we have brought them to our shores and manufactured them into finished products, they must be transported in the form of munitions, planes, and so on to the equally far-distant areas where the battles of combat rage. Further, the raw materials, finished products—and men—must pass over certain routes on the oceans, routes which are the lifelines of the democratic world.

This term *lifeline* is not new. Students of history and of international affairs have been familiar with it for years as applied to the Mediterranean Sea and to British policy and power within that region. But a lifeline for the United States is new indeed, at least in terms of its present exigency. True, for some years the significance of the Panama Canal has been recognized, and proper steps to insure its defense have been taken. But we are only beginning to perceive that there are several others, in the wastes of the South Pacific and South Atlantic, in the dangerous North Atlantic and the White Sea, and in the tumble of mountains which forms the border between Russia and Iran.

OUR LIFELINES

The maps at pages 102 and 336 demonstrate the problem of the lifelines of supply, or the "logistical problem" of the United

States as Navy and Army men would term it. Study of these maps
will give the reader a hint of the nature and the scope of our problem. Briefly, where are these vital routes? They number five.

(1) In the Pacific, a line may be drawn from Pearl Harbor
southwest to Samoa and west and south again past the protective
cover afforded by the ports and bases on the eastern and southern
coasts of Australia. Before the Japanese captured Amboina, the
Dutch naval base, and threatened to neutralize the value of the
northern Australian base of Port Darwin, the route might have
been shortened by passage through the Dutch islands. Until Allied
air supremacy is established in this region, and probably until the
time has come when the United Nations can take the offensive to
regain the critical points along this lifeline, this route must be considered closed. Assuming that Australia can be held by the Allies,
the destination of the supply ships will be India. Obviously this is
a long route, and one beset with dangers on every hand. (2) The
North Atlantic is more familiar to us, north and east from Halifax
past our leased base in Newfoundland, Iceland, northern Ireland,
and so to Great Britain and even on around the North Cape,
through the White Sea to the Russian ports of Archangel and Mur-
mansk. (3) In the South Atlantic, a triple-purpose route may be
noted. As the war progresses, it is bound to increase in significance.
From eastern ports it lies past the United States-leased base in Bermuda, over the Atlantic, past the present neutral islands such as the
Azores, Cape Verde, and the Canaries, owned by Portugal and Spain
respectively, down the west coast of Africa, past the French port of
Dakar, which can either be a danger point or a valuable point of
protection, and around the Cape of Good Hope at the southern
tip of Africa. Beyond that point, the merchantmen and warships
divide along three separate routes. If the supplies are destined for
the British, the line, of course, goes through the Red Sea and Suez
Canal to Egypt; if they are marked for Russia, to the Persian Gulf
and the port of Basra in Iran; if they are supplies and reinforcements for our Allies in the East, then across the Indian Ocean to
India. (4) The fourth route is on land, from the port of Basra
mentioned above, along the overloaded railroads and poor highways of Iran and over the treacherous heights of the Caucasus
Mountains to Russia. American technicians and engineers are work-

ing there today; this route may well become the "Burma Road" of the Middle East. (5) Finally, there is a route within our own hemisphere up and down the coasts of South America bringing vital mineral supplies from the mines of Peru, Chile, Bolivia, and Brazil to us and transporting vital manufactured products to the Latin American countries. The west coast route is guarded in part by our strong defenses within the so-called "American Mediterranean," the Caribbean Sea, and by potential bases such as the Galápagos Islands off the coast of Ecuador, owned by that country. The route on the east coast to Brazil and Argentina is more open; the desirability of Brazilian-North American coöperation in the development of base facilities in certain Brazilian ports is easy to see.

This is the simple basic picture of the lifelines. Certain considerations about them which are frequently overlooked must be especially noted. One must be clear as to the nature of the "lines." In the first place, the direct red line which can be, and usually is, drawn on the maps between the places which have been mentioned is somewhat deceptive, for after all the so-called "line" is wide. Many leagues of sea and many miles of adjacent coastline are equally parts of the "line," which more accurately might be termed "zone." Even in the days of sailing vessels, any single point within a fairly wide radius of the course plotted by the navigators might be a lurking place from which enemy raiding vessels might harass or try to destroy the convoys of the other power. Air power, which is proving to be such a vital and potent weapon in the present global war, has influenced and even changed the nature of lifelines, as it has affected so many other aspects of conflict. Surely the width of the zone, on the sea and on land, from within which the merchant vessels may be attacked has been widened to previously undreamed-of degrees. The smallest coral atoll, if the harbor can be developed to accommodate seaplanes or if runways may be constructed on the sand, may become a base of operations for aërial marauders. The Japanese-mandated islands are testimony to this fact. Planes operating from aircraft carriers are a constant danger on the ocean highways. Patrol planes with ranges of several hundreds of miles, and bombers which can fly with heavy loads for thousands, may be based on mainlands which formerly were no great threat to the ocean routes of the world. Thus, hardly a sea mile on the route through the South Atlantic and around Africa will be free from the danger of aërial attack by planes based at numerous possible points along the West African coast. The problem, then, has been immensely complicated. Not only the blows of surface raiders but quick, unexpected, devastating attack from the air must always be a possibility.

How can the far-flung lines or zones be protected? Obviously, if an aircraft carrier laden with fighters could be assigned to every convoy, the problem would be far less acute; such an eventuality is, to say the least, highly remote. Rather must protection be based upon skillful development and use of those points, on sea and land within and near the zones, which are or could be at the disposal of the United Nations. Before noting certain of the key points in this strategy of sea routes, however, it is well to consider as a whole the general areas within which the zones fall.

THE PACIFIC AREA

Within any of these regions, the objectives of the United States are two: (1) to protect and defend any of the territory which actually belongs to us or to our allies which may be of strategic value; (2) to defend and to keep open the trade routes which have been noted. Stating the problem broadly, there are at least three general regions within the Pacific area as a whole which are vitally important to the United States. The *immediate* significance of the different regions will shift as the war develops; all of them are of immediate or ultimate importance for one or both of the general American objectives.

The first area, that of the West and Southwest Pacific, was of preliminary importance in the war and may be of ultimate and decisive importance. In the first days and weeks of hostilities, interest of the American people centered about the possibilities of successful defense of the Philippine Islands, held by this country since 1898, a possession which we were committed to defend. It may be presumed that the interest of the officers of the armed forces of the United States, who had long recognized that it would be difficult if not impossible to hold the Philippines against great odds—given our failure, up to December, 1941, to fortify or garrison them sufficiently—revolved about the possibility of holding as much as possible of the Philippines and the city and port of Hong Kong for as long as possible. The possession of those two points athwart the Japanese route of attack on southeast Asia would have constituted a threat against Japanese "lifelines" which could not be minimized.

Obviously, this preliminary significance of the West Pacific area to the United Nations was nullified by the rapid conquest of Hong Kong and the neutralization of the Philippines as a base for operations against the fleet of Japan. Yet, in the last phase of the war, when the power of the United States has been mobilized, trained, and made available for combat, this area must again be the decisive one. The Philippines must be retaken, or neutralized as a Japanese base, both for the sake of a national commitment and because of strategic demands. Whether the offensive be carried to Japan through the medium of a war of attrition, shutting off the vital lines of communication between the Japanese mainland and her armies, naval bases, and sources of raw materials in Malaya and the Indies, or whether the war will be carried by various means to the archipelago of Japan itself, this region will be one in which American and Allied planes, ships, and men must see action. Notation of this widely held belief, however, suggests that the conclusion may have been stated before the argument. How, after all, are the forces of the United States to reach this area of the ultimate decision? Are not other regions of the Pacific of more basic importance in the immediate problem of the prosecution of the war?

Answers to these questions will be found in a consideration of a second Pacific region which for purposes of simplification may be called the *Central Pacific*, a term which includes all of the ocean area and islands between the Philippines and a line drawn due south from Alaska to the Hawaiian Islands. This is the vast expanse over which the trade routes and the military supply routes pass; thus today it possesses double and immediate significance. The fact must be frankly faced that our outposts of the Philippines are far distant (over 6,000 miles) from Hawaii and farther from bases of supplies and troops from the United States. What are the routes which might be used? The first alternative would take the form of following what might be called a "Great Circle" route from Seattle, Washington, north and west along the coast of Alaska and the Aleutian Islands, American territory which stretches out in a long string of small islands to within a short distance of the continent of Asia. But then between the oncoming Americans on this route and the destination, the Philippines, lie the island of Sakhalin, the southern half of which is owned by Japan, the mainland of Japan itself, and the island of Formosa, where Japan has a large naval base. The route invites attack from the enemy. Further, both aërial and naval operations, and especially the former, are difficult along many parts of this route. Ice, snow, cyclonic storms, and especially fog harass shipping and endanger the movements of planes during much of the year. There are few less propitious spots on the globe for the prosecution of war.

The second and most direct route, though it is a long one, lies directly across the Pacific westward from Hawaii. Here is our problem: to make this route safe against the many pinpricks which the Japanese are in a position to be able to make against it. We must first hold or retake our own bases, the islands of Midway, Wake, and Guam, for those are our only positions of support on the route. But we are faced with a more difficult problem. Throughout the western part of that area lies a great gridwork of small islands, some of them being little more than sandy strips of land a few miles long and hardly twenty feet above sea-level. These island groups, called the Marianas or Ladrones, the Carolines, and the Pelew, were until 1919 owned by Germany. After the last war they were taken away from her and given to the League of Nations. Like many other former German colonies, these islands were given as "mandates" to another country—unfortunately Japan. By solemn agreement among all the members of the League, Japan promised not to fortify or develop these islands in any military way. Japanese operations against Pearl Harbor, Wake, Midway, and Guam, as well as American naval operations against the islands have demonstrated how well the promises and covenants were kept. These islands, or at least many of them, are nesting places for Jap submarines, torpedo boats, and planes. They will have to be cleaned out before this vital route is finally safe.

The third and longest route is, of course, through the South Pacific from Hawaii to Australia and eventually beyond. A brief glance at the map will show the chief reason for the fact that this is not desirable: the simple geographic fact of distance makes it impractical to use unless absolutely necessary. The Japanese would surely find it very difficult to operate in this area, for they have no bases nearby; but our own bases where ships can find fuel and food and repair of damage are also few and far between. We own a base at Samoa and possess the very small islands of Baker, Johnston, Howland, Canton, and Enderbury, and others too small and numerous to mention; yet Samoa is not well developed and the others are too small to offer much possibility for development as important naval bases.

In other words, the *middle part of the central Pacific*, the route westward from Pearl Harbor, where our bases are now under attack and where we will find the Japanese bases from which first treacherous attacks were launched—*that* is the most important area of the Pacific for our geographic interests.

The third section of the Pacific area to which we must give some attention is the *East Pacific*, the region between a line from Hawaii to Alaska and thence eastward to the mainland of the North and South American continents and especially to the Panama Canal. The question of the significance of the Canal, however, is linked to both Pacific and Atlantic areas, and will be considered below.

BASES

So far we have mentioned the word *bases* several times. Not only are many of the places mentioned in the Pacific important chiefly as bases which guard more valuable possessions or routes, but in Latin America and in the Atlantic that is equally true. Here is a word which seems simple yet demands some explanation. What is a base and what geographic factors are important in selecting its location? Used in the broadest sense, of course, it means any kind of military, naval, or air station. A base may be a fueling station, dockyard, airfield, fortified harbor, or anchorage. There are few base sites in the world which offer ideal conditions; even such fine bases as Gibraltar, Pearl Harbor, and Singapore have some imperfections, as events have demonstrated. In general, officials of a country must ask questions something like the following in selecting or deciding to develop a base, whether it be on the mainland or an island somewhere at sea. (1) Does it strengthen the defense of the United States or some vital interest of the United States; or must the United States contribute to its defense without any equal gain? (2) Is it situated in the right place to guard some vital area? (3) Can it be easily supplied and maintained? Is it, or can it be, linked with the United States by a string of connecting bases? (4) Are water depths in the harbor, features of the terrain, and weather conditions satisfactory? Apply these questions to some of the places and regions which have been noted, and some of the problems of the armies and navies of all the warring countries in the Pacific will be clear.

THE PANAMA CANAL AND THE CARIBBEAN AREA

Any discussion of the eastern part of the Pacific or the western part of the Atlantic in regard to American strategic geography must center about the Panama Canal. The "Big Ditch," forty-six miles long and in the center of a Zone of United States territory ten miles wide, has often been called the key to the defense of the United States. This is an exaggeration only in the sense that it seems to imply that the United States could not defend itself without the Canal. There is no truth in such a statement, but without the Canal how much more difficult defense would be! The fleet could then move from Pacific to Atlantic or vice versa only around Cape Horn, or through the Strait of Magellan at the southern tip of South America, a movement which would probably take about forty days in contrast to the time of approximately ten days necessary for a trip by way of the Canal. Further, the Canal is important as a route not only for movement by the Army and Navy of the United States but for many of those vital raw materials which have been discussed. The copper of Peru and Chile, the tin, tungsten, and antimony of Bolivia are within eighteen days of New York by way of the Canal; it would be forty days and more if the products from the west coast were forced around the Cape or through the Strait. The longer the movement, the more vulnerable this traffic would be for submarine attack.

Here, then, is a key point. How does geography protect the Canal? The answer must be given in several points, each of which relates immediately to the location of the Canal. In the first place, we are fortunate in the fact that no strong and possibly hostile country surrounds or is near the Canal. Panama is friendly, and if there should ever be anti-American groups in Panama, American police and soldiers are always on duty in the Canal Zone. Costa Rica, to the north of the Canal, is one of the most friendly of the "good neighbors" and was the first Latin American nation to declare war on Japan. Colombia, nearest country in South America, has long ago forgotten past difficulties with the United States and coöperates fully with us today. One danger to be guarded against, of course, is the possibility that enemies of the United States might establish air fields in a country such as Colombia from which attempts might be made to bomb the Canal. For over a year now no German or Italian planes have been allowed to fly in Colombia; their former fields and their planes have been taken from them, the former pilots sent home or put in jail. Constantly the far corners of the country are being patrolled to prevent any secret fields from being established. This, coupled with the intensive and very far-reaching work which the Army has done in Panama, especially in the last three years, permits us to assume that the land surroundings of the Canal, while demanding watching, are safe.

What of the adjoining seas? Some one has rightly said recently that unless the seas are protected by bases and ships and men they are avenues of attack rather than barriers against an enemy. Considering the situation with regard to the Canal, we find a very different situation on the Pacific and Atlantic sides. On the Pacific side there is little but distance by way of protection—distance from the Asiatic enemy. Pearl Harbor is the nearest large base, about 5,000 miles away. Destroyers and planes of course operate constantly out of Balboa at the Pacific end of the Canal. But we need more outlying bases. At least two are close at hand and only await the political arrangements which will grant them to us and the following development. To the southwest of the Canal, about 800 miles away, lie the Galápagos Islands, barren, windswept, inhabited by only a few men and millions of turtles and sea gulls. While harbors there would not be suitable for large vessels, they could accommodate our smaller patrol boats and seaplanes which could sweep the seas by day and night on a large radius in search of enemy prowlers. Owned by the small country of Ecuador, there is no reason why they should not be put at our disposal, rented or purchased by this country. To the northwest of the Canal, not as far away as the Galápagos, is another small and little-known group, the Cocos Islands, owned by Costa Rica. As mentioned before, this little republic is one of our best friends and has already put the islands at our disposal when and if we need them. If these two groups of islands are developed into patrol bases, that fact, plus the tremendous distance from Japanese bases to the Canal area, plus the coöperation of the adjoining countries, plus our great defense preparations around the Canal itself should make it impossible to attack with any hope of success.

In the region to the east of the Canal, geography has given us a great opportunity to protect the Canal, in the form of the ring of islands which surrounds the Caribbean Sea, sometimes called the "American Mediterranean." The passages through which enemy ships could enter the Caribbean are few in number—if there are bases on those islands, which are in the perfect position to protect this vital American interest, the sea should be a "Mediterranean" in the sense that we would have *relative* control over all means of entrance or exit. *We do.* Our strategic geography of the sea is dominated by three main bases, one at Key West on the tip of the mainland in Florida, one leased from Cuba at Guantánamo, and one at San Juan in our own territory of Puerto Rico. Since September, 1940, by one of the wisest international agreements ever made by the government of the United States, we have leased from Great Britain certain sites where we have been building new bases that will make the screen against attack complete. We have the right to a base in the island of Jamaica, to one in the group of the Bahamas, especially valuable for anti-submarine patrols, to several in the tiny islands in the eastern ring, Antigua and Santa Lucia; we are building a larger base in a fine harbor of the island of Trinidad and finally a land base in the mainland colony of British Guiana. Further, we have a new base in our Caribbean possession, the Virgin Islands. The narrow passages can be mined and are, of course, constantly patrolled. Gray ships of war sweep the seas for many thousands of miles out into the Atlantic, and planes of all types aid in the task, all operating from these bases which nature provided and wise politics secured for us. Thus the possibilities of naval attack in any form against the Canal, especially from the east, are about zero. The greatest danger might be from aircraft based in some Latin American country; that danger is also lessening every day.

THE ATLANTIC AND HEMISPHERE DEFENSE

Two other regions of American concern which were mentioned at the beginning of this chapter were the Atlantic and Latin America. It is desirable that they be discussed together. Reason for this will be found in answering the question, What are American vital interests in these regions? In the first place, there are sea routes again, this time of two types. It is certain and well known to all that our British allies and we ourselves are most concerned with the problem of safeguarding the route across the North Atlantic from eastern American ports to the British Isles, with the objective of providing the food necessary for the British people and the materials of war which they need. Interest in this route has increased in the last year because of the desirability of getting aid to Russia in her fight against Hitler. That "Battle of the Atlantic," against Germany's submarines and raiders, will be won through the joint action of the American, British, and Canadian navies, by use of our advance outposts of Iceland and bases leased or used jointly in Newfoundland and Nova Scotia.

In the South Atlantic are other lifelines—from Brazil to the United States, from West Africa to this country, from our eastern ports to the Red Sea and the areas of the Near East and Egypt—remote outposts where the battle for freedom is also being waged. Another group of islands, Bermuda, long the vacation land of many American citizens, is now a leased base of this country and is being developed to serve as a great aid in keeping the Middle Atlantic free from danger. One other group bears watching— the Azores. Today they are in the hands of a friendly and neutral nation, Portugal. In unfriendly or enemy hands they could serve as a base for attack on our shipping, that of our allies, and all of our naval vessels. This must be prevented.

One final aspect of the Atlantic must be mentioned, and here we also return to Latin America. No one will question the statement that every part of this hemisphere, from Greenland to Tierra del Fuego, south of the Strait of Magellan, must be defended against any possible attack from our European enemies. But defense of this hemisphere cannot be restricted to these shores, as we all know now; if we wait, the seas will be the avenue of attack which has been feared. In the first place, the seas must be kept clear, as we are strenuously endeavoring to keep them now. But further, what of the jumping-off places on the other side of the seas? In West Africa on the unhealthy coast of Senegal, a colony still loyal to Vichy France, is the port of Dakar—hardly known to Americans two years ago, today the necessary concern of all. Dakar, approximately 1630 miles from the "bulge" of Brazil, is the logical place for the Nazis first to try to endanger the sea routes in the South Atlantic and, perhaps some day, to launch attacks against Brazil itself. Here in Dakar, it is known, is a part of the former navy of France. Can any one doubt that America must watch this port and prevent its occupation by the Nazis?

Finally, there is the question of the defense of the hemisphere itself. A few years ago this might have been a cause for real concern on the part of Americans. Most of the people of Latin America, including countries like Brazil and Argentina, were suspicious of the United States and even actively disliked us. This dislike had its roots in many things; in part it was the result of interventions by this country in Latin American countries many years ago—they feared that we would attack them. In part it was the result of very deep differences between us, symbolized by the fact that they speak Spanish or Portuguese, that they are Latin and not Anglo-Saxon nations. Partly it was due to the fact that up until a few years ago they sold more of their goods to European countries than to us. But today that is generally changed, a direct result of the policy of the "Good Neighbor" begun by President Roosevelt in 1933. They tend to believe us and know us to be their friend, and they have taken measures against the Nazis in their midst who have tried to stir up hatred and worse against the United States.

Probably only one more thing is necessary, the development of bases on the eastern coast of South America—in Brazil, Uruguay,

Argentina. The best would be at the city of Recife, near the bulge of Brazil which juts out so far toward Africa. South America, which is not only south of us but EAST of a large part of this country, is nearly united in the fight against aggression. Thus the diplomats of this country have, in the last eight years, gone far towards the defeat of geographic dangers to all the Americas.

Within the general framework of these areas, certain aspects of the global war must be noted; the aforementioned total war has given new significance to certain points near the lifelines, within the zones.

A general fundamental of Axis strategy throughout this war has been early recognition of key points on land and sea. Once the Axis partners have recognized and evaluated these points, they have not been slow in concentrating on seizing them first, to the usual surprise and inevitable dismay of the Allied Powers. But there are a few key points left along or adjacent to some of our lifelines which can be developed by the United Nations into powerful and valuable points of support; if they be lost to the enemy, by whatever means, our supply problem will become much more difficult and the victory in the Battle of Transportation will be much further away. Where are some of these points, which are far off the usual beaten path of man?

In the Indian Ocean, a few hundred miles south of Burma, are two groups of islands, the Andamans and the Nicobars. They have been held by the British for over fifty years and have been used chiefly as a penal colony. What significance may they have in the near future? They lie directly athwart the supply line from India to the East Indies. The Andamans have been taken by Japan; they are a deadly threat to that line. The geography of the islands is suited for that purpose. There are many inlets on the coasts where hostile warcraft could lie in wait, and above all in the Nicobar group there is a splendid harbor at Nancowry, well-protected, capable of sheltering large warships. That this harbor could be used for enemy operations is evidenced by the fact that the famous German raider *Emden* tried to use it in the last war.

In the South Atlantic, several hundred miles west of the Union of South Africa is another of Britain's neglected children, the island of Tristan da Cunha. Cold, barren, unproductive, without a harbor, it has sometimes been cut off completely from the world for as long as ten years. Yet it was originally acquired by the British, in 1815, because a British admiral advised it, arguing that this route might some day be an important lifeline and that without the use of the island and another, the more famous St. Helena, the route would be "like a ship without a mast." Its particular value today might be a result of its topography, for the interior of the island consists of a broad, flat plateau, where an admirable air base could be developed.

Other points must at least be watched. Dakar, the Azores, the Canaries, the Cape Verdes, Madagascar, in the hands of the Nazis, or used by them, would constitute a grave threat to this route, which is trebly important to the United Nations as has been pointed out.

Certainly it must be clear that these routes *are our* lines of life. It will avail us little to win the Battle of Production, to call ourselves the arsenal of democracy, if the blue-water highways of the world are filled with death and destruction with which we are not in a position to cope! Cool and calculating planning is of the essence of total war; recognizing the key points in our lifelines, developing them, defending them are essential milestones on the road to victory.

CHAPTER VI

THE NAZI-AMERICAN CONFLICT

Having presented in detail the substance and nature of materials entering into world trade, and particularly that of the United States, and further having considered the different geographic regions of the world in which the United States is interested, either as a source of supply or as a market or as a vital spot on the sea routes of the world, we must finally raise some questions regarding the broad geographic objectives of certain states in the world. This inquiry will take the form of a comparison of the objectives and methods of Germany, as the leader of the Axis countries, and those of the United States, as the leader of the Allied nations. There are many ends which countries try to achieve through their foreign policies: many are political; some are what is called ideological, such as our own desire to see democracy flourish in the world rather than dictatorship; some are economic and geographic. We will confine ourselves to the last two categories.

All countries are interested in finding a market abroad for those products which they cannot use at home; all are interested in obtaining, as cheaply and efficiently as possible, those raw materials which cannot be produced at home. There are, of course, other economic-geographic objectives, such as obtaining an outlet for population if there are too many people for the land within your own country. We are not concerned with these here, however, and will consider only the two objectives described, which have been our particular concern in these pages. The fundamental question to be asked about the *methods* used by countries to arrive at these ends must be: Will it be by force and attack against other countries or by the many peaceful means available?

GERMANY'S GEOGRAPHIC OBJECTIVES

Germany is probably the one country in the history of the world, or at least one of the very few, which has ever used the

51

study of geography both as a basis for conquest and as an explanation of plans for conquest. Ever since their country was defeated in 1918, there has been a group of so-called students in Germany working on the subject of geography. Through the years they developed certain ideas as to the type of world which would most suit Germany, and they thought up very elaborate schemes and methods for bringing that German world into being. It will pay us to examine their ideas and their methods in some detail.

Though it must sound very strange to American ears, the first feature to be noted about the German idea is that it assumes that *countries are alive;* to them a nation is not simply a territory with a certain number of people living in it, with definite boundary lines and a government running it, but is rather a living thing in itself. The nation has an organic, biologic nature, the meaning and power of which are greater than those of any one individual within the nation, and greater than all of them put together. The people, one by one and all together, exist only for the state according to this idea; they are servants of the state. The state is not a form of government which exists to aid and protect the people, as we think of it here and in the British Empire.

Now, if you believe that the nation is something alive, it is to be supposed, they say, that a country will pass through various stages of life. It is born, becomes adolescent, matures, and finally passes into old age. This is convenient indeed for the German, for he then goes on to say that when a country is adolescent it wishes to begin life and must expand from the place of its birth. Of course, he concludes, Nazi Germany is adolescent! Further, these writers who, as we shall see, have enjoyed a direct pipe-line to Hitler's ear for many years, always have pointed to England and the British Empire as being in the stage of old age; they claimed, before this war, that England was no longer able to take care of all her territory and that therefore it should be handed over to other and younger countries. This is, of course, propaganda, but it is much more. It is a philosophy of international politics based on one idea of geography and leading to geographic objectives.

It is much more, first of all, because these "geopoliticians" (as they are generally called) try to analyze how a country ought to behave. Just as the psychologists try to analyze people and to discover why we do certain things, they have studied countries. Much to their own satisfaction, they find that the basic urge within a country is toward expansion. They usually claim that there are too many people within a nation such as Germany was within her boundaries of 1933, though they never explain why the same government which claims to suffer in this way also gives prizes and medals to mothers of more than ten children. At any rate, they claim this and then come to the point of their argument: the people must have *room to expand*, to spread out into farms and factories, to develop all sorts of raw materials to feed the population and the centers of industry. Some areas, according to this thought, such as Africa and above all southeastern Europe and Latin America, are destined by geography to be forever merely areas producing raw materials which are needed by countries which are more industrially advanced. They propose, of course, that one big industrial country should own and dominate all of this territory.

Note here, then, one of the most important results which the world would face if such a system of ideas were ever to succeed in being put into operation. While countries are emphasized in this German idea, it is only in the sense of one or two big countries expanding and dominating large areas of the world. The day when the people of a region would be free to decide under what form of government they wished to live would be over. In other words, the inevitable end result of these ideas lies in the direction of the establishment of large areas in the world dominated by one great country, denying all freedom of thought, expression, and political choice to the peoples within it. Look at Nazi-occupied Europe today as an example. The relations between Germany and Japan are also an example: two fairly advanced industrial countries agree on the limitations between their so-called "living spaces" and upon the methods by which they hope to snatch this region from the other countries. Were two such regions under these countries to be established, any one can see that the United States would be left in the middle, where an economic and military vise could be applied against us.

Now, it may be asked, just how seriously does the Nazi government take these ideas? And how were they transmitted from the men who thought them up to those who are trying to put them into practice? Taking the second question first, the line to Hitler is very direct. The man who has done the most thinking and writing along these lines is one *Dr. Karl Haushofer*, at one time a professor in the University of Munich. Before·the last World War he entered the army and served for some years in many posts as an army officer in the Far East. After the war he wrote a tremendously long and difficult book on the geography and politics of the Far East. Some of the ideas which he put forth there the Japanese are trying to put into practice today. After 1918 he became a professor at Munich, teaching his ideas about world geography. One of his first and most interested students there was one *Rudolf Hess*, who astounded the world in 1941 by his airplane trip to England. Hess, of course, as early as 1923 was one of the most intimate friends of Adolf Hitler. When the first attempt of the Nazis to seize power failed in 1923 and Hitler was thrown into jail, one of his frequent visitors was Dr. Haushofer. While in jail, as everyone knows, Hitler wrote a rambling and ungrammatical book called *Mein Kampf*. Many of Dr. Haushofer's strange ideas as just explained are in those pages. Since 1933, when the Nazis came to power, Haushofer at least until very recently was in the inner circles of the party; he wrote constantly, and hundreds of other so-called students followed his teachings. His ideas are in many if not most of Hitler's speeches, and the idea of "living space" has been swallowed hook, line, and sinker by the German people. Many of the basic policies of the Nazis are the direct result of the proposals and ideas of these men, led by Haushofer; the idea and the policy of dominating central and southeastern Europe—Austria, Czechoslovakia, Hungary, Yugoslavia, Rumania, Bulgaria, and Greece—was of course step number one. They always favored close alliance with Japan. They favored a peaceful agreement with Russia, as it was put into effect in August, 1939. They always stated, however, that some day it would be necessary to make a division of land with the Russians; the Germans would take the western part, especially the rich and fertile Ukraine area, and then allow the Russians to dominate central Asia and Siberia. Here, for the first time, Hitler "jumped the gun" on the geopoliticians. From *his* point of view, perhaps, that was his fatal mistake.

These concepts of "living space" have, of course, been merged with another basic idea peculiar to the Nazis—that of a superior so-called "race." They claim that some peoples are fated to be better than, and the rulers of, others. It is interesting to see that as a rule the peoples whom they claim to be inferior are those who live in the "space" which the Germans have picked out to be theirs.

Thus the Nazi geographic pattern of the world emerges. Is it not clear that these men, with their strange ideas, have paved the way for the entire policy of Nazi aggression and enslavement of most of Europe and intended aggression against many other areas of the world? This is the pattern of the Nazi "New Order," by which *their* geographic objectives would be achieved—a world composed of great blocs of land each dominated by one enslaving power, where liberty and all of the values which we have associated with civilization for many years would be destroyed.

Let us turn to the American alternatives.

AMERICAN GEOGRAPHIC OBJECTIVES

The United States has no geographic objectives which are different from those of other great countries of the world; the only notable difference is to be seen in the manner by which we set out to achieve those objectives, as contrasted with the manner and methods of certain other countries, i.e., Germany, Japan, and Italy. In the first place, we certainly are interested in obtaining markets for many of our products in other nations. Most countries, due to their geographic position and their geographic endowments especially, are usually classified either as agricultural or as industrial states. We are one of the very few states that can be called a "mixed" economy, for as we all know and as was pointed out above, the factors of raw materials, climate, and soils have combined to make it possible for us to produce not only many different kinds of crops in great abundance but an enormous number of manufactured products of all kinds as well. In such quantities are we producers of many of these materials, both agricultural and industrial, that a surplus of many is always at hand which we are naturally interested in exporting abroad. Some readers may know the figure, frequently quoted, that of all American products entering into trade, only from 7 to 10 per cent enter into foreign trade. While this is true, the figure is misleading, for one must ask *what* products of *which* industries enter into the export trade on the world markets. If one investigates, one sees that the surplus cotton exported, the surplus automobiles, typewriters, electric refrigerators, etc., in many cases spell the difference between profit and loss for the industry—and certainly not only for the employer, for if profits go down so do the wages of labor. Further, it should never be forgotten that trade works in a kind of spiral: if the cotton farmer sells less abroad, his workers are paid less; they can buy less chewing gum, see fewer movies, buy fewer shoes; and then in turn the employers and the workers in all of those industries and hundreds of others are affected. If the foreign trade of the United States were to be cut off permanently or if we were forced to trade on their own terms with the Axis powers, selling to them only what they wanted and pretty much at their own price, as some countries have already been forced to do in recent years, a very great change in the standards of living of the American people as a whole would be inevitable.

Let us be quite realistic about the significance of this objective to all Americans. There are great and fundamental issues in this war of a moral and an ideological character. There can be little doubt that, if the Axis were victorious in the global war, *political* democracy as we know and practice it, as the British, French, Dutch, Danes, Belgians, Norwegians, and others have known and practiced it too, would be dealt a fatal blow. Nazism wars against most of the institutions of the Western World; even organized religion has suffered and would suffer more from the attacks of the new paganism. Yet there are other institutions, other phases of the "way of life" of the United Nations which could not withstand the onslaughts of a militarily triumphant Axis. *Economic* democracy would die as well. This is not one of those terms which are meaningful only to college professors in their classes held in the quiet isolation of the campus. This is a term which means the full dinner pail, the ability to trade in the old "jalopy" for a new model, the ability to send Joe to college. All these, and many more, are incompatible with the Axis economic pattern of the world.

It may be argued that if Japan controlled all or most of Asia, while Germany's "Eurafrica" had been realized, that we could still trade with those regions. Probably true, but along what lines? We have already seen in practice the nature of trade relations between Germany and countries which were dependent on her for export markets. Rather than pursuing the normal channels of trade, affording fair sale and distribution of products, the so-called "barter" system was developed. There was no use of foreign exchange; for a certain quantity of Argentine or Brazilian or Yugoslav products shipped to Germany, the producing country could obtain only a stipulated quantity of German products, the nature of which was chosen by Germany. German harmonicas, Harz mountain canaries, and Bayer aspirin flooded those countries.

Everything in the world economy, in brief, is to be ordered. How could the United States resist the process of adjustment to the new order? With the western hemisphere virtually encircled after the military triumphs of the Axis, the United States would possess very little bargaining power indeed. Our products, with few exceptions, would not be absolutely indispensable to Europe or Asia; we rather would be dangerously dependent on areas within those regions for those raw materials which have been discussed in previous chapters. It would be inevitable that we would have to adjust our economy to compete with that of German-controlled Europe and Japanese-controlled Asia in the one remaining "free" market of the world—Latin America. Yet even the most summary glance at the nature of the standard of living of most of the people of that region demonstrates that their purchasing power is low indeed. For our exports, a large proportion of which are finished manufactured products which would be of a "luxury" category to Latin Americans, those countries offer no solution.

Even relatively successful competition in Latin America failing to solve the problem, it would be inevitable that we would have to bend our economy to the demands of "coöperation" with the Axis. This implies a state-controlled economy in the United States. There would be "ceilings" on production, curtailments of every kind on that free enterprise which has been at the very basis of the development of American prosperity and power. No worker, however humble, would be able to escape the impact of the new order. Free channels of trade having been broken, raw materials hoarded by the Axis for the purpose of using them for further destruction and conquest, the American dream would perish. We must preserve the American alternative.

Before coming to the methods by which we have tried in the past to achieve our objective of obtaining foreign markets—methods which we will use again in the future when victorious—let us look briefly at other purposes which have geographic bases. One is the objective which has been stressed in these pages—access to sources of raw materials. The conclusion suggested in the first chapter was: "No nation can live alone." This is partly true because of the necessity of trading in exports with the rest of the world as just mentioned; it is wholly true because we are not sufficient unto ourselves in many of the raw materials which we need.

The third and final major geographic objective of the United States is one which is common to all of the countries of the world, the maintenance of our territorial security. Here are two words which, though seemingly simple enough, demand some definition; men have been arguing as to what "security" means since the dawn of history, but at no time more violently than in the last twenty years. The meaning itself is fairly plain for all to see —the difference of opinion comes when one decides what *methods* are necessary to achieve security—which is of course a position in which you are safe from attack, a position in which you can defend yourself. But what different methods are used by different countries, all in the name of being secure! Hitler claimed that he must have Austria, Czechoslovakia, Poland to be "secure" against attack from somebody—no one was ever quite clear as to who the attacker was supposed to be. Russia must have a slice of territory belonging to Finland to be "secure"; later, Finland must have a slice of Russian territory in order to be "secure." Fortunately for American honor, there are no examples in our history of the seizure of territory belonging to another country by *force* in order to be "secure." We have used the honorable methods of peace. It has meant to us the security of our land borders; on the approximately 3,000-mile border with Canada, there has been an example for over 100 years for the world to marvel at and try to follow— 3,000 miles of border with not one fort! Security to us has also meant the safeguarding of the ocean approaches to our shores; for that purpose and others we have followed the idea and doctrine of "freedom of the seas." But this is a *method*, and to this and others we must turn.

AMERICAN METHODS

Let us go back for a moment to the first objective which was mentioned above—that of finding markets for our surplus products abroad. The nature of America's ideas as to how those markets could be found, not only for our own products but for those of all countries, is very clear from the policy regarding world trade which we have followed since 1933. Previous to that time, the United States had adopted the policy of erecting tariff walls charging heavy duties on the import into this country of the products of many other countries; the others, in turn, had raised tariffs against our products. This process of give-and-take was giving little to anyone and taking much from many. It had been one of the causes of the general decline in world trade after 1929. These facts were recognized by President Roosevelt and Secretary of State Cordell Hull when they came into office in March, 1933. One of the first steps in foreign policy which they took had the purpose of improving this unhappy situation. Recognizing that if you wish to sell abroad you must also buy, they began the policy known as the "reciprocal trade agreements" program, by which we signed treaties with other countries, reducing duties on the import into the United States of some of their products, while they in turn reduced duties on many of our products. Nearly thirty such agreements were signed between 1933 and the outbreak of the European War in September, 1939. Trade between the United States and those countries with which we signed agreements had improved in every case. The program was, of course, dealt a heavy blow by the wars all over the world, for ordinary trade declined, trade routes were broken off or threatened, new markets had to be found, and new sources of supply of many products had to be opened up. But the fundamental aim remains. The United States is dedicated to the policy of making general free international trade possible. As opposed to the German method of breaking the world into blocs, one area trading with another on what amounts to a barter basis, we try to lower barriers throughout the world, to encourage the development of those products for which a region of a country is "best fitted" according to its geographic environment, to make it possible that those products can be exchanged as cheaply and as easily as possible. Here, then, is one great and basic difference between German and American methods and plans for the economic-geographic future of the world.

In regard to the second objective, we have made our methods equally clear, partly by our failure to take any kind of steps such as the aggressor nations have taken, partly by our own recent statements as to the future. The Nazis, Japanese, and Italians, as we know, have decided that *they* will obtain their raw materials by war and conquest. They say that they must have them, yet it is with the eventual end of being in a better position to fight future wars against the world. We have, throughout the stormy years which lie just behind us, not only refrained from any such steps—and they are surely unthinkable to any American—but we have condemned such Axis policies in every possible way. Further, we have shown a way to reason in the future. When President Roosevelt and Prime Minister Churchill met at sea in August, 1941, it will be remembered that they drafted a list of eight points or principles which will guide the Allies, after we win this war, in the organization of the kind of world which we believe to be just. Among the points in this document, which is coming to be known as the "Atlantic Charter," is one which states that the Americans and British and their Allies will take steps which will guarantee to ALL countries equality of access to the raw material supplies of the world. No longer will it be possible for a small group of producers to hold up the world by charging too high prices for products on which they may happen to have a monopoly. The Nazi idea, that one or two large units should control the raw materials of the world, is rejected. By international coöperation a method will be found which will free the products of the world to all who wish them—and on the FREE SEAS of the world, where the ships of all nations will have the right to ply their way and chart their course unchallenged and unmolested, those goods will reach their peaceful destination. In this world to come, it might be added, it may be presumed that the raw materials of the world can be used not to make weapons of death, but instruments of welfare and of comfort.

Finally, how have we tried to safeguard our territorial security, and how shall we do it in the future? In sharp contrast to the methods of those who achieve what they call their security through the attempted conquest of others, the United States has followed this simple line of reasoning. Your geographic security is threatened only if somebody attacks or threatens to attack you; if there are agreements between nations and *the mutual will to live up to them*, there need be no conflict. Further, if there is law between nations—and there is a great body of international law, just as there are laws which rule the conduct of individuals within a country —and nations are willing to live up to this law, there will be no conflict. Countless treaties have been signed by all the countries of the world, promising that no one will attack another, especially in the last twenty-one years; all kinds of international laws have been agreed to by the majority of nations. What countries have been the lawbreakers, and what ones have lived up to the treaties and the agreements? Japan signed a treaty with eight other nations in 1922 stating that none of those nations would ever attack China; Hitler signed an agreement in 1938 stating that he would never use force against another European state. These are only glaring examples of the broken promises and the broken laws. Yet laws and treaties and their faithful observance remain our method of maintaining territorial security, and not only our own security but that of all the peaceful nations in the world. Fruitful use of the geographic endowments of the world, prosperous world trade, can be assured only through reason, law, and the faithful observance of that law; these can flourish only when the lawbreakers are crushed.

PART II

The World Crisis

by

Second Army Board

CHAPTER VII

TREATY OF VERSAILLES (1919) TO INVASION OF POLAND (1939)

A boy born in the early part of 1919 came into a world weary with war and hopeful for a peace that would continue for many years. As that boy grew to manhood it is more than likely that he realized his manhood by shouldering a rifle in some army in the service of some nation in a world again at war. What is the story of the world during those few years that saw a boy grow to become a soldier?

It is the purpose of this series of three lectures to present, briefly, that story. The first lecture will be concerned with the years between the end of the World War in 1918 and the start of the second World War in 1939. The following lecture will deal with the second World War from 1939 to December 7, 1941, and the third lecture will present the successive steps that have influenced the position of the United States from strict neutrality to its present active participation.

It is true that there is no real beginning for anything in history, just as there is never any end. But the end of the first World War seems to be the best place to start the story of the second World War. The Armistice in 1918 marked the close of one great age of civilization and the beginning of a period of great change. This period of change has continued through the last twenty-odd years—vital, crowded, immensely significant years. Their story may be presented by a brief discussion of four following general topics:

(1) the magnitude of the first World War and its influence upon the world in the years that followed;

(2) the failure of the peace system for Europe set up by the Treaty of Versailles;

(3) the enthroning of a spirit of blind selfishness in nations that placed the interest of a single nation or of a political clique or party above the cause for peace in the world; and,

(4) the assumption of power by Adolf Hitler and his march towards war, dragging the world in with him.

When the Armistice was declared on November 11, 1918, the peoples of the warring nations felt inexpressible relief at the end of the unparalleled slaughter and waste. Thirty nations had waged the war. Sixty-five million men bore arms in it; 8,500,000 of them were killed, and 29,000,000 were wounded, captured, or reported missing. Nearly every family in these warring nations suffered loss of relatives or close friends. The financial cost is almost impossible to estimate, but the direct cost has been figured at over 200 billion dollars and the indirect cost at more than 150 billion dollars.[1]* The world was exhausted, its productivity crippled. Labor and living costs rose tremendously. The resources of the earth were mortgaged for years to come. A picture of this cost to the major powers in lives and dollars is shown in the accompanying chart.[2]

However, these directly accountable losses were not nearly the total losses. Equally serious if not more so were the losses due to starvation, the wrong kind of food, and disease. In some parts of Europe the peasants were living on roots, grass, and acorns during the war. In Germany in 1918 the number of births was actually less than the number of deaths.[3] In Serbia half the male population had been killed.[3] It is difficult to bring before the imagination the results of these dreadful conditions and to estimate their effect on Europe for the years that followed.

All this suffering produced in the public mind a desire for a world organized on a new and better plan. So, after a few weeks necessary to bring the war machines to a full halt following the Armistice on November 11, 1918, the statesmen of the Allied governments and their advisers met to write this new and better plan. After a number of weeks of hard labor and at times almost hopeless differences, their product, the Treaty of Versailles, was ready for signing.

* Reference numbers printed in this manner refer to numbered reference notes at the end of the chapter.

COST OF WORLD WAR I IN MEN AND MONEY

$ REPRESENTS $5,000,000,000
✝ REPRESENTS 200,000 MEN KILLED OR DIED FROM ANY CAUSE

SECOND ARMY EDUCATIONAL PROGRAM CHART NO. II

PREPARED IN ENGINEER HEADQUARTERS, SECOND ARMY, 1942

UNITED STATES

$ $ $ $ $
✝⌐

BRITISH EMPIRE

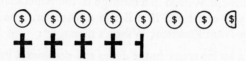
$ $ $ $ $ $ $ $
✝ ✝ ✝ ✝ ✝⌐

FRANCE

$ $ $ $ $
✝ ✝ ✝ ✝ ✝

GERMANY

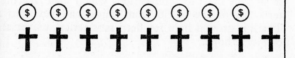
$ $ $ $ $ $ $ $
✝ ✝ ✝ ✝ ✝ ✝ ✝ ✝ ✝ ✝

RUSSIA

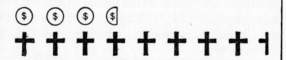
$ $ $ $
✝ ✝ ✝ ✝ ✝ ✝ ✝ ✝ ✝⌐

ITALY

(ACCURATE ESTIMATES OF MONEY NOT AVAILABLE)

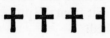
✝ ✝ ✝ ✝⌐

SOURCES:
HALL & DAVIS, COURSE OF
EUROPE SINCE WATERLOO
ENCYCLOPEDIA BRITANNICA,
"WORLD WAR"

AUSTRIA HUNGARY

(ACCURATE ESTIMATES OF MONEY NOT AVAILABLE)

✝ ✝ ✝ ✝ ✝ ✝

It was just five years to the day since the shot that had opened the war was fired when the representatives of the warring nations gathered to sign the treaty. On June 28, 1914, the Archduke Ferdinand of Austria was assassinated, eventually plunging the world into war, and on June 28, 1919, the treaty of peace ending that war was signed at Versailles.

Two opposing ideas of the meaning of the treaty are significantly illustrated by two statements made that same day. One was by President Wilson in a message to the American people, and the other was contained in a Berlin newspaper. The following is an excerpt from President Wilson's message [4]:

It is a severe treaty in the duties and penalties it imposes upon Germany, but it is severe only because great wrongs done by Germany are to be righted and repaired. And it is much more than a treaty of peace with Germany. It liberates great peoples who have never before been able to find the way to liberty. It ends once and for all the old and intolerable order under which small groups of selfish men could use the peoples of great empires to serve their ambition for power and dominion. . . . It makes international law a reality. . . . It lays the basis for conventions which shall free the commercial intercourse of the world from unjust and vexatious restrictions. . . . There is ground here for deep satisfaction, universal reassurance and confident hope.

One of the few German newspapers that had anything to say at all began its article with the words, "Lest We Forget." The German people, it said, "will again strive to attain that place among the nations of the world to which it is entitled. Then, vengeance for 1919!" [5]

After the treaty was signed, the statesmen of the world went about the immense task of trying to reorganize the ruins of Europe according to the plan of the treaty. The new system for Europe was founded on four pillars built from the provisions of the treaty. These four pillars may be called:

(1) The League of Nations
(2) Financial or reparations settlements
(3) Military or disarmament settlements
(4) Political or territorial settlements

It is in the first of the fifteen parts of the treaty that the Covenant of the League of Nations is found. A world community of nations was formed by this covenant in order to promote international coöperation and achieve international peace and security. Every member state assumed the obligation to submit any quarrel to the League before going to war. But the League had no police power to force any member to do anything. The basic thought was to have arguments between nations settled by arbitration, not by war. This was the first pillar.

The financial or reparations provisions of the treaty formed the second pillar. Germany was to acknowledge responsibility for the war and to make financial payments for all damage done to the Allies by the war. The total amount she was to pay would be announced by a committee that would determine what Germany was able to pay. This was the second pillar.

The military or disarmament settlements were aimed to destroy the existing German fortifications and war materials and to maintain Germany permanently ineffectual as a military power. Conscription was abolished, a standing army of but 100,000 men was authorized, and a small navy of about thirty-six vessels with no submarines was allowed. No air force was to be permitted. This was the third pillar.[6]

By the terms of the political or territorial settlements Germany lost, in Europe, about 25,000 square miles of territory and 6,000,000 population. The land taken from her was rich in coal, iron, zinc, and lead. Overseas she lost about 1,000,000 square miles of colonies and 12,000,000 natives. This was the fourth and last pillar.[7]

The after-the-war European system was thus set up, a structure resting upon the Treaty of Versailles as upon a hand with four fingers upstretched. However, it was one thing to write up such a system; it was to be another and far more difficult thing to make it work in the ruins of Europe left by the war.

Europe under her leaders set to work to clear away the wreckage of the war and to rebuild on the four pillars of the Treaty of Versailles. But the effectiveness of the treaty was dealt a serious blow when America failed to ratify it. Despite the pleas of President Wilson, this nation isolated itself from Europe and its problems and thus deprived the cause for world peace of responsible counsel by a powerful and impartial country. The first few years were hopeful ones nevertheless, but gradually hope faded and dis-

illusionment set in. The gradual weakening, then crumbling, of
each of the four pillars went on concurrently, but it was the financial pillar that was the first to crash.

The economic situation in Europe during the years immediately
after the war was almost hopelessly grave. Nations were overloaded with war debts; severe unemployment resulted from the
return of millions of soldiers to their homes; and each country
was naturally concerned with protecting its own interests. Since
the signing of the peace treaty the diplomats and politicians had
been roaming around Europe from one international conference
to another. They were trying to decide how much Germany
should pay for the almost incalculable damage she had caused
during four years of war, trying to determine how the payments
would be divided among the nations that had suffered; and endeavoring to decide how to finance their own debts. In May, 1921,
a commission finally determined that the amount Germany should
pay should be thirty-two billion dollars.[8] The United States asked
for no reparations.

Payments on this sum were never made in full or anything like
it. Germany could not or would not find the money, and when
payments were allowed in goods there was constant trouble with
the deliveries of goods. Finally, in 1922, although German industry
was again operating efficiently, the Allies allowed Germany a six-
months' suspension. Still Germany made no satisfactory adjustment, and instead asked for a two-year moratorium in 1923. The
British agreed. But France still viewed with bitterness the contrast
of her ruined and devastated countryside with the reviving and
untouched Germany across the Rhine. The answer of France was
to send troops into the Ruhr, the industrial heart of Germany.

New committees were formed to study the reparations problem.
In 1924 the Dawes Plan was presented. This plan kept the total
German debt at thirty-two billion dollars but stretched German
payments over a period of decades.[9] This was still unsatisfactory
to Germany, although payments were made from 1924 to 1928.
In 1929 the Young Plan was worked out and took the place of the
Dawes Plan. Under its provisions Germany was to pay roughly
from $400,000,000 to $600,000,000 a year for fifty-nine years until
1988, when the debt would be all paid.[10] The plan seemed to offer

a workable solution to the debt problem, but before it could be tested the Great Depression started and the world was plunged into a financial crisis. The Hoover Moratorium in June, 1931, was one attempt to relieve the crisis. Under its provisions, all reparations payments by Germany and war debt payments by the Allies to the United States were to cease for a year. This year might as well have been forever, because no more payments, with a few exceptions, were ever made; none were made by Germany. Thus in 1931 the first of the four pillars had fallen.

The disarmament pillar was the next to go. There was no general disarmament after the World War. True, the once-great war machines of Germany and her allies were dismantled; but in spite of general demobilization in Germany, England, and the United States, other countries retained large standing armies.

A series of conferences on the limitation of naval armaments finally came about: the Washington Naval Conference in 1921-1922, one at Geneva in 1927, and another in London in 1930. Under the terms of the Washington conference, the United States did scrap, between 1922 and 1926, thirty vessels, twenty-two of which were battle-ships or battle cruisers. How well could these ships have been used in December, 1941!

But none of the conferences contributed anything leading to a permanent solution of the problem of naval armament limitation. By 1937 the naval race was undisguised.

Attempts to negotiate a general limitation of land armaments were even less successful. In 1925 the League of Nations created a special commission to study the problem, and after five years it brought forth a report which merely exhibited the failure of the commission. A conference on disarmament met in Geneva in 1932, but after two years of futile discussion it faded away in 1934. By that time it was bound to die. Hitler's star had risen.

The collapse of all conferences to limit or balance land and naval armaments cracked the second pillar of the system, and Adolf Hitler dealt it a final crushing blow. Military preparations had been going on in Germany ever since the end of the war, in spite of the Treaty of Versailles. Many of Hitler's various organizations, for example, were military in nature though unarmed. All secrecy or indirectness was abandoned, however, when on March 16, 1935, he announced to the world, in effect, that he had abolished the disarmament clauses of the Treaty of Versailles. Universal military service was reëstablished in Germany, and a peacetime army of thirty-six divisions was set up. "The memory," said a Nazi manifesto, "of the glorious German Army with its glorious history is now no longer a pale, historic phantom." [11]

So crumbled the second pillar, disarmament.

In January, 1920, the League of Nations was formally inaugurated at Paris, with a membership of forty-two nations. However, from the outset a very serious handicap to the League was the fact that the United States was not a member. A long fight on the part of President Wilson and his supporters to have the Treaty of Versailles ratified, with the United States joining the League, raged between 1919 and 1921. Many issues were raised, but the fight was decided against Wilson when the American people elected Warren G. Harding president of the United States. In March, 1921, the President declared that "in the existing League of Nations, world-governing with its super-powers, this Republic will have no part." [12] The child of President Wilson had been abandoned on the European doorstep.

France, Britain, and the United States seemed joined together in the common interest of preserving world peace by means of the League. They were the victors in the war. They had jointly shared the responsibility of carving up Austria-Hungary and of creating new nations—Poland, Czechoslovakia, Yugoslavia, and an enlarged Greece and Rumania. But the United States withdrew and Britain reverted to her traditional policy of avoiding commitments on the European continent. This was partly due to the fear on the part of Britain that the League might blockade the seas in trying to settle a dispute and America would object because of her strong belief in freedom of the seas. This might involve Britain and the United States in a naval or commercial collision which Britain did not want.[13] Moreover, pacifism rode a high tide in both Britain and the United States, accompanied by cynicism and disillusionment.

This left France as the dominant power in the League. This League became to her but one of a limited number of means of protecting her 40,000,000 people against a restless, revengeful nation of 70,000,000 Germans. Thus, it is understandable that she used the League to help strengthen any alliances she could make to ensure security against an always-to-be-feared German revival.

The League did perform some services in gathering and publishing useful data about world conditions,* but in the adjustment of disputes between nations and in the prevention of war, the League was less successful. After a few failures, such as in a Polish-Lithuanian dispute in 1923 and an Italian-Greek dispute the same year, the League pillar began to crack. On September 19, 1931, Japanese troops invaded Manchuria. The League did not and could not prevent Japan from forcibly appropriating Manchuria and conducting military operations against China. Japan thus initiated the first successful assault of major proportions on the collective security system of the League.

The Japanese incident signaled the end of the League, and in 1935, when the League failed to prevent Italy from undertaking the conquest of Ethiopia, the League of Nations pillar crumbled, and the European system began to fall. Only the pillar of territorial settlements remained, and this was soon to crash.

The end of the war in 1918 saw the crumbling of two great empires, the dual monarchy of Austria-Hungary and Imperial Germany. Several new states or transfers of territory to already established countries resulted. Revolutions and civil wars formed other countries, and the British Dominions assumed roles as independent nations. Eight new countries were formed in Europe, and six countries received additions to their territories. About 2,000 miles of new frontier were created, and the total number of countries in Europe became twenty-seven, as against twenty-two before the war.[14]

The new system fixed European boundaries, and the peace of the new Europe depended upon these boundaries remaining as such. There were a bewildering number of incidents, conferences,

* Yeoman work was done by the Labor office of the League in its studies and recommendations, but the latter could not be implemented. League studies of the narcotics trade were also illuminating, but the chief beneficiaries of the trade were not inhibited by these revelations. The World Court adjudicated some minor disputes. The professional and technical services of the League functioned faithfully while the political branch compromised the League away.

secret alliances, and diplomatic meetings designed either to maintain the map of Europe or to attempt to change it. (The Little Entente, for example, an alliance between Czechoslovakia, Romania, and Yugoslavia, became a part of the French security system. You may see the reason for this on the map. It is also easy to see how this system could have been completed—by Poland's entering the Little Entente. This she refused to do, although Poland was allied to France. There was friction between Poland and Czechoslovakia.) In 1934, Poland signed a ten-year non-aggression pact with Germany. However, one culminating event tumbled the whole system. On March 7, 1936, as Adolf Hitler's frenzied oratory thundered through loudspeakers, columns of German troops were rolling across the Rhine bridges, spreading steadily through the Rhineland zone demilitarized by the Versailles treaty. It is said that Hitler's generals had two sets of orders: one to occupy the Rhineland, the other to withdraw if the French Army marched across the frontier to meet them. But the French did not march. Here, finally, was actual territorial change in Europe, and as the last of the four pillars crumbled, the whole system came down in ruins. To the German people, Hitler had delivered a tremendous bloodless victory.

The post-war system, put together at Versailles and in the years that followed, had fallen at last. Reparations had gone, disarmament had gone, the League had gone, and territorial settlements had gone. Hitler's move into the Rhineland on March 7, 1936, had signaled this complete collapse and, as though in echo, there followed the victorious shouts of the Italian troops storming into Addis Ababa a short two months later. "In the flames which greeted the Italian troops as they rolled down from the Ethiopian hills into Addis Ababa much more had perished than the ramshackle houses of a barbarian capital. Those flames were now to spread across a world." [15]

One of the main results of the first World War was the political grouping together of people of the same racial group either to form a new nation or to strengthen one already in existence. To the family of world nations of the Germans, French, English, Italians, and other countries in existence before the war there were added new nations. The Poles established the independence of

Poland; the Irish demanded and exacted from the British an Irish Free State; the Finns carved out Finland; the Serbs, Croats, and Slovenes and their southern Slav brothers joined Yugoslavia. This logical tendency to group peoples of the same nationality to form countries may be called nationalism. It is well for the people so to group themselves, because people of the same nation have identity in their background of culture and history and much the same interests. However, when this nationalism becomes too narrowly selfish and when the nation thinks only of itself, then arrogant nationalism may become a menace to world or international peace. This is what happened during those years that saw the crumbling of the four Versailles pillars. In some countries, especially those that lost a lot by the war, recalcitrant forces saw a way to gain power by exploiting this selfish nationalism. The national state was exalted above humanity and above the individual. The carrying-out of the ideals and glories of the nation became the total life. While it is desirable that every nation conserve and develop its national ideals, some are more fanatical than others; and we shall note this by examining briefly the foreign policies of Russia, France, Italy, Germany, Japan, and England during the twenty-odd years between the wars.

Inefficiency, corruption, pro-German influences in high places, and terrific losses at the front led to rioting and rebellion in Russia in 1917. The Germans went so far as to transport the leaders of the revolution through Germany into Russia in a sealed train to take command of the revolution. Under these leaders, a radical group known as the Bolshevists rose to power during the stormy days of the revolution. After several years of bloodshed and constant turmoil, the Union of Soviet Republics was formed January 1, 1923, and complete control was placed in the hands of the Communist Party. Of course, this party already controlled the Red Army. After the first leader of the Bolshevists, Lenin, died in 1924, the present dictator of Russia, Stalin, came to power.

The Bolshevist government claimed to be anti-nationalistic. They considered the organization of the workers of all nations of the world into one group more important than nationalism. Gradually, however, after Stalin's coming into power, Russia became increasingly nationalistic. The idea of world organization of the proletariat became of secondary importance to the idea of organizing Russia first, and then perhaps the world, on a Communist basis. Russia became occupied at home with carrying out a series of five-year plans.

At the end of the World War France was devastated and exhausted. The practical French realized that Germany remained the source of gravest danger to France in the future. Hence the French foreign policy revolved around the desire and purpose to keep Germany encircled by French alliances and helpless to make a future war of revenge. This extreme attitude was softened a bit in 1925-1926 when the Locarno Treaty was signed, guaranteeing the borders between Belgium, Germany, and France, and marking the first time since the end of the war that Germany was treated as a near equal.

As a result of alliances and treaties and with the prestige of her large army, France may be said to have kept the peace in Europe until 1935. However, Britain had remained aloof. The United States was entirely withdrawn—and critical of the French system of alliances. Russia was no longer an ally, but on the contrary influenced the growth of communism in France. Italy was jealous and bitter. And every German effort was devoted to the goal of cancelation of the Treaty of Versailles. As time went on, France had fewer friends, less confident allies.

The story of Italy between the two wars is largely a story of the career of Benito Mussolini. The pressure of population as opposed to resources is great in Italy. As a result of her participation in the war, she received little territory. This fact was played up by her politicians. An intense nationalism was stimulated within the country. Mussolini rose to power by the exploitation of this nationalism and was named Prime Minister of Italy on October 30, 1922. A former socialist and radical, he gradually assumed the role of dictator. Since 1922 the foreign policy of Italy has been bombastic and aggressive. The past glories of Rome were paraded before the people, and future return to pomp and glory for Italy was promised. Mussolini did unite the Italian people and raise the standard of living at home.

Then by a series of small wars and alliances Mussolini pushed Italy to the front line of nations. Too late, England and France realized the rejuvenation of Italy, and it was to Germany that the now militaristic country turned for alliance. Thus was formed the Rome-Berlin Axis which functioned during the Spanish Civil War and is at present the enlarged Rome-Berlin-Tokyo Axis in a world at war.

Opinion differs as to the degree of harshness of the Treaty of Versailles to a conquered Germany. Whatever opinion may be on that score, it is safe to say that the peace Germany would have imposed upon Europe had she won would have been far more excessive in its exactions of wealth and territory. An example, for instance, is the Treaty of Brest-Litovsk, signed in February, 1918, that the Germans imposed upon the Bolshevists as the price for peace for Russia. In that treaty Germany not only disregarded the welfare of her ally, Austria-Hungary, but took from Russia vast territories with a Slavic population of tens of millions of people. And we see today the pattern of German methods after conquest, which is evident to the world in the colossal demands and exactions of Germany wherever the Nazis have succeeded in conquering free peoples.

To return to the Treaty of Versailles, German foreign policy thereafter revolved around one central goal: to make up for the supposed wrongs of that treaty. The German people after the war were led to believe that the calamities of Germany were due to the peace and not to the war. All propaganda within Germany devoted itself to that idea. They were indifferent to the ravages their armies had visited upon other countries. They forgot the tremendous damage caused Germany by her all-out war effort. The Germans had had a war plan which mobilized every resource and every energy for war use. The country had been stripped of men and materials. The result of the four years of terrific drain and strain was the exhaustion of Germany. When peace came, Germany blamed all her misfortunes on the peace, not on the fact that she had exhausted herself with war, and her ruling thought was the abolishment of the Treaty of Versailles. German preparation for the next war began before the ink on the treaty was dry.

The army permitted by the treaty, although a mere 100,000 in size, became the training ground for professional leaders. It became an army of experts constantly being replaced that others could be trained. Hundreds of millions of dollars were "borrowed" for the "reconstruction" of Germany. Something like half a billion dollars of American money went into what proved at last to be a reconstruction for war. Meanwhile, even inflation was cleverly used, despite the terrible effect it had on the German people in the years immediately following the war. Germany paid her immense internal debt—everything the government had borrowed from the people before and during the war—by simply printing paper money. By wiping out her internal debt, Germany was able to start afresh, while France and particularly England labored under colossal debts owed to their own people. Thus the Nazis could put huge sums into building and equipping a powerful military machine that ravaged Poland in 1939 to put the world again at war.

British foreign policy is influenced largely by the fact that hers is an island empire. The center of the empire, England, is linked to the rest by sea. Therefore, England must dominate the seas and trade and ensure free pursuit of commerce. However, this domination is challenged today, for other powerful navies have been built and other nations have developed great trade systems. Moreover, land-based airplanes can now operate hundreds of miles from shore to challenge sea power in oceans where it formerly was supreme. The British Dominions, too, have become independent commonwealths, with fewer ties to the island center. Thus, the traditional position of Britain as World Power No. 1 was mightily changed between the wars. War no longer was an instrument of policy in Great Britain. Her policy since the last war was a "live and let live" policy. This was the background for the famous appeasement policy pursued by Neville Chamberlain.

Appeasement had three main ideas:

(1) The dictatorships should be encouraged to do business with others. They would then be satisfied with peaceful trade and intercourse with the rest of the world and solve their problems by gradual adjustment.

(2) The peace treaties had not solved European organization; maybe the recovery of Germany would be for the good of the continent.

(3) In the face of a changing world, Britain must now find se-

curity and prosperity in coöperation with others, for she cannot have it alone.[16]

Appeasement ended after the swallowing of the remnants of Czechoslovakia; and Britain's stern refusal to retreat any further before Hitler's aggressions put her at war in 1939.

Japan fought in the first World War on the side of the Allies. She received a number of former island possessions of Germany in the Pacific north of the equator at the peace treaty. For ten years or so after the war Japan gave evidences of coöperation in the interest of world peace. She joined the League of Nations and was present at the 1922 Washington Naval Conference, which checked a naval race among the nations. In 1929 she signed the Kellogg-Briand Peace Pact by which fifty-seven nations "outlawed" war, and she was a member of the 1930 London Naval Conference, which extended the naval truce. However, her military party, always strong —for Japan has often been called a nation of soldiers and was ruled for 650 years by military government [17] —came back into power and started the island empire on its road to war in 1931. In that year Japan invaded Manchuria and received the censure of the United States as well as that of the League of Nations. Our present Secretary of War, Mr. Stimson, was then Secretary of State. In 1933, Japan withdrew from the League that had not checked her in Manchuria. In 1937 Japan undertook her war on China and soon after announced her determination to dominate Asia. Since then, this may be called the heart of Japan's foreign policy—to rule Asia to the exclusion of all the white powers. By her treacherous attack on the United States on December 7, 1941, Japan indicated that her chips were all down and her militarists were resolved on a fight to the finish.

THE RISE OF HITLER

The crumbling of the peace machinery set up by the Treaty of Versailles enabled a man like Adolf Hitler to rise to power.

Hitler blamed all of Germany's ills on the Treaty of Versailles and announced himself as the leader who would destroy that treaty. He outshouted his competitors, and his private army of

storm troopers had its elements organized in every community.
Not only did he capitalize on the willingness of the German people
to forget the effects of the devastating war and blame the peace
instead, but there are other characteristics of the German people
that helped him to rise to his position as dictator.

As the war drew to a close, the Germans found that all their
sacrifice and suffering of four long years had brought only defeat
and utter exhaustion. This caused a great wave of sentimental self-
pity to sweep over the German nation. This was aided by propaganda fed to the German people by the Prussian military class
known as the Junkers, and by members of the so-called intellectual
class. This propaganda maintained that the German Army was not
defeated in the first World War, but was stabbed in the back by
revolution at home. The state of mind resulting was made worse
by the fact that Germany was defeated when she was at the height
of her power, when she was proudest of her achievements as a
nation, when she had no justifiable reason to go to war. But far
more dangerous was the German tendency toward militarism.
The heart of militarism in Germany is based on a history and a
way of thinking which accepts war as the instrument of the nation's policy. It believes that victory means advantage; therefore,
victorious powers suffer less than the vanquished. How easy it was
for Hitler and other men of his kind to paint a false picture of
wealth, fortune, and happiness in England and other Allied countries because they were the winners, in contrast with poverty and
pain in Germany, the loser.[18]

Hitler seized upon this militarism and used it as an important
instrument in the building of the Nazi system. He also turned the
German mind to the belief that only through military preparedness
on a gigantic scale could he liberate Germany from the direct
source, so he claimed, of her troubles—the Treaty of Versailles.
Hitler's early struggle and rise to power need not be mentioned
here. The bloody purge by Hitler in 1934 is typical of his ruthless
climb. During the middle of that year, according to an official list,
seventy-four persons were summarily killed with little or no hearing. In this way, Hitler swept aside opposition within his party,
including men who had been his closest friends. He still seemed
something of a mountebank to the outside world. But it was on

March 7, 1936, that the nations of the world realized that he was a direct threat to the peace. You may remember that it was on that day that the last of the four pillars was tumbled by the German occupation of the Rhineland.

The years 1936 and 1937 ran out. The bloody Spanish Civil War continued, there was vast misery in China. Jewish persecution was raging in Europe; all nations were feverishly arming, and the whole air of Europe seemed poisoned by savagery and gangsterism, by violent policies and barbaric teachings. "Men more and more were coming to feel that this could not last; that sooner or later there was bound to be an explosion somewhere. But as yet nothing definite or final had happened." [19]

Then Hitler resumed his march. The early part of 1938 saw a purge in Germany which removed possible domestic and military opposition to Nazi plans. After a rapid succession of dramatic events, the union of Germany and Austria was announced to a fearful world on March 13, 1938. The German Army had moved in. Austria was dead, and the French and British threw up their hands and accepted the situation. They reasoned that after all Austria was really a German state, Hitler himself was an Austrian; and why should young Frenchmen and Englishmen die to prevent a logical union? And Hitler announced himself as satisfied with expansion.

But Hitler's eyes turned next toward Czechoslovakia, and the attention of the world followed. What about 3,500,000 Germans living in the Czech nation, and what would the British do about Czechoslovakia were she attacked? Russia and France declared they would come to the aid of the Czechs in that event, but the Germans solemnly told everyone they wanted only peace with the Czechs. Neville Chamberlain, Prime Minister of Great Britain, made a curious speech on March 24, 1938, which outlined the now famous appeasement policy. He had no desire to get Britain into a war on the continent. Britain would not promise Czechoslovakia aid were she attacked, but on the other hand Germany was not to think that nothing would make Great Britain fight. Mr. Chamberlain clearly thought there was still time to make a deal with the dictators, and that a deal was still possible. After a flurry of Nazi insults and Czech mobilization reviving fears of war, things quieted down, and by July the Czech question seemed to be fading away. Then suddenly it was revived, loudly, violently—the "war of nerves" was on.

Then came a series of conferences between England and Czechoslovakia, England and Germany, England and France, the ultimate end of which was a shameless call on the Czech government on September 19, 1938, to hand over to Hitler all of its territory in which even as many as half the inhabitants were Germans.

The Czechs gave in under bitter protest, and the Germans took over the territory assigned to them, but it was only the beginning. Hitler failed to live up to the clauses of the agreement which provided for non-military occupation and declared his troops must march into the German part of Czechoslovakia by October 1, 1938. War again seemed inevitable. The situation was saved at the eleventh hour by a request from Hitler on the 28th of September, 1938, for a meeting at Munich. Chamberlain represented Britain; Daladier, France; Mussolini, Italy; and Hitler, Germany. The meeting resulted in a complete surrender by the British and the French, and the German Army rolled across the Czech border into the new German territory on October 1, as Hitler had said it would. However, Chamberlain was hailed in Britain and Daladier in France as the saviors of peace, "peace in our time." The one real bit of appeasement brought from Munich was a guarantee of safety and independence for what was left of Czechoslovakia, a Czechoslovakia now robbed of its frontier fortifications and natural defenses. Also, Hitler had declared to Mr. Chamberlain, "I have further assured him, and I repeat it here, that when this problem is solved, there is for Germany no further territorial problem in Europe. And I have further assured him that at the moment when Czechoslovakia solves her problems, that means when the Czechs have come to terms with their other minorities and that peaceably and not through oppression, then I have no further interest in the Czech state, and that is guaranteed to him. We want no Czechs!" [20]

This appeasement was to prove not worth the paper it was written on. It was the same Hitler who had no further claims after occupying the Rhineland and no further claims after occupying Austria.

German and Italian gestures became more warlike, more cocky

after Munich. The people of their countries were promised more glory, greater power. This began to make the democracies wonder what sort of appeasement had been given at Munich. After a series of moves and speeches, now a familiar pattern to the world, on March 15, 1939, German troops marched into the rest of Czechoslovakia. It was one year exactly since Hitler had made his entry into Vienna.

The democratic countries were shocked. With one bold movement Hitler had torn up the Munich pact, had proved he would not be bound by treaties, had proved he was not bound to seize only those lands containing German minorities. What would he do next? What limits were there to his ambition? Chamberlain spoke to his people, and Daladier to the French. The words of Daladier to the French Senate may be used to indicate the feelings of the people of both countries:

The present circumstances call less for speeches than for action. . . . We are now in the trench which we must defend at the cost of whatever sacrifice. The Munich Agreement? Destroyed. The mutual declaration of Franco-German coöperation [signed in December, 1938]? Violated in letter and spirit. . . . Today, and in the hours to come, we shall have to face events that may develop dangerously. . . . This is the storm, gentlemen, and we must face it with all the means the situation requires and with our will and the will of the people of France.[21]

This was the end of appeasement. The retreat was over.

One week after the fall of Czechoslovakia, Germany demanded and got from Lithuania its chief city and only seaport, Memel, which had belonged to Germany before the World War. At the same time, Hitler focused his systematic pattern of conquest on Poland, and so began the last phase before war. The Polish Corridor was demanded—that strip of Poland on the sea separating East Prussia from the rest of Germany. Poland refused to comply with German demands, remembering what had happened to other nations that had so agreed. She sent recommendations of her own to Germany. The French and British attitude that no more appeasement would be tolerated stiffened Poland's position. Negotiations dragged on. Britain and France hoped to line up Russia against Germany. The summer came and slipped by, filled with discussions, speeches, and uneasiness. The Germans began to intensify their familiar system of attack on Poland. There were stories of brutality and minority mistreatment, and there was fifth-column activity. Finally, a stupendous sensation broke on August 21, when it was announced suddenly from Moscow that Germany and Russia had made a non-aggression treaty, thus knocking the bottom out of all the long British and French negotiations for Russian aid.

Ten hectic days followed. France and Britain were irrevocably pledged to come to Poland's aid should Hitler attack. However, with relentless tread, Hitler resumed the march, and on September 1, 1939, German bombs were crashing on Polish towns and the German-Polish war had begun.

Over and over again France and England had declared that if a showdown were made, the two democracies would fight without hesitation. One last warning was handed to Germany by London and Paris. The Germans paid no attention. Great Britain declared war on September 3, and the French, on the same afternoon, followed the British action.

It was just twenty-one years lacking two months since the great silence had fallen over the Western Front and World War I had reached its bloody end. The babies who were being born as the statesmen assembled in Paris to establish their new world, were just coming to their manhood as that world went up in the flames of still another general conflict; and they were now filling, in their thousands, the ranks of the new armies whose task it would be to make yet another peace.[22]

The boy had become a soldier.

REFERENCE NOTES

[1] C. J. H. Hayes, *A Political and Cultural History of Modern Europe* (The Macmillan Company, 1939), p. 622.

[2] W. P. Hall and W. S. Davis, *The Course of Europe Since Waterloo* (D. Appleton-Century Company, Inc., 1941), p. 644.

[3] H. A. L. Fisher, *A History of Europe* (Houghton Mifflin Company, 1939), pp. 1189-1190.

[4] From *Why Europe Fights*, by Walter Millis, copyright 1940 by Walter Millis, by permission of William Morrow & Company.

[5] From *Why Europe Fights*, by Walter Millis, copyright 1940 by Walter Millis, by permission of William Morrow & Company.

6 Lawrence Martin, ed., *The Treaties of Peace, 1919–1923* (Carnegie Endowment for International Peace).

7 A. P. Watts, *A History of Western Civilization* (Prentice-Hall, Inc., 1940), p. 984.

8 C. J. H. Hayes, as above, p. 660.

9 Same, p. 662.

10 Walter Millis, as above, p. 76.

11 From *Why Europe Fights*, by Walter Millis, copyright 1940 by Walter Millis, by permission of William Morrow & Company.

12 C. J. H. Hayes, as above, p. 754.

13 W. R. Sharp and G. Kirk, *Contemporary International Politics* (Farrar & Rinehart, Inc., 1940), p. 527.

14 A. P. Watts, as above, p. 977.

15 From *Why Europe Fights*, by Walter Millis, copyright 1940 by Walter Millis, by permission of William Morrow & Company.

16 F. J. Brown, C. Hodges, and J. Roucek, *Contemporary World Politics* (John Wiley & Sons, Inc., 1939), pp. 142-144.

17 J. A. B. Scherer, *Japan Defies the World* (The Bobbs-Merrill Company, 1938), p. 44.

18 J. T. Shotwell, *What Germany Forgot* (The Macmillan Company, 1940).

19 From *Why Europe Fights*, by Walter Millis, copyright 1940 by Walter Millis, by permission of William Morrow & Company.

20 Adolf Hitler, ed. R. de R. de Sales, *My New Order* (Reynal & Hitchcock, Inc., 1941), p. 531. Reprinted by permission of Reynal & Hitchcock, Inc.

21 From *Why Europe Fights*, by Walter Millis, copyright 1940 by Walter Millis, by permission of William Morrow & Company.

22 From *Why Europe Fights*, by Walter Millis, copyright 1940 by Walter Millis, by permission of William Morrow & Company.

CHAPTER VIII

POLAND TO PEARL HARBOR

The last chapter gave the highlights of the development of the crisis in Europe between two wars. The years from 1918 to September, 1939, were years that led to war again instead of to a lasting peace. The many reasons and causes may be indicated by a general summary of four main ideas.

The magnitude of the first World War so drained the earth of manpower and resources that the nations of Europe were weakened and disorganized. The peace treaty ending the war was designed to reorganize the ruins of Europe and to ensure peace for the world, but it failed in that mission. Short-sighted selfishness among some nations, envy and bitterness among others, and a desire for revenge among the defeated prevented the establishment of an enduring peace. Finally, Adolf Hitler, as head of a nation of 80,000,000 revengeful people regimented by the Nazi Party, led those people, step by step, into a second great conflict that has spread from continent to continent.

FROM THE INVASION OF POLAND TO THE FALL OF FRANCE

This chapter will continue the story of a Europe at war from the time of the invasion of Poland in September, 1939, to the event that spread the flames of war all over the world—the treacherous Japanese attack on Hawaii in December, 1941.

There has been one fundamental idea in Hitler's plan for conquest—to attack and defeat his enemies one by one. And one by one the nations he invaded fell to the concentrated power of German surprise attack with mechanized might. The list of his victims is a long one. Its length alone points to the need for united action by those nations aligned against the Axis powers. The foes of Hitler must remember Poland, Denmark, Norway, the Netherlands, Belgium, France, and the Balkan countries—remember their doomed single stands against the spread of dictatorship.

How does Hitler work? How was he able to single out his victims one by one in an ordered world? How did he keep his victims from uniting against him? How did he utilize other nations' fears and self-interests to further his schemes?

His methods have been applied so many times that they fit into a surprisingly definite pattern of conquest. First, a particular nation is singled out. Then there is the arousing of fear in the victim; its people are made aware of the dictator's reputation for aggressiveness; their attention is called to the readiness of the German armies for action; so-called "well-informed sources" broadcast the strength of this army. Perhaps some motion pictures are shown leading officials of the devastating power of this army. Some problem, real or invented, is played up as requiring adjustment. Threats and aggressive actions increase the apprehension of the victim nation. Then peace feelers or mediation rumors are thrown out. This causes widespread confusion and disunity. A war of nerves follows, and usually at a superbly timed moment—when possible friends of the victim are busy with other problems—Hitler strikes the jittery, confused, weakened country and gobbles it up.

After such a campaign of mental terror the German Army invaded Poland, without a declaration of war, on September 1, 1939. This act was in defiance of the promises made by Britain and France that they would go to war were Poland invaded. And of course, it was in abrogation of the German-Polish non-aggression pact. After a last ultimatum ignored by Germany, Britain and France joined Poland in her hopeless fight. At least they declared war. More than that they were unprepared to do. The Allies immediately occupied their own Western Front defenses, but for geographical reasons and because of lack of preparedness could give little aid to Poland. Poland was lost from the time Hitler outflanked her by taking over Czechoslovakia. The speed of the German war machine in its "blitzkrieg"—lightning war—made any possible later aid of no avail. The powerful German Army quickly crushed the Polish forces at all points along the militarily undefendable Polish border. In fact, the Polish Army was still in process of mobilization when the blow was struck.

Then Russia entered the arena. Back in 1920 Poland had taken advantage of defeated Russia's armies practically at the gates of Warsaw. In the settlement that followed, Poland seized territory largely populated by Ukrainians and White Russians. The Polish ambassador was now informed that as far as Russia was concerned the Polish government had ceased to exist; that the Soviets deemed it necessary to send troops into Poland to protect Russian interests. So Russian troops crossed the frontier and occupied roughly the area which had formerly belonged to Russia and that Poland had taken over in 1920. Hitler took the rest, including Warsaw and the heart of Poland.

Hitler hailed his victory and challenged Britain and France to a peace on his own terms or a fight to the finish. In a speech made on September 19, 1939, Hitler said: ". . . The British assertion as to the unlimited character of German foreign policy is a lie. I am happy now to be able to refute this lie for British statesmen. British statesmen, who continuously maintain that Germany intends to dominate Europe to the Urals, now will be pleased to learn the limits of German political intentions." This was the old, familiar Hitler song that Europe had heard after every German seizure of territory—that this seizure was to be the last, that Germany wanted peace.

What bitter memories arose! In 1934, Hitler had declared that Germany had no territorial ambition beyond the return of the Saar. In 1935 he had promised that the German government would unconditionally respect the other articles of the Treaty of Versailles, including territorial clauses, and would bring about only by peaceful arrangements the revisions that are unavoidable as times change. He had stated at the same time that Germany had neither the wish nor the intention to mix in internal Austrian affairs, or to annex or unite with Austria.

But what had happened in spite of Hitler's fine promises? In March, 1938, Hitler had swallowed Austria, followed by another scream to the high heavens that *now* his territorial demands were satisfied. But soon following had come the assertion that certain parts of Czechoslovakia must be surrendered, the demand being sugar-coated with the most solemn promise that now Germany was making her last territorial demands in Europe. England and

France had given in; *appeasement* had become a world-renowned word. But in March, 1939, Germany had gulped the rest of Czechoslovakia. Hitler had broken each of his promises in turn. He had used each compromise as a basis for demands on his part, and for further concessions and surrenders on the part of England and France.

What bitter memories indeed, when peace was proposed after the conquest of Poland! The British and French were resolved to make no peace with Hitler, but they were not resolved to make joint war upon him either. They had not yet learned the lesson from Hitler's conquest of nations one by one. Of course, Britain was feverishly rearming and was unprepared for an offensive war. France sat behind her supposedly impregnable Maginot Line and hoped she would not have to sacrifice her soldiers. Thus the months went by in what came to be called the "phony war," the "sitzkrieg"—from October, 1939, to April, 1940.

Although there was no major military action during this period, Hitler's war of nerves on Britain and France continued. His strategy of threat-making followed by peace offers continued and led to much confusion among the Allies. This served to disunify their war effort as well. By the time the spring of 1940 came, Hitler was in an excellent position both militarily and psychologically to start what he thought would be the final operations which would force a decision by the end of the year. The Allies and the European neutrals were at once hypnotized with fear of Hitler's unpredictable next move and at the same time hopeful that he in turn was too scared to move at all. They listened with secret eagerness to the reassuring voices of those who still said there would be no real war.

The "phony war" bubble was pricked when on April 9, 1940, the German armies invaded Denmark and Norway. For some time the situation in Norway had been a cause of concern to the Allies, especially the British. The 800 miles of Norwegian coast offered many hiding places for roving German warships and submarines, despite Norway's friendliness to Britain. Swedish iron ore came to Germany from Norwegian ports. About the same time that Britain decided to take action, Germany struck in her usual ruthless, thoroughly prepared fashion. Again the element of surprise was successfully employed, but this time linked to German military efficiency was a Norwegian fifth-column movement. Two Norwegians, Major Quisling and Colonel Lundlow, had organized this group, which enabled the Germans to capture strong military and naval positions without opposition. Large numbers of so-called German "tourists" had infiltered throughout Norway, prepared to act when the signal was given. After three weeks of futile resistance, the Norwegians asked for an armistice. Their king fled to England.

A British expeditionary force was hurriedly sent to Norway, indicating finally some joint action against Germany. But this force was soon compelled to withdraw, and Norway was added to the growing list of German conquests—which already included Denmark, attacked the same day as Norway but surrendering at once to the German invaders.

Hitler did not stop. On May 10, 1940, German troops crossed the frontiers of the Netherlands, Belgium, and Luxemburg—all neutral countries that had leaned over backward endeavoring to keep from being involved. While Dutch troops fought heroically on the frontier, bombing and parachute attacks destroyed sections of their cities and caused great confusion in their rear. Moreover, there was extensive, coördinated fifth-column activity, which added to the confusion and enabled the Germans to move with fearful rapidity. Overwhelmed by sheer numbers of German bombers, tanks, parachutists, and troops, the Dutch surrendered on May 15, five days after the blitzkrieg struck. The frightful bombing of the heart of the great city of Rotterdam after it surrendered was an object lesson that horrified the world. Thirty thousand civilians were destroyed in that one bombing operation against the undefended city.

Simultaneously with their attack on the Netherlands the Germans struck at Belgium and the tiny country of Luxemburg. The latter was completely overwhelmed the first day. The Dutch story was repeated in Belgium despite brave resistance, and on May 17 German troops marched into the main Belgian cities of Antwerp and Brussels.

But the greatest military disaster occurred farther south. The Germans concentrated the full force of their attack on that part of the French border that first joins the Belgian frontier. This was a weak section, for the French had believed Belgium offered buffer protection here. The German mechanized forces broke through and fanned out to their right to the English Channel. By establishing this new line, the Germans isolated the Allied forces that had rushed into Belgium, and those in northern France, from the main body of the French armies. The German forces then turned and began to advance north against the trapped Allies, who were still being pounded by that part of the German pincers in northern Belgium. Gradually the penetrating and hammering German forces closed in. On May 27 the trapped Belgian army was surrendered by King Leopold. The remaining Anglo-French forces retreated to Dunkirk to attempt escape—evacuation from Dunkirk to England over the Channel.

Then followed the miracle of Dunkirk. In the face of continued pressure by land and air, the British evacuated an astonishingly large percentage of the trapped troops to England, concentrating their limited air forces to maintain local air superiority. However, besides the men they lost, the British Army lost a large amount of guns and mechanized equipment, in fact all the equipment of the expeditionary force. The Battle of Flanders may have ended in a miracle, but nevertheless it left the British in a desperate position as they waited tensely for Hitler's next move.

In twenty-four days Hitler's armies had overrun and conquered the Netherlands, Belgium, Luxemburg, and an important section of France, and the German dagger pointed now at Paris, the heart of France. The French now faced the German armies alone, and those armies were already around the left flank of the Maginot Line and deep into France. The expensive and elaborate defense system was no longer between Paris and the German threat.

A new German offensive hurled itself at the remade French line —of men, now, not concrete, and the line crumbled. Wholesale surrenders were taking place. On June 10, Italy declared war on France as a "stab in the back" action and thus eliminated the possibility of sending reinforcements from the Italian border to aid the hard-pressed French troops in Paris. By June 14, Paris, declared an open city to save it from destruction, had fallen. By June 25 fighting had ceased on French battlefields and an incredulous world realized that independent France was no more. The greatest land army among the democracies had been crushed.

The world was appalled. Seemingly the impossible had happened. How could it be that a great power, a power that had boasted of the "finest army in Europe," could crumble in less than two months of fighting?

Those at the head of the French government and her military forces had mistakenly put their reliance in the defensive strength of heavily fortified lines. Yet they failed to build up the Maginot Line to full strength along the Belgian frontier, despite the fact that the Germans had remilitarized the Rhineland as early as March, 1936, and despite Belgium's severance in 1936 of her military alliance with France, a movement Belgium undertook in the vain hope of assuring herself of a neutral position. Moreover, France's political leaders had signally failed to grasp the significance of the Nazi movement. While it gathered strength in and for Germany, France was weakened by political bickering and economic strife. The workers and employers of France, during those years that saw the workers of Germany regimented to pour out military products, were demoralizing French industrial life by a succession of quarrels and strikes. Public opinion was divided by the Spanish Civil War. Communist and fascist elements strove for control of government offices and positions. The structure of the French democracy had been progressively weakened. When the war came, there was no spirit of the offensive.

Now Britain alone remained to carry on the war. Would Britain give up and accept a German peace while Germany prepared for her next move toward world conquest?

"Bearing ourselves humbly before God," Prime Minister Churchill declared on July 14, 1940, "but conscious that we serve an unfolding purpose, we are ready to defend our native land against the invasion by which it is threatened. We are fighting by ourselves alone. But we are not fighting for ourselves alone. Should the invader come to Britain, there will be no placid lying down of the people before him. . . . We shall defend every village, every town, and every city. . . . *we* would rather see London in ruins and ashes than that it should be tamely and abjectly enslaved. . . .

Thus only in times like these, can nations preserve their freedom." [1]

This should have been no surprise to Hitler, but probably it was by this time. He had by now become accustomed to seeing the spirit of resistance break. But he had been aware of the character of the people with whom he would have to deal from then on. Many years before he had included in *Mein Kampf* his estimate of the British character, an estimate that was now to challenge his march to world domination. In his book he had written:

> The spirit of the British nation enables it to carry through to victory any struggle it once enters upon, no matter how long the struggle may last or however great the sacrifice that may be necessary or whatever the means which have to be employed; and all this though the actual equipment at hand be utterly inadequate when compared with that of any other nation.[2]

Nevertheless, as always following a Nazi victory, Hitler launched a peace offensive. In a speech made on July 19, 1940, he pointed out the invincibility of German arms and the inevitability of German victory. Hence further war, with its great cost and sacrifice, would be unnecessary. But there were no specific peace terms; if accepted the peace would mean a Germany lording it over the other peoples. More likely, it was an attempt to cloak his schemes in a certain righteousness before his own people.

The British answer was short, simple, tough, and to the point: "We realize the struggle may cost us everything," Foreign Secretary Halifax declared, "but we shall not stop fighting until freedom for ourselves and others is secure." [3]

GERMANY VERSUS BRITAIN

The stage was now set for the German invasion of Britain. Each side had certain advantages. In manpower, Germany had a population of 80,000,000; Great Britain without its Dominions had 48,-000,000. The British Army consisted, in July, 1940, of 1,500,000 partially trained, poorly armed men, plus another million hastily organized home guards. The German Army consisted of about 3,500,000 magnificently armed men, trained by actual warfare, with plentiful reserves of manpower and equipment. On the other hand, the British Navy, greater by far than the combined navies of Germany and Italy, stood ready to defend the island to the last ship. But unlike 1914, the new war was fought as fiercely in the air as on land and sea. At the opening of the battle, Germany possessed a tremendous superiority in airplanes. Because of her conquests, she had air bases much closer to Britain than Britain had to the heart of Germany. Germany had the advantage on land and in the air; Great Britain on the sea.

Two months after the fall of France the Germans launched their air offensive against Britain. This air campaign consisted of three phases. First, effort was made to crash through the British defenses by using unescorted bombers in great numbers; the result for the Germans was that they sustained heavy losses, 180 planes being lost in the vicinity of London in a single day. The resistance of the British fighter forces was an epic of courage and fortitude. Next the Germans turned to daylight bombing, with fighting ships escorting the bombers. This, too, proved too expensive to be sustained. The third phase consisted of night air raids, with the maximum effort directed against London, the night raids later changing to mass efforts against a single city, Coventry being the first victim, later Plymouth, Liverpool, and others. But British morale was not broken; neither were profitable targets such as power plants, railroad installations, and so on fatally damaged.

In the meantime, the R.A.F., confined to raiding at night because of German numerical superiority, carried out raids on German industry and repeatedly bombed the "invasion ports." Invasion by the German Army did not materialize, perhaps because of the R.A.F.'s efforts.

By June, 1941, however, it appeared that more serious than the threat of a Nazi invasion of Britain was the intensive German campaign against British and neutral shipping. In May, 1941, the British admiralty announced that since the beginning of the war Britain and neutral shipping in British service had lost more than 1400 merchantmen, totaling more than 6,000,000 tons.[4] This was a real threat to Britain. She must transport to her shores the foodstuffs and supplies which were necessary for her war effort. Although the British still remained supreme on the high seas when it came to naval combat, numbering besides lesser victories the sinking of the *Bismarck*, Germany's newest and most powerful battle-ship, the attack on her shipping became a bitter and ominous threat to her existence as an island fortress dependent upon ship bottoms for food, raw materials, and other supplies.

FRANCE AFTER THE FALL

Let us turn back to France—to the conquered France of June, 1940. After the fighting ended, the German forces occupied over half of France, with Paris as the headquarters. The entire Atlantic coastline was occupied, and its ports were made bases for German operations against British shipping. The rest of France, with the city of Vichy as capital, was unoccupied, and came to be called, somewhat ironically, Free France. But that name did not endure for long. On July 9, the French parliament, meeting at Vichy, conferred upon Marshal Pétain full power to create the plans for a dictatorship. By a number of decrees the Third Republic of France, born as a result of a German victory in 1870, died as the result of a German victory in 1940. The government of Unoccupied France became the Pétain dictatorship. Former Premier Laval was named Vice-Premier of the new government.

The France of Vichy was to have a strongly fascist cabinet, a single party, and a parliament the duties of which would largely be advisory. France was to become a "peasant country." Thus it would seem France would be an agricultural province of industrial Germany. Anti-Jewish measures were adopted, another sign of the strong German influence. A number of the leaders of the old France were imprisoned and ordered to trial for taking France to war when they knew the French were unprepared to fight. Among their accusers were men as guilty of France's unreadiness for the war, if not more guilty.

Not all Frenchmen approved of the actions and policies of the Pétain government. General Charles de Gaulle was one who did not. He believed that France, though conquered on the Continent, should still fight as an ally of Britain, continuing to use her navy, her air force and her colonial power. He appointed himself leader of the French outside France, and so served as a rallying point for the French who still wanted to and could fight Hitler. Many distinguished French officers from the army and the navy rallied to his colors. Their properties at home were confiscated. Many were tried and sentenced to death *in absentia*.

Relations between Great Britain and the Pétain government soon came to a definite break. The French fleet, contrary to promises made to Britain, was to be collected, demobilized, and disarmed under German or Italian control. Although the German government solemnly declared it had no intention of using the French fleet during the war, the British had learned by painful experience that Hitler's word was of no value. Nor were the French leaders at Vichy trusted. On July 3, two French battle-ships, two light cruisers, eight destroyers, a number of submarines, and about 200 smaller craft which lay in British harbors were seized. Several units at Alexandria also fell into British control and were immobilized, their ammunition removed. But at Oran, Algeria, two French battle cruisers and a number of other warships refused a blunt demand to surrender, and the British blasted them, all but destroying the whole fleet. A few days later the largest French battle-ship, the *Richelieu*, was disabled by British fire at Dakar, French West Africa. By these and other measures Great Britain safeguarded her supremacy at sea.

Within conquered France everything was not harmonious. Laval, the leading exponent of collaboration with Germany, apparently wished to have France join Germany against Britain, but Marshal Pétain maintained that honor forbade the French to fight against their former allies. This clash in policy resulted in the removal of Laval on December 13, 1940, and the appointment of Admiral Darlan as his successor. Negotiations for collaboration with Germany were broken off for a time following Laval's dismissal, although Darlan's opinions were believed to be similar to Laval's. In the meantime, approximately 1,500,000 French soldiers were still held prisoners by the Germans, food stocks in France were running low, the budget situation became hopeless, and lack of communication between Occupied and Unoccupied France all tended to further the split in the country and the demoralization of the French people.

Moreover, in Occupied France the Germans applied certain financial practices which have subsequently been used in other conquered territories and can be accepted as the German pattern for looting conquered peoples. Her soldiers were issued so-called "occupation marks" with which they were permitted to purchase goods. These marks had no value in Germany, and were supposed to be presented to French banks for payment by those that accepted them in payment for merchandise and produce. By this process French goods were removed from storekeepers' shelves and sent back to Germany, but Germany did not pay for them. They were paid for by the French banks, by the savings of millions of Frenchmen. It was and is the loot not only of merchandise but of banks as well. Besides this, Germans became majority directors in French industry so that it would respond to the fuehrer's war effort, with the profits being siphoned off by German officials. The whole scheme was thoroughly planned and organized looting. In addition, quantities of food were shipped to Germany, causing not only hunger, but dire want. (In Greece this policy has caused actual starvation; in France malnutrition and near-starvation.)

Early in 1941 the Pétain government sought to resume negotiations with Hitler through Darlan, whose views did not greatly differ from those of Laval. After a few months it was indicated that the Pétain government would collaborate with Hitler, perhaps even to the possibility of war with Great Britain. This was France, in May, 1941.

FROM THE BALKANS TO CRETE

We have followed the course of France and Britain from the fall of France in June, 1940, to May, 1941. During this time another section of Europe entered into the spreading war. In the southern part of the Continent lie several nations that we usually group together under the term *Balkan countries*. Rumania was the earliest of these countries to feel the pressure of Nazi intervention. During and since the first World War, Rumania had taken advantage of her neighbors' difficulties to add to her territory. Return of these territories was now demanded by Russia, Bulgaria, and Hungary. After frantically seeking the advice of Hitler and Mussolini, who urged acceptance to avoid war, Russia's claims were reluctantly granted in June, 1940, and Bessarabia was returned to Russian control. By August Bulgaria had what she wanted. But accord between Rumania and Hungary for the Transylvania region was not reached so easily. After much bickering, despite a German decision in favor of Hungary early in October, German troops entered Rumania and occupied that country in a bloodless conquest. Hitler had at last reached the Black Sea, one of the principal objectives outlined in *Mein Kampf*.

The next move in the Balkans was made by Mussolini. Following the German pattern of building up a case for attack, Italian troops massed in Albania suddenly invaded Greece on October 28, 1940. The attack was no surprise, but Greek resistance was. This fierce resistance, aided by mountain roads and winter weather which bogged down Italian mechanized equipment, and also aided by British warships and bombing planes, enabled the Greeks not only to hold out stubbornly during the first three months of 1941, but actually to push the Italians back.

Meanwhile, Hitler was attempting to persuade the small states of Central Europe and the Balkans to support his "new order." Passage through Bulgaria and Yugoslavia would enable Hitler to come to the aid of the fleeing Italians. Bulgaria joined the Axis on March 1, 1941, and German forces moved in to occupy the Bulgarian-Greek frontier.

The pressure now turned upon Yugoslavia. Great Britain hurriedly transferred men and supplies from Egypt into Greece in order to encourage Yugoslavia to resist Hitler. But after Bulgaria succumbed and Yugoslavia saw herself nearly surrounded, the government of Regent Prince Paul of Yugoslavia entered the Axis organization by signing a pact on March 25, 1941, in Vienna. This news was immediately received with anger in Yugoslavia, particularly in Serbia; and the Nazi-influenced government was overthrown by the Serbs and the Yugoslav Army ordered mobilized. Unfortunately for the Yugoslavs, before mobilization was well under way the Nazis launched terrific attacks upon both Yugoslavia and Greece. After a twelve-day campaign, the defeated and scattered Yugoslav Army laid down its arms. And Belgrade, although declared an open city and not defended, was laid in ruins by ruthless German air attacks. But not all the Serbs of Yugoslavia laid down their arms. Thousands fled to their mountain fastnesses. From there they are waging guerrilla warfare to this day.

Meanwhile, the Greek section of the German blitzkrieg swept over the Greeks, who were now aided by 60,000 British, New Zealand, and Australian troops. As in all their other campaigns, the Nazis possessed an overwhelming superiority in air and mechanized forces and troops especially trained for this type of campaign. This inevitably decided the campaign in German favor despite the mountainous terrain and the valiant stands of the Greek and Anzac troops. On April 27, after a three-week campaign, the Nazis occupied Athens. The British, as at Dunkirk, managed to evacuate a large percentage of their troops, though they left much precious equipment behind.

Although the invasion of the Balkans was costly to the German armies in men and materials, the net result of the campaign appeared to be distinctly favorable to Hitler, despite the poverty of those countries. Even the poor can be further looted. The seeming invincibility of his panzer divisions was maintained; the Allies were now swept off the Continent of Europe except for Gibraltar. The occupation of Greece enabled the Nazis to menace the eastern Mediterranean and threaten the flank of Turkey, and there were new agricultural and mineral resources added to the German holdings, more stores of supplies to be drained from the helpless conquered countries.

But the Germans did not stop with the Balkans. On May 20 they launched the first completely air-borne invasion in history against the British occupied island of Crete, some sixty miles out in the Mediterranean. Following a terrific attack by bombers, Nazi troops were landed in Crete by parachutes, gliders, and transport planes. The British Navy smashed all German attempts to land men from ships. But hundreds of airplanes shuttling back and forth between Greece and Crete carried men, supplies, and light equipment to the German troops already on the island. British naval forces were roughly handled by air attackers, and many vessels were lost. By early June the under-equipped British were forced to carry out again an overseas evacuation as at Dunkirk and in Greece. The outcome of the battle for Crete seemed to be a clean-cut victory for air power. By taking Crete, Hitler pushed his air bases farther into the Mediterranean, gaining for the Axis an important aërial base for attacks on the British in Africa.

THE WAR IN NORTH AFRICA

This was in June, 1941. After the Nazi victory in Crete, the world wondered where Hitler would strike next. It was thought he might strike through Syria and Iraq to secure Near East oil, or that he might drive across North Africa in order to oust the British from Egypt and the control of the Suez Canal. However, there soon came reports from England of the massing of Nazi troops along the Russian frontier from Finland to the Black Sea. Were these reports only propaganda? Both Berlin and Moscow denied any German pressure on Russia. Suddenly on June 22, without a declaration of war the Nazi air and land forces struck at Russia. Rumanian forces collaborated in the south. The attack apparently was launched along the whole western frontier of the Soviet Union. Before continuing with the story of the gigantic struggle between the forces of Russia and Germany, the story of the war in Africa and Asia should be brought up to June, 1941.

During the first two years of the war, the conflict raged in Africa as well as in Europe. There were two general areas in which Axis and Allied forces struggled for supremacy on the Dark Continent. These were East Africa and North Africa.

Between June, 1940, and August 20, 1940, the British and Italians fought in East Africa. The first important Italian conquest after a series of preliminary skirmishes was to conquer British Somaliland.

Early in 1941, after months of preparation, the British swept into Italian Somaliland in a counter-offensive to the earlier Italian drive. Spearheads of attack driven from the British Sudan and Kenya Colony arrived at the heart of Italian territory. Italian Somaliland was conquered, British Somaliland recaptured, and Addis Ababa wrested from the Italian Army which had crushed Ethiopia several years earlier. On May 19, 1941, the last large Italian military unit in East Africa surrendered at Algi in Eritrea. By June, 1941, practically all of East Africa was cleared of Italian troops.

In North Africa the war fluctuated on a grand scale in Italian Libya and Egypt. On September 12, 1940, Marshal Graziani with about 300,000 Italians forced the attack from Libya into Egypt. After pressing forward for five days the Italians paused to consolidate their gains at Sidi Barrani, about sixty miles within Egypt. The British fleet bombarded their bases at Bardia and Tobruk as the Italians rested. Their rest was needed, for they never got beyond Sidi Barrani. On December 9, 1940, the British General Wavell struck with British, Australian, and New Zealand troops. The Italians were badly smashed and surrendered by tens of thousands. Tobruk, then Derna, and finally on February 6, 1941, Benghazi fell into British possession. Again there was a pause. Then the pendulum swung against the British. General Wavell had sent reinforcements to the Greeks during the Greek campaign, and the Italians in Libya, now heavily reinforced with German mechanized units, roared eastward once more, recapturing Benghazi and Derna. Grimly Tobruk held out. On April 14 the Axis forces were inside Egypt again and had nullified British gains. Early in June, 1941, the Italians and Nazis halted. The British still held Tobruk and Solum. The German supply line was now 1,000 miles long back to Tripoli. Both sides paused to re-form for a final effort. This was June, 1941, in Africa.

JAPAN'S AGGRESSIONS IN CHINA

And now let us return to the Far East. At the time Germany invaded Poland Japan had already been engaged for more than two years in an undeclared war against China. During these two years, the Japanese had captured the great commercial cities of Tientsin, Peiping, Shanghai, Nanking, Hankow, and Canton; they also controlled the main railways of China, and they had closed the Chinese ports. But the Chinese under the leadership of Chiang Kai-shek refused to surrender, and in practically every Japanese-occupied province of China guerrilla warfare was being relentlessly carried on against the invaders. In 1911 the United States and Japan had concluded a commercial treaty which regulated all trade relations between the two countries. It was provided in the treaty that its provisions would remain in effect until one nation or the other gave six months' notice of cancelation. Subsequently Japan had signed a treaty in which she agreed to equal trade opportunities in China. That meant that the United States, as well as other countries, would have equal trade rights with the Japanese in doing business with China. The United States became disgusted with Japan's failure to live up to the provisions of this latter treaty; the American nation was disgusted with Japan's whole expansionist scheme. It was obvious to the United States that treaties meant nothing to Japan except a temporary convenience or a mask to cover her other intentions.

So, in the summer of 1939 the United States gave the necessary notice of cancelation. This meant that a Japanese ship could not even be unloaded in an American port without specific permission. But the United States continued to permit war materials to be sold to Japan up to September, 1940.

In the meantime, toward the end of 1939 and the early part of 1940, Japan was not doing so well in China. Not only had her army failed to capture Chungking, the Chinese capital and new industrial center, or to make other important gains, but her troops were actually being driven back in some places by the Chinese. The Chinese, it seemed, could fight if they could continue to secure munitions and war supplies in sufficient quantities.

There still remained in 1939 three major avenues of importation for war supplies to China—from Indo-China, from Burma, and from Soviet Russia through outer Mongolia. In November, 1939, the Japanese cut the road from Indo-China, and in early 1940, Japan made attempts to cut the Russian route, but bitter fighting stalemated her effort. The Burma Road remained open, under British control.

On March 3, 1940, Japan set up a puppet government at Nanking to administer the Japanese-conquered area in China. The United States, however, immediately announced it would continue to recognize the government at Chungking as the government of China.

Following Germany's blitzkrieg successes in Europe against France and the Low Countries in May and June, 1940, Japan soon moved toward establishing her control over not only East Asia but the South Seas as well. By late summer, her government was organized and ready to carry out the Japanese-announced intention of domination in Asia.

Japanese pressure was brought to bear upon Great Britain in Asia, and Great Britain was forced to accede to Japanese demands. At a time when the British Empire was engaged in a life-and-death struggle with Hitler, it was felt necessary to prevent Anglo-Japanese tension. Pressure was also brought to bear upon the Netherlands and on France, and Japan took advantage of every event in Europe favorable to the Axis to strengthen her own position and to increase her demands in Asia.

As though to balance Japan's aggressive move, on September 25, 1940, the United States announced that a loan of $25,000,000 had been made to China. On the next day President Roosevelt announced an embargo on all scrap and steel to Japan. The Japanese press raved and said war was now inevitable between the United States and Japan. It was not surprising that on September 27 in Berlin, Japan, Germany, and Italy signed a ten-year military alliance. In it they pledged mutual assistance in the event any one of them were attacked by any power not then at war. Japan's role as the dominant power in the East was recognized by the other two Axis partners. It was obvious to all but the blind that this alliance was aimed against the United States.

Japan's armies, toward the end of 1940 and the first of 1941, were bogged down in China. The Chinese had been bolstered by Britain's reopening of the Burma Road on October 18, 1940, at America's insistence and by United States shipments of lend-lease supplies since March 11, 1941. This was the Far East in June, 1941.

THE GERMAN ATTACK ON RUSSIA

We may now pause a minute to review the situation in the various areas of the war in June, 1941. Germany was dominant on the Continent of Europe west of Russia. On the Russian front the two largest modern armies in the world, the German and the Russian, were locked in a gigantic struggle, strongly favorable to the Germans, who again seemed to have got the jump on another victim. Britain with ever-increasing strength fought Germany and Italy in the air over Europe, on the sea throughout the world, and on the land in Africa. The opposing forces in Africa paused near the border between Libya and Egypt, preparing for a continuance of the struggle. Japan, stalemated in China, intensified her fight for domination of the Far East, no matter what power might oppose it, and her press was indulging in a campaign of hate against the United States. The story moves on swiftly from June, 1941, to the climax of December, 1941.

The German invasion of Russia began on June 22, 1941, and swept on in typical vigor for a short time. The daily list of Russian towns captured grew larger. Large Russian forces were encircled and annihilated. Finally Moscow itself was threatened, and Leningrad was three-fourths encircled early in the campaign. In September, Hitler's front forged ahead in the south, where the Crimea again knew the bloody struggles of war. By October 8-11 the Nazis reported a 300-mile break in the Soviet lines and boasted that Russia had been decisively beaten, its best armies annihilated, destroyed. The Soviet admitted its armies were everywhere in retreat and ordered partial evacuation of Moscow. The part of the world still resisting Hitler felt the approaching doom of Russia and consequent prolonging of the war if not total German victory. All through October the giant Nazi offensive slowly pressed on as the hopes of the democracies sank lower. Suddenly a new note began to enter the once completely confident German communiques. Explanations were being made as to why the German offensive was slowing down. Gradually news leaked out that the offensive had not only been slowed down but stopped. To an incredulous world, wary of believing Russian or German communiques, the truth dawned that the offensive had not only stopped, but that Germany's mighty machinery of attack and conquest was in reverse. During the week of November 10-17 the Germans admitted that bad weather and Soviet resistance had brought all their attacks to a standstill.

On December 5, 1812, Napoleon Bonaparte got into a coach that was headed back toward France, not toward Moscow. Napoleon was leaving the remnants of his Grand Army in Russia and returning to France. The greatest adventure of the "Little Corporal" was over. One hundred and twenty-nine years later to the day, on December 5, 1941, a German spokesman in Berlin an-

nounced that the great battle to take Moscow had been abandoned
and that the "war of movement" had ended on the entire front.
For Adolf Hitler, another former corporal, it also represented the
end of a mighty effort. Only two months before he had promised
the German people the end of the war was in sight.

STALEMATE IN NORTH AFRICA

The war in North Africa was stalemated in June, 1941, following the Axis counter-offensive that nullified previous British gains.
Both sides rested and gathered strength for continuing the war.
During the week of November 16-24, the British Army, strengthened by American arms, particularly light tanks, struck first. The
attack was directed west into Libya. One week later a junction
between the main British forces and troops from Tobruk, which
had held out during a long siege, was made. It was believed that
large Axis forces under the German General Rommel were
trapped. But Rommel escaped and cut between Tobruk and the
main British forces again. This was a heavy blow to British hopes
for a speedy victory. But the British continued to press forward,
even though winter had come to the desert. Heavy rains and cold,
bitter winds caused a temporary lull in the battle. Both sides were
bringing up supplies and reinforcements as 1941 drew to a close.
Tobruk was again relieved and the Axis forces driven toward
Tripolitania. The British R.A.F. continued to dominate the air,
and the Navy claimed that a large part of the ships sent from Italy
to Africa were sunk on the way. This was Africa in December,
1941. In late January, 1942, Rommel counter-attacked in force,
driving the British back from their advance positions to approximately forty miles west of Tobruk. Meanwhile violent air attacks
had been in almost continuous operation against Malta, drastically
weakening British operations against Axis transports and supply
convoys bound for Tripolitania and indicating the possibility of an
all-out Axis attempt to seize Malta.

JAPAN STRIKES SOUTH AND EAST

In the Far East, remember that Japan's war in China seemed
bogged down in June, 1941. But the Tokyo war machine struck

out in other directions. On July 23, 1941, Japan received the permission of the Nazi-controlled Vichy government of Unoccupied France to move into Indo-China. In reply, Washington on July 25 froze Japanese assets in the United States. This action, joined by the British and by Batavia in the Dutch East Indies, established an economic blockade of Japan which steadily sapped her strength. The Japanese press raved. On November 15, Saburo Kurusu, a special envoy from Japan, arrived in America in a professed eleventh-hour attempt to reach a peaceful settlement. But during these negotiations, and indeed long before, Japan was preparing its war machine for the treacherous attack in December. On December 6 President Roosevelt appealed to Emperor Hirohito in a final attempt for peace. The Japanese answer came—in the form of bombs on unsuspecting American Pacific outposts. On December 7, 1941, the murderous surprise attack on Pearl Harbor and the American islands even shocked a world already accustomed to ruthless German warfare and plunged America into war. The flames that rose in Poland had now spread around the world, and raged in Europe, Asia, Africa, and the Americas.

REFERENCE NOTES

[1] From F. L. Benns, *Europe Since 1914* (F. S. Crofts & Co., 1941), p. 848.
[2] Adolf Hitler, *Mein Kampf* (Houghton Mifflin Company, Boston).
[3] F. L. Benns, as above, p. 849.
[4] Same, p. 856.

CHAPTER IX

EVOLUTION OF UNITED STATES FOREIGN POLICY AND DEFENSE PREPARATIONS, 1934-1942

In the two preceding chapters events and conditions that form the background of the present World War have been related in the briefest possible outline. No attempt was made to present theoretical conditions or those that are argued from a set ideological position. The purpose was to present as nearly a factual statement as possible.

The first chapter of this series sketched in compact form the story of Europe between two wars, from 1918 to 1939.

The second continued the story of a Europe at war again and of Japanese aggression in the Far East. It continued from the invasion of Poland in September, 1939, to the attack upon Pearl Harbor in December, 1941. Hitler's series of blitzkriegs paraded in ruthless fashion through these two years; Poland, Denmark, Norway, Luxemburg, the Netherlands, Belgium, France, and the Balkan nations became but slaves to the German will. By the time Japan launched her treacherous attack upon the United States, the German invasion of Russia had gone into reverse and Hitler, like Napoleon before him, had a retreat from Moscow on his hands, with the Russian armies maintaining steady pressure as the Germans withdrew from hard-won territory. Britain and her Dominions were continuing to wage stubborn warfare against the Axis in the air, on the land, and at sea—in Europe, Asia, and Africa. The conquered nations were growing restless under the iron hand and economic exactions of the Nazis, and trouble flared continuously. Finally, the gigantic strength and immense resources of the United States were thrown whole-heartedly by a united people into the war against the Axis.

It is the purpose of this chapter to trace the successive steps that have influenced the position of the United States in the present world conflict, the recent foreign policy of this nation, and

America's reactions to the startling events and changing conditions
of the war years, 1939, 1940, and 1941.

There is no provision in our Constitution for the making of a
foreign policy or for the conduct of foreign relationships as such.
But there are four parts of our government system that may be
called, together, the machinery of foreign policy, the agencies that
make and express policy. They are the Department of State, the
foreign service, the Presidency, and the Congress. It is necessary
to explain the functioning of these divisions of government in relation to our foreign policy.

The head of the Department of State, the Secretary of State,
functions in three somewhat different ways—as a political ap-
pointee of the President, as a department chief, and as a sort of
Foreign Minister of the United States.

While the appointment of the Secretary of State is political, in
that the Secretary of State is always a prominent member of the
President's party, his chief task is not the building and mending
of political fences but the heading of that complex organization
known as the State Department. As chief of that department he
assumes the duties of a Foreign Minister for the United States.

The department is composed of a number of divisions, such as
Far Eastern Affairs, Current Information, Treaties, and so forth.
A chief for each division advises the secretary. To assist the Secretary of State in the administration of this elaborate organization
there are an Under Secretary of State and three assistant secretaries. It has become the practice for the secretary to delegate the
routine of administration to his many assistants, leaving him free
for his third and most important function, handling foreign affairs.
The secretary maintains constant contact with foreign representatives and with the President, with the embassies and legations that
represent foreign nations in Washington and with our embassies
and legations in all quarters of the world. Normally, he is the President's chief adviser in matters of foreign policy; while he does not
originate, he often develops the foreign policies of our country.

The Foreign Service of the United States is made up of two
separate services, the Diplomatic Service and the Consular Service.
Diplomatic officers, such as ambassadors and ministers, represent
the United States in foreign countries. Consular officers are con-

cerned chiefly with commercial matters. However, this distinction may not always be sharp. Many of our consular officers have performed and are performing diplomatic duties in addition to carrying on their regular duties.

The diplomatic mission in a particular foreign country is the channel through which communications are made from one government to another. It must also gather all possible information about the policies and affairs of the country to which it is assigned and report them faithfully to the State Department. The diplomatic mission also protects and assists American citizens in the country where it is located. It seeks to extend in a friendly way the influence and prestige of the United States.

The officers of the Consular Service are stationed at foreign trade centers. They gather and report to the State Department information as to tariffs, trade practices, business conditions, and other matters which help American foreign trade. They assist in the administration of the immigration, tariff, sanitary, and merchant marine laws of the United States. They also act as legal agents of the United States, assisting American citizens in distress.

You can see how this network of Foreign Service plays a vital role by supplying the State Department and so the President with daily, fresh information from all over the world. This information enables our government to form and keep up to date our foreign policies.

The parts the President and Congress play in determining and expressing our foreign policy may be considered together. Every nation has a definite representative authority to speak and act for it in foreign relations. *A country must speak with a single voice to the outside nations of the world.* In the United States, that authority and that voice is the President. The President is the only mouthpiece of this nation for communication with foreign governments, and communications from foreign nations to this country must be addressed to him. Therefore, the State Department and the Foreign Service are simply agents of the President, deriving their authority from him.

The Constitution provides that the President shall have the power to make treaties, but with the advice and consent of the Senate, two-thirds of the members present concurring. It likewise declares he shall appoint ambassadors, consuls, and other public ministers, with the approval of the Senate. Other authority over foreign relations accrues to him because of his position as chief executive.

However, Congress maintains a check on presidential leadership. Congressmen make the President aware of the opinions of their constituents concerning foreign policy; hence the members of Congress serve, indirectly, to influence the President's actions. Only the President and the Secretary of State are more prominent in matters of foreign policy than the chairman of the Senate Committee on Foreign Relations. The Senate may reject treaties negotiated by the President. It has done so more than once. An example, the Treaty of Versailles, which President Wilson signed in Paris, was turned down in the Senate and therefore never ratified by this country.

Nevertheless, it is the President who officially formulates the chief principles of American foreign policy. He can do this in messages to Congress, he can do it in dispatches to foreign diplomatic representatives, or he may give his views to the world in public addresses. The office of the President, therefore, is the key to the *expression* of foreign policy. The Congress is the branch in which foreign policy is incorporated into law.

To repeat, various branches of government contribute to the machinery by which our policy is set up and set forth. It is the pooling of the intelligence of our executives and their appointees, of the representatives of the people, and of our trained Foreign Service men. The next question to be considered is, "What are the basic policies that this combination has formulated that have developed during our years as a nation?"

The chief principles of our foreign policies may be expressed under three main headings. First, we stand upon our rights as a nation under international law and believe it the duty of our government to back up this stand. Secondly, we believe in freedom of action for this country in its own interests. Finally, we believe in the principles and theory of the Monroe Doctrine.

We stand upon our rights as a nation. This means that we abide by treaties in our relationship with other countries and expect others to do the same. The United States has entered into a large group of pledges and contracts with other nations as individual nations or as groups of nations. These pledges and contracts form a relationship that is entered into voluntarily by both sides. This relationship continues until there is mutual consent to end it, or until it is ended by certain provisions contained within the treaties themselves. With this policy as a mode of behavior, we claim the following rights as a nation: We desire to promote and upbuild our foreign trade; we are committed to protection of American citizens in foreign countries and on the high seas; we are concerned in maintaining our own independence and that of our territories; we seek peaceful relations with all nations and believe in the harmonious adjustment of international disputes without recourse to war.

The second basic policy is our intention to have freedom of action for Americans in relationship with the nations of the world. This policy erroneously has been called the isolation policy. *Isolation* is an inaccurate and narrow name for it. The concept of isolation usually is traced to opinions expressed by President Washington in his Farewell Address, in which he said, "Europe has a set of primary interests which to us have none, or a very remote, relation. Hence, she must be engaged in frequent controversies, the causes of which are essentially foreign to our concern. . . . It is our true policy to steer clear of permanent alliances with any portion of the foreign world." [1] It is to be noted that Washington said *PERMANENT* alliances. A truly great statesman, he weighed his words carefully. The narrow interpretation of this theory through the years gives the impression that, in reality, it is a policy of nonparticipation in the affairs of the world except as it pleases our fancy to act. The late Senator William E. Borah performed a most useful service when in a speech made on January 8, 1934, he pointed out in the following words that such was not the case:

It is not isolation, it is freedom of action. It is independence of judgment. It is not isolation, it is free government. There can be no such thing as free government if the people thereof are not free to remain aloof *or to take part* in foreign wars. . . . In matters of trade and commerce, we have never been isolationist and never will be. In matters of finance, unfortunately, we have not been isolationists and probably never will be. When earthquake or famine, or whatever brings human sufferings, visit any part of the human race, we have not been isolationists and never will be. In all matters political, in all commitments of any nature or kind which encroach in the slightest upon the free and unembarrassed action of our people or which circumscribe their discretion or judgment, we have been free, we have been isolationists. And this, I trust, we shall ever be.[2]

The third of our basic policies is contained in the theory and interpretations of the Monroe Doctrine; and to see how that doctrine came to be pronounced, let us look for a minute or two at the times, six score years ago.

Napoleon had been defeated and exiled to St. Helena, and a wave of reaction had engulfed Europe. The Hapsburgs were again in control of Spain, just as another branch of that liberty-hating family ruled Austria with an iron hand. A Bourbon had been restored to the throne of France. Drastic measures were taken all over the Continent of Europe to suppress minorities and eliminate the seeds of republicanism sown by the French Revolution.

But in South America an opposite trend had set in. The great Simon Bolivar of Caracas was leading the struggle of liberation from Spain in Colombia; Mexico was breaking her bondage to her Spanish masters. A British seaman-adventurer, Lord Cochrane, aided Peru and then Brazil in throwing off the yoke of European control; and British merchants were enjoying a growing, prosperous trade with the rebels of the New World.

It was with jaundiced and threatening eyes that the autocrats of Europe looked upon these events in South and Central America. Fortunately a brilliant English statesman, George Canning, was directing the foreign policies of Great Britain. He was a Tory at home but a liberal in recognizing a new world in the Americas and the advantages to British trade if the independence of the American republics could be maintained. Therefore, in the name of Britain he recognized the South American rebels and suggested to the United States that a joint declaration be made from London and Washington on that subject.

But the United States determined to make a strictly 100 per cent American pronouncement. Spain's ambition to recover dominion over her colonies and again monopolize their trade to the exclusion of all others was looked upon in Washington as a threat to this country and to its growing commercial relationships with Latin America. Moreover, it was feared that the reactionary regimes of Europe would endeavor to set up one or more monarchies in the New World.

President Monroe, therefore, called attention to the impending danger in a message to Congress in December, 1823, and said: "We owe it, therefore," he said, "to candor and to the amicable relations existing between the United States and those powers to declare that we should consider any attempt on their part to extend their system to any portion of this hemisphere as dangerous to our peace and safety. With the existing colonies of any European power we have not interfered and shall not interfere," but, declared the President, "the American continents, by the free and independent condition which they have assumed and maintain, are henceforth not to be considered as subjects for future colonization by any European powers." [3] Britain immediately supported the attitude of the United States; Spain did not reëstablish her dominion in the Americas. Perhaps European respect for the British fleet in those years had something to do with our early success in upholding the Monroe Doctrine.

Thus, the third basic policy of our foreign relations was derived from this statement of doctrine. The United States, while observing the existing rights of European nations in this hemisphere, would oppose any interference with self-government in any independent country on this side of the Atlantic.

These three general ideas, then, include our basic foreign policies. The reader should not get the idea, however, that they are as simple and as fundamental as they appear in the statements above. During the many turbulent periods of our history and under our different presidents, these basic policies have been interpreted in different ways. Our democracy was keeping up with rapidly changing world affairs. Essentially, basically, however, they remain the same. *We stand upon our natural rights as a nation under international law; we demand freedom of action in foreign relations; and we believe that no foreign power should interfere with the self-government of the independent nations of the Americas.*

OUR RELATIONS WITH EUROPEAN NATIONS
SINCE 1939

Now that we have seen who determines and expresses our foreign policies, and also have considered the basic attitudes that our government has maintained during our history, we have the foundation needed to understand the policies of recent years.

Since the World War the foreign relations of the United States have varied, depending on circumstances. There have been different ways of interpreting the three fundamental policies just discussed. Our policies took seven different leads [4]:

(1) Plans to maintain neutrality or the attempt to build walls against the spread of other people's wars: (2) the renunciation of war by treaty or the endeavor to establish world peace among nations by the signing of a pledge to do away with armed conflict; (3) the limitation of naval armament in order to eliminate sea-power rivalry as a cause of war; (4) coöperation with the League of Nations in matters mostly non-political, such as labor problems or opium traffic control, but not coöperation with the League in any action against a nation that might involve us in a war; (5) peaceful settlement of international disputes through arbitration; (6) the withdrawal on our part of controls and intervention in the affairs of other nations in the Americas, such as the recall of the Marines from Haiti and Nicaragua; (7) the building-up of peace and coöperation in the Americas through the "good neighbor policy."

But in 1939 the world was once more plunged into war. The "realistic" powers had taken advantage of the inclinations towards pacifism of the idealistic. The conference on naval limitations in 1921, held in Washington at the invitation of the United States, had more severely handicapped the United States than any other world power. It was our nation, the one most able to bear the cost of naval armament, that gave up the most. The League of Nations' "disarmament" conferences in 1926 and 1927 bore negligible results. As time went on, there was growing suspicion that Japan was secretly evading the terms of her agreements, including the prohibition against fortification of mandated islands in the Pacific. And finally, British appeasement of Germany permitted that country again to stir German naval shipyards to intense activity. The idealism and love for peace (together with a substantial degree of wishful thinking) of the democratic countries had played into the hands of the enemies that were to seek their destruction.

A tremendous task confronted the administration of President Roosevelt as the Hitler scheme for world conquest was unrolled, as the German armies moved into defenseless Bohemia and Moravia in the spring of 1939 and stormed ruthlessly across the frontiers of Poland in September. The realities of a second World War came home. Fortunately for several years the President had sponsored modernization and increase of the naval establishment, and much headway had been made in the strengthening of our naval forces. But in the face of diverse sentiments at home, the problem of 1939 was how to adjust towards realism the foreign policy of the United States and bring it abreast of the times?

Immediately after the outbreak of European hostilities in September, 1939, President Roosevelt announced the neutrality of the United States. He followed this with a proclamation of a limited national emergency and defined American territorial waters as extending as far to sea as the nation's interests required. The President also appealed to the heads of warring nations not to bomb civilian populations. The United States government, after the quick success of the German invasion of Poland, denied Germany recognition of her conquest and opened relations with the new Polish government in Paris. Toward the end of the year, Great Britain established a purchasing commission in the United States to coördinate purchases of war supplies in the United States and Canada.

These were the actions of our government at the outbreak of the war. What was the opinion of the American public during the last few months of this fateful war year? There was almost universal antagonism toward Hitler and Nazism. He and his aides were the authors of a stream of abuse against democracy. The Nazi methods and characteristics of government were fairly well known to Americans. The contempt for tolerance, the ridicule of peaceful settlement of disputes, the use of lying and false reports, the terror of the Gestapo and concentration camps were familiar concepts of Nazism to most Americans. An agreement between Germany and Japan was a threat to United States interests in the Far East. Nazi methods of trade made American trade interests uneasy. Nazi agents were busy in the Americas, and it was believed here that there was fifth-column activity in numerous places in the Americas.

The hostile attitude toward Nazism was a slow outgrowth of sober thinking, made possible in a way of living that afforded the public a free and honest press and provided for the privilege of open discussion. The large demand for books and magazines on European affairs showed the extensive public interest in this field.

But Americans, while well-informed and interested, were not affected by the new war in the same way as those whose lives and fortunes were immediately involved. The Americans in the fall of 1939 could be described as more anti-Hitler than pro-Ally. They felt that a definite stand by America might lead to an eventual A.E.F. Their formula for peace was to keep American ships out of the danger zone, avoid loans to Allied governments, and keep on the alert to detect sources of both Allied and Axis propaganda and immediately label them as such.

It was generally assumed that Americans favored an Allied victory. The British Navy stood between the British Empire and the schemes of Nazi Germany. The destruction of this navy would mean the destruction of the empire. The German system of trade would be forcibly extended, and our commerce would suffer heavily. We were accustomed to a certain degree of taken-for-granted teamwork between the United States Navy and the British Navy. We had only a one-ocean navy.

Nevertheless, at the end of 1939, although public opinion in the United States still was overwhelmingly against Hitler, it also was overwhelmingly opposed to our participation in war. Hitler was warring against democracy, against our civilization and way of life, but still only a few would use American forces to stop him.

Following the fall of Poland, a military quiet set in that lasted well into the spring of 1940. A previous chapter commented on the references to this period as the "phony war." You will remember that in April world affairs again suddenly became critical. The "phony war" was over; and German invasion and conquest of Norway, Denmark, the Netherlands, and Belgium followed in an amazingly short time. During this spring blitzkrieg President Roosevelt condemned the aggressor Germany, and twenty-one other American nations followed his lead. Moreover, he froze the assets of the victim nations deposited in the United States. Had he not done this, Germany would have been able to use these assets to make purchases to add to her war machine.

Prior to the fall of France in June, 1940, Premier Reynaud appealed desperately to President Roosevelt for support, asking for clouds of warplanes. The sudden turn in the war had eased restrictions in the United States on Allied purchases of war materials. The Allies were able to obtain almost any type of plane, for example, then in production for the United States government. But there was no time for clouds of warplanes. Clouds of planes were not yet in production. And anyhow it was too late.

The lesson of the German successes in the spring and summer of 1940 sank home; restrictions were eased still further, and Great Britain, now fighting alone, was greatly aided. Under the interpretation of already existing laws, arms and munitions were sold to Britain, replacing in part the equipment she lost at Dunkirk. Congress required that military experts certify that certain of these items classified as surplus were not essential to our own defense. Congress thus sought to strike a balance between aid to the Allies and due regard for national defense.

America continued to give aid to China in her fight against Japan. During the summer, a loan of $25,000,000 was granted China. President Roosevelt also placed restrictions on the export of petroleum, iron, and scrap steel, in a move that was obviously aimed at Japan.

During the summer months of 1940, the parade of events seemed to continue to increase the power of the Axis. Unoccupied France became a Pétain dictatorship strongly influenced by the Nazis, who held nearly 2,000,000 French soldiers as hostages. Rumania joined the Axis, and toward the end of the summer mighty German air raids were launched over England. The United States was warned that after the war she would have to trade on victorious Germany's terms or be barred from a Europe entirely part of the

Nazi system. Germany advised neutrals that Great Britain was under total blockade, and warned them to keep their ships out of the war zone. American aid to Great Britain increased, however.

Not only did we maintain and increase our flow of war aid to Britain, but passage of the Selective Service Act showed the concern of the country with its own defense. By the fall of 1940, the first peacetime citizen army in United States history had been inducted into federal service. Our small regular army took over the huge task of training many hundreds of thousands of selectees and National Guardsmen in the shortest possible effective time.

Paralleling the growing flow of war materials to Great Britain was an alarming increase in the number of ships sunk by German submarines and planes. At one time there were three ships being sunk for every new ship being built. This problem became a matter of grave concern to both Washington and London, for at this rate much war material and urgently needed foodstuffs would be lost en route.

In World War No. 1 Allied convoys had solved the problem of getting through submarine-infested waters with small losses, but conditions had changed. New weapons were now employed to supplement the submarine, such as the airplane and motor torpedo boats. The British needed small, fast ships for convoy, particularly destroyers. Over 100 old World War destroyers were tied up in American ports. They still could be used effectively for convoy work. A campaign followed to enlist public support to sell some to Britain. In August, General Pershing broadcast a warning. "All the things we hold dear are gravely threatened," he said, and advocated all possible aid to Britain, including placing at least fifty destroyers at her disposal. Several other prominent men supported the proposal. Some, however, feared that this move would be an act of war; others felt that it would weaken United States defenses. Sentiment took a favorable turn when Great Britain announced she would give, in return for destroyers, long leases on islands in the Atlantic and Caribbean for use as naval bases. The administration was eager to get such bases for hemispheric defense.

Doubts as to the effect on United States defenses were dispelled. The Attorney General ruled that the President could complete the deal through an executive agreement with Great Britain. Assurances were required from Great Britain that, in the event the British Isles should fall to Germany, the British Navy would not be surrendered.

Public sentiment, as measured by the Gallup Poll, was 61 per cent in favor and 39 per cent opposed to the trade of destroyers for strategically located naval and air bases. In the American press the majority of the newspapers supported the trade of destroyers for bases. The Nazi government-controlled press claimed sardonically that the United States was taking advantage of the fact that Britain was tied down and on the verge of defeat to improve the American position. These newspapers claimed that the United States was now beginning to take over the remnants of the British Empire. According to the Italian press also the trade was proof of the beginning of the collapse of Britain.

Meanwhile the presidential campaign was under way in America. The candidates of both the Democratic and Republican parties were in substantial agreement as to foreign policy. "Aid to Britain" was as fervently espoused by Mr. Wendell Willkie as it was by President Roosevelt. The November election was, nevertheless, considered a popular endorsement of the President's foreign policies; and he took immediate steps to increase the flow of war materials to the Allies. It was announced that production of implements of war would be divided equally between the United States and Great Britain. A British order for a large number of additional planes was approved, and several "flying fortresses" were traded to Great Britain.[5]

In the meantime, sales to Britain had been on the basis of "cash on the barrelhead and come and get it." By late 1940, however, the dollar reserves of Britain were running low. Mechanized warfare proved expensive. Late in November, the British Ambassador to the United States reported that his country was near the end of her cash resources and that some form of financial arrangement with the United States would be necessary. Both the Johnson Act and the Neutrality Act prohibited financial credit to England. President Roosevelt proposed that the United States government take over a large part of future British orders, pay the manufacturers, and lease the goods to Great Britain under mortgage, to be returned or replaced in kind after the war. The British Purchasing

Commission in the United States was immediately advised to proceed with orders totaling about three billion dollars.

In addition to government aid to Britain, there was widespread private assistance that indicated the support of public opinion. The Red Cross and the British War Relief Society sent large quantities of clothing and blankets. Some English children were provided homes here. There were Bundles for Britain. The Committee to Defend America by Aiding the Allies gave moral support, as did numerous other organizations. These movements grew as German exactions on conquered peoples and the utter ruthlessness of German methods in dealing with subjugated populations shocked the conscience of the American people and drew a stark picture of "things to come" if Germany were to emerge victorious over a slave Europe.

Congress supported the President and was eager to further domestic preparedness. There was a determination to keep the Axis out of the Americas and even a willingness to defend the Philippines. But above all, Congress wanted to keep the country out of war. More than twenty years of pacifistic teachings and propaganda of disillusionment had had their effect upon the public opinion that is reflected in the halls of Congress.

While the mighty thrusts of the Axis military machines during 1940 left only Great Britain resisting and standing between Hitler and further world conquest; while gallant Greece was heroically stemming the Italian invasion; while the overwhelming majority of Americans was bitterly opposed to Hitlerism in all of its ugly forms, the sentiment of the nation was still strongly against participation in war. Only a minority of our people at the close of 1940 was in favor of American intervention in a "shooting war."

As 1941 opened, the question of aid to Britain, how much and what kind, was recognized as the most urgent problem of the period. Extension of financial help was being brought more to the fore. The subject of domestic preparedness was no longer a matter of debate. While an increasing number of people seemed to read war's handwriting on the wall, there was also some bitter opposition to aid for Britain.

In the first phase of the Axis-Allied struggle of 1941, British success in Africa had been countered by successful Axis counter-attacks. In the Balkans the British attempt to aid Greece ended in defeat, and the Allies were driven off the Continent of Europe except for Gibraltar. The administration at Washington took steps to bulwark British resistance in the face of this acute situation. In his annual message to Congress President Roosevelt asked for all-out aid to the nations resisting aggressors. The Lend-Lease bill became law in March. The United States took Greenland under its protection April 10, and the following day the President lifted the ban on American shipping in the Red Sea area. In May, Secre-- tary of War Stimson urged the use of warships to convoy war cargoes.

It appeared Americans were awakening to the fact that, for the second time in a quarter of a century, they were becoming in-volved in a world war and would be forced to choose whether to fight with allies or later fight alone. The position of the United States had shifted by degrees from complete isolationism to the Lend-Lease Act, which has been described as the most positive internationalist legislation in our history. Eighteen months earlier the nation had rocked with controversy over the adoption of a neutral "cash and carry" policy toward belligerents. Now the question had become the extension of aid short of war. Public opinion actually had been changing rapidly. German firing squads throughout Europe were helping to consolidate this opinion. The United States had not blindly followed isolationism into a *cul-de-sac*.

The passage of the Lend-Lease Act indicated that America was following a course based on an awakened concept of the realities —most of all the reality that the collapse of Britain would bring this nation face to face with Germany in an American isolation without allies. Another reality was the importance of the preser-vation of British sea power.

Therefore the next logical step after the adoption of the lend-lease principle was the extension of protection for the delivery of the goods, a step that opponents of aid to Britain advertised as one that might readily lead to war.

But Germany, Italy, and Japan had already signed a pact aimed directly at the United States. They had declared in 1940 that any act of war against one of them by a nation not already engaged in the world struggle would be considered an act of war against them all. Moreover their interpretation of the act of war was one that would give effective aid—effective aid according to their definition of the term—to one of their enemies. That meant war with the United States at any time they chose to put this country on their timetable. They alone would determine when and where their blows would be delivered.

The state of mind of the American public at the time of the lend-lease debate has been investigated by numerous polls, revealing certain definitely marked sentiments and opinions. If Germany won the war, the great majority felt sure of three results:

1. There would be an unjust and oppressive peace.

2. The world would be a hard place to get along in for any democratic country.

3. Hitler would go further for world domination and would not be content until he had achieved domination of the western hemisphere.

Practical considerations of what would happen to the American people, their country, and their world if Britain fell and Hitler consolidated his subjugation of an enslaved Europe were uppermost in the minds of the people polled. Two-thirds of them believed that Hitler wanted to dominate the United States and one-third or more felt he could invade the United States. There was no general belief in American invincibility. About half thought that Hitler would ruin the United States if he wrecked our foreign trade and had control over world markets and strategic materials. The nearer Hitler might seem to come to world domination, the more likely would be the growth of a popular majority who believed the United States would have to fight to defend American institutions. Meanwhile German military commanders in occupied countries continued to seize hostages, continued to give public notice of shocking mass executions as reprisal measures. No propaganda invented atrocities in this war. They were official admissions, and they stirred America deeply.

In his address of May 27, 1941, President Roosevelt reaffirmed the determination of the American people to see Hitlerism defeated. In January Hitler had threatened to torpedo any United States ships approaching the British Isles. As though in answer to the President's speech, an American vessel, the *Robin Moor*, was sunk. The administration showed no disposition to force a crisis. The press and the country were indignant but calm. The President knew that so-called "incidents" are but tools for an aggressor. In a message to Congress the President condemned the sinking as a part of a "declared and actively pursued policy of frightfulness and intimidation, which has been used by the German Reich as an instrument of national policy." [6] The United States held Germany responsible, and it was indicated that reparations would be expected. On July 6 the United States took over eighty-four ships belonging to the Axis and occupied countries. These ships had been seized earlier in March to prevent sabotage. Axis assets were frozen and the consulates closed. Germany and Italy promptly retaliated by freezing American assets and closing United consulates.

Closing of the Axis consulates helped to disrupt the Axis propaganda program in the United States. Another important step followed soon after. A blacklist of South American firms with pro-Axis connections or sympathies was published. The assets of these firms in the United States were frozen, and American commercial dealings with them were subjected to a licensing plan. The use of American trade and money for the support of propaganda in Latin America and other nefarious Axis activities were thus stopped.

British shipping losses continued to run high—approximately 400,000 tons monthly. So far the United States Navy had gone no further than limited patrolling. Now the question was presented: How far would the United States go to guarantee the delivery of goods to Britain? The President issued an order to the Navy to assure safe communication between the United States and Iceland. This move permitted the British Navy to concentrate on the zone of greatest danger. Sinkings at once dropped sharply. To replace the 2,000,000 tons of shipping Britain already had lost the United States assembled an equal amount of American tonnage for the British. United States ships also took over all British shipping service from North America to Australia. The occupation of Iceland as well as the other policies were generally approved throughout the United States.

Hitler's invasion of Russia in June, 1941, did not give him the important support among anti-Communist elements in the democracies which he expected and for which he made a world-wide propaganda play. The extent of Russian preparedness and resistance was a surprise to both the Axis and the Allies. As Russia proved a worthy foe of the Germans there was a willingness to extend aid to her. The United States pledged aid late in June, and Britain followed early in July.

The authorization of forty-seven billion dollars for defense purposes during the fiscal year ending June 30, 1941, indicated the extent of the determination of the United States to build up home defenses to aid the nations fighting Hitler. The importance of this protective program not only to the United States but to the entire western hemisphere is revealed in a report of the Brookings Institution. The study demonstrated that Hitler never could make his new order work in an economic sense even if it included Russia. He would be forced to seek the really vast surpluses of wheat, meat, cotton, coffee, and oil of South America; and "so long as there is liberty in the United States, Hitler's ultimate object must be the United States." [7]

RELATIONS WITH JAPAN

Another nation was becoming more and more a part of the picture of aggression for world domination. Across the Pacific, Japan was following a policy of opportunity. She had indicated her alignment with the Axis. Early in the year she had requested that the United States recognize Asia and Asiatic Pacific waters as Japan's natural sphere for development. In July Japan demanded military control of French Indo-China, which Vichy was forced to accept, as she must accede to Nazi wishes. Japanese occupation, which amounted to virtual seizure, followed immediately.

This appeared to be the last step, short of war, which Japan would be permitted to take on her road toward conquest of the South Pacific. The vital British base at Singapore, the Philippines, and the Dutch East Indies, source of important strategic materials, were endangered. Realizing Japan must be checked, President Roosevelt ordered the freezing of her assets in the United States. This move was also popularly approved. The British countries made a similar move, terminating also their trade treaties with Japan. The United States took immediate steps to bolster the Philippine defenses.

The conference at sea between President Roosevelt and Prime Minister Churchill marked the high point in the development of United States foreign policy during the summer of 1941. Long-term aims and peace ideals were drawn up. Points agreed upon included disarmament of aggressor nations, equal access for all to international trade and raw materials, freedom of the seas, and liberty for all. Further gains were planned for labor and social security. There would be no change of sovereignty without the consent of the governed, and no aggrandizement at the end of the war for either the United States or Great Britain. Further discussion included aid to Russia and coördination of measures to be taken.

Significant developments followed. Pan-American pilots began flying planes to the British in the Near East. Prospects of close collaboration between Vichy and Berlin created a demand for recognition of General de Gaulle's government of the Free French. American diplomacy endeavored strenuously to convince Vichy that further collaboration with Germany would not pay, that France should not risk her honor on the wrong horse. Allied and American opposition to Japan on the economic front made that nation anxious for a respite, but still unwilling to relinquish any of her spoils. The Japanese press was violent in its attacks on the United States. The attempted torpedoing of the American destroyer *Greer* and the German admission of responsibility led President Roosevelt to order the Navy to eliminate the submarine responsible. Other American-owned and American-operated ships were sunk by the Axis. On November 11 the President declared that from then on if German and Italian vessels of war entered any waters whose protection was deemed necessary for American defense they did so at their own peril.

The Neutrality Act of 1939 had stipulated that American ships could not carry passengers or cargoes to any belligerent nations nor enter any combat zone. The arming of American merchant ships also was forbidden. During the summer and fall of 1941 American public opinion increased its pressure for added assistance to Great

Britain and to Russia. The administration, the press, and the public were growing increasingly aggravated over the sinking of American-owned and American-operated ships by the Axis. In line with the change in the international situation and under the pressure of public opinion, Congress in November modified the Neutrality Act to permit the arming of American ships; it also lifted the ban on their sailing into the combat zone.

Since the outbreak of the war in Europe, the problems confronting America in her foreign affairs had increased in number and had become more and more complex. The success of the German war machine, its ruthless methods, and the triumph of Germany over country after country that had stood in the Nazi path had brought a sense of solemn foreboding and appreciation of stern reality to the American people. The great majority had loyally supported the nation's leaders as, step by step, they had been forced to modify the policy of declared neutrality until it closely approached belligerency. There was the establishment of a neutrality zone, the first American peacetime conscription, the destroyer deal, the Lend-Lease Act, the Latin-American blacklist, the taking-over of Axis-controlled ships, the freezing of Axis credit, the assumption of jurisdiction over Iceland, and the modification of the Neutrality Act. The United States had disposed of any pretense to neutrality in this war. The American people approved the ending of neutrality restrictions. They had backed every strong act of the government and had demonstrated their dislike for hesitation and obstacles to action.

With this final determined attitude emerging by degrees from the confusion of the past, the American people, toward the end of 1941, faced the culminating act in the drama "From Peace to War." Japan came to the forefront of the stage on which she had been playing an opportunistic and threatening part in the background.

With her armies bogged in China and an economic blockade sapping her strength, Japan sent a special envoy to the United States in a professed eleventh-hour attempt to reach a peaceful settlement. Saburo Kurusu arrived in this country during the latter part of November and, ever-smiling, ever-hopeful, promising to do everything possible to prevent spread of the World War to

Asiatic waters. Little did Americans believe that his mission was but a mask.

Negotiations and conferences at the White House and the State Department followed, long conversations that dragged on and on without any compromise on Japan's part. Finally, on December 6, President Roosevelt appealed to Emperor Hirohito in a final attempt for peace, a dramatic effort to promote a spirit of conciliation. Mr. Kurusu continued to smile for the newsreels. The Japanese envoys met again with members of the State Department December 7, but shortly before dawn on December 7 the Japanese answer to negotiations and personal appeals was made. Bombs were her answer, bombs raining down in a murderous, treacherous attack upon American Asiatic outposts. The United States, in December, 1941, was at war; and the bombs that crashed on the Island of Oahu and in Pearl Harbor heralded the immediate unity of the American people, the galvanizing of their energy and their spirits in a war effort destined at whatever cost to destroy the forces of evil that had combined against the freedom-loving peoples of the earth.

REFERENCE NOTES

[1] C. A. Beard, *American Government and Politics,* 8th ed. (The Macmillan Company, 1939), p. 265.

[2] C. C. Maxey, *The American Problem of Government,* 3d ed. (F. S. Crofts & Co., 1941), p. 531.

[3] C. A. Beard, *American Government and Politics,* 8th ed. (The Macmillan Company, 1939), p. 267.

[4] F. J. Brown, C. Hodges, and J. S. Roucek, *Contemporary World Politics* (John Wiley and Sons, Inc., 1939), p. 250.

[5] *Fortune Survey,* Vol. XXXVII, p. 104.

[6] *Current History,* Vol. I, No. 1 (September, 1941), p. 26.

[7] *Fortune Magazine,* Vol. XXIII, No. 6 (June, 1941), pp. 58-59.

PART III

American History and the Constitution

by

Ralph H. Gabriel

Larned Professor of American History, Yale University
Formerly (1917-18) First Lieutenant of Infantry,
United States Army

CHAPTER X

THE OLD WORLD AND THE NEW

The United States is today one of the most important nations in the world, with a population of more than 130,000,000, larger than that of any nation in Europe save Russia, and possessed of great natural wealth in fertile soil, beds of minerals, oil pools, and water power. The American people lead the world in manufacturing. The citizens of the Republic have called into being a large army and are creating a navy and air force that will surpass in power any similar establishments the world has ever seen. As a result of these factors the United States today is playing a vastly important role in the course of the twentieth century. The decision as to what the world of tomorrow shall be rests to a great extent with the United States.

The present importance and power of the United States seems almost unbelievable when we remember that our nation had its tiny beginnings only a little more than 300 years ago. Three hundred years may seem a long time, but it is short when compared with the extent of the history of China. And in Europe the ancestors of the present Spaniards, Frenchmen, Germans, and Englishmen have lived in the regions we call Spain, France, Germany, and England for more than 2,000 years. Europe is old; the United States is young. So also are the other nations of the New World—Mexico, Brazil, Chile, the Argentine Republic, and the rest. The New World is the child of Europe.

The history of the New World begins in the fifteenth century, a period when the people of Europe were bringing about important changes in their civilization. They were passing out of that era known as the Middle Ages, the time of armored knights and strong castles surrounded by moats. Europeans in the Middle Ages had been divided into a great number of small political groups, each governed by a lord, or a duke, or a baron. In those days Europeans knew little of any world outside their own continent.

Among the many changes which ended the Middle Ages and brought in the modern period, four inventions were of particular importance. The discovery of gunpowder made possible the development of firearms. Cannon could batter down castle walls and so ultimately made these forts almost useless, and new weapons helped to make it possible for the stronger barons to increase the size of their domains by conquering their neighbors. Gunpowder, then, helped to bring about the modern type of nation. The invention of printing was a great achievement of the fifteenth century. Johannes Gutenberg, a German, printed the first book, a Bible, in 1456. Printing was important as a background for the discovery of America because one of the earliest printed books was *The Travels of Marco Polo*, a widely read book which brought to the Europeans much information about distant India and China. The third and fourth inventions were the compass and the astrolabe, the latter being an instrument to assist the sailor to determine his location at sea. Before the compass and the astrolabe the Atlantic Ocean had been a barrier, full of mystery and danger, holding the Europeans on their continent. These instruments transformed the sea into a highway.

In the twentieth century the oceans have been and are the most important international trade routes. The growth of ocean navigation has taken place in the same period which has seen the development of civilization in the western hemisphere. Today the United States insists on the principle that these highways shall be free to the use of American ships.

THE DISCOVERY OF THE NEW WORLD

In 1492 Christopher Columbus, sailing for the King and Queen of Spain, led an expedition of three small ships on the first voyage of discovery to cross the Atlantic. He found and landed on some of the islands now known as the West Indies, and, believing these islands to be off the coast of Asia, he called the red men who inhabited them Indians. Columbus made other voyages to the newfound lands. Other explorers began to trace the irregularities of the coastline. Then in 1513 a Spanish adventurer named Balboa made his way through the jungle of the Isthmus of Panama and saw before him the mighty Pacific Ocean. A few years later an expedition led by one of the greatest sailors of all time, Magellan, rounded the continent of South America, crossed the Pacific, and finally reached Spain by sailing around the southern tip of Africa. The discovery of the Pacific by Balboa and Magellan made it clear to Europeans that Columbus had discovered a new world. To this new region the name America was given, for an explorer, Americus Vespucius, who first became convinced that Columbus had reached a new continent blocking the way by sea from Europe to Asia.

For Europeans the discoveries of Columbus, Balboa, and Magellan made the world grow suddenly big. The pioneering mariners robbed the Atlantic of its ancient terrors. But the New World was full of mystery; it lured men of adventurous spirit to come to find out what opportunities it offered.

THE SPANIARDS IN THE NEW WORLD

Spain founded colonies in America almost a hundred years before the French and the English began to establish homes on the western side of the Atlantic. The Spaniards sought wealth, particularly gold and silver. The principal Indian people of the highlands of Mexico were known as Aztecs, a tribe with a civilization much further advanced than that of any Indians living within the present boundaries of the United States. The Aztecs were farmers and also miners of the precious metals which they used for vessels and for ornaments. Another Indian people, known as the Inca, lived in the high mountain valleys of Peru near the west coast of South America. In the sixteenth century Spanish adventurers conquered both the Aztec and the Inca and won great wealth for Spain. The story of the conquest of Mexico illustrates the methods and the strength of Spain in the sixteenth century.

Hernando Cortés, a Spanish soldier of fortune, sailed with a fleet of small vessels along the east coast of Central America and Mexico in the year 1519 searching for an opportunity to conquer wealth. He led a force of about 500 soldiers who had joined the expedition in the hope of getting a share in any riches that might be won. While his fleet was anchored in the harbor of what is now Veracruz, Cortés learned of the existence of that rich and powerful

Aztec empire whose capital city was deep in the interior of Mexico. The Aztec chieftain, whose name was Montezuma, commanded thousands of fighting men and exacted tribute from many conquered Mexican tribes.

Cortés, determined to overthrow the inland ruler and to win the treasures of the Aztecs, ordered his ships to be destroyed. This cutting-off of all possibility of retreat in the face of an opponent whose power was unknown was one of the boldest acts in the history of North America. The Spanish soldiers wore armor which reached from the shoulder to the hip, and were equipped with steel-pointed spears, called pikes, and with clumsy guns that were fired by holding a burning fuse to powder in a little pan beside the barrel. The flash of the powder in the pan was carried to the powder inside through a small hole. The gun, called an arquebus, would shoot neither far nor accurately. Cortés had a few horses and some primitive cannon.

The Indians did not attack as the Spaniards marched on Montezuma's capital because the wavering Montezuma could not make up his mind whether or not the white chieftain who rode on a horse was a god. Cortés found the Aztec capital to be a city of about 70,000 people, built on some islands in a large lake with three raised roads or causeways joining the city to the mainland. The military tactics of the Aztecs emphasized defense; they apparently believed their city in a lake to be impregnable. Cortés met Montezuma on one of the causeways and accepted his invitation to enter the city. Then the Spaniard with incredible audacity not only led his force into the city but seized the chieftain, Montezuma, and made him prisoner.

There followed two years of bloody fighting during which the Spanish army was driven from the city with heavy losses, but in the end the white men won, and in 1521 Mexico became a Spanish colony. The success was a victory of iron weapons over those of stone. It was also an illustration of what a daring offensive carried out by courageous and determined men can sometimes accomplish. One admires the leadership of Cortés, while at the same time wishing he had had a better cause. The Spanish conqueror made the Indians of Montezuma's empire virtual slaves. The red men were divided into groups and given to Spanish leaders who used them to work either in silver mines or on great plantations. The remainder of the Spanish Empire in the New World was, like Mexico, conquered by force. Wealth from the Americas made Spain in the latter years of the sixteenth century the most powerful nation in Europe.

Everywhere in New Spain the priest came with the soldier, and in addition to the priests religious brotherhoods, particularly the Order of Saint Francis, called the Franciscans, and the Society of Jesus, known as the Jesuits. The brotherhoods befriended the Indians and attempted not only to lessen the harshness of the conquest but to teach the conquered red men the civilization of ·the Spaniards.

When it was finally completed, the Spanish Empire was a collection of Spanish colonies on the continents of South and North America and in the West Indies. It included all of South America except Brazil, a region which was settled by Spain's neighbors, the Portuguese. Spain controlled not only all of present Central America but Mexico and a considerable part of what is now the United States. The Spaniards possessed California and built a fort on San Francisco Bay, named for St. Francis. They occupied what is now Arizona, New Mexico, Texas, and Florida. St. Augustine, the oldest town within the present boundaries of the United States, was in the beginning a Spanish frontier fort. The Spanish Empire, the largest and richest empire in the world of its day, collapsed in the first quarter of the nineteenth century, and from its ruins have risen eighteen independent nations, not including Brazil, which freed itself from Portugal about the same time the Spanish Empire broke up.

The creation of New Spain was a marvelous achievement. During the three and a quarter centuries of its history only a relatively few Spaniards came to the New World to make permanent homes. In New Spain white Spaniards were a small ruling class. Many of these intermarried with the Indians. Negro slaves were brought to some colonies. The mass of the people of New Spain were Indians and mixed-bloods; yet though they were few, the Spanish overlords gave to New Spain the Spanish civilization. Everywhere south of the Rio Grande Spanish is the ruling language except in Brazil, where Portuguese is spoken, and everywhere again, except in Brazil, the customs of the people are Spanish. Their church is the Catholic Church; their music, literature, and theater are all of Spanish origin. Graciousness in manners is much more important in Spanish America than it is usually in the United States.

Today the people of the United States are drawing closer to the neighboring nations on the south which came originally from the old Spanish Empire. Americans have always been handicapped, and still are, in dealing with these neighbors because too few citizens of the United States understand that the Spanish civilization of Central and South America is quite different from our own and that it has much to contribute to us. Likewise the Latin Americans have failed to realize that the civilization of the United States has much more to offer than stores and factories. The United States is today attempting to found the defense of the western hemisphere not only on political and military agreements with its Latin-American neighbors but on the mutual understanding and respect of the peoples who enjoy those two great civilizations, the Latin-American and the Anglo-American.

THE FRENCH IN THE NEW WORLD

The French established themselves on the St. Lawrence River in 1608, when Champlain founded Quebec, and this settlement gradually grew in size until French farmers occupied the St. Lawrence Valley from Quebec to Montreal. Other French farming communities grew up in Nova Scotia. But the real life of New France was the fur trade, not agriculture. French fur traders pushing into the forests around the Great Lakes and in the northern Mississippi Valley made New France for more than a century the chief fur-producing region in North America.

French explorers followed the Mississippi and discovered its mouth; France founded New Orleans; and some Frenchmen dreamed of a great empire in the New World that would extend from the mouth of the St. Lawrence to that of the Father of Waters. In the eighteenth century France planned to consolidate and hold this empire by building a chain of forts from the Great Lakes to the mouth of the Mississippi.

Today the descendants of these old French settlers in the St.

Lawrence Valley make up about a third of the population of our Dominion neighbor on the north. Canada should always be thought of as a nation made up of two quite different peoples, the French-speaking one-third and the English-speaking two-thirds, a fact that has in the past sometimes made it difficult for Canadians to achieve unity of feeling and purpose.

THE ENGLISH IN THE NEW WORLD

The English began making permanent settlements in the New World early in the seventeenth century, almost a century after the Spaniards had begun taking advantage of the opportunities of the western hemisphere. The English founded Jamestown in Virginia in 1607, only a year before the French established themselves at Quebec, and in the seventeenth century Englishmen established a line of colonies along the eastern coast of what is now the United States. The vast extent of land from Maine to Georgia was claimed because much of it had been explored by Englishmen, but the Hudson River and the harbor at its mouth had been first visited by an expedition sent out by the Netherlands, and naturally the Dutch had founded New Amsterdam on Manhattan Island. Because England and Holland were keen rivals in the seventeenth century for trade on the sea, Britain was unwilling to permit a Dutch colony to cut its American empire into two parts. In 1664 a British fleet sailed into the harbor and compelled the Dutch officials to surrender the colony. New Netherlands was awarded to the Duke of York and was renamed, in his honor, New York. But Britain had other colonies in the New World besides those on the continent of North America. The English founded a colony on the island of Bermuda and others in the West Indies and the Bahamas. The most important British colonies in the West Indies were Jamaica and Trinidad.

Americans are apt to forget that in the seventeenth and eighteenth centuries the people of England were probably more interested in the colonies in the West Indies than in those on the mainland of North America, the reason being that the colonies in the West Indies were on the edge of the tropics and could produce sugar. In the seventeenth and eighteenth centuries the West Indies was the most important sugar-producing region in the world, and they still remain today the center of the world's production of cane sugar.

Bermuda, the British West Indies, and the Bahamas did not join the rebelling Americans on the mainland in the Revolutionary War, and the colonies founded so long ago on those islands still remain possessions ruled by Britain. The United States has never attempted to interfere with the management of any of these settlements, but in recent years a change of vast importance has taken place in the relations between these English possessions and the American Republic. Bermuda, the Bahamas, and the West Indies all lie near the coast of the United States, and in these days of swift warships and of airplanes, these islands have become essential to the defense of our nation. It was, therefore, an event of great importance when, in 1940, Great Britain permitted the United States to lease sites for the building of air and naval bases on these island colonies. Bases on Jamaica, Trinidad, Bermuda, and other islands bring America into close relations with the ancient British Empire.

The English colonies in North America were begun as private enterprises, the British government granting specific areas of land to different groups of Englishmen desiring to establish colonies in the New World. One such group called itself the London Company and was made up largely of business men who had invested money in the concern. The King gave the London Company a charter, just as a State legislature gives a charter to a corporation today, and the company, sending settlers to Virginia, founded the Virginia colony in 1607. But the London Company was never successful in its management, was reorganized, and again did not succeed. Finally, in 1624, the English crown revoked the charter and turned Virginia into what was called a royal colony. The change meant that Virginia ceased to be a venture intended to make money for stockholders in a British company and became a colony of men and women who were carving out careers for themselves in the New World. After Virginia became a royal colony in 1624, the crown, instead of the company, appointed the governor of the colony.

Not all the English colonies in North America began as undertakings by commercial companies. Sometimes a tract of land was awarded to a single person, who was called a proprietor. Maryland was so awarded by the King to Lord Baltimore, who assumed the responsibility of getting colonists to come to the colony. The proprietor granted land to settlers and appointed the governor of the colony. Pennsylvania was a similar colony, and there were other forms of colonial organization.

A majority of the Englishmen who made their way to America in the seventeenth and eighteenth centuries came primarily to find new and better ways of making a living. Some were farmers who had been driven off the land when large areas in England, which had once been used for raising crops, were turned by their owners into pastures for raising sheep. Other colonists were men who had failed in business and wanted to make a new start. Many young Englishmen believed that the new communities in America offered more opportunities for speedy advancement than did the settled communities in Britain. The men and women who sought to take advantage of the opportunities offered by the English colonies had to have the courage to break away from a kind of life they knew well and to take the risks of living in a strange and almost unknown land. The voyage across the Atlantic was dangerous and might last three months; only the more ambitious and venturesome were willing to undertake an enterprise so hazardous as abandoning a familiar life for a home in an unknown wilderness.

These men and women who came to make careers in the English colonies were seeking freedom of opportunity, and many of them were trying to escape from the rigid and cramping restrictions of the class system of the Old World. A man in Europe was born into a low or a high class, and normally he expected to live all his life in the class to which his father belonged. There were some young men of ambition and ability who sought to break out of such a regimented system by coming to Massachusetts, New York, Pennsylvania, Maryland, or Virginia. In the English colonies in America a man was free to rise as far as his industry and abilities would take him. What he, as an individual, was and did counted more than who his father was.

Many of those who came to the English colonies sought freedom of another sort; they were men and women who were persecuted, sometimes mildly and sometimes severely, because they held fast to certain ideas. Some of these people were Catholics who suffered in many ways in seventeenth-century England, and who found a refuge in the New World in Maryland; others were of several different varieties of belief who got into trouble because of their differences with the Church of England. The Puritans and the Pilgrims, both nonconforming groups, came to New England; the Quakers, looked upon as radicals in seventeenth-century England, founded Pennsylvania and settled in several other colonies.

For most of the immigrants who came in the seventeenth century to the English colonies America meant freedom. For some it meant the freedom of the individual man to make of himself what he could. For others it meant the freedom of the individual to direct his life in accordance with the moral and religious principles he thought right. For many people the America of the English colonies meant both these freedoms.

William Penn, the founder of Pennsylvania, expressed in the seventeenth century the ideal of freedom which the Quakers followed. Penn, in England, had spent months in jail because he had left the Church of England to join the Quakers, who insisted that all churches should be entirely separate from the government. Penn knew the value of freedom from having lost it because of his beliefs. Speaking of America, he wrote: "We lay a foundation for after ages to understand their liberty as men and Christians . . . for we put the power in the people."

CHAPTER XI

THE FOUNDING OF AMERICAN INSTITUTIONS

MONARCHY AND THE ENGLISH COLONIES IN NORTH AMERICA

Today we often forget that Americans have in their history lived longer under a monarchy than under the government of the Federal Republic. Between the Declaration of Independence in 1776 and the present lies a period of 166 years. But between the first permanent settlement in Virginia in 1607 and the Declaration of Independence lies a period of 169 years. During those 169 years Americans were the subjects of monarchs of England. A suggestion of the importance of monarchy in the lives of early Americans may be found in some place names on the east coast of the United States: Virginia suggests Queen Elizabeth, the Virgin Queen, who ruled in Shakespeare's day; Charlestown, now a part of the Boston metropolitan area, was named for Charles I, and Charleston, South Carolina, for Charles II. Annapolis, the site of the United States Naval Academy, was a compliment to Queen Anne.

Monarchy is that form of government in which a king is the head of a nation. The position of kings in former centuries is difficult for modern Americans to understand. Monarchs were looked up to with something like reverence by the common people, and men and women who suffered from diseases asked the king to touch them in the hope that this act would make the patient well. When Shakespeare near the end of the sixteenth century remarked that "divinity doth hedge a king," the phrase did not mean that the great dramatist thought of the king as a god, or even that the ruler derived all of his powers from God. The words meant, rather, that Shakespeare and his fellow-Englishmen thought of the monarch as a person apart from and above common men. For Englishmen

141

the King still is the symbol of England, and loyalty to the King is loyalty to England. The British national anthem is "God Save the King."

THE ENGLISH KING AND HIS SUBJECTS IN THE SEVENTEENTH CENTURY

Most of the English colonies in North America were established in the seventeenth century, and in that same period the foundations of American constitutional government were laid down. When the century opened, the English monarchy was strong but the crown did not have absolute power because the king had for a long time been assisted in his rule by a council of nobles called the Parliament, and, shortly before the opening of the seventeenth century, the common people had demanded and secured the right to send representatives of their own to Parliament. When these representatives assembled they were called the House of Commons while the nobles made up the House of Lords. In the seventeenth century Parliament was made up of two houses: the older House of Lords and the newer House of Commons. Parliament assisted the monarch in the government of the kingdom.

During much of the first half of the seventeenth century England was disturbed by the attempts of two kings, James I and his son Charles I, to make the power of the King more nearly absolute. Charles I even dismissed Parliament and tried to govern without its consent and advice. For a time he succeeded, but after several years he was forced to call Parliament together again because he could find no way to raise money without its help. Parliament at once challenged the powers the King had assumed; the conflict became a civil war; and Charles I was not only driven from the throne but was beheaded on the charge of treason.

More than half the English colonies on the North American continent were established during the reigns of James I and Charles I when the strife between the King and the Parliament was developing. The Englishmen who went to America to live did not forget in the New World the rights for which the supporters of Parliament were contending against the dictatorial tendencies of James I and Charles I.

EARLY AMERICANS AND
THE RIGHTS OF ENGLISHMEN

The settlers who came to Virginia, Maryland, Massachusetts, and the other colonies assumed that in their new homes they enjoyed the same rights as they had possessed in the Old World. The Pilgrims who established Plymouth and the Puritan leaders who came to Massachusetts had left England because of persecutions at the hands of royal officers in the days when James I and Charles I were trying to increase the royal power. Persecuted Catholics had also come to Maryland. It was natural that men and women who had fled to America for refuge from tyranny should be keenly aware of the rights they claimed as Englishmen.

What were these rights? Two were of primary importance. Englishmen insisted on courts independent of the will of the King. Old and firmly established law and custom in England required that the decision as to whether an accused person had or had not committed a crime must be made by a jury of free men and not by the King or any of his officers. The right of trial by a jury of his equals was one of the basic rights of the Englishman. The objective sought in maintaining this right was the protection of individual men or women who might otherwise be helpless against tyranny and oppression at the hands of an arbitrary monarch.

The second right was even more far-reaching. Englishmen in the Old World demanded that subjects of the King should have a share in the management of government, and they insisted, in particular, that no taxes be levied unless voted by the representatives of the people. One of the rights which Englishmen carried to America was the right of the people to choose representatives from among themselves to share in the government of the respective colonies in which they had settled and to vote their own taxes.

These two basic rights may be put together into one idea; Englishmen had created a law that was above the King. This law required the monarch to grant his subjects the right of trial by jury and the right to choose representatives to assist in managing the affairs of the nation. The law, in short, governed the King; it still exists and is called the British Constitution. This constitution, however, is not set down specifically in writing; much of it is made up of customs that have the force of law. Because the Constitution guarantees the fundamental rights of Englishmen, the colonists who sought to establish and maintain these rights in the New World were laying in America the foundations of constitutional government. The essence of constitutionalism is the existence of a law above the government that the government is not permitted to break. A constitution is sometimes referred to as the fundamental law because it creates the basic pattern of political society.

THE IMPORTANCE OF THE INDIVIDUAL
IN THE ENGLISH COLONIES

One of the important differences in the seventeenth century between the English and the American way of life was the emphasis in the colonies upon the importance of the individual man or woman, an attitude which grew naturally out of the fact that the wilderness was vast and almost overwhelming and that the men and women to tame it were few. Forests had to be cut away and the ground cleared of stumps and roots before the land was ready for crops. For this great labor only the crudest tools were available; there were, of course, no power machines. What work was done had to be done by hand. Manpower was the sole resource, and as a result men were important; human life was valuable; it was not to be lightly thrown away.

The effects of this importance of the individual soon appeared in punishments meted out to convicted criminals in the colonies. At the time in Europe and in England barbarous and cruel punishments were still a common practice; men convicted of crimes were often punished by cropping or cutting of the ears, and by being branded or maimed. Execution was the penalty for a large number of crimes, in the list of which thievery was often included. In many of the seventeenth-century English colonies the cruelties and barbarities of these old European punishments began to disappear and the offenses calling for execution were greatly decreased in number. Because in America men were too valuable to maim and human life was too precious to destroy except for extreme wrongdoing, the individual in America took on a dignity that the masses of men possessed nowhere in the Old World. This importance and dignity of the individual became the foundation of American democratic institutions.

ENGLISH CUSTOMS BECOME DIFFERENT IN AMERICA

Though English colonists brought with them basic ideas of liberty and of the management of government, the way of carrying out these ideas in the New World began almost at once to differ from the practices of the mother country. Not all English laws, for example, could be used in the colonies. Both the famous common law (custom) and governmental regulations in England had grown up in old and well-established communities and fitted a complex society. Communities in America were new and were founded on the edge of an untamed wilderness; life in them was simple. As a result, only a small part of the famous common law of England could be used in the earliest settlements; the colonists in America began to establish customs of their own.

Equally important was the growth in the American colonies of a different idea of the meaning of representation in a lawmaking body. A member of the House of Commons thought of himself, first of all, as representing all the people of England; but a member of one of the colonial assemblies considered his task to be to represent the country or district in which he lived and whose voters sent him to the legislature. In America, representation was said to be on a geographical basis. This difference between English and American practice remains true today.

The tendency for American institutions to move away from likeness to those in England has resulted in great differences between the two countries, the greatest of these unlikenesses growing out of the fact that the United States more than a century and a half ago abandoned the monarchy. Yet the basic principles underlying the institutions of the two countries remain practically the same, a condition of vast importance in the twentieth century, for it makes for easier and more complete mutual understanding on the part of the peoples of the two nations. Englishmen and Americans mean the same thing when they speak of political liberty.

DUTIES OF THE ENGLISH COLONISTS

If the early colonists asserted that they possessed the rights of Englishmen, they were also forced quickly to assume the responsibilities of citizenship that went with life on a dangerous frontier. In the forest, stretching endlessly westward from their tiny villages built near the sea, lived Indians, some of whom, such as the Iroquois of New York, were able fighters. From the point of view of the red man the white man was an intruder who threatened to drive him from his homeland and to rob him of his hunting grounds. Naturally fighting occurred again and again on the frontier.

The colonists fell back upon an ancient English institution, the militia. Colonial laws required able-bodied men of military age, usually between eighteen and forty-five, to enroll as militiamen and to stand ready to defend the community in times of emergency. In some colonies militiamen were required to provide themselves not only with guns but with powder and bullets. The fact that a large proportion of the early colonists were poor made it difficult to enforce the regulation that the militiamen provide their own military supplies.

There were times when these early militiamen faced hard fights. In 1675 war flamed up along the New England frontier which then stood in northern Massachusetts. A chieftain whom the whites called King Philip led his braves in devastating raids that extended from the Atlantic coast to the Connecticut valley; in these forays the hostile Indians burned many houses and wiped out many families. After more than a year of fighting the war was ended by the killing of King Philip. Of the 5,000 men of military age in Massachusetts one in ten was either killed or captured in the war against Philip. It was a heavy price, and it brought home to these seventeenth-century forefathers of ours the fact that if they would claim the rights and privileges of free men, they must also assume the responsibilities of working for the common good and of defending the public safety.

When a period of danger had passed, the militia of the colonies usually declined. Training days, when companies were supposed to learn the military art, tended to become public holidays. Nevertheless, the principle remained that the community had the right to call upon its manpower to defend it in time of emergency.

The foundations of constitutional liberty were laid in America, as in England, under a monarchial form of government. The voters who debated about a new road in the town meeting in a New England village were subjects of the British King; the members of the Assembly in the royal colony expected a King to review the acts they passed. The institution of monarchy does not, in itself, prevent the growth of constitutional liberty and democratic institutions, a fact which the last three centuries of English history have made abundantly clear. No king can be a tyrant when there is a law or constitution above him, which both he and his subjects must obey.

A COMPARISON OF GOVERNMENTS IN THE ENGLISH COLONIES AND IN THE SPANISH COLONIES

While there were some minor differences in the form of government set up in the different colonies which England established on the continent of North America, the basic principle of permitting a large amount of self-government was common to all of them.

Self-government was carried furthest by the colonists who settled in New England. This region in the seventeenth century was in reality several clusters of small farming or fishing villages. It became the custom for the villagers to decide at town meetings on the management of local affairs such as laying out new roads or providing for stray animals. The citizens would assemble, discuss their problems, and decide by vote what to do. Such government by the people themselves is complete democracy. The early New England town meeting is one of the foundation stones on which our modern democratic institutions rest.

The most common form of government in the colonies was that of the so-called royal colony. The governor of such a colony was appointed by the crown in England and was usually an Englishman, who came to America for the period of his term of office. The executive chose from the leading men of the colony a council to advise him concerning the problems of the region. Those persons in the colony who possessed property were allowed to elect representatives from among themselves to sit together in what was called an assembly, where the representatives of the people voted taxes within the colony and passed such laws as were thought to be necessary for the welfare of the colony. The governor could veto bills passed by the assembly. If the governor approved a bill by signing it, the measure still did not become valid until it had been sent to England and approved by the crown. The King usually acted through officers charged with the responsibility of studying the enactments of the colonial assemblies.

The government of the Spanish colony called Mexico presents an interesting contrast to that of the English colonies. The governor of Mexico, called a viceroy, was appointed by the King of Spain and was assisted by officers who took their orders directly from the viceroy. The chief executive and all his assistants of high rank must have been born in Spain; white Mexicans, no matter how rich or able, were not permitted to hold high office. There was no organization similar to the assembly in the British colonies which enabled the people of the colony to share in its government. There was no town meeting. Under the command of the viceroy was a standing army enabling him to enforce the will of the King of Spain throughout the colony.

In the Spanish Kingdom and Empire there was no law or constitution above the monarch. Colonial rule was autocratic, that is, the viceroy and the King above him were supreme. The government rested not on the will of the people, most of whom in Mexico were conquered Indians, but on military force.

THE CONFLICT OF EMPIRES IN NORTH AMERICA

Americans in recent years have tended to forget how familiar their colonial ancestors were with the fact of war. The British and French empires in North America were near to one another, and British and French were rivals for that rich country of the Great Lakes and Mississippi valley which is now the heart of the United States. The English colonies stretched along the Atlantic seaboard from Maine to South Carolina and after 1732 included

Georgia, founded to give opportunity to British debtors to make a new start in life and also to serve as an outpost against the Spaniards in Florida. The empire which France claimed and tried to hold extended through the continental interior in a vast arc from New Orleans to what is now Nova Scotia, which the French called Acadia. The chief settlement of French colonists was in the valley of the St. Lawrence, with smaller population groups in Nova Scotia and at the mouth of the Mississippi. In population the English colonies greatly outnumbered the French, but their superiority in numbers was partially neutralized by the fact that British manpower in North America was divided among thirteen colonies, each independent of all the rest. New France was separated from the British continental colonies by a mountain system, with very few passes across it, extending from the highlands of northwestern Georgia to the White Mountains of New Hampshire. The most important single route across this upland area was the valley in which are to be found the Upper Hudson, Lake George and Lake Champlain, a way that in the French and Indian Wars came to be called the Great Warpath.

France and England were rivals in Europe as well as in North America; four times in less than a hundred years their armies and navies fought in the Old World, and each of these European conflicts saw fighting in North America. The present war is not the second European war to extend to North America, as some people have supposed; it is the seventh. And there was an eighth war, the American Revolution, that broke out in North America and extended to Europe.

The first of the four Franco-British wars began in 1689; the last ended in 1763. Between those two dates stretched a span of seventy-four years. Thirty-three of these, almost half, were years of war. For three-quarters of a century there was not a generation in the North American colonies that did not know war. The first three of the French and Indian Wars did not, to be sure, involve bitter and extensive campaigns in North America, but there was important fighting and loss of property and life in each. The fourth was a long and desperate conflict with heavy fighting in the New World. And the hardest conflict of all, the American Revolution, which continued nearly eight years, broke out only twelve years

after the close of the last French and Indian War. The foundations
of our American civilization were laid in times of war and suffering. Ours is not the only American generation to know strife and
bloodshed.

THE LAST FRENCH AND INDIAN WAR, 1754-1763

The French in the eighteenth century depended heavily upon
fortifications to defend their extensive empire in North America.
They erected a powerful fort according to the latest designs at
Louisbourg on Cape Breton Island in the eastern part of Nova
Scotia, intending this strong point to be a Gibraltar to defend the
entrance to the Gulf of Saint Lawrence. But their principal citadel
in the New World was the fortified town of Quebec, the center
of the power of New France. West of this stronghold the French
erected a chain of frontier forts on Lake Ontario, the Niagara
River, and at the beginning of the Ohio where Pittsburgh now
stands. On the Great Warpath the flag of the *fleur de lys* flew
above the powerful fort Ticonderoga, on the shores of Lake
Champlain.

In the opening phase of the war the British made a thrust against
Fort Duquesne on the present site of Pittsburgh, entrusting the
mission of taking the fort to General Braddock, who commanded
a substantial army of trained, regular troops from England. He
was assisted by a force of colonials and had on his staff George
Washington, a colonel in the military establishment of Virginia.
Braddock's service train was made up of wagons and animals collected mostly in Pennsylvania. The British commander cut his way
through the forest to the neighborhood of the French fort, where
he was attacked in the forested terrain by a smaller force of French
and Indians. The enemy used a primitive form of open-order fighting in which cover was emphasized. General Braddock was trained
in the close-order fighting without use of cover which characterized the European armies of his day. In those days companies
three ranks deep marched into battle as though maneuvering on
the parade ground. The British general had refused to listen to
advice from his colonials that he be prepared for the Indian fighting that had developed in the American forest, and when the battle
was joined he compelled his troops to stand in close column on

the road, helpless except for an occasional salvo which they fired into the trees. The hidden French soldiers and their Indian allies maintained a murderous fire at the men standing shoulder to shoulder on the open road. The losses became too great for any force to endure, and Braddock's soldiers broke and fled. The General, who was personally a very brave man, was killed. This disaster to British arms suggests the importance for the military man of being able to adapt himself swiftly to new conditions.

The French were finally defeated, and their North American empire was captured, by operations based on masterly strategic conceptions. The British leaders in London came finally to see that Quebec was the center of the French Empire and that the fall of that stronghold would mean the collapse of New France. The city could be approached from the east by the St. Lawrence and from the south by the Great Warpath. Moreover, William Pitt, the chief of the British statesmen, understood that sea power must be the determining factor in overthrowing the French Empire. By a series of brilliant operations early in 1758 British fleets won such supremacy over the French naval forces in European waters as to prevent them from crossing the Atlantic. This supremacy was maintained during the next two years.

One British army in 1758 laid siege to Louisbourg and captured it, an operation which British control of the sea made possible. Another British army advanced northward along the Great Warpath but failed, due to the incompetence of its commander, to take Ticonderoga. The following year General Amherst captured the great fort on Lake Champlain and opened the way for an advance on Montreal. In this same season, the summer of 1759, a naval force sailed up the St. Lawrence and landed troops near Quebec. General Wolfe led his army of British regulars against the French defending force commanded by Montcalm; the battle was fought in close-order formation after the approved style of eighteenth-century Europe, the fight beginning when the armies were about 100 yards apart. The British won the day and forced the great French stronghold to surrender. In the hard-fought battle both commanding generals were killed. The British occupation of Montreal a year later brought hostilities to an end, and the treaty of peace in 1763 made Canada a part of the British Empire.

SOME CONSEQUENCES OF
THE TREATY OF PARIS, 1763

The United States occupies today a unique position among the great powers of the world. It has no rivals in the western hemisphere capable of challenging seriously its power. And this freedom from potential enemies near at hand has been true for most of the course of our history as an independent nation. The result has been a sense of security that has played an important part in the attitude of the American people and of their government toward the Army and the Navy. Prior to the twentieth century the United States tended to neglect both branches of its armed forces save in time of actual war.

Had France been able to retain Quebec and to hold the Mississippi River, Americans would have known what it means to a nation to face, year in and year out, across an international boundary a strong people speaking a foreign language. Across such a line France and Germany faced one another for many decades in Europe; Americans were spared a similar situation by the defeat of the French Empire in North America. The destruction of French power in North America in the last French and Indian War brought the beginnings of this sense of security which has been the foundation of the isolation sentiment of the nineteenth and particularly of the twentieth century.

A sense of relief from the menace on the north followed immediately upon the signing of the treaty of peace. Almost overnight Americans in the British colonies began to feel that now, with France gone from North America, they had little need for protection by the military and naval forces of the British Empire; the only enemies near at hand were the Indian tribes, and Europe was at least six weeks away, when distance was measured by the time it took a sailing ship to cross the North Atlantic. This new sense of security was part of the background of that growing feeling of independence which finally resulted in the Revolutionary War.

CHAPTER XII

ORIGINS OF THE REVOLUTIONARY WAR

THE BRITISH EMPIRE IN 1763

The British Empire after 1763 was the most important in the world, its only rival being that of Spain. The Spanish Empire included South America (except Brazil), and colonies and claims in North America as far north as San Francisco on the west coast. The British held India, wrested from France in the last French and Indian War, Gibraltar at the straits which the ancient Greeks called the Gates of Hercules, and in North America not only that vast fur-trading country about Hudson Bay but all the eastern half of the continent from Labrador to Florida. In addition the British flag flew above Bermuda and many islands in the West Indies. Australia and New Zealand were not parts of this empire, for they were then wilderness areas inhabited by uncivilized tribes of brown or black natives. These dominions of English-speaking white men did not come under the control of Britain in the middle years of the nineteenth century.

The most important part of the British Empire of the eighteenth century was the thirteen colonies on the continent of North America; they were populous, and each year saw them increase in wealth. New England was a farming, fishing, and trading region where many ships were built for merchants who carried on extensive trade with the other continental colonies, with the West Indies, and with England. The Middle Colonies from New York to Maryland were primarily agricultural regions, but from the cities of New York and Philadelphia many trading vessels put out bound for the same ports to which New Englanders went. The Southern colonies were a region of plantations and small farms. Virginia in the eighteenth century was the greatest tobacco-producing area in the world; and South Carolina had large and prosperous rice plantations. In the seaports of Boston, New York, and Philadelphia the American colonies had, in the terms of the eighteenth century, important and very modern cities. In England only London was larger than the capital of Pennsylvania and nowhere in Britain was the solution of city problems, such as fighting fires or lighting streets, further advanced than in the coast towns of America.

There was little unity, however, among these thirteen colonies; each colony was separate and different from all the rest. New England life had a Puritan flavor, and Dutch influence was strong in New York long after the conquest of New Netherlands. The plantation of South Carolina with its fine plantation house, its village of slave cabins, and its field gangs of Negro slaves was vastly different from the simple farm of Connecticut. But in spite of the differences there were factors which made unity among the colonies possible to achieve: their people spoke a common language, and in every colony lived educated leaders who were familiar with what the people of England and of Europe were reading and thinking.

England had established, mostly in the seventeenth century, a system of rules known as the Navigation Acts to regulate trade within the Empire. One law required that such trade be carried on in British-owned-and-operated ships and that a large proportion of all crews of merchant vessels must be subjects of the King. The purpose of this measure was to prevent Dutch ships and traders from participating in the trade between England and her colonies, for Holland was, at the time, the chief commercial rival for the carrying trade of the oceans. The regulation which sought to exclude the Dutch benefited American colonists because, since the Americans were subjects of the British crown, ships built in the Middle Colonies and New England and manned by American crews were, according to the law, British ships. Colonial traders, moreover, were freed from Dutch competition. The act stimulated shipbuilding in the more northern of the American colonies, and each decade of the eighteenth century saw the American-owned and American-manned merchant marine increase in size.

Another advantage that membership in the British Empire gave to the colonists was protection, particularly against the French. This need for defense seemed, however, to most Americans somewhat remote after French Canada had become part of the Empire. The American attitude at the time was conditioned by a lack of understanding on the part of the colonists of the importance of sea power and of the role played by the British Navy in the conquest of New France. Nor was it clear to the masses of the people that after 1763 the British Navy still stood in the way of a sudden French effort to reconquer its lost American empire. The Americans, looking eastward from their shores across the broad Atlantic, felt secure, and the military advantages of membership in the Empire seemed to them to have disappeared.

The disadvantages of colonial status were mainly economic. Britain had early established a list of goods which colonials were permitted to import only from England. Americans, moreover, were hampered by high duties in their efforts to trade with the sugar-producing colonies which the French retained, even after 1763, in the West Indies, for the British trade regulations naturally favored the English West Indian colonies that produced sugar.

More important than these trade restrictions, however, was the determination of Britain in the eighteenth century to prevent, if possible, the development of manufacturing in the American colonies. These were the days when manufacturing was done mostly by hand. Machines and factories in the modern sense did not exist in colonial America, but were appearing in Britain. In general the English attitude toward the colonies in North America was that these communities should produce raw materials, such as tobacco, naval supplies, furs, and foodstuffs. But the colonies were not to become regions in which raw materials were fabricated into finished goods; this task was to be carried on in England. The chief disadvantage, then, of membership in the British Empire lay in the fact that the mother country sought to control the growth of the economic life of the American colonies in such a way that England would be benefited; the Americans were not to be left free to work out their destiny in such manner as they chose.

Such a colonial policy was not limited to Britain in the eighteenth century; the idea that colonies existed for the benefit of the nation that established them was held even more strongly by France and Spain than by Britain. Of all the empires of that period, the regulations of the British Empire were the lightest. But the time came, after 1763, when Americans, freed as they thought from the immediate menace of France, were no longer willing to accept this commonplace of European imperial thinking. Sensing the economic possibilities of their continent, so rich in natural resources, the people of the colonies began to believe that they should be permitted to take advantage of their opportunities and be allowed to develop their communities in their own way. The basic cause of the American Revolution was the inability of the British politicians in power during the period from 1763 to 1775 to realize that the time had come in American development when it would no longer be possible for Britain to control in its own interest the economic life of America.

PARLIAMENTARY SUPREMACY IN BRITAIN AND AMERICA

Political as well as economic issues lay behind the American Revolution, and the chief of these was the question as to whether the British Parliament was supreme over the American colonies. To understand this claim of supremacy made by the Parliament, it is necessary to know the story of a seventeenth-century victory for civil liberty in England.

That contest between Parliament and the King in early seventeenth-century England which finally resulted in the conviction and beheading of Charles I has already been mentioned. The issues raised by this conflict were not finally settled, however, until the end of the century. In 1688 the British Parliament, angered at certain policies of James II, forced that monarch to abdicate the throne and invited two new sovereigns, William and Mary, to become respectively King and Queen. The affair is known in English history as the Revolution of 1688. The event established the supremacy of Parliament over the crown, and since that time Parliament has been the ruling power in England.

In the eighteenth century Parliament began the practice of appointing what was, in effect, an executive committee, called the Cabinet, to carry on the executive functions once performed by the King. The head of the Cabinet came to be known as the Prime Minister and he became the real executive in the British government. He derives his power from the Parliament and resigns when Parliament is no longer willing to support him.

Parliament naturally assumed during the eighteenth century that it was supreme in the Empire as well as in England. But before the last French and Indian War the British government in exercising general control over its colonies had done little more than pass the Navigation Acts already mentioned. The situation changed, however, after 1763, when the acquisition of Canada and India had made the Empire much larger. The long French and Indian Wars, moreover, had burdened Britain with debt, while France, defeated but not destroyed, continued to be a danger. The British leaders decided that the American colonies needed defense and were persuaded of this necessity by a sudden Indian attack, called the Pontiac Conspiracy, upon the frontier fur-trading posts in the region of the Great Lakes.

As a result of these various factors the Cabinet devised a plan for colonial management in 1765 which Parliament approved almost without debate. It provided that regular troops be sent to America for purposes of defense and that a stamp tax be levied in America to support them. There were other aspects of the plan, but these were the essential points.

The Stamp Act roused a storm of opposition in the American colonies that was wholly unexpected by the British government. Americans, enjoying their new sense of security, did not feel that they needed the army, and some Americans suspected that the army was not really intended for defense but rather was meant to strengthen the power of the royal governors and of the British government in the management of American affairs. Such colonists feared that the troops might become, like the armed forces in the Spanish colonies, an instrument by which an autocratic rule could be established in the colonies and the civil liberties of the Americans destroyed. The opposition was founded on a constitutional principle. The colonial assemblies had long possessed the right and power to tax the people of the colonies. If Parliament could tax Americans directly, would not the assemblies disappear as institutions of importance and would not Americans be subjected to the rule of a legislative body in which they had no representatives and which sat in a far-away land? To this last query the British answer came back that, of course, Americans were represented in Parliament because every member of that body represented not only the whole Kingdom but the entire Empire. So the issue was drawn between the American and the English idea of representation.

The importance of the Stamp Act controversy in the story of events leading to the American Revolution is that it brought about a number of beginnings. It led to the calling of a congress of representatives from several, but not all, of the colonies to discuss measures to be taken to oppose the Stamp Act. This was a long step toward that confederation of colonies which ultimately came out of opposition to the mother country. The Stamp Act Congress recommended that Americans boycott British goods and so bring pressure to bear on Parliament, a measure which proved in the end to be effective enough to cause the repeal of the Stamp Act. This boycott was the first general attempt of Americans to defy the authority of the British government. Parliament repealed the Stamp Act under pressure from British merchants who were suffering serious loss of trade. But Parliament accompanied the repeal with a Declaratory Act, the first measure formally to assert the supremacy of Parliament over the entire Empire.

The issue of taxation was raised again in 1767 when Parliament levied new taxes in the form of import duties on a list of specified articles that included tea. Americans boycotted the taxed commodities. The growing conflict between Americans and the Parliament leaders was aggravated in 1768 by the quartering of a detachment of British regulars at Boston, a town that had been a center of opposition to the plans of the British government. It was plain to all that the soldiers were sent to the Massachusetts seaport to uphold British authority and that the troops were intended to remind American opponents of British imperial policy that, if resistance went too far, force was at hand to deal with it.

The presence of the soldiers did not have the result desired. New Englanders, far from being frightened, were angered. They began to reorganize their militia and to train so as to be ready if a crisis should come. A fight occurred in 1770 between some soldiers on guard in the streets of Boston and a group of citizens, and during the fracas the soldiers fired and killed some of the crowd. This so-called "Boston Massacre" so enraged the people of Boston that the governor of the colony ordered the troops removed from the city to barracks on an island in the harbor.

In this same year the leaders of Parliament attempted to check American opposition by a policy of conciliation. They removed all the obnoxious new taxes save the duty on tea, retaining this merely to uphold the principle of the supremacy of Parliament over the American colonies. Quiet prevailed in America, but the colonials continued the boycott on tea. If parliamentary leadership had been wise, the American difficulties might, after the conciliatory moves of 1770, have been smoothed over and the unity of the Empire retained unimpaired, for, in the early 1770's, there was no important demand among American leaders for independence. Americans thought of themselves as fighting to preserve the constitutional privileges of Englishmen. They believed in particular that they were striving to maintain the age-old right of Englishmen to share in their own government. They insisted that they were not represented in Parliament and that the acts of that body taxing them amounted to nothing less than tyranny. After 1770, the only way that Parliament could have satisfied the opposition in the colonies would have been to set up guarantees by which the power of the colonial assemblies would be recognized. In short, the time had come when, if England wished to retain her colonies without a fight, she must grant them control over their own affairs.

AMERICANS PROPOSE A CONSTITUTION FOR THE BRITISH EMPIRE

During this revolutionary struggle the quality of American political thinking was high. At least three men, Madison, Jefferson, and Franklin, pointed out the only principle that would make imperial unity possible, but Americans were never given a chance formally to discuss or propose it. This American suggestion for a constitution for the British Empire would have made the crown the one unifying element in the Empire. In 1775, George III was as much the King of Pennsylvania as of England. Let the fact that they are both subjects to the same King, said Franklin in effect, be the bond which ties Pennsylvanians to Englishmen. Let the British Parliament be supreme in Britain, but make the Pennsylvania Assembly supreme in Pennsylvania. These two bodies would then become, in a sense, equal. They would be united in the fact that they both served the same King. The suggestion was ignored by the parliamentary leaders of the 1770's.

The quality of the proposal of these Americans is suggested by the fact that in 1926, after more than a century and a half, it was adopted as the constitution of the British Empire at the London conference in which were represented the great self-governing Dominions of Canada, Australia, New Zealand, and British South Africa. That conference changed the name of the British Empire to the British Commonwealth of Nations and adopted the following statement: "[The Dominions are] autonomous communities within the British Empire, equal in status, and in no way subordinate to one another in any aspect of their domestic or external affairs though united by a common allegiance to the crown and freely associated as members of the British Commonwealth." The bonds which unite the independent nations of Great Britain, Canada, Australia, New Zealand, and British South Africa are three: common interests, common ideals and civilization, and a common fealty to the same King. This idea originated in the 1770's in the thirteen British colonies on the continent of North America. Its rejection by the leaders of Parliament was one of the chief reasons why the British Empire of the eighteenth century broke apart and the United States of America came into being.

THE BOSTON TEA PARTY AND ITS CONSEQUENCES

The long tension between the American colonials and the British government passed from the stage of debate to that of action in 1773 when a group of Boston men boarded some British merchant ships tied up at the wharves of that city and openly and willfully destroyed property by throwing a large quantity of tea into the water. Back of the act lay a blunder by the Prime Minister, who was at that time Lord North. North, to help out a great British commercial company known as the East India Company, gave it such special privileges in trading in America that the company could sell tea more cheaply in the American market than could any American merchant. North did not stop to think that his act established a precedent which, if followed for other commodities, might make it possible for English trading companies to put American merchants completely out of business. The Boston merchants were behind the violence of the Boston "Tea Party," and the possibility of war became very real.

The party of Lord North in control of Parliament made no thorough effort to discover the nature of the American opposition to British policy. They did not send a fact-finding commission or official to the colonies to investigate the trouble and to suggest a remedy. In a later crisis in Canada in the nineteenth century the British government sent out such a representative to discover on the ground what was the reason for a little colonial rebellion. The report of this official was of great benefit to the Empire. After the Boston Tea Party no such official was sent. Lord North, instead, attempted to punish the Americans; he closed the port of Boston and appointed a major general of the regular British Army to be the royal governor of Massachusetts.

The American colonists promptly chose representatives to an intercolonial congress known in history as the First Continental Congress. This body sent a petition to the King, George III, asking him to restore those rights of Englishmen which Parliament seemed determined to take away. The Congress also called upon Americans to establish a most rigorous boycott of English merchandise.

So the die was cast. Lord North attempted coercion backed by the threat of a regular army in Boston. The First Continental Congress turned to the weapon of economic coercion. Behind the Congress, however, was the militia of the colonies, training more earnestly each day.

WHIGS VERSUS TORIES IN ENGLAND

The policy of Lord North with respect to the American colonies did not reflect the will of the English people or even of all the parliamentary leaders. It was primarily the action of an ultra-conservative party known as the Tories. They were opposed in Parliament by a more liberal party known as the Whigs, most of whom disapproved of North's policy toward the Americans. In the spring of 1775, less than a month before the outbreak of the Revolution, one of the greatest of the Whig orators, Edmund Burke, rose in the House of Commons and made a powerful appeal for the abandonment by Britain of the policy of force with respect to America and asked for the adoption of a genuine attitude of conciliation and compromise as the foundation for a lasting imperial unity. His speech has been accepted as one of the classics of English literature, and his argument has significance even today.

". . . the people of the Colonies are descendants of Englishmen," said Burke. "England, sir, is a nation, which I hope respects, and formerly adored, her freedom. The Colonists migrated from you when this part of your character was most predominant, and they took this bias and direction the moment they parted from your hands. They are, therefore, not only devoted to liberty, but to liberty according to English ideas and on English principles. . . . As long as you have the wisdom to keep the sovereign authority of this country as the sanctuary of liberty, the sacred temple consecrated to our common faith, wherever the . . . sons of England worship freedom, they will turn their faces toward you. . . . Slavery they can have anywhere. It is a weed that grows in every soil. They may have it from Spain, they may have it from Prussia. But until you become lost to all feeling of your true interest and your natural dignity, freedom they can have from none but you. . . . Magnanimity in politics is not seldom the truest wisdom, and a great empire and little minds go ill together. . . . We ought to elevate our minds to the greatness of that trust to which the order of Providence has called us."

Burke's appeal failed, partly because it came too late. Events in the spring of 1775 moved swiftly to a crisis. The determined citizens of Massachusetts confined the authority of General Gage, the newly appointed royal governor, to the area of Boston where his soldiers could enforce his decrees, while in the outlying towns the people turned for government to the local authorities they had chosen. The militia gathered powder for possible conflict. When Gage sent a detachment of soldiers to Concord to destroy there what would today be called an ammunition dump, the news of the enterprise brought about the hasty mobilization of the militia of eastern Massachusetts. On April 19, 1775, the Minute Men of Massachusetts met and fought the Redcoats at the battles of Lexington and Concord. The long period of debate as to American rights came to an end. American farmers and artisans had challenged the armed might of the British Empire.

THE FIGHT FOR THE RIGHTS OF ENGLISHMEN

From April, 1775, until July, 1776, the Revolutionary War was an uprising within the British Empire in which the American rebels thought of themselves as fighting for their ancient rights under the British Constitution. They considered that their war was part of that centuries-old struggle of Englishmen for political liberty, which had in the seventeenth century brought about the beheading of Charles I and later the abdication under compulsion of James II. A number of English Whigs, among whom was Burke, felt that Americans were carrying on the ancient British battle against arbitrary authority.

If Englishmen were divided as to their attitude toward the rebellion in the American colonies, sharp differences of opinion separated Americans also into two groups. There were the Patriots, popularly known as American Whigs, who were convinced that the course of the British government left Americans no choice but to fight for their fundamental rights. Opposed to them were the Loyalists, called in their own day the American Tories, who put loyalty to King and Empire above every other consideration. Many of these Loyalists were as bitterly opposed as the Patriots to the acts of the British government, but the Loyalists tried as a matter both of principle and of policy, to avoid going to extremes. The Loyalists supported the principle that discussion is better than force, that rebellion is a great evil, and that in the long run discussion would achieve the ends desired by Americans and at the same time preserve imperial unity. They opposed the war as a matter of policy on the ground that it bred anarchy and that, if it succeeded, it would bring about a weak nation which might not be able to support its independence. No one will ever know how the Loyalists and the Patriots compared in numbers. Particularly in the phase of the war before July, 1776, the two parties are generally supposed to be roughly equal in size. The influence of the Loyalists was not, however, as great as their numbers; the Patriots took the initiative and determined the destiny of America.

THE REASONS FOR INDEPENDENCE

The question as to why a rebellion of loyal subjects developed into a war for national independence focuses attention upon George III, King of England during the fateful months between Lexington and the Declaration. He was an able and often a generous King but determined and shortsighted. When the American Revolution was in the making he was attempting to increase the royal power in the actual government of the realm. George III, King, and Lord North, Prime Minister, worked closely together in the months which preceded independence. Of course all the acts of government at this time, as at all other times, were announced and carried out in the King's name, and among these acts two were of especial importance in destroying the loyalty of American subjects for their monarch. The first of these was the effort of the North government to coerce Americans by destroying their ocean-borne commerce. It was mentioned in the Declaration of Independence as "cutting off our trade with all parts of the world." The second was of vastly greater psychological importance. The North government went to one of the German States and hired mercenaries to fight American subjects of George III who were contending for the civil and political rights they claimed under the British Constitution. News of this act determined thousands of Americans to quit their allegiance to a monarch who would permit such an act to be done in his name and caused them to espouse the cause of national independence. A paragraph in the Declaration suggests the intensity and bitterness of the American feeling about the hiring of the Hessians. "He [George III] is at this time transporting large armies of foreign mercenaries to complete the works of death, desolation and tyranny already begun with circumstances of cruelty and perfidy scarcely paralleled in the most barbarous ages, and totally unworthy the head of a civilized nation." On July 4, 1776, the Declaration of Independence, passed two days before by the Continental Congress, was made official and the United States of America came into being.

THE DEMOCRATIC PHILOSOPHY OF
THE DECLARATION OF INDEPENDENCE

The Declaration was the greatest statement of the principles of democracy to be made in the eighteenth century, and one of the greatest of all time. It was considered so dangerous in France that the French King for a long time would not permit it to be published and circulated in his realm.

The Declaration affirmed in the first place the theory of natural rights which for present purposes may be stated as follows: The God of Nature created all men equal in one fundamental particular, namely that Deity endowed every man with the natural and inalienable right to his life, his liberty, and the opportunity so to develop himself that he will gain that sense of achievement and of well-being which is called happiness. The Declaration set forth in the second place what is known as the compact theory of the origin of government, a doctrine that may be summarized as follows: The God of Nature created man with reason and therefore capable of setting up a government for the regulation and direction of society. Government, therefore, is established by free agreement or compact among reasonable men endowed with natural rights, and the prime purpose and the chief task of government is to defend and preserve the natural rights to life, liberty, and the pursuit of happiness. Government can exist only with the consent of the governed. When a government ceases to defend and preserve the natural and inalienable rights of the governed, then, in the words of the Declaration, "it is the right of the people to alter or abolish it, and to institute a new government, laying its foundation on such principles, and organizing its powers in such form, as to them shall seem most likely to effect their safety and happiness."

The implications of the Declaration of Independence are of as great importance as its positive affirmations. They are: (1) that the individual man is of such great value that nature has endowed him with inalienable rights, (2) that he and his fellows create the political state, and (3) that among those ultimate principles or laws, which are the very foundation of society, is the principle that the political state exists for the individual, not the individual for the state.

CHAPTER XIII

THE NATURE OF THE AMERICAN REVOLUTION

OUTLINE OF MILITARY OPERATIONS

The military operations of the Revolutionary War may conveniently be divided into those of the different years because the important campaigns were carried out in successive summers. Washington became Commander-in-Chief of the American forces in the summer of 1775, and established his headquarters with the army at Boston, and held the British regulars at Boston. These abandoned the port in the spring of 1776 and went to Halifax to join in the main operations of that year.

Learning in 1776 that the British blow was to fall at New York, Washington moved his headquarters to that important seaport and prepared defenses on Long Island. The importance of British sea power in the war is suggested by the fact the English could move troops and supplies by water to any point on the coast they chose for an attack. British ships landed an army on Long Island in August, 1776.

General Sir William Howe, commander of the land forces before New York, was a British Whig in politics and a friend of the Americans by family tradition. To the memory of a brother of his, who had led a force of American troops in the last French and Indian War and had been killed at Ticonderoga, Americans had erected a tablet in Westminster Abbey. Sir William was given by his government the difficult mission of waging peace and war at the same time. He was ready to guarantee the liberties the Americans desired before 1775 but was quite unprepared, when he arrived at New York, to deal with the fact of American independence, proclaimed only about a month before. Howe, of course, had no instructions from his government as to the manner of meeting this changed situation. His peace move failed because of the refusal of Americans to treat on any other basis than independence.

Howe then moved against Washington, drove him from New York, and compelled him to retreat across New Jersey. Because the American force had little training and was badly organized, Washington's army dwindled rapidly and alarmingly in the summer and fall of 1776. Militia detachments would march off when their periods of enlistment terminated, and men deserted because of the discouragement and disorganization of defeat. Washington crossed the Delaware into Pennsylvania with about 3,000 men, a force not much larger than a modern regiment. December, 1776, was the crisis of the war; Howe then had it within his power to disperse completely the main armed force of the rebellion. For reasons which have never been fully explained, he gave up his chase of the American army at the Delaware and retired to New York to go into winter quarters, leaving advanced detachments at Trenton and at Bordentown on the Delaware.

Washington, knowing that desperate measures were needed to restore the shaken morale of his army and of the country and realizing that with the end of the year the enlistments of many more of his men would run out, planned and executed a surprise counter-attack. Recrossing the river, he fell upon a detachment of Hessians at Trenton on the dawn of Christmas Day and captured them. At the same time he took Bordentown. When Howe sent a force under Cornwallis to capture Washington's army, now assembled on the east bank of the Delaware, the American commander found himself with the river at his back and a powerful enemy on his front. In the darkness before the day on which Cornwallis expected to fight the decisive battle, Washington eluded the trap by a night march around the British flank. Defeating at Princeton a detachment of British hurrying to reinforce Cornwallis, Washington moved into northern New Jersey and took up a strong position at Morristown. Cornwallis was forced to retire to New York. The counter-attack ended discouragement both of the army and of the people; it impaired the prestige of the British forces; and it rewon New Jersey. Cornwallis, after the fighting in the Revolution was over, expressed the opinion that Trenton and Princeton were Washington's most brilliant achievements in the war.

The year 1777 brought defeat to both sides. The responsibility for the British disaster, which was more important in the sense of

grand strategy than American setbacks, lay with the blundering
War Office at London. London permitted Howe to attack Philadelphia, the American capital, and at the same time London ordered
a British army under Burgoyne to move south from Montreal by
way of Lake Champlain into the Hudson valley to join forces with
Howe. A third British army at Newport, Rhode Island, was kept
inactive. Washington sent part of his army north to meet Burgoyne, and these troops plus a force of militia and volunteer companies assembled before the advancing British army. Burgoyne
pushed southward as far as Saratoga, New York, but his army
was weakened by the fact that his line of supplies from his base at
Montreal was dangerously long and also by an unsuccessful fight
to get supplies stored at Bennington, Vermont. He failed, moreover, to get aid from the small force Howe had left at New York.
After two hard-fought battles with the American army, commanded by General Gates, Burgoyne found himself completely
surrounded and therefore surrendered.

Meanwhile, Washington had not been strong enough to prevent
Howe from occupying the capital. After considerable unsuccessful fighting the Americans withdrew into winter quarters at Valley
Forge, some twenty miles west of the city. The fact that Valley
Forge was an entrenched camp located in a position of great natural defensive strength brings out the point that Washington made
it an unvarying practice to fortify as strongly as practicable every
position where his army made an extensive pause. Lack of supplies,
however, so weakened the American force at Valley Forge that
a determined British winter attack might well have caused the
destruction of the American army.

The capture of Burgoyne persuaded France, ancient enemy of
Britain, that the Americans both could and would fight, with the
result that the French King signed an alliance in 1778 with the new
United States and entered the war. The immediate importance of
this event was a challenge to British sea power, hitherto undis-
puted in American waters. The British first met the changed situation by concentrating the British army at New York, pulling in to
this center the forces at Philadelphia and at Newport. Before the
evacuation of Philadelphia, however, Howe, relieved of command,
had been replaced by General George Clinton. A French fleet ap-

peared for a time in 1778 in American waters, and later a French army under General Rochambeau was landed at Newport.

The story of the rest of the war can be quickly told. After their initial scare in 1778, the British reëstablished enough sea power to make it possible for them to undertake new land operations. Having failed to conquer New England and the Middle States after four years of war, the British strategists decided to try their luck in the South; Clinton planned the move, but the campaign was under the command of Cornwallis. The operation got fully under way in 1780 and was based on Charleston, South Carolina. The first American army assembled in the South to meet Cornwallis was commanded by General Gates, the victor of Saratoga, and was decisively defeated at Camden. The victory made it possible for Cornwallis to accomplish his mission of conquering South Carolina. He was opposed in the latter part of this operation by a hastily assembled American force for the command of which Washington had sent south his trusted and able subordinate General Nathanael Greene.

Greene's operations are among the best of the American Revolution. With a force much inferior to that of Cornwallis, Greene retreated northward, luring his enemy almost to the northern boundary of North Carolina and dangerously far from his base. Then the American struck and fought a hard battle at Guilford Court House. The engagement was a technical defeat for the Americans, who at the end of the day withdrew from the field. But they had inflicted such damage upon the British force that Cornwallis retired to the sea at Wilmington, North Carolina. Greene then led his little force back into South Carolina and in a determined and brilliant campaign won back that State.

Meanwhile, Cornwallis, hoping the British forces left in South Carolina would be able to hold out, advanced northward from Wilmington into Virginia and attempted to conquer that State. He was soon opposed by Lafayette with a force which steadily grew in size. After much maneuvering to little purpose, Cornwallis retired again to the sea at Yorktown to reëstablish contact with Clinton at New York.

When Washington, whose army was holding Clinton in New York, learned that Lafayette had accomplished his mission of driv-

ing Cornwallis to the sea, the American commander sprung the
trap he had begun to prepare early in this year, 1781. Learning in
the spring that a French fleet was to set out in early summer for
the defense of the French colonies in the West Indies, Washington
had urged that during the hurricane season, when operations in
the West Indies would be impossible for sailing ships, the fleet
come northward to the American coast. The French coöperated,
and Count De Grasse appeared with his fleet off Yorktown not
long after Cornwallis had retired to that seaport. The British naval
forces in the waters off the United States were taken by surprise
and fatally erred in their measures to meet the new situation. An
English fleet, inadequate in size and poorly handled, challenged
De Grasse and suffered defeat, with the consequence that the
French won a temporary naval supremacy at a vital spot. Meanwhile Washington pushed his part of the campaign. Joined by
Rochambeau with his French army, the American Commander-in-
Chief marched to Virginia, taking with him the larger part of the
force about New York. The movement was so well concealed that
Clinton did not know what was happening until the American
troops were on their way almost as far as Philadelphia. Washington confronted the trapped Cornwallis with vastly superior
strength. During a brief siege preparations were completed for
assaults on two of the chief outworks of the beleaguered English.
When these bastions were taken, Cornwallis surrendered.

The war was ended by an overwhelming local concentration of
land power and sea power, and the victory was made possible by
effective coöperation between the army and the navy. The surrender of Cornwallis ended the war in North America and established
the independence of the United States.

A PEOPLE'S ARMY

The armies of eighteenth-century France, Prussia, and England
were made up of professional officers and enlisted men. In England and France too many men who were without military qualifications bought high military commissions or obtained them through
some kind of favoritism. There were, however, particularly in the
English army, many able and courageous officers, among whom
must be numbered General Cornwallis. But in practically all the

armies of eighteenth-century Europe the quality of enlisted men was poor; they were frequently the down-and-outers who had to choose between the army and starvation. Particularly on the Continent men were frequently shanghaied and forced into military service. In the British Army the enlisted men were poorly fed and housed. Except in battle they were under the almost exclusive control of the non-commissioned officers, and a harsh and frequently brutal discipline characterized all the professional armies of Europe; the officers appeared only to lead their companies or regiments in battle. Such professional armies had done most of the conclusive fighting in the French and Indian Wars.

The tactics of the time made it possible to use enlisted men of such caliber. They could be taught to maneuver in close order and to fire salvos at the enemy, an entire rank shooting at the same time. After firing the company was supposed to close in a bayonet charge with the enemy, who also was in close order. The artillery was drawn up on the flanks of the fighting line or in the intervals between regiments and was on the same line as the infantry. Such tactics required endless drill that transformed the soldier into a virtual automaton. Probably the best-trained soldiers in America were the Hessians hired by the North government to help put down the rebellion in America. No irregulars or half-trained force could stand in the field against such professional soldiers.

In contrast to the professional troops used by the British government the American Army was a people's army, the first great people's army in modern history. It was followed a few years later by the people's army of the French Revolution. The forces of these two revolutions were the forerunners of the mass armies of today, recruited from all callings of civilian life. In this development of modern times the American Army pioneered.

Two illustrations will suggest the nature of the Revolutionary army that won our national independence. When the war broke out in 1775, a young man in Boston by the name of Henry Knox was just getting started in the bookselling business and had recently opened his own shop. But for several years before Lexington he had been studying, by himself, engineering and artillery and had been training in a Boston military company. Soon after the battle of Bunker Hill he gave up his business and left Boston to

join the American force that was holding the regulars of General
Gage within that city. Knox quickly rose to be Washington's chief
of artillery. In later life he was the first Secretary of War of the
United States.

More striking than that of Knox was the story of Daniel Morgan,
a frontiersman who lived in the Shenandoah Valley in western
Virginia. Thirty-nine years old in 1775, he had the qualities that
made for leadership in a frontier community: he knew the woods,
he was an expert with the hunting rifle, and he had had experience
in Indian fighting. Within a few weeks after it assembled, in 1775,
the Continental Congress commissioned Morgan a captain with
orders to raise a rifle company. He recruited his frontier riflemen
in ten days. Immediately after the last man had signed, Morgan
started a march which began at Winchester, in the Shenandoah
Valley, and ended twenty-one days later at Boston, Massachusetts.
The distance on the straight, through highways of today is 510
miles. The detachment must have averaged more than twenty-five
miles a day. Morgan's riflemen, who were later greatly increased
in number, became famous in the Revolution for their individual
fighting prowess. They helped materially to defeat Burgoyne at
Saratoga. They did not normally fight in close order. Deploying in
open formation in wooded country, they were deadly marksmen
with rifles that outranged the smooth-bore musket carried by the
British infantry. Burgoyne's subordinates complained that Morgan's sharpshooters lacked sportsmanship because they concentrated their fire on the commissioned officers, who in eighteenth-
century armies were clearly distinguishable.

The smooth-bore musket, with an effective range of about the
distance between goal posts on a present-day football gridiron, was
the weapon of the military automaton of the professional army
whose individuality was lost in a close-order machine. The rifle,
of much greater range, was the weapon of the individualist, and it
was developed, not in Europe, but on the American frontier. It was
introduced into war by Morgan's pioneer rifle company and its
successors in the American Revolution. Because there were not
enough rifles to be had, it was impossible to arm all the American
forces with this gun, and as a consequence it remained throughout
the war an auxiliary but very important weapon.

TRAINING AND HANDLING A PEOPLE'S ARMY

Washington and his officers had the responsibility of training American civilians and transforming them into soldiers who could stand against the mass formations of the British and the Hessians. The American leaders understood that they had to perfect close-order fighting in the American service to avoid destruction and dispersal of their armies in battle. Of necessity in the early years of the war Americans imitated British practice, the only practice with which they had any familiarity; American officers even imitated the English custom of turning over the care and training of enlisted men to the non-commissioned officers while the commissioned officers tried to perfect themselves in the art of fighting battles and conducting campaigns.

The training of the American soldiers was made more difficult by the policies of Congress. It should always be remembered, however, that the blunders and inadequacies of Congress were due in part to the fact that this body was a hastily improvised *de facto* government created by an emergency. While in the early years it included in its membership the ablest leaders in America, these men were untrained in the management of the affairs of a nation and had no national experience or precedents to guide them. They were, moreover, fighting a new kind of war, a people's war, with a new kind of army, a people's army.

The first of the military problems confronting Congress had to do with recruiting. In 1775 the troops about Boston were members of the old colonial militia. Very few of the soldiers had any training of value, and militia enlistments were usually for a few months. Early in the war Congress began recruiting and organizing a Continental Army, the beginning of our American Regular Army. At first enlistments in this Continental Army were for a year, but later the period was extended and many men signed up for the duration of the war. Down to the latter years of the conflict there was a rapid turnover of men in the American Army, a fact that vastly complicated the training problem.

The second of the problems confronting Congress had to do with supply both of food and equipment. It was almost impossible for the Quartermaster General to bring food to an army from any distance because the roads in America were few and bad and because wheeled vehicles were relatively scarce. For long-distance transportation Americans had before the war generally depended upon coastal vessels sailing from colony to colony, but after 1775 the British control of the sea put a stop to most of this sea-borne trade. An army had to get its food from the neighborhood in which it operated.

As a consequence, from the beginning to the end of the war the Army was compelled to endure privations. The hardships at Valley Forge are familiar to us, but not so well known is the fact that the conditions at Valley Forge were duplicated in other winters and it many other cantonments. A few figures suggest the Valley Forge story. On December 23, 1777, 2898 men, a high percentage of Washington's relatively small army, were unfit for duty because of lack of shoes and clothing; and in February, 1778, the number had increased by more than a thousand. This was the winter when Lafayette joined the American cause and Army. The young French nobleman reported of many soldiers that, due to lack of clothing and shoes, "their feet and legs froze until they grew black, and it was often necessary to amputate them." Yet the Army did not quit. Instead it was at Valley Forge that the basic problems of training were solved and certain principles were established which have ever since been a part of the tradition of the American Army.

The two men who wrought the change were Washington and Von Steuben, the latter a German officer trained in the army of Frederick the Great of Prussia. Von Steuben was a master of close-order maneuvering and fighting. One of Washington's many gifts was his ability to judge men. He saw at once, when Von Steuben appeared at Valley Forge, that here was the drillmaster the American Army needed, and the Commander-in-Chief promptly persuaded the Congress to commission the German as Inspector General. Von Steuben sensed that one important weakness in American methods lay in the fact that the commissioned officers had so small a part in the actual training of their men. He himself, with a general's rank, set the example by instructing enlisted men in things as elementary as the manual of arms. At first the officers were scandalized. They then grasped a truth which Von Steuben had sensed more quickly perhaps because he came from outside the country. The Inspector General understood that in America the people's army, from enlisted men to generals, was made up of free men who prized their individualism and who were in the Army to fight for the cause of independence. They were not the offscourings of society so frequently found in the ranks of European professional armies. In such an army the commissioned officer had the heavy responsibility to give unsparingly to his men the benefits of his better training or abilities. The Von Steuben example and policy caused an immediate transformation throughout the cantonment; drilling became the order of the day. But Von Steuben, backed by Washington, insisted that the officers take charge of more than drill; they were held responsible for the well-being of their men. The results were astonishing. An improved camp discipline cut down the number of men unfit for duty, and in spite of privations the morale became high. The thoroughness of the Von Steuben drill revolutionized the Army at Valley Forge; when spring came it was a fighting force capable of standing against any regulars. It is a significant fact that after the winter at Valley Forge, no British general of his own volition attacked Washington's army. On the contrary, Washington engaged in two offensives, the second being the affair at Yorktown.

The spirit of the revivified Army is suggested by a paragraph Von Steuben wrote and Washington approved as a result of the experience at Valley Forge. Congress charged Von Steuben with the responsibility of preparing the formal instructions for drill and discipline which were to govern the American Army. The paragraph in question was included under the heading, "Instructions for the Captain," and was repeated with appropriate variations in the instructions for other officers. "A Captain cannot be too careful of the company the state has committed to his charge. He must pay the greatest attention to the health of his men, their discipline, arms, accoutrements, ammunition, clothes and necessaries. His first object should be to gain the love of his men, by treating them with every possible kindness and humanity, inquiring into their complaints, and when well founded, seeing them redressed. He should know every man of his company by name and character. He should

often visit those who are sick, speak tenderly to them, see that the
public provisions, whether of medicine or diet, are duly administered, and procure them besides such comforts and conveniences
as are in his power. The attachment that arises from this kind of
attention to the sick and wounded, is almost inconceivable, it will
moreover be the means of preserving many valuable lives." These
regulations of Von Steuben suggest the strategy of Washington
in trying to alleviate as much as possible the sufferings of Valley
Forge. The essence of these instructions is respect and regard for
the individual human being, principles that made it possible for free
men of all military ranks to accept with dignity and enthusiasm
the discipline necessary for effective coöperation in achieving the
ends for which they fought. In the professional armies of eighteenth-century Europe, the private soldier was an object of contempt both to his officers and to the civilian population. Von
Steuben, under the guidance of Washington, founded the discipline
of the people's army of the Revolution on the basic principle of
democracy, namely, respect for the individual human being. The
first American drill regulations set forth the principles on which
the fighting forces of democracy must be founded.

THE LEADERSHIP OF WASHINGTON

It is true, as has often been said, that French aid was a vital factor
in winning the American Revolution; both a French army and a
French fleet participated in the capture of Cornwallis which ended
the war. But more important than the aid of France was the leadership of one man. There was one military mistake the Continental
Congress did not make: it did not divide command and, hence,
responsibility. From the appointment of Washington in the summer of 1775 to the end of the war, the Americans had the ines-
timable advantage of unity of command; all important military
decisions were made at Washington's headquarters. The Virginia
planter from Mount Vernon was the very heart of the Revolution.

As a general Washington had a sound sense of strategy and also
of the importance of timing in military operations, as he demonstrated in the brilliant counter-attack at Trenton and Princeton.
But his battle plans have been criticized sometimes for too much
complexity. He was, after all, virtually a self-taught soldier and,

without doubt, the best in the American Army. His leadership was founded on other qualities as well as his competence in the military art. He possessed a physical courage which he demonstrated in more than one crisis, the best example occurring in the Battle of Princeton. In this engagement, on one occasion when the American lines seemed about to break, Washington rode forward and took a position between the firing lines until he had rallied the faltering troops. His greatest strength, however, was a peculiar moral quality that enabled him to draw to himself a group of devoted officers and men who stuck to him in every crisis. Washington and this nucleus of men and officers were the core of the Revolution. The quality of the political leadership in Congress declined as many able men returned from the national capital to their States to take office in the new State governments. But the quality of military leadership improved as the Commander-in-Chief and his officers grew in experience and in mutual confidence.

THE FATE OF THE LOYALISTS

The Revolution was one of the most terrible of American wars in its consequences. In many communities it was a civil war in which neighbors were aligned against neighbors. There were many Americans who held fast throughout the conflict to their old loyalty to King and Empire, and, when the war was over, an estimated 50,000 of these Loyalists left the country. For most of them the defeat of the British in the Revolution meant that they must begin life afresh in some other country. Some went to England, and a few to the West Indies. The greater part went to Canada, some to the country north of Lake Erie and Lake Ontario, but most of them to Nova Scotia in the region about Halifax. These American Loyalists represented the first large English-speaking migration into Canada after that part of North America was taken from the French in 1763. In Canadian history and tradition these refugees from the United States, known in Canada as "United Empire Loyalists," have an important and honored place.

THE TREATY OF PEACE

The treaty of peace was signed in 1783, two years after Yorktown; in this interval the war between France and England, which had begun when the French King entered into a treaty of alliance with the new United States, was finished. The settlement was unexpectedly favorable to the Americans. It established the southern boundary at the northern limit of the Spanish colony of Florida. The establishment of the Mississippi River as the western boundary gave to the new republic a broad territory west of the Appalachians. It is true that Americans had fought for at least a part of this region. George Rogers Clark had led a successful campaign in Illinois and Indiana that finally resulted in the defeat and capture at Vincennes of the principal British force in the West. But the treaty gave to the United States territory far to the north and south of the Ohio country where Clark had campaigned. This treaty was won partly by the skill of the American peace commissioners, John Jay, John Adams, and Benjamin Franklin, in taking advantage of the fact that Britain in the American Revolution was also fighting France and outside of France facing a hostile Continent. The settlement provided room for expansion and so made sure that the Americans, if they could organize an efficient government, would be able to establish a strong nation on the continent of North America.

CHAPTER XIV

LAYING THE FOUNDATIONS OF THE
AMERICAN NATION

OBSTACLES TO NATIONAL UNITY IN THE
LATE EIGHTEENTH CENTURY

The United States as a nation emerged out of a common effort to overcome a common danger. The thirteen States, so long as the war lasted, were held together by the fact that only through union could they hope to stave off or defeat the invader. When the fighting ended, certain obstacles to national unity became more evident than they had been while the war was still in progress.

The first of these was size. In attempting to estimate the importance of size as a factor in the founding of the United States, distances should be measured, not in miles, but in time required to go from one place to another. If we wish to know how far Boston was from Virginia in the latter decades of the eighteenth century, we should remember that it took Morgan's company of riflemen twenty-one days to go from Winchester to the Massachusetts capital. Going by horseback or by stage-coach would have cut down that surprising time very little. Almost an equal length of time would have been required from Winchester to Savannah, Georgia. Today in an automobile we can cross the continent from New York to San Francisco in less than ten days. By airplane we can fly today from Los Angeles to Philadelphia in much less time than it took Benjamin Franklin to go from Philadelphia to New York. When distance is measured in terms of time, the thirteen States that declared their independence in 1776 made a nation much larger than our present country. The United States could not become strong until this vast area could be brought together under an efficient central government.

The second obstacle to national unity was the fact that people in the different States lived and thought differently. Eighteenth-

century Americans tended to think of themselves first as Virgin-
ians or Pennsylvanians or New Yorkers. The States, moreover,
were of different sizes. Virginia and Pennsylvania were large,
while Connecticut and Rhode Island were small, and the small
States did not always completely trust the large States. They were
particularly afraid of Virginia, which claimed because of provisions in its colonial charter much of the huge territory that lay west
of the Appalachians and north of the Ohio River.

When the obstacles of size and of the rivalries and suspicions
among the thirteen States are considered, we must look upon the
establishment of a single United States of America as an extraordinary achievement. Europeans who were familiar with American
affairs were inclined to think in 1783 that, not long after independence had been won, the American States would form themselves
into two or three nations. The fact that the new union did not
break up in the latter years of the eighteenth century is evidence
of the high quality of American leadership in those critical years.

ESTABLISHING LIBERTY IN THE STATES

Before the machinery of the central government of the United
States could be perfected it was necessary to set up governments
for the States, for the Declaration of Independence in effect destroyed the legality of the old colonial governments. Independence
had hardly been proclaimed when the people of the States turned
to the task of framing constitutions.

They thought of themselves as entering into a compact or contract with one another, and for the purpose of drawing up this basic
compact the people of the various States chose delegates to meet
in conventions to decide upon the kind of government the State
would have. There were two exceptions. The old colonial charters
of Connecticut and Rhode Island were so liberal that it was necessary to do little more than to strike out all mention of the British
crown from those instruments. So changed, they continued in
force as State constitutions well into the nineteenth century. In
the remaining States the conventions drew up constitutions which
described the form and set forth the powers of the new State governments. In general these governments looked much like those
of the old colonies. In every State there was an elected legislature.

The great difference between the new States and the old colonies lay in the fact that the governor, normally appointed in colonial days by the crown, was now elected by the people of the State.

The Declaration of Independence had affirmed that government rests on the consent of the governed. By voluntarily agreeing among themselves what kind of government they would have, the people of the States carried into effect in the early years of the Revolutionary War the principle which Thomas Jefferson had written into the document announcing independence.

But there was another principle of equal importance in the Declaration, namely that men, because they are men, possess certain natural and inalienable rights. The delegates who framed the constitution of Massachusetts included in that instrument what they called a "Declaration of Rights," the first article of which reads as follows: "All men are born free and equal, and have certain natural, essential and inalienable rights; among which may be reckoned the right of enjoying and defending their liberties; that of acquiring, possessing, and protecting property; in fine that of seeking and obtaining their safety and happiness." After this opening statement there followed twenty-nine other articles listing the fundamental rights of the citizens of the Commonwealth of Massachusetts. These were enumerated in the constitution of the State in order to protect the citizen against acts of tyranny or injustice at the hand of the government which the people of the State had set up. The fact that Americans in 1776 took pains to protect themselves against governments of their own making and whose officers they elected suggests the importance they gave to the idea of the rights of the individual man and woman.

The Massachusetts Declaration of Rights and other similar affirmations in other State constitutions illustrate the point, suggested in the Von Steuben regulations, that American democracy is founded on the idea of the sacredness of the individual human being and that the political state exists for the benefit of the citizen and not the citizen for the state. The latter position, that the individual man lives for the state and must be ruled in every phase of his life and thought by the state, became in the second quarter of the twentieth century important in European thought. It is the philosophy of dictatorship and totalitarianism. When put into practice through regimentation of the behavior and thoughts of a people, it drags in the dust the dignity of human nature.

THE REVOLUTION AND THE GROWTH
OF AMERICAN DEMOCRACY

During the Revolution about 90 per cent of Americans lived on the land. Most of the people were small farmers, but there were large plantations in the South and equally large estates in some of the northern States. The Fairfax holdings in Virginia at one time amounted to some 6,000,000 acres; the Van Rensselaer manor in New York near Albany was two-thirds the size of Rhode Island; probably the largest landholding of the late colonial period was the manor of Lord Granville in North Carolina, which comprised about one-third of the colony. There was a tendency to try in many colonies to hold such estates together by laws modeled on the custom in England for the estate of a member of the nobility to pass at his death to the eldest son, or on other British practices which tended to keep large landholdings intact. Because of the emphasis on democratic principles after the Declaration, the laws which tended to perpetuate in America a permanent landed aristocracy disappeared rapidly during the Revolution, and within fifteen years after the end of that conflict they were practically gone. The aristocratic principles which came from England were replaced by the more democratic practices in the inheritance of property which we know today. The favored position of the eldest son disappeared. Many, but not all, of the large estates in the North, moreover, were held by Loyalists, and in most cases the owners of these estates were driven into exile and the land confiscated by the State. Almost invariably such a property was broken up into small holdings, so that in one New York case 300 owners bought farms out of the land held before the war by one man. The Revolution, therefore, tended to bring about a more democratic land tenure. The ideals of the Declaration of Independence were given a base of economic democracy.

SLAVERY AND THE REVOLUTION

In the period of the Revolution Negro slavery existed in practically every State, and many of the men who signed the Declaration of Independence were slave-owners. These leaders in the fight for liberty did not ignore the fact that the institution of slavery denied the liberty they sought for themselves. Even as early as 1773 Patrick Henry, that fiery leader of the Revolutionary movement in Virginia, spoke his mind on this evil which his generation had inherited from their fathers. "Is it not amazing," asked Henry, "that at a time when the rights of humanity are defined and understood with precision, in a country above all others fond of liberty, that in such an age and in such a country we find men [by holding slaves] . . . adopting a principle as repugnant to humanity as it is inconsistent with the Bible and destructive of liberty? . . . Would anyone believe that I am master of slaves of my own purchase! I am drawn along by the general inconvenience of living here without them. I will not, I cannot justify it. . . . I believe a time will come when opportunity will be offered to abolish this lamentable evil. Everything we can do is to improve the opportunity, if it happens in our day, if not, let us transmit to our descendants, together with our slaves, a pity for their unhappy lot, and an abhorrence of slavery."

The American crusade for the rights of free men brought about, however, an attack upon the evil of slavery. This institution was not limited to the thirteen colonies but was widespread in the western hemisphere, and it was particularly bad in the sugar islands of the West Indies. Americans of the thirteen rebelling colonies took the lead in attacking the institution. In July, 1774, Rhode Island passed a law that all slaves thereafter brought into the colony should be free. The preamble of this enactment contained significant words. "Whereas the inhabitants of America are generally engaged in the preservation of their own rights and liberties, among which that of personal freedom must be considered the greatest . . . those who are desirous of enjoying the advantages of liberty themselves should be willing to extend personal liberty to others."

In the Northern States, where slaves were few, the Revolution put the institution in the way of extinction. In the South, where slavery was of greater economic importance, the independence movement tended to check the importation of slaves. In Virginia slave-owners were given the right to free their slaves by will, and within eight years after this enactment some 10,000 Negroes were given their liberty through the wills of their masters. All was not done, however, for the ending of slavery. There continued to be glaring contrasts between the principles of liberty and the fact of slavery. But much honest progress was made. And it should be remembered slavery was one of the most complex and difficult social problems that Americans have ever confronted.

THE FIRST EFFORT TO SET UP A GOVERNMENT OF THE UNITED STATES

The first constitution of the United States was called the Articles of Confederation. It was drawn up while the war was in progress and was agreed to by the thirteenth State in 1780, in which year it went into effect. In spite of the threat of the enemy and the consequent need of unity, the States were not willing to commit themselves at once even to the small obligations required in the proposed plan of confederation. Maryland, in particular, held out because that State was afraid of Virginia. Virginia, Massachusetts, and Connecticut all had claims derived from their colonial charters to the country between the Ohio River and the Great Lakes, and Maryland insisted that all States having such claims must surrender them to the central government proposed by the Articles of Confederation. After Virginia, Massachusetts, and Connecticut had complied and had turned over their claims to the United States, Maryland ratified (1781) and the Articles became the first constitution of the United States. The new Confederation, therefore, became possessed of a vast wilderness region to which was given the name Northwest Territory.

The Articles of Confederation represented an adjustment to the great distances of America and to the individual peculiarities of the separate States. This first constitution did not attempt to go too far toward national political unity; under the Articles the States retained almost the power of independent nations. They could coin money; they could establish tariffs for imports into the State; and they could raise armies like the old colonial militia. But in agreeing to the Articles these independent and sovereign States set up a central Congress which should consider and legislate for concerns of a general nature that affected all the commonwealth. The Congress moreover appointed ministers to represent the United States in the capitals of foreign countries, and it had the sole responsibility for the management of the Northwest Territory.

The old Articles of Confederation repay study because of the continuing importance of the idea of federation in our own world. The drift of world events since 1939 makes it clear that the world which will come into existence after the present war will be an organized world. The Third German Reich has attempted to organize Europe on the basis of a super-state surrounded and supported by vassal states. The policy of the United States in attempting to organize the defense of the Western Hemisphere has been to guarantee every nation, no matter how small, its independence. The policy may well serve as a precedent of an organization of the world in some manner on the confederation principle. There is still some value in looking back at the first American experiment in confederation.

Under the Articles of Confederation, the Congress which had begun in 1775 as a *de facto* revolutionary government was given constitutional standing, for the Congress of the Confederation was almost identical with the old Continental Congress. In the Congress each State might have one or more representatives, but, when decisions were made, a State had but a single vote. Little Delaware was, therefore, the political equal of large Virginia. No important decision could be made except by vote of two-thirds of the States, and any change in the Articles required the unanimous consent of the States. Two aspects of this Confederation proved to be of vital importance. The Congress of the United States had no funds of its own; it received its revenue from the State treasuries. The expenses of the government were divided into thirteen parts and each State was asked to pay its just share. Sometimes the States were slow, with the result that the Congress was financially embarrassed. Measures passed by the Congress were, moreover, in the form of recommendations to the governments of the several States. Congress could not pass a law that applied to a citizen of the United States; congressional enactments were directed toward the State governments. The one exception to the general rule was the ability of the Congress of the Confederation to legislate directly for the people of the Northwest Territory.

Because the Articles of the Confederation ultimately did not

work well, this first constitution of the United States has often
been treated as a failure. Far from being a failure, it was a great
achievement. It held together thirteen different and often jealous
States scattered over a vast area long enough to enable them to see
more clearly the kind of government the United States must have.
In addition to this accomplishment, the Articles made forever
impossible the danger of a super-state among the American States,
for the Articles first established in American constitutional law the
principle of the political equality of all the States that were con-
federated to form the American Republic.

THE CONGRESS, THE ARMY, AND THE COMMANDER-IN-CHIEF

As the Revolutionary War neared its end the United States
found itself threatened from within the country with new perils
that had to do with the Army. Eighteenth-century Americans
were very much aware of these dangers; but in the nineteenth
century historians were inclined to feel that the fears of the men of
the eighteenth century were exaggerated. The rise of totalitarian
dictatorships in the twentieth century has given us a new perspec-
tive from which to view the anxiety of our forefathers of the
eighteenth century. The 1930's saw a dictator who rose to power
in Germany largely through the skillful use of an armed force
existing within the Reich itself. For many years the dictator-to-be
had been organizing his own army of storm troopers and with their
aid had fought his way to absolute power over every German man
and woman. In the same period the high officers of the Japanese
Army increased their power until the Japanese military became the
rulers of the Japanese nation. What our eighteenth-century forefathers feared, when all governments in the world were ruled
either by princes or kings, and when the principle of absolutism
was still powerful in Europe, was that some one in America would
try to make himself king and would use an army to gain and to hold
his power. This fear provides the background for three acts of
Washington of very great importance for the future history of the
United States.

After the surrender of Cornwallis, the prestige of Washington, who had led the armed forces of the Revolution to ultimate and complete victory, was tremendous among Americans, while at the same time that of the Congress of the Confederation was low. Most of the delegates to Congress were mediocre men because the outstanding political leaders of the country, such as Thomas Jefferson, Governor of Virginia, preferred to hold office in the States, where they possessed real power. A dangerous situation results in any nation when the prestige of political leadership is low and that of military leadership is high.

After the defeat of Cornwallis and when the army of Washington was stationed outside of New York watching the inactive troops of General Clinton, a small group of men secretly proposed a plan to the Commander-in-Chief. They wrote him a letter which was signed by a certain Colonel Nicola in which they pointed out what was becoming clear to all, that the Congress was weak and that this weakness might become so serious as to threaten the nation with disaster. Under such circumstances, the letter suggested, it would be a patriotic duty to establish a strong central government, and of course Washington was the only man who could do this. Let him step forward, make himself the head of a strong government, and assume some appropriate title, perhaps that of a king. This is the episode of the so-called offering of the crown to Washington. The General rejected the suggestions in the letter with some heat, pointing out that the proposal to set up by force the rule of a strong man was contrary to all the principles of liberty for which the war had been fought.

The second episode was more serious. Because of the weakness of the Congress of the Confederation, the officers of Washington's army had a real grievance: Congress could not get the States to provide the central government with sufficient funds, with the result that for months Congress was unable to pay the officers their salaries. This failure to pay brought acute suffering, particularly to the men who had families, and naturally such hardships bred discontent. Washington's headquarters at the time were at Newburgh on the Hudson north of New York. One day in 1782 a paper was circulated among the officers of Washington's army. The men who wrote it are unknown, but their number was small. The paper called upon the officers to assemble on a certain day in the church at Newburgh to make plans to compel the Congress to do them justice and proposed further that the Army, before it was demobilized, as everyone knew it soon would be, should march on Philadelphia and demand financial justice of Congress at the bayonet's point.

Washington, informed of the call to action, sensed at once that the proposal, if successfully carried out, would put the military power above the civil power in the United States, and that such an event would certainly bring disaster to the new nation. Americans would see in the supremacy of the Army a threat to their liberties, and the result, Washington believed, would be a new and terrible civil war. The Commander-in-Chief promptly ordered his officers to assemble in the church at an hour earlier than that set in the circular. When they had gathered, he entered and stood before them. When he spoke, it was with the authority of a victor, and he addressed those who were bound to him by ties of long comradeship. It was his greatest speech. He appealed for patience and forbearance, and he pointed out the dangers to liberty of any attempt to establish military supremacy. He ended with these words: "Let me request you to rely on the plighted faith of your country, and place full confidence in the purity of the intentions of Congress. . . . And let me conjure you in the name of our common country, as you value your own sacred honor, as you respect the rights of humanity and as you regard the military and national character of America, to express your utmost horror and detestation of the man who wishes, under any specious pretences, to overturn the liberties of our country, and who wickedly attempts to open the floodgates of civil discord and deluge our rising empire with blood." The voice of the Commander-in-Chief prevailed. The Army of the United States continued its role as defender of the liberties of the American people.

The third episode occurred in 1783 after the news of peace and the terms of the treaty had been brought to America. Then Washington in full military regalia appeared before the Congress and formally returned to that body the commission as Commander-in-Chief he had received from it in 1775, eight years before. He left the meeting a private citizen and hastened to Mount Vernon to take up the management of his neglected plantation. The drama of the ceremony made a deep impression on his fellow-countrymen. When the victorious military chieftain gave up his power, paradoxically he increased his influence among the people of the nation.

The French Revolution which followed so soon upon the American Revolution saw also in its later years the decline of the prestige of the political government. When that occurred in France a dictator, Napoleon Bonaparte, arose to mastery over the nation. One of the reasons why no dictator came out of the American Revolution was that the only possible dictator refused to depart from the democratic principles for which the war had been fought.

THE FAILURE OF THE CONFEDERATION

After peace came in 1783 troubles increased in the United States. A post-war depression set in and brought with it, particularly in 1785, hard times. The foreign trade of the Americans was almost destroyed for a time by the fact that the United States was now, as an independent nation, outside the British Empire and so was excluded from the old trade, which had been very profitable in colonial days. Quarrels arose among the States. There was a dispute among New York, Massachusetts, and New Hampshire over the territory which became Vermont; Connecticut quarreled with Pennsylvania over a Connecticut claim to land in the northeast corner of Pennsylvania; a tendency grew up for States to establish tariff barriers against imports from other States. The Congress, of course, had no power to settle these disputes. When the Congress sent John Adams to England as Minister, it was humiliated to learn that a British official had asked Adams where the other twelve ministers were. The implication was clear that the United States was not one but rather thirteen nations, and the British refused to make a trade treaty, knowing that the Congress could do nothing about it by way of reprisal.

The most serious event, however, occurred in Massachusetts in 1786, when an internal political battle within that State in that year flamed into an open insurrection, known in American History as Shays's Rebellion. Discontented farmers in the western counties of the State under Daniel Shays raided and took arms from the United States arsenal at Springfield. The affair made clear to all the weakness of Congress. That body in 1784 had reduced the Army of the United States to eighty men, the highest ranking officer being a captain. Its function was to guard military stores at Pittsburgh and West Point. (Incidentally, this unit was Battery D, 5th Field Artillery, which was recently transformed into a tank destroyer battalion.) The Congress, therefore, had no force with which to defend the national property against the Shays insurgents. A government so weak and ineffective could not serve the purposes for which it was established. Shays's rebellion sent a wave of fear among American conservatives; even Washington was much disturbed. He began to feel, with many others, that with the failure of the Confederation the future was dark and uncertain.

MOVEMENT FOR A STRONG CENTRAL GOVERNMENT

After 1785 a movement got under way to amend the Articles of Confederation and to set up a stronger central government. One of the leaders was Alexander Hamilton, a brilliant young lawyer of New York. Hamilton while still in his teens had raised an artillery company in the Revolution, and Washington had later chosen him to be his aide. To the end of their lives the relations between the two men continued close. Hamilton went to Mount Vernon and persuaded the former general of the necessity of lending his support to the movement to strengthen the central government. Washington's influence was so great at the time that any cause he opposed was doomed and whatever he favored was by his support half won. As a result of his support a convention was called by the Congress to amend the Articles.

THE SIGNIFICANCE OF THE CONSTITUTIONAL CONVENTION

During the Revolution Americans assumed that the States would be the principal defense for the liberties to be won with independence. The States were not so large that the voters could not understand the problems to be considered. The electorate could, moreover, keep an eye on the officials chosen.

The calling of the constitutional convention signified that a large group of Americans had become convinced that the weakness of the central government threatened the States themselves. A strong central government appeared to be the greatest need of the hour. Without such strength, those who called the convention feared that the nation would disintegrate as a result of internal dissension aided, perhaps, by foreign intrigue, and there were foreign observers who were convinced that such disintegration was already well under way. When the convention met, it faced the difficult task of creating a central government that would be strong, and at the same time so hedging its power about as to prevent its officers from transforming it into a tyranny.

CHAPTER XV

CREATING THE FEDERAL REPUBLIC

We think of the United States as a young nation, and when compared with some it is. England goes back beyond 1066, and China is more than a thousand years old. In comparison with these the United States, with a history of 166 years in 1942, is young. But, paradoxically, the government of the United States is old. The Constitution, drawn up in 1787, had by 1942 been in force 154 years. This Constitution has been the supreme law of the land since it was ratified in 1788; the Federal Republic established by it has undergone some modification and has developed greatly, but there have been no basic changes. It has never been set aside by a revolution. This record of stability and success makes a contrast with that of the governments of most other nations. In the last century and a half France has had more than half a dozen constitutions. The present constitutions of China and of Russia date from the twentieth century. The Fascist organization of Italy and the Nazi dictatorship in Germany have come into being since the first World War. It is literally true that in the world today there is only one important governmental system that is older than that of the United States; the British democracy in which the Parliament is master of the crown is about a hundred years older than our federal republic.

This aspect of American history suggests the high quality of the statesmanship at the Constitutional Convention at Philadelphia. It emphasizes the continuing capacity of the successive generations of America to govern themselves, for no matter how sound the work of the framers of the Constitution, their instrument must have failed if their successors had proved unable to meet the responsibilities of self-government. The age of our American form of government is evidence of the strength and self-control of the American people. But this long period of success emphasizes a third important truth, namely that free institutions make for political stability.

The free governments of Britain and the United States have out-lived all other important governments of Europe.

THE CONSTITUTIONAL CONVENTION

The constitutional convention met in Philadelphia in the sum-mer of 1787 in the beautiful brick building now known as Inde-pendence Hall. The body was made up of delegates chosen by the legislatures of the States. The group was small; there were rarely over forty men in the convention at one time. The seriousness with which the delegates took their responsibility is suggested by the fact that they decided at the outset that all sessions should be secret. The convention as a matter of course chose Washington, one of the delegates from Virginia, to be the presiding officer. The former general was also impressed with the extreme gravity of the task which the convention confronted. On one occasion in the de-liberations a paper was handed to him which had been picked up on the floor after a session had closed. The next day the chairman, sternly reminding the convention that premature publicity might wreck their whole enterprise, laid the paper on his desk and an-nounced that the careless delegate who had dropped it could have it by claiming it. It was never claimed, and the offense was not repeated.

In accordance with the fashion of the time the members of this typically eighteenth-century gathering wore breeches, long silk stockings, and either wigs or long, powdered hair. They were, on the whole, young men or men in middle life. James Madison of Virginia, who played a leading role in the deliberations, was thirty-eight. Washington, one of the older delegates, was fifty-five. In the group were many able men, but they were in no sense super-men. Their ultimate success lay in the fact that they were con-vinced that the nation, the United States, would ultimately break up if they failed, and as a consequence they conceived their first task to be the achievement of sufficient unity among themselves to make possible a constructive result.

Purposes of the Convention

The primary purpose of the convention was, as set forth in the Preamble to the Constitution, to establish a more perfct union among the States, to ensure peace at home, and to provide for defense against enemies abroad. The members of the gathering believed that all three objects could be achieved by setting up a strong central government to replace the old Congress of the Confederation, but the early debates on the convention floor demonstrated that beyond this common agreement in principle were broad differences of opinion as to the nature of this proposed strong central government.

The central problem before the convention was the question as to how much power the sovereign States should surrender and how much authority the proposed new central government should be given. The Virginia delegation proposed a plan which would have made the United States virtually a consolidated nation and would have left the States in a weak position. Opposed to this suggestion was a determined group who insisted that American liberties were best defended by State governments and who proposed a plan of their own that would have continued the confederation principle as it was under the Articles of Confederation but would have given Congress more power than it had under the Articles. The debate over these two divergent proposals came near ending in stalemate.

Finally a compromise was reached, the first of many important compromises in the history of the American nation. The two plans were, in effect, put together. The Virginia scheme for a consolidated nation gave to the Republic the House of Representatives, in which each State is represented in accordance with the population of the State. The plan of those who wished to keep power in the governments of the States led to the creation of the Senate, a body in which each State is represented equally. Small Rhode Island has the same voting power in the United States Senate as vast Texas. In establishing the Senate the Constitution emphasized the principle of confederation and of State power, while in the House of Representatives it gave to the United States a legislative assembly which was much like the House of Commons that was appropriate to a consolidated nation such as England. The central government created by the Constitution is, therefore, both a nation and a confederation of States. We speak of the United States as a single nation when we say the United States is at war with the Axis powers, or we may with equal propriety say, as did Prime Minister

Churchill in his historic address to the Senate on December 26, 1941, that these United States are at war with the Axis powers. The skill and sagacity of the framers of the Constitution was nowhere better shown than in this Great Compromise, as it has come to be called. In the Constitution the framers set forth many specific powers that should belong to the central government and consequently should be denied to the States. The members of the convention did not, however, try to answer all questions; they left an area of uncertainty between the powers definitely belonging to the States and those granted to the central government. In other words, the framers of the Constitution left for future generations the decision as to whether the States should grow in power relative to the central government or whether the authority of central government should be augmented at the expense of the States, and for the first half of the nineteenth century the dispute over the relation of the powers of the States to those of the nation remained one of the central issues in American politics. The changes which the twentieth century have brought to our way of life and to the world in which we live have required Americans to make the central government powerful in order to meet dangerous enemies, but the States have remained essential, if subordinate, agencies in the American political system.

The Powers of the Central Government

There is no citizen, civilian or soldier, who does not come every day into contact with the power of the United States. We buy a package of cigarettes carrying the blue stamp of the excise tax, and we know that part of the money we pay goes to the government at Washington; the coins in our purse which we pass over the counter were minted by the national government. Under the Articles of Confederation the coining of money was one of the most important and prized powers of the States. The existence of the Army in the present crisis springs from a clause in the Constitution giving to the central government the power to raise and to maintain armed forces. After the Revolution and before the Constitution the only important American armed forces in the nation were the State troops, that is, the militia.

One difference, then, of vast importance distinguished the Constitution from the Articles of Confederation. Under the Articles the Congress could deal only with the governments of the States; Congress could ask the States for money or for troops and could advise the States to do this or not to do that. Under the Constitution the central government deals directly with the citizen; it taxes him; and it calls him to military service. This power to deal directly with its citizens is the principal factor that has made it possible for the citizens of the Republic to create a strong central government with the Constitution as a foundation.

The Presidency

After the Great Compromise the most difficult task confronting the convention was to decide on the nature and powers of the office which should form the apex of the government of the United States. Here the convention had few precedents for guidance because, as already brought out, the heads of practically all the nations in the world known to Europeans and Americans were princes or kings. The framers evolved the office of President, investing the Presidency with great powers, but limiting the term to four years. The delegates at Philadelphia were convinced that the central government could not be strong unless the office of chief executive were given great authority, but though they set up safeguards which they believed would prevent a President from abusing his powers and making himself a tyrant, they put their trust ultimately in the patriotism and love of liberty of the American people to achieve this end.

In a democratic government faith in the people is fundamental to all political thinking. No governmental machinery will safeguard a weak people from disaster; no political devices will keep a corrupt people from the tyranny it deserves. In giving great powers to the office of chief executive the framers of the Constitution thought they took the risk that a man of ill will might seek to gain and use that office for evil ends. But they were willing to make an adventure of faith—of faith in the men who had won their independence in the Revolution and in the children of such men, reared in the tradition of liberty. The framers of the Constitution sometimes spoke of that instrument as an experiment. They could not foresee exactly how it would work. But basically they considered it an experiment because it put before Americans the question as to whether a free people, without calling upon hereditary monarchs for aid, could and would use it as a means for governing themselves. The record of the years which have passed since the Constitution was written have more than justified the faith of that group of eighteenth-century men who met at Philadelphia. In the long list of American Presidents no individual has ever sought to make himself dictator.

The Constitution made the President responsible for the enforcement of the laws of the land. It charged him with the task of taking the lead in dealing with foreign nations, but it required that he could enter into treaties with foreign powers only with the consent of the Senate. The delegates at Philadelphia gave to the President the power to disapprove by a veto measures proposed by Congress, but refused to make the power absolute by laying down the rule that a two-thirds vote in both houses can override a veto.

The Constitution made the President the Commander-in-Chief of all the armed forces of the nation, yet when he reviews the Army or the Navy, he does not appear in uniform in spite of the fact that he is the supreme commander who issues orders to the highest ranking generals and admirals. Nor is this failure to wear a uniform an accident; it has been the deliberate policy of the chief executive from Washington to the present. The President is a civil officer, and the Chief Executive in civilian garb reviewing the armed forces of the nation is a symbol. He is, of course, the servant of the people of the whole nation, charged by them with the performance of the duties necessary to the continuance of the national life. When he reviews the armed forces, he not only represents the people but signifies that the people of the nation who are his masters are also the masters of the Army and the Navy. He is no military dictator; democracy cannot survive when the head of the nation uses the armed forces to compel the populace to conform to his will. The dictatorship of the German Fuehrer is symbolized by his constant practice since he first seized power of wearing the military uniform of the armed force that enabled him to make himself master of the Reich. By the same token in the Republic of the United States the

President wears the garb of the people who with their votes elevated him to responsible office and from whom he derives his
authority. Yet by wearing the garb of the citizens when he reviews
the Army or Navy of the United States the Commander-in-Chief
enhances the dignity of the uniforms of the armed forces, for in a
democracy the uniform is the symbol not of tyranny or dictatorship but of service on the part of free men in the preservation of
the ideals and the protection of the homes of a free people.

The Federal Courts

The framers of the Constitution felt that the executive branch
and the legislative branch of the government were only two of the
foundation stones on which the structure of the Federal Republic
must rest; the third was an independent judiciary. Americans have
developed their courts beyond those of any other nation. The Constitution provides that no man may be put in prison and held there
by the arbitrary act of any executive officer; the citizen has the
right to know the charges against him and to defend himself against
those charges. The institution which safeguards these rights is the
court, for the judge can compel the jailer to produce a prisoner in
court and to tell publicly what the charges against the man are.
The case is then tried before judge and jury. This right of every
citizen is called the right to a writ of habeas corpus, and the Constitution provides that it can only be suspended by act of Congress.
But such a right would be of no use if the court were an instrument
in the hands of a tyrant.

The condition that has prevailed for nearly ten years in Nazi
Germany illustrates vividly the kind of situation the framers of the
Constitution sought to make impossible. In Germany the subordinates of the dictator have put and held in concentration camps
thousands of men and women because the Fuehrer and his party
did not like the religion, the race, or the politics of the imprisoned
individual. The courts were of no use for the defense of a man or
woman, for they were not independent but were the tools of the
dictator. To make such tyranny impossible the framers of the Constitution provided in that instrument that the justices of the federal
courts should hold office during good behavior; they cannot be

dismissed by the President or the Congress for any official act or opinion. They can only be unseated if they commit the sort of crimes for which the ordinary citizen is sent to jail. If they are honest and high-minded men, as almost without exception they have been and are, they hold office for life. The President or any other official of the government has no influence over the courts save that which comes from arguments presented to the judge in open court session. The officer of the government can try to persuade the judge that what the government desires is right and just, but the judge makes his own decision knowing that he cannot be dismissed or driven from power for ruling as he thinks right. This independence of the judiciary is the foundation of American freedom.

The Constitution Is the Supreme Law

The framers of the Constitution did not look upon the instrument which they drew up at Philadelphia as a collection of recommendations; they considered that they were engaged in the work of formulating a law, the supreme law of the United States. From this law all branches of the federal government derive their power. This law stands above every officer of government; it is no more binding on the common citizen than it is upon the Chief Justice of the Supreme Court or the President of the United States. Before this law all Americans, whether in or out of office, are equal. The Constitution stands above any and all enactments of Congress and any and all rulings by officials of the executive branch of the government.

The framers of the Constitution created what has been called a government of laws. They were trying to make impossible a situation in which the law of the land would be the will of a single irresponsible individual. Such a situation, so familiar to us in the totalitarian nations, has been called a government of men. The principle of constitutional government, the foundation underlying all democracies, is that the people, through their representatives, decide upon the law which shall govern all the officials of government. More than once dictators have drawn up and promulgated what they called constitutions. But such instruments do not make a constitutional government. A constitutional government exists only when the head of the nation must obey a law higher than himself; it does not exist when a leader writes a constitution in accordance with his own particular ideas and purposes.

Checks and Balances

One of the outstanding characteristics of the government set up by the Constitution was and is the arrangement which the framers spoke of as checks and balances. The planners of the Federal Republic divided its government into three branches, the executive, the legislative, and the judicial. These branches are independent of one another, but at the same time they are so closely bound together that they comprise a composite whole. Each branch has, however, one or more checks on the activities of the other branches.

The legislative branch has important powers which enable it to check the executive. If the President vetoes a bill that has passed both houses of Congress, the veto may be overridden by a two-thirds vote in both houses. The President, therefore, must submit his negative judgment to the Congress, which can then make its will prevail over his if two-thirds of both houses deem such a course wise.

The Senate has checks of its own with respect to the executive. The President must submit for the approval of that body his nominations for justices of the federal courts, for members of the President's Cabinet, and for a large number of other important offices. These nominations to be effective must be approved by a two-thirds vote of the Senate. The President, moreover, must submit to the Senate for its approval all formal treaties made with other nations, and these, before they become legally binding, must be approved by a two-thirds vote of the Senate. These peculiar powers of approval that belong to the Senate are sometimes spoken of as its executive functions. The Senate, when exercising these powers, is sometimes thought of as being part of the executive branch.

Of course, the ultimate check of Congress over the executive branch is that involved in the power to impeach, convict, and remove the President or other official from office. The House of

Representatives is given the power by the Constitution to impeach the President or any official of the executive branch or any federal judge for committing high crimes or misdemeanors. The word *impeach* is similar to the word *indict* in ordinary courts of law. When the House impeaches, it brings formal charges. The Senate sits as a court, listens to the evidence presented by the House and by the defense, and renders a verdict. To convict an officer who has been impeached a two-thirds vote of the Senate is required. In ordinary trials before the Senate the Vice-President of the United States presides, he being the regular presiding officer of that body. But in the case of a trial of a President the Chief Justice of the Supreme Court presides over the Senate. The Constitution does not give to Congress the power to impeach and remove an officer of the executive or judicial branch for his political opinions or acts. The framers of the Constitution put the power or impeachment and conviction in the hands of Congress in order to make possible the removal from office of men who take bribes, steal public funds, or are otherwise morally delinquent.

But the system of checks works both ways. The President has a powerful check over Congress in his power of veto even though it is possible for Congress to override that veto. The Supreme Court has also a check over both the executive and legislative branches in its power to declare unconstitutional and therefore null and void such acts passed by Congress and signed by the President as the Court finds to be in conflict with the provisions of the Constitution.

By this system of checks a balance of power is maintained among the three branches of government. The framers of the Constitution hoped that this system of checks and balances would prevent any one branch of the government from usurping supreme power. Checks and balances were intended to protect the citizen against tyranny.

RATIFICATION OF THE CONSTITUTION

It is true that the framers of the Constitution looked upon themselves as writing the supreme law of the land, but from the beginning of their deliberations they always remembered that the document they wrote could only be made law by the people. When they had completed their instrument, they planned the manner in which it should be passed on by the people, and the scheme they hit upon was that of the State ratifying convention. In State after State special elections were held in which the central issue was whether the voters favored or did not favor the proposed Constitution. The delegates chosen in such elections met at the capital of the State, and the State convention debated whether or no the State should ratify the plan drawn up at Philadelphia.

Long experience with the Constitution has given our generation a great admiration for that document, but the delegates who assembled in the ratifying conventions had no veneration for it. They did what they were elected to do; they subjected the proposed constitution to the most searching criticism of which they were capable. There were large numbers of honest and able men who did not like it, who were, in fact, afraid of this powerful central government which the Constitution proposed. These men insisted that the framers had gone too far toward creating a powerful nation, that the Constitution, in spite of its safeguards, would set up a government that would endanger the liberties of the American citizen. These critics made a telling point when they asked: Where is the bill of rights? The constitutions of Virginia, of Massachusetts, and of many other States, the objectors added, have bills of rights, but this proposed constitution has none. To such an attack the framers and advocates of the Constitution could only reply that they felt they had put in enough safeguards for the citizen to make a bill of rights unnecessary. The advantages of the Constitution were so great, however, that it was ratified finally in 1788 by eleven States. But many of the conventions ratified with the explicit understanding that one of the first acts of the new government would be to draw up a bill of rights in the form of amendments to the Constitution which then could be submitted to the States for their approval.

Two States, Rhode Island and North Carolina, preferred to remain loyal to the Articles of Confederation. Their refusal to ratify was a demonstration of the fact that the principles of democracy dominated the discussion and adoption of this new supreme law of the United States. Later, however, after Washington had become President and the new government was actually in operation, the two dissenting States decided that it was to their interest to ratify the Constitution and take their place beside the other States in this new union.

THE BILL OF RIGHTS

The Bill of Rights, added to the Constitution in the first ten amendments, was intended to protect the individual citizen against a government created by the people and whose officers were elected by the people. The fact that eighteenth-century Americans felt it necessary in the new federal government, as they had done earlier in the State governments, to protect their rights and liberties against a political power of their own creation suggests the jealousy with which they guarded the rights won in the American Revolution. When these rights were written into the Constitution, they became part of the supreme law of the land, and it became the function of the courts to see that the citizen was protected by them in his dealings with his fellows and with all public officials.

There are ten articles in the Bill of Rights. Article I guarantees religious liberty, freedom of speech and of the press, the right of citizens to assemble peaceably, and the right to petition the government. Article II affirms the right of the citizen to keep and to bear arms. Article III recalls a grievance of the colonies before the Revolutionary War when British officials in time of peace attempted to quarter troops in private houses and prevents the recurrence of the evil. "No soldier," declares the amendment, "shall, in time of peace, be quartered in any house without the consent of the owner, nor in time of war, but in a manner to be prescribed by law." Article IV is a reaffirmation of the principle that a man's house is his castle and that he has a right to privacy. It secures the people "in their persons, houses, papers and effects, against unreasonable searches and seizures." The purpose of Article V and of Article VI is to give specific meaning to the guarantees contained in the Constitution in connection with the writ of habeas corpus. These two amendments make it impossible to hold any person for alleged crime unless he has been charged with wrongdoing by a grand jury. They protect a defendant from being compelled to give testimony against himself; they guarantee him the right to speedy and public trial before a jury; they make sure that he is informed of the charges against him and that he is permitted to confront those who give testimony against him; and they give him the right to compel to come into court persons who can testify in his favor. In other words a person charged with a crime is given full protection against arbitrary and unjust treatment. In addition, Article V prevents the government of the United States from depriving a person of "life, liberty, or property, without due process of law," and adds, "nor shall private property be taken for public use, without just compensation." Articles VII and VIII also have to do with the courts. Article VII guarantees the right of jury trial in civil suits in which the matter in dispute is more than twenty dollars, and Article VIII forbids excessive bail or fines and also "cruel and unusual punishments." Articles IX and X seek to make clearer certain aspects of the Constitution. The former affirms that the mentioning specifically of certain rights in the Constitution "shall not be construed to deny or disparage others [not listed] retained by the people." The latter provides a protection for the States as against the central government. It reads: "The powers not delegated to the United States by the Constitution or prohibited by it to the States, are reserved to the States respectively, or to the People."

Such is the charter of liberties that eighteenth-century Americans insisted must be written into the supreme law of the land, and the liberties constitute the core of what has sometimes been called the American way of life.

PUTTING THE CONSTITUTION INTO OPERATION

The first Congress under the new Constitution was supposed to meet March 4, 1789, at New York City, chosen as the temporary capital. But travel was difficult in those days and the men of the eighteenth century moved in a leisurely way. The House of Representatives got a quorum on April 2, and three days later the Senate organized. Then the votes cast by the Electoral College were counted and it was found that Washington had been unanimously elected President, with John Adams of Massachusetts as Vice-President. On April 30, 1789, the Virginia planter delivered the first presidential inaugural address in American history.

CREATING THE FEDERAL REPUBLIC 205

Congress turned at once to the task of organizing the government in accordance with the outline set forth in the Constitution. In quick succession it passed and the President signed measures organizing the Department of State, of the Treasury, and of War. Another act organized the federal courts. And a tariff law began to bring in an income. The Constitution had been turned into a living government.

This Federal Republic was created in a day when monarchy was the normal way of organizing governments. Outside of England there was at that time little popular government in the world. But Washington had hardly been inaugurated when, in 1789, the oppressed people of France rose in revolt against the absolute monarch who reigned over them. Parliamentary government in England, the creation of the American Republic, and the French Revolution all operated to stimulate the growth of liberalism in Europe. During the nineteenth century many European nations limited the authority of kings and centered governmental power in parliaments elected by the people. In twentieth-century Europe, however, parliaments have been overthrown by ambitious leaders and nation after nation has experienced tyranny as complete as that of the absolute monarchs of the days before the founding of the American Republic. Through all these changes the government of the United States has passed without suffering essential alteration. Today it is challenged by the most formidable combination of armed force that the Republic has ever confronted. Its record of more than a century and a half of stability and success suggests that it will not now be overthrown by the temporary dictatorships which are undermining the civilization of Europe and are seeking to destroy the ancient culture of Asia. The ultimate power of free governments is the majesty of the principles on which they are founded.

CHAPTER XVI

THE FRONTIER AND AMERICAN DEMOCRACY

When the Revolution ended, a wilderness lay between the Appalachians and the Mississippi. The Ohio divided this region into a northern and a southern half, known in history as the Old Northwest and the Old Southwest. In both these areas powerful Indian tribes retarded the westward advance of settlement.

One of the most unfortunate aspects of the history of the American frontier is to be found in the relations between the advancing Americans and the red men. The Indians cannot be blamed for holding fast as long as possible to their old hunting grounds. Nor can they be criticized for preferring their own ways to those of the white men. But the Old Northwest, where tens of millions of people now make their homes, could only support a few thousand Indians with their primitive manner of life. The red men lived by hunting and gardening, and the struggle between the races on the frontier was really a conflict between an undeveloped and a developed civilization. Numbers, military strength, and economic power were on the side of the whites. The history of the American frontier had two aspects; it was the story of the advance of the whites and of the retreat of the Indians. The defeated red men have now been segregated on reservations and in many cases the government aids in the support of the people. Many of them in Oklahoma have been absorbed in the general population.

Settlement west of the Appalachians first began in Kentucky, a region where no Indian tribes lived but which was a common hunting ground for the tribes living to the north and to the south of the region. Settlement spread quickly into Ohio and into Tennessee. The power of the Indians was broken early in the nineteenth century by decisive fighting both in the Old Northwest and the Old Southwest and the red men were ultimately compelled to move west of the Mississippi. Before 1820 settlement had already pushed beyond the Father of Waters into what is now the State of Missouri and that region was filling up.

THE ORDINANCE OF 1787

The management of the Old Northwest passed into the hands of the Congress under the Articles of Confederation as soon as Virginia and the other States ceded to the central government whatever claims they had in the region, and soon after the close of the Revolution the Congress of the Confederation took steps to set up a government for this western country. The Congress first decided on a method for surveying the territory so that land could be sold in an orderly fashion to settlers. Finally in 1787, the year in which the Constitutional Convention drew up the Constitution, the Congress of the Confederation enacted the famous Ordinance of 1787, sometimes called the Northwest Ordinance.

This ordinance established what was, in reality, a colonial policy for the United States, for, as England had once settled the thirteen continental colonies, so the United States was in its turn settling the wilderness which lay west of the Appalachians. The English had laid out colonies with definite boundaries, such as Pennsylvania or Georgia; the Americans marked out with definite boundaries what were really colonies but what they called territories. The Ordinance of 1787 provided a government for these territories.

The framers of the Ordinance worked out a government which would change and develop as the territory filled with people. In the first stage, when settlers were few, the territory was to be managed by a governor and judges appointed by the central government at the national capital. When the people in the region became more numerous, the second stage of territorial government appeared and the settlers elected a legislature that passed laws for the territory. But the governor was still appointed by the United States. One result of this arrangement was that all laws of the territorial legislature must, in effect, have the approval of the central government. There are today three important territories still in this second stage—Alaska, Hawaii, and Puerto Rico. The law provided finally that, when a territory reached a population of 60,000 or a number of people equal to that of the smallest State, it could draw up a constitution as a State and ask for admittance to the Union. When the first new States—Kentucky, Tennessee, and Ohio

—came into the Union, they entered on a footing of equality with the thirteen original States.

The Ordinance of 1787 established a policy that lasted throughout the entire history of the frontier. It was the most liberal colonial policy the world had ever seen because it provided that the colony (territory) should pass through successive stages of developing self-government until at last it was incorporated in the parent nation with all the rights and privileges of the older members of that union of States.

One of the most striking characteristics of the Northwest Ordinance was its affirmation of democratic principles. It included what was in effect a bill of rights. But the Ordinance of 1787 added a point not found either in the earlier bills or rights of the States or in the later one added to the Constitution. When the Congress of the Confederation in the Northwest Ordinance recognized the importance of widespread and public education as a foundation for democracy it affirmed the principle that the democratic form of government cannot succeed unless it is founded on educated citizens. When in 1784 the plan for surveying the western lands was worked out, the Congress stipulated that in each township, as it was surveyed, one lot of land was to be reserved for "the maintenance of public schools within the said township." The Ordinance of 1787, reaffirming the importance of education, declared that "Religion, morality, and knowledge, being necessary to good government and the happiness of mankind, schools and the means of education shall forever be encouraged." These two enactments are part of the beginnings of that system of public schools and universities which is one of the finest aspects of American civilization and without which the principles of popular government established by our eighteenth-century forefathers could scarcely have survived.

EXPANSION TO THE PACIFIC

The selection in 1942 of Washington as the war capital of the powers fighting the Axis suggested not only the vast power of the American Republic but also the importance of its strategic location. The United States lies between the two most important oceans on the globe. The world position of the United States, where in 1942 the United Nations began planning the moves in a war being fought on every continent and in every ocean, is the result not only of the size and character of its population or even the wealth of natural resources within its boundaries, but of the fact that it fronts on both the Atlantic and the Pacific. When looked at from such a point of view it becomes clear that the story of the advance of the American frontier in the nineteenth century, westward to the Pacific, is one of the most important events in modern world history.

Expansion of the United States began in 1803 when commissioners whom President Jefferson had sent to France purchased from Napoleon the vast territory known as Louisiana. Behind this event lay a period of anxiety for Americans. Since 1762 the Louisiana Territory had belonged to Spain, a weak power which the United States did not fear. The United States was vitally interested in the fate of Louisiana because the Mississippi provided a channel of commerce of increasing importance for the growing settlements in Kentucky, Tennessee, and Ohio west of the Appalachian Mountains; the river, in fact, offered these western people the only good trade route for their products to outside markets. Spain through its control of both Louisiana and Florida had dominated the mouth of the Mississippi, and after considerable negotiation Americans had won from that nation the right to deposit goods for transshipment in warehouses at New Orleans without paying the customs duties. Tennesseans and Kentuckians had looked upon this "right of deposit" as a most important victory for them, but one that might be nullified at any time by a change of Spanish policy.

The arrangements had hardly been concluded, however, when Napoleon of France began that spectacular rise to power which culminated in a temporary mastery over Europe. With the opening of the nineteenth century Bonaparte had begun to dream not only of European conquest but of a vast new French empire in the western hemisphere, the center of which would be the sugar islands which France still held in the West Indies and which would include on the continent the territory of Louisiana. In pursuance of this plan Napoleon had forced Spain to cede Louisiana to France.

Jefferson was President when news of this transfer was received at Washington. He rightly said that the power which held the mouth of the Mississippi was the natural enemy of the United States because of the ability of that power to close the Mississippi to trade and so to undermine the prosperity of the western settlements. Two events, however, played into Jefferson's hands. The first was the successful termination of a slave insurrection in the most important of the French West Indian colonies. The victorious ex-slaves founded an independent nation that is today the Negro republic of Haiti, on the western half of the island of the same name. The collapse of the chief French colony in North America made Louisiana of little use to France. The second event was a drift toward war in Europe. Napoleon became anxious to get rid of Louisiana because he faced a conflict with England, and he preferred to sell the region to the United States rather than to have it captured by the British fleet. So Jefferson was able to acquire not only New Orleans but all of Louisiana and to push the western boundary of the United States to the foothills of the Rockies in the country north of Texas. Texas still remained Spanish. But the Mississippi became an American river.

The second acquisition of territory came in 1821 when Spain finally ratified a treaty of transfer which had begun two years before and Florida was added by purchase to the territory of the United States. The weakness of Spain had long prevented effective government in that region, and it had become a refuge for runaway slaves from Southern plantations. It was also the home of Indians who were inclined to plundering expeditions into Georgia. By 1819 conditions had become so bad that the United States forced Spain to sell.

The third important addition of territory was Texas, a region that was at first part of the Spanish colony called Mexico. Because it was too far removed from the main settled region of the Spanish colony only a few Spaniards or Mexican mixed-bloods had ever lived in Texas. Mexico declared and made good its independence of Spain in 1821, a time when that country was losing most of its empire in the New World. Under arrangements made with the new Mexican government American settlers began migrating to Texas and, before many years had passed, a large American population had appeared in that region. In the 1830's Mexican officials began to be afraid of the Americans and oppressive measures on the part of the Mexican government brought on the Texas revolt of 1836. In this struggle an army of Texas frontiersmen, after retreating before an invading Mexican force almost to Louisiana, suddenly turned on its pursuers, defeated the Mexicans, and captured their commanding general, who was also the head of the Mexican government. For eight years Texas was an independent nation and then it was annexed, as from the beginning it had wished to be, to the United States.

Mexico from the beginning refused to recognize Texas independence, and the annexation in 1845 was the real cause of the war which broke out in 1846 between the United States and her southern neighbor. The war ended in the complete defeat of Mexico when the American troops captured the national capital, Mexico City. In the treaty of peace of 1848 Mexico ceded to the victor the vast areas of New Mexico and California and the United States in return assumed the obligation to pay a considerable number of claims owed by Mexico to American citizens and, in addition, paid Mexico $15,000,000 for the territory acquired. Though Spain, and later Mexico, had long held New Mexico and California, Spaniards had done very little about settling them. Save for the Spanish towns of Santa Fé in New Mexico and Monterey in California, both regions were still largely Indian country. The final establishment in 1854 of the present boundary between the United States and Mexico completed the rounding-out of the territory within the present boundaries of the United States.

In the year in which the Mexican War broke out the United States and Great Britain agreed to divide between them that region of the Far Northwest vaguely known as Oregon, a fur-trading country which they had been occupying jointly for nearly thirty years. The United States took the southern half including the Puget Sound region and the Columbia River valley.

Between 1803 and 1848, a period of forty-five years, the United States completed its occupation of the Atlantic seaboard and pushed its western boundary from the Mississippi River to the Pacific Ocean. No other country in the nineteenth century underwent such an expansion of territory. The nation by 1848 was larger in area than all of Europe west of Russia. Expansion on the part of the United

States, moreover, did not involve the enslavement of conquered peoples. The Indians were made wards of the nation and, at the present time, are being protected and many of them supported by the government at Washington. The rights of the handful of Spaniards in New Mexico and California were guaranteed and they have been absorbed in the American population.

What really happened was that the United States acquired a virtually empty wilderness which was reclaimed for civilization by the pioneers of the Republic who established their homes in the West. By the middle of the nineteenth century the ample foundations had been laid for the powerful nation that has emerged in the twentieth.

HOLDING THE NATION TOGETHER

We have already considered the importance at the end of the eighteenth century of the great distances that make the United States so different from all European nations save Russia. Forty-five years of expansion increased these distances so much that some thoughtful Americans doubted whether so vast a nation could be held together. In 1828 a member of Congress, discussing the Oregon territory, then jointly occupied by Britain and the United States, argued that it would be impossible for that far-away country to be an effective part of the American Union. The Congressman pointed out that if a man in Oregon were elected in November to the House of Representatives and set out for Washington on the day after the election, he would reach the national capital in about a year, and, if he were to start back home on the day after he arrived in Washington, he would get to Oregon just about in time to make the next congressional election. The calculations were reasonably accurate for 1828. There were in that year only two or three railroads, not one of which was longer than a few miles.

Americans succeeded in holding the nation together by tremendous accomplishments in improving the means of transportation. Early in the century they built a great road, called the National Pike, across the Appalachian Mountains connecting the eastern seaboard at Baltimore with the Ohio River at Wheeling. In the same period Robert Fulton perfected a practicable steamboat, and this invention, rapidly improved, made it possible to use those tremendous waterways, the Mississippi and its tributaries and the Great Lakes. Meanwhile canals were being built. The Erie Canal in New York State united the Hudson River with the Great Lakes. Within little more than ten years after the Congressman expressed his doubts about Oregon and the Union it was possible for a man to travel entirely by inland waterways from New York City to New Orleans, or from New York City to the fur-trading posts on the Missouri River in Montana.

Important as the waterways were, they did not solve fully the problem of binding distant regions together. The greatest of the material achievements of the first half of the nineteenth century was the railroad. The tiny beginnings of railroad experimentation and building came in the 1820's, but in less than thirty years enough progress had been made so that the young city of Chicago was connected with the Atlantic seaboard by an all-rail route. In this same decade of the 1850's ambitious schemes were launched looking toward the building of railroads that would connect the Mississippi Valley with the Pacific coast, and the first transcontinental line was completed in 1869. It was one of the greatest of all American achievements, a victory over rugged mountain ranges and arid deserts. It tied the Far West to the older part of the nation. The railroad provided the first real solution for the American problem of great distances. The railway network which came into being after the middle of the century laid the foundation for that industrial development after the Civil War which became the chief strength of the United States in the twentieth century.

AMERICAN FRONTIER TYPES

Many different types of pioneers appeared as settlement moved westward across the continent. The first on every frontier was the hunter, the fur-trader or trapper, his occupation varying somewhat with the region in which he operated. One of the most famous of these backwoodsmen is Daniel Boone, who, just before the American Revolution broke out, crossed the Appalachians to spend a winter alone hunting and exploring in the forests of Kentucky. As the War of Independence was beginning Boone led a party of settlers over the mountains and into the new country. Men of the Boone type were known to the Indians as the "long rifles" because of the long barrels of the hunting pieces they carried. They were the borderers of the leather leggings and fringed buckskin shirts. They lived, as the Indians did, as much by the hunt as by farming. When Kentucky filled with people and life on that frontier became more civilized, Boone left it and moved west into the wilderness to build his cabin on the Missouri River in prairie country.

Boone was an Eastern hunter. His counterpart in the Rocky Mountains was Jim Bridger, the most famous free trapper of the Western highlands. Bridger had been born in Virginia and had had no opportunity for schooling as a boy. He went West because he loved the free life of the wilderness. He came to know the Rockies better than almost any other man and was one of the earliest explorers of what is now Yellowstone Park. Though he could not read or write, he learned to speak French and Spanish from other trappers or settlers in the mountains. He knew several Indian languages and on one occasion entertained a party of Indian visitors, whose tongue he could not speak, for an hour beside his campfire by telling them a story in the sign language of the Plains. His name is perpetuated today at Fort Bridger in Wyoming, a successful trading post which he established on the Oregon Trail.

Another frontier type was the prospector and miner who came to California in the gold rush in 1849. For the next twenty years prospectors were found almost everywhere in the Western mountains. Yet another pioneer was the cowboy of the old free cattle range when herds were driven from Texas north to Wyoming and Montana. To the list should be added also the missionary who went to the frontier settlements or to the Indians. The greatest of the Western missionaries was a doctor, Marcus Whitman, who established a station in what is now eastern Washington, where he tried to help the Indians. At a rendezvous of free trappers in Jackson's Hole in Wyoming, Whitman, when he was on his way to Oregon, astonished the redskins who had come to the camp to trade by performing an operation on Jim Bridger and removing from his back a flint arrow-point which had been embedded there for some time. Whitman, who was later killed by the Indians he tried to serve, illustrated in his life the fact that idealism played an important part in the westward advance. Among the most important of the pioneers were the soldiers, two of whom led exploring expeditions. Captain Zebulon Pike followed up the Arkansas River, discovered the peak in Colorado that bears his name, crossed into what was then Spanish territory in New Mexico, and was made prisoner by the Spanish officials. When he was released, he brought back valuable information concerning the Southern plains and mountains. The most celebrated of the explorers of the Rockies was John C. Frémont, who made his first expedition when he was a lieutenant. His long and well-written reports about the Western mountains were very popular in the East, and these volumes brought to thousands of Americans their first authentic knowledge of those Western ranges and canyons which in later years have become famous for their minerals and their scenery.

FRONTIER CHARACTERISTICS

Life on the frontier emphasized individual strength, ingenuity, and resourcefulness. The frontier was not a place for weaklings; it bred hard and tough individuals; it emphasized the fact that, if a man would survive, he must learn to stand on his own feet. This characteristic of frontier life tended to develop and strengthen one of the basic aspects of American democracy, namely its emphasis on individual rights and individual responsibilities.

The freedom of the frontier also bred a spirit of independence which expressed itself in a dislike of restraints. There was much lawlessness on every frontier, but also in every case the frontiersmen themselves ultimately devised methods to curb criminal acts. Among the best-known stories of the Old West are those of the Vigilantes of the mining camps and the cattle country, and of that summary frontier code which decreed that thieves should be driven out of the country or hanged. Every frontier community quickly assumed the responsibilities and established the discipline without which community life is impossible. Ordinarily, however, the job of maintaining order was done by the local frontiersmen and not by distant national authority. An illustration of frontier independence comes out of Oregon, whither American settlers began moving while the country was still jointly administered by Britain and the

United States. Before the final arrangements for dividing the country had been completed, the American settlers, without asking permission, organized a government and began making rules and setting up courts. The American capacity for self-government was demonstrated again and again on the frontier.

The frontier of the American West differed vastly from the complex life of a European community, where streets and churches were old and people were separated into sharply defined social classes with an hereditary aristocracy at the top. American frontier communities were new; life was usually hard and society was simple. A man was judged by what he was and what he could do. On the American frontier men looked upon themselves as basically equal; the inequalities that existed were the result of individual achievements or failures. This sense of equality had important political consequences, particularly in the matter of voting. At the time of the Revolution and the framing of the Constitution only those male citizens in America who owned property could vote. In the States that came out of the Western frontier this property qualification was abandoned and universal manhood suffrage, a long step toward a completely democratic political system, was adopted.

On the nineteenth-century American frontier the emphasis on the individual was inevitably carried too far, for the survival of American democratic institutions depends not only upon sound individuals but upon the ability of these individuals to think in terms of coöperation and to work in team. The small beginnings of community coöperation appeared on the frontier when the neighbors gathered to help a man build a house or barn or to harvest for him his crops when he was sick. But larger and more far-reaching community planning did not occur, and as a result the men of the twentieth century have made the unhappy discovery that our pioneer ancestors from the Atlantic to the Pacific not only robbed the land of its fertility but sometimes used such farming methods as to destroy the soil altogether. Because of lack of foresight and planning, the soil resources of the Republic have been seriously impaired, and for that reason the national government has put into operation in recent years a long-range policy intended to repair as much as possible of the damage done by too much individualism and too little foresight on the part of our frontier ancestors of a century and more ago.

FRONTIER CONTRIBUTIONS TO AMERICAN DEMOCRACY

The importance of the frontier for American life is suggested by the fact that of the forty-eight States in the Union thirty-three lie west of the Appalachian Mountains and so had their origins in the nineteenth-century frontier. To the life of these States and, through them, to the life of the nation the frontier contributed basic ideas and attitudes. What was more important, it strengthened the democracy which had originated in the colonies and had matured in the period of the Revolution and the Constitution.

The frontier with its wealth of varied resources emphasized the ideal of equality of opportunity. The best-known illustration of this ideal of the frontier is the story of Abraham Lincoln. His parents were poor people in Kentucky who moved early in the nineteenth century to a place called Pidgeon Creek on the Indiana frontier. Here Thomas Lincoln and his wife, Nancy Hanks, with their son spent a winter in an open-faced camp, that is, a shelter enclosed on only three sides, the open side facing the fire. Later the family drifted to the Illinois frontier. Young Lincoln made his way by running a store and keeping a post-office. The poverty of the frontier gave him little opportunity for formal schooling, yet educating himself he became a lawyer. From the office of a frontier attorney he made his way to the responsibilities of leadership in the crisis of the Civil War.

The ideal of equality of opportunity was firmly established in American society by the development of the public school system, foreshadowed by the Ordinance of 1787 and fixed in American civilization through the leadership of older States, particularly Massachusetts and New York. The community provides at public expense educational training from the kindergarten through the university. The system of public schools, high schools, and universities in the United States surpasses that of any other nation, and the roots of this educational system lie in that idea and ideal of equality of opportunity so important in the thinking of every American frontier from the seventeenth century onward.

In nineteenth-century America the emphasis was on progress. Americans could see their nation going ahead in a hundred ways: the country was growing larger as new territory was added; as the decades succeeded one another Americans achieved new triumphs in canals, steamboats, and railroads; and on every frontier primitive settlements were growing up into civilized towns. Nineteenth-century Americans took progress for granted, and men fixed their eyes on a tomorrow that would be better than today. This emphasis on progress is a fitting background for the middle years of the twentieth century, when Americans are entering upon a new era. The world of yesterday can never rise again. September 1, 1939, brought to an end an epoch in world history, and the men and women of America in the 1940's are struggling through blood and tears toward a new day. Behind them is that tradition of the American frontier, reaching back to the seventeenth century, that men are not pawns, helpless before the tides of fate, but are rather masters of their destiny. Eighteenth-century Americans transformed thirteen separate and subordinate colonies into an independent and united nation; their successors in the nineteenth century tamed a wilderness of continental proportions and extended the national area from ocean to ocean. Americans of the twentieth century, with soldiers and sailors fighting on every continent and every ocean, are engaged with their allies in the task of remaking the world. The frontier still beckons, but this time it is the hope of a new age in which free men throughout the world can live in peace and dignity.

CHAPTER XVII

NATIONALISM AND THE WAR OF 1812

The men who framed the first State constitutions during the American Revolution believed that the governments of the States were the proper seat of power and were the principal instruments for the protecting of those individual liberties to be won by separation from Britain. Later the dangerous weakness of the central government under the Articles of Confederation, disclosed by the events of the years immediately following the treaty of peace in 1783, convinced the men who wrote the Constitution in 1787 that a strong national organization was needed also, if the bills of rights in the State constitutions were to be of any use. Obviously, a bill of rights in a State constitution would be of little value to the citizen if the State were defeated and overthrown by a foreign enemy. The purpose of the central government, therefore, was among other things to make possible an adequate national defense. But the framers of the Constitution did not attempt to decide for all time the exact relation between the national government they were creating and the older State governments and wisely left this problem to be worked out as later generations of Americans faced the changing problems of an unfolding national life. Early in the nineteenth century a difference of opinion appeared between those citizens who wished to make the national government stronger and those who wished to put their faith in the States. The latter group called the idea for which they contended the principle of States' rights.

Thomas Jefferson, who in 1801 became the third President of the United States and held that post for eight years, was the greatest among the leaders of the eighteenth-century American movement for democracy. Jefferson, like Washington, was a Virginia planter. Jefferson's father had begun life as a small farmer and had accumulated a modest property, and agriculture was one of his son's chief interests. Thomas Jefferson was always searching for new ideas for the betterment of farming methods; for example, he invented an improvement for the plow. His lifelong interest in agriculture and the association with men and women of the soil gave Jefferson the foundations of his political thinking: he believed in political democracy because he believed in the character and the intelligence of the American farmer. Jefferson saw the farmer as the independent and self-reliant manager of an important enterprise. The husbandman was his own boss; he took orders from no man; he not only had to manage his fields and his animals, but also he had to sell his crops wisely; he had to take the consequences of his mistakes; the varied nature of his occupation tended to develop his mind and to strengthen his judgment. Jefferson, a farmer himself, understood the qualities of rural Americans. He believed American husbandmen could make democracy work. From Jefferson's day to the present, American farmers as a group have exerted a powerful influence in support of that kind of political democracy which has grown up in the United States.

The Virginia planter thought the farmers could most easily make their opinions felt in the State governments, and as a consequence Jefferson believed that the States should be as powerful as possible and that the central government should not be permitted to grow too strong. These were the dominant political ideas in the mind of Thomas Jefferson in 1801 when he stood before John Marshall, Chief Justice of the Supreme Court, and took the oath of office. Yet when Jefferson left the Presidency, eight years later, he had helped to make the government of the United States stronger than it had ever been under either of his predecessors, George Washington or John Adams. Of course Jefferson's enemies charged him with being inconsistent. Actually, however, the Virginia democrat changed his mind in the matter of the powers of the central government slowly and reluctantly; he had been forced to change it by the drift of world events.

When the French dictator, Napoleon Bonaparte, offered to sell the vast territory of Louisiana to the United States, Jefferson could not find that the Constitution specifically gave the United States power to buy land from a foreign power. But it was obvious to the President and the Congress that Napoleon's offer must be accepted. Jefferson remarked a little ruefully, as he completed a deal which practically doubled the territory of the United States, that he was stretching his power until it cracked.

Napoleon was seeking to conquer Europe and to humble England, and Britain, its fleet commanding the sea, was fighting desperately against the war lord on the Continent. The situation had many similarities with those that developed after 1939. In this war of the early nineteenth century the United States was neutral, but Jefferson was compelled to take action when he saw the ships and the citizens of America suffering blows from both contestants. In the first decade of the century both England and France seized American property and injured American citizens. Jefferson believed that an economic boycott would compel the warring nations of Europe to respect American rights, and as a consequence he asked Congress to establish an embargo which would forbid American ships from leaving American ports. To enforce this drastic measure it was necessary for Congress to give great power to the President, and in his efforts to carry on economic war in defense of American rights on the sea Jefferson vastly increased the powers of the whole central government. The President learned the hard lesson that, if the United States would deal successfully with foreign powers it must be strong. He might have added, though he did not, that the value of the guarantees to the citizen in the national Bill of Rights depends on the strength of the United States. Jefferson's policy of boycott failed, and his successor, President James Madison, saw the United States drawn in 1812 into the Napoleonic wars.

THE WAR OF 1812 AND AMERICAN NATIONALISM

In the summer of 1812 Congress at the request of President Madison declared war on England. Several causes brought on this struggle. As already mentioned, both England and Napoleon had done injury to neutral American ships and men in their titanic and prolonged struggle for power. But the wounds inflicted by Britain upon the United States were more numerous and more serious because Britain had control of the sea. British warships, faced with a problem of desertion among their crews, stopped American trading vessels to search for deserters. There were times when the searching parties took American citizens from the decks of American ships and forced them into service on British men-of-war. The British felt themselves justified because of the desperate character of their fight against the military tyranny of Napoleon. The American government protested vigorously and continuously against the invasion of its sovereign rights involved in the searching of peaceful and neutral American merchantmen. The British government finally yielded to American pressure and rescinded certain orders to which President Madison had objected. But the change of policy came too late. While news of England's move toward conciliation was being carried in a sailing ship across the Atlantic, Congress declared war. A paradox of this war may be discovered in the fact that the shipping men of New England, where most of the American merchant fleet had its home ports, were bitterly opposed to the war in spite of the fact that they were the owners of the vessels being stopped and searched for men and for contraband.

Another chain of events was even more important than injuries on the high seas in bringing on the War of 1812. The men of the frontier of Ohio, Kentucky, and Tennessee were hostile to the British for reasons of their own. English fur-traders still carried on a lively business with the Indians who dwelt in the forests south of the Great Lakes. The frontier of the Ohio valley was a farming frontier; as it pushed westward, the forests and necessarily the fur trade disappeared. The American frontiersmen suspected British traders of inciting the redskins against the American settlements in the West in an effort to slow up the advance of the westward march of settlement.

But the ideas of the pioneers who lived west of the Appalachians were not limited to suspicion of the English fur-traders. These men of the West saw visions of a mighty American nation to be. The acquisition of Louisiana had recently (1803) carried the boundary of the United States to the Rockies, and some Western political leaders believed that the next outward movement of the United States should be to the north. A young man from Kentucky named Henry Clay, elected to Congress in 1810 and taking his seat, according to the custom of those days, in December, 1811, declared on the floor of the House of Representatives that Canada could and should be taken and incorporated into the American Union. The aggressive party from the West that appeared in Congress as a result of the election of 1810 came to be known as the "war hawks." Their desire was to acquire Canada. A member of Congress from the West declared on the eve of the War of 1812: "The waters of the St. Lawrence and the Mississippi interlock in a number of places; and the Great Disposer of Human Events intended these two rivers should belong to the same people." It was these young Western leaders, rather than the more cautious Madison, who actually tipped the scales for war in June, 1812.

THE ARMY IN THE WAR OF 1812

In June, 1812, the British regular force in Canada was less than 5000 men, and the actual strength of the Regular Army of the United States was at the time under 7000. The training of the United States Army was inadequate, partly because of the inferior military education of its officers, for though West Point had been established as a feeble institution before the War of 1812, it did not give its cadets proper military training until after the conflict. Because of the weakness of the regular forces the nation had to depend heavily on the virtually untrained militia of the States. The United States in 1812 was, therefore, in a military sense almost completely unprepared for war with a major power.

Throughout the two and a half years the war lasted the American Army did better than a realistic military observer could have foreseen in June, 1812. The weapons and tactics of this conflict were the same as those of the Revolution. American commanders had the same difficulties as in the former struggle (before the days of Von Steuben) in getting militia to stand up against the military machine represented by regular troops trained in close-order maneuver. The army did not conquer Canada as Henry Clay expected it would, but in 1813 it fought well along the Niagara frontier and north of Lake Erie.

The one decisive triumph of the American Army occurred in January, 1815, at New Orleans after the treaty of peace had been signed but before the news of the event had crossed the Atlantic. The battle of New Orleans is worth studying because it illustrates the point that in actual operations, while rules and principles are of basic importance, commanders must show originality and ingenuity in applying them to particular situations. New Orleans was defended by an army of frontiersmen recently recruited from the Mississippi Valley and commanded by General Andrew Jackson. This force had not had time to perfect the close-order training that would enable it to march into open battle against the strategic seaport under the command of General Pakenham. Jackson, therefore, depended upon prepared defensive positions which could be taken only by frontal assault.

Pakenham faced a difficult task, but he knew that, if he could once reach and penetrate the American defenses, the inadequately trained frontiersmen might well be sent fleeing from the battlefield. He apparently felt that he had a chance. He knew that the infantry musket still in use would carry effectively only about a hundred yards. He knew also that his American adversaries were in part armed with rifles, but the British commander doubtless felt that the superior range of the rifle was offset by the fact that it was slower to load than the smooth-bore musket. It took some time to hammer home the tight-fitting bullets in those long-barreled muzzle-loading rifles that American frontiersmen used for hunting. Pakenham decided to risk the fire-fight, believing apparently that enough of his men would survive the final hundred-yard charge to carry the works and throw out the enemy.

Jackson, recognizing the danger confronting his army, felt that his main hope lay in taking full advantage of the many superior guns and expert marksmen his force contained. The rifle would carry accurately to about 500 yards, but it could only be effective if it could be transformed into a rapid-fire weapon. Jackson's solution of his problem was to put his best marksmen in protected but advanced positions in his defense line. Available to each of these marksmen was a half-dozen or more rifles with a squad whose sole job was to load and pass them forward to the sharpshooter. By such a scheme Jackson transformed the slow-loading rifle into a rapid-fire weapon. The effect was decisive. The British troops were badly cut up before they came into musket range and were finished by the volleys from that weapon. Pakenham himself was killed. The British withdrew with heavy losses, leaving the American force scarcely more than scratched. The battle made Jackson the greatest national hero to emerge from the War of 1812.

SEA POWER IN THE WAR OF 1812

In the last five years of the eighteenth century the United States had built a few powerful oak-sided frigates for use against pirates, particularly in the Mediterranean, and also against France. Due to insults of the French government to American envoys and the aggressions of that nation against American commerce, the United States had fought an undeclared war against France from 1798 to 1800. The frigates came into being during this conflict.

Presidents Jefferson and Madison unfortunately had no realization of the importance of sea power and, as a consequence, no interest in a sea-going navy. Jefferson advocated and brought about the building of some gunboats that were supposed to go into action in time of war and prevent enemy ships from landing soldiers on American shores. These tiny coastal warships proved to be quite useless in the war, and the frigates were too few to challenge British control of the waters off the Atlantic coast of the United States.

From a naval point of view the War of 1812 was a defeat. It is true that there were several individual engagements between single American and British frigates, and these encounters frequently resulted in victories for the Americans, whose ships carried more guns than similar British craft. In these duels the frigate *Constitution* won such glory as to make it still, after more than a century, the most famous single warship in American naval history. Not many years ago the President of the United States, in the interest of strengthening the memory of a great tradition, put the old *Constitution* again in the list of commissioned vessels in the American Navy.

But the single-handed victories of the *Constitution* and other American warships over their hard-fighting adversaries could not prevent the British Navy from establishing a blockade of the Atlantic coast which finally extended from Georgia to Maine. The blockade denied to the Americans the use of the sea either for purposes of commerce or for transporting armies or their supplies. Control of the sea made it possible, moreover, for the British to strike wherever they chose along the coast. In 1814, when the power of Napoleon in Europe was declining and his final overthrow was near, the British planned knockout blows against the United States. Bringing to North America troops freed from campaigns in Europe, the English assembled a powerful army at Montreal to invade the United States from the north and another in the Gulf of Mexico to take New Orleans. At the same time the British made harassing attacks along the coasts of Maine and of Maryland and Virginia. A particularly well-planned and well-executed raid resulted in the capture of Washington and the temporary dispersal of the American government. The slightly trained militia called out for the defense of the national capital fled so precipitately when the small force of the enemy reached Bladensburg, just outside Washington, that the affair came to be derisively known as the "Bladensburg Races." The two main blows from north and south and the harassing coastal attacks were all made possible in 1814 by the command of the sea possessed by the British Navy.

The war demonstrated that, while commerce raiding such as Americans effectively carried on against British merchant ships may seriously injure the enemy, it cannot be decisive while warships retain essential control of the sea; the conflict also made clear that sea power can be won only by navies organized into fleets. The War of 1812 completely discredited the older American naval theory which had emphasized the importance of single ships.

One of the most curious things, however, about the War of 1812 is the fact that almost as soon as it was over and peace had brought back the status quo in North America of the years before 1812, the legend grew up in the United States that in a naval sense the recent conflict had been a successful struggle. Americans remembered the victories of the *Constitution*, which were without strategic value, and forgot the defeats represented by the blockade, which was of the utmost strategic importance. Not until the end of the nineteenth century did an American naval officer, Captain Alfred T. Mahan, point out the real lessons to be learned from the American naval defeat in the War of 1812.

STATES' RIGHTS AND THE WAR OF 1812

Life for an individual or a nation is never secure, but when a country embarks upon war it faces deadly peril. The War of 1812 was begun with the confident expectation on the part of the "war hawks" that the conquest of Canada would be an enterprise requiring few regiments and fewer months. Before it ended, however, the struggle brought the United States to the verge of dissolution. The grave and almost fatal cause of American weakness in this conflict was lack of national unity. Those who dissented from the policies of the Madison administration made effective use of States' rights in which both Jefferson and Madison believed. The center of disaffection was New England, a section in which the political party of Jefferson and Madison was in a minority. The New England leaders of the political opposition charged that Madison of the agricultural State of Virginia had brought on the war for the evil purpose of destroying New England commerce and so of destroying the important position of that section in the Union of States.

When the words of criticism and dissent were translated into action, matters became serious. At the outset of the war, because of the smallness of the regular army and the slowness of recruiting, President Madison called upon the States to furnish quotas of militia to be added to the national armies charged with the mission of overcoming the enemy. The militia were, in those days, State troops under the immediate control of the governors of the States. Their primary reason for existence according to law was to defend against invasion. The governors of Connecticut and Massachusetts refused to furnish to the United States the militia units for which they had been asked. Both governors argued that it was the function of the State governments to decide whether or not a threat of invasion existed. They told the President that they saw no threat of invasion and that, if one came, Massachusetts and Connecticut preferred to have their troops at home where they could protect their own homes and firesides.

The disaffection in New England increased as the war progressed. It expressed itself in some trading with the enemy on the part of New England shippers. Boston, moreover, one of the most important financial centers of the country, did not coöperate fully with the administration at Washington. This fact was one cause, although not the only one, for the collapse in the Treasury of the United States which brought the Madison administration to the verge of despair in the fateful year of 1814.

In 1814 the young American Republic almost broke up, and in the summer of that year great destinies hung on small events. A powerful army of veteran British regulars moved southward into New York State from its base at Montreal. In preparation for this campaign the British had hastily built a flotilla of warships on Lake Champlain, knowing that the invading army must advance through a narrow lowland between the rugged Adirondacks on the west and the lake on the east. For the third time in American history the Great Warpath of the French and Indian Wars and of the Revolution was to see decisive action. The British shipbuilders gambled, in their bid for naval control of Lake Champlain, on one large frigate which they called the *Confiance*. She was supported by a few small vessels. The Americans were not caught napping and built a defending flotilla of their own. They put their bid for victory in two ships of war, of which the largest was the *Saratoga*. But neither of these vessels nor the batteries they carried equaled the power of the *Confiance*. The British lake force was commanded by Captain Downie; the American commander was Commodore Thomas McDonough.

The narrative of the resulting campaign is a fantastic story of blundering and of heroic efficiency. The first of the mistakes was committed by the distracted general command in Washington. A large army had been stationed at Plattsburg on the western shore of Lake Champlain, where the mountains come close to the lake, and this force had organized a strong defensive position. After these preparations the Washington high command, due to the inadequacy of the American service of information, got the idea that the British thrust would be made west of the mountains by way of Lake Ontario, where the English also had a naval flotilla. As a result of this error, a large part of the army at Plattsburg was moved across the mountains to Lake Ontario not long before the British campaign of invasion began. When General Prevost, commanding the British regulars, reached Plattsburg, he faced a force capable only of delaying action. Prevost understood, however, that he could not advance with safety until the naval forces of Britain had control of the lake and were in a position to protect his line of communications with Montreal. Prevost sat down, therefore, before Plattsburg and ordered Captain Downie, who was under his command, to dispose of the American flotilla which had placed itself in Plattsburg Bay on the American right flank.

Prevost was no naval officer and had no understanding of the necessities of naval tactics. He saw only that in weight of guns and ships Downie was somewhat superior to his adversary. Downie was confident that, if he got the Americans out into the open lake where he could maneuver, he could defeat their two principal ships singly or jointly. But McDonough refused to come out. He drew up his flotilla in line of battle across the mouth of Plattsburg Bay, an arm of the lake shaped like a round bag, with a narrow mouth made by two projecting promontories. The American army planted batteries on these promontories to protect the flanks of McDonough's battle line. With his ships in such a defensive position McDonough felt equal to his opponent. The fatal blunder that Prevost made was to order Downie to attack the Americans in their strong position. Prevost with his vastly superior numbers could have moved against McDonough's flanking land batteries and could have driven the American ships into the open water. But Prevost made no such move to give Downie aid. Captain Downie, an efficient and gallant officer, obeyed orders. He moved the *Confiance* against the *Saratoga* and her sister ship and opened battle. As both commanders had anticipated, the heavier weight of the metal of the British warship finally silenced the guns of the *Saratoga* on the side of the ship turned toward the enemy. But in accomplishing this result the *Confiance* took heavy punishment. At this juncture, when the American ship could not fire a shot and the battle appeared lost, McDonough executed a maneuver which he had carefully planned before the engagement began. To understand this maneuver it should be remembered that this was, because of McDonough's defensive position, a battle in which the warships were almost stationary floating batteries and were lying parallel to one another. McDonough dropped the anchor of the *Saratoga* and ordered into action the boats, propelled by oars, that he had prepared to swing the ship around in order to bring into action the guns which before had been on the opposite side of the vessel from the enemy. The anchor provided the pivot on which the ship was turned. Downie was taken by surprise. He attempted to execute the same maneuver with the damaged *Confiance*, but McDonough brought the *Saratoga* around first and caught the *Confiance* at a disadvantage. When McDonough put her hitherto unused batteries into action, she practically blew the *Confiance* out of the water. Never in American history have the foresight, skill, and determination of an officer of the armed forces been of greater service to the nation thon those qualities in Commodore McDonough. The defeat and death of Captain Downie brought the British campaign of invasion to an end. Prevost took his army back to Canada. Relieved of command, he was put down for court martial but died before his case was heard.

DISUNITY IN NEW ENGLAND

What might have happened to the nation if Prevost's invasion had succeeded, as it should have done, is suggested by a book written by a prominent business man in Philadelphia and published on November 8, 1814. Matthew Carey, the author, called his volume *The Olive Branch, or Faults on Both Sides*. He did not refer to both sides of the war. What Carey meant by "both sides" was that, in spite of the failure of the Prevost invasion, disaffection in New England and New York had gone from bad to worse. News had reached Philadelphia that New England leaders were calling a convention in which it was generally assumed the question of New England's secession from the Union would be discussed. "About one half of the papers published in New England," said Carey in the *Olive Branch,* "are opposed to the present administration. Hardly a single number of any of them appears without accusations of the foulest description. . . . The national vessel is on rocks and quicksands, and in danger of shipwreck. . . . While the parties are more and more inflamed against each other, the vessel bulges on a sharp rock—down she goes—pilot—and supporters—and mutineers—and peacemakers—all in one common destruction." Carey concluded with an extraordinary appeal. "This, I am fearful, will be our fate. It may be prevented. All that is necessary is for a few influential men in different states to step forward—to bury the hatchet—lay aside all minor considerations while the vessel of state is in danger. This policy is so obvious that one hundred individuals throughout the union setting the example would have sufficient efficacy to accomplish the blessed object of saving their country."

Carey made clear the deadly peril that lurks in national disunity. The dissension that endangered the safety of the Union was from the beginning of the War of 1812 a blight tending to paralyze the war effort of the nation. Not only did it help to bring about defeat at the hands of the enemy, but enemy victories made the evil worse. In such a scene it is not difficult to imagine the consequences for the Union of a victorious march by Prevost even as far as Albany on the Hudson. Contemplation of such consequences gives us a sense of the importance of McDonough's contribution to American history. At a moment of dire crisis his victory helped to save the Union and, incidentally, to make it possible for our present United States, powerful and united as never before, to play its role against aggression and tyranny.

THE BEGINNING OF A CENTURY OF PEACE

The War of 1812 came to an end with the virtual close of the Napoleonic wars in Europe. Britain and America agreed to quit fighting and to return to the situation in North America that had existed before the war. After the treaty of peace two changes in the international scene took place. The first had to do with the impressment of American seamen; never again did Britain or any other nation violate the sovereignty of the United States by taking American citizens from American ships. The second modification of an earlier practice related to the boundary between Canada and the United States. England and the American Republic agreed that Canada and the United States should live side by side as friendly neighbors. The two nations entered into an understanding that they should do away with all armed vessels on Lake Champlain and the Great Lakes save those needed for police purposes, and further undertook to build no forts along the international border.

For more than a century the Canadian-American border has been unfortified. With the advance of the frontier it has become the longest unfortified boundary between two nations in the world. It has been and still is a symbol suggesting that two democratic peoples, though of unequal strength, can live beside each other as peaceful neighbors. But Americans, in dealing with Canadians, should remember that in Canada boys and girls study history in school just as they do in the United States. And Canadian history books have unpleasant things to say about our American ancestors of more than a century ago. The school histories of Canada teach that the first important migration of English-speaking people into Canada were the Loyalist refugees driven out of the United States as a result of the success of the Revolutionary War. And these same school histories emphasize that, so far as Canada is concerned, the War of 1812 was an unsuccessful attempt on the part of the United States to conquer that country. The Canadians are and have long been our friends. But international friendships are strengthened by understanding on the part of peoples on each side of the traditions and points of view of the other country.

THE END OF STATES' RIGHTS IN NEW ENGLAND

The convention to discuss secession which Matthew Carey feared assembled in Hartford in December, 1814, but the course of the war and particularly the failure of the Prevost invasion tended to prevent extremists from controlling the gathering. Yet the leaders of the Hartford Convention were angry and threatening. They criticized the national government not only for the war but for the failures of the war. They demanded peace. The men at Hartford drew up resolutions demanding important changes in the Constitution that would give New England more power, relative to other sections, in the councils of the nation. The convention sent these demands to Washington by special messengers. As the emissaries neared the national capital, however, they were met first by the news that a peace treaty had been signed and second by the tidings of Jackson's victory in New Orleans. The messengers suddenly found that they had become ridiculous. The dissenters in New England were completely discredited, and the political party to which they belonged died. The War of 1812 was followed by an upsurge of national feeling. Americans, including New England, turned to the great task of conquering and developing the wilderness which lay beyond the western frontier.

CHAPTER XVIII

THE BACKGROUND OF THE DIVISION OF THE NATION IN 1861

The issue between the rights of the States and the powers of the nation continued after the close of the War of 1812. It is true that States' rights sentiment gradually died in New England until by 1825 that section supported the movement to strengthen the central government, and in 1829, Daniel Webster, senator from Massachusetts, made one of the most powerful arguments for a more fully developed nationalism ever to be delivered in the Senate. But the doctrine of States' rights did not die; under the leadership of John C. Calhoun of South Carolina it gained great strength in the South in the second quarter of the nineteenth century. After 1850 it acquired such importance that in 1861 it led directly to the secession of eleven Southern States from the Union.

THE AMERICAN DEMOCRATIC FAITH OF THE MIDDLE OF THE NINETEENTH CENTURY

The background for the combat between the champions of nationalism and of States' rights was made up of the democratic ideas of the American people in the middle years of the nineteenth century. By 1850 the foundation of American political institutions had been broadened by the adoption in almost every State in the Union of the practice of universal manhood suffrage. The old property qualifications of the eighteenth century were abolished, and the poor man was given equality at the ballot box with his richer neighbor.

There is no better or more typical expression of the ideas of Americans about the middle of the nineteenth century than those set forth in a little book called *Democracy*, written by an obscure author named George Sidney Camp. It was widely sold and read. "It is part of man's nature to be free," said Camp. "Natural liberty

. . . consists in the uncontrolled disposition of our persons and our property, agreeably to our own will, provided that we do not transgress the natural or moral law. . . . The law of justice between man and man establishes the republican principle. Let every man accord to every other the possession and enjoyment of his own rights as well as his property, and a republic will be the necessary consequence. . . . The government provides for a community of men; of equals, not of inferiors; of moral beings, and of beings endowed with the right voluntarily to regulate their own conduct agreeably to the dictates of their own will. It provides for government by moral considerations and not by force. The people are the sovereigns, the government their servant. . . . The question, then, as respects the progress and eventual supremacy of . . . [democratic] principles, is not more nor less than this: will justice be maintained in the public relations of man to man . . . or will society be surrendered up to force? Will men, like brutes, be governed, or, like rational and moral creatures, govern themselves? . . . The essence of republican government, its peculiar and distinguishing principle, is the supremacy of the popular will. It is this that constitutes a republic. . . . That a people have a moral right of self-government is equally true of every people in every age and country. . . . The people of a republic never can . . . be at a variance with their government. In its essential principles it is a transcript from their nature; in its practical character it is a creature of their will. A thousand years hence, if we should so long endure as a nation, a republic will be as proper for us as now. . . . It possesses a principle of permanency which monarchical government can never acquire."

Camp and the Americans of his generation believed that the United States had a mission in the world. They were convinced that the peoples of the world were looking to the American experiment in democratic government to see whether such a form of political organization was practical, whether, in short, democracy would work. The great mass of Americans of the middle of the nineteenth century felt that the national mission was to make a convincing demonstration before the world that free men could govern themselves. Two illustrations of this belief in the mission of America held by our forefathers of a hundred years ago are worth noting. A citizen of western New York named A. A. Bennett, addressing his neighbors in 1827, prophesied: "We may look forward to the period, when the spark of democratic liberty kindled in America, shall spread and spread, till the whole earth be illuminated by its light." Bennett saw a future Europe accepting the liberal principles on which the American Republic was founded. Joseph Story, distinguished Justice of the Supreme Court, agreed with him. "We stand," said Justice Story in Boston in 1826, "the latest, and, if we fail, probably the last experiment of self-government by the people." But Story did not think Americans would fail, and he was convinced that American liberal institutions would transform the world. "Already," he said, "has the age caught the spirit of our institutions." Story believed that civilized men were leaving tyrants and despots forever behind them. Yet the Justice was sure that democratic government must have strength, and he insisted that the way to perpetuate constitutional liberty in the American Republic was to make the national government powerful within its sphere. As a member of the Supreme Court Story supported nationalism as against States' rights, and in this policy he followed the leadership of his chief, Chief Justice John Marshall.

JOHN MARSHALL, CHAMPION OF NATIONALISM

John Marshall of Virginia, the first great Chief Justice of the Supreme Court of the United States, was appointed to that position in 1801 by President John Adams. When Marshall died in office thirty-four years later, he had strengthened vastly the power of the central government. The forces that turned his mind toward nationalism and made him the champion of the cause of the United States as against the States are to be found in his youth and early manhood.

John Marshall was born in 1755 on the frontier of Virginia. While he was still a child, his family moved even further westward to establish a home on the eastern slope of the Blue Ridge. The Marshalls were poor, and the family was large. John was the eldest of fifteen children. He recalled in later life that there were times when his mother and sisters used thorns for buttons. Marshall was a frontiersman, and on the frontier he derived an independence and a spirit of initiative that expressed themselves later in decisions which broke away from old precedents and traditions and struck out into new paths. His frontier home was not barren of books, for his father, whom Marshall always admired, had a small but well-selected library. The son, making the most of his reading opportunities, brought a well-stocked mind to his judicial task.

The second force in the life of Marshall was the Revolutionary War. He was just under twenty when the Battle of Lexington occurred. Enlisting almost as soon as the news of this clash reached his neighborhood, he entered the service in Washington's army. Staying with Washington for most of the long struggle, young Marshall fought in five battles and endured the rigors of the winter at Valley Forge. "I had grown up at a time," he wrote later, "when the love of the Union and the resistance to Great Britain were the inseparable inmates of the same bosom; . . . when the maxim 'United We Stand, Divided We Fall' was the maxim of every orthodox American. I had imbibed these sentiments so thoroughly that they constituted part of my being. I carried them with me into the army, where I found myself associated with brave men from different states, who were risking life and everything valuable in a common cause believed by all to be most precious, and where I was confirmed in the habit of considering America my country and Congress as my government."

Marshall had read law before he joined the army, and he continued his legal studies in the last year of his active service. Soon after the defeat of Cornwallis he hung out his shingle in the undeveloped town of Richmond, the new capital of Virginia. As a young lawyer Marshall watched with growing dismay the decline in the prestige of the Congress of the Confederation after the treaty of peace in 1783. Becoming fearful that the Confederation would break up in ruin, he strongly supported the Constitution written at Philadelphia in 1787, and as a delegate to the Virginia ratifying convention he played an important part in the hard fight to get the Old Dominion to accept the new plan. Marshall's success in the law was a stepping-stone to success in public life in John Adams' administration. His legal and political prominence led to his selection by Adams as the leader of the highest court in the nation.

Marshall's first great achievement as Chief Justice was to make clear the Supreme Court's power to declare unconstitutional acts of Congress that the Court found to be in conflict with the Constitution, a power that is implied but not specifically stated in the Constitution. As a result of this achievement by Marshall in constitutional law, the Supreme Court of the United States has become, with the development of the nation, the most influential judicial body in the world; no other nation has a court of such power and prestige as the Supreme Court of the United States.

Marshall's second important achievement was to strengthen in a series of remarkable decisions the powers of central government. He insisted that the Constitution had created the United States a nation and not a mere confederation, and his unvarying policy in deciding the cases that came before the Court was to see to it that the central government was given the powers necessary to permit it to govern. Marshall's ideas of the nature of the American Republic are summed up in the following selections from opinions in which he repudiated the idea that the Constitution was a compact among the sovereign States and insisted rather that it was the work of the American people: "The government of the Union, then, is emphatically . . . a government of the people. In form and substance it emanates from them. Its powers are granted by them, and are to be exercised on them for their benefit. . . . [The Constitution] marks, with lines too strong to be mistaken, the characteristic distinction between the Government of the Union and those of the States. The General Government, though limited as to its objects, is supreme with respect to those objects. This principle is part of the Constitution, and none can deny its authority." The protection of the liberties guaranteed by the Constitution, Marshall believed, could only be accomplished by making the nation and its government strong.

THE NATIONALISM OF ANDREW JACKSON

The victory of New Orleans made Andrew Jackson of Tennessee a national hero. On March 4, 1829, after an impressive triumph at the polls, he became the seventh President of the United States. His eight years in office were marked by hard-fought political battles, for he had many enemies who disagreed both with his policies and with his acts. But Jackson was not a man to be turned aside either by criticism or by opposition. He made mistakes. But when he left the White House in 1837, he had accomplished two things of great importance in the development of the American nation.

The first of these had to do with the office of President. The Constitution was very clear as to certain functions of the Chief Executive, namely, that he must assume leadership in seeing that the laws of the land are enforced and also that he is responsible, with the advice and consent of the Senate, for dealing with foreign powers. But the relations of the President to Congress and the President's part in framing the laws were not so certain when Jackson was elected. It is true that the Constitution had expressly given the Chief Executive the power to veto bills passed by Congress and had required a two-thirds vote in the two legislative houses to override a veto. But the first six Presidents had used the veto sparingly, and practically all the presidential vetoes before Jackson's time were of measures that the President considered unconstitutional. Jackson made the presidential veto an instrument of the first importance in national political life. He disapproved bills on the grounds that he thought them unwise, and he maintained that the veto power makes the President important in shaping the national policies set forth in congressional statutes. His enemies charged him with trying to be dictator. They called him King Andrew I. They asked him why he thought his individual opinion should outweigh the collective opinions of a majority in both houses of Congress. To this question Jackson made an effective answer. He pointed out that a United States senator represents the State from which he comes and that a member of the lower house speaks for the district that chooses him. The President, on the other hand, is elected by the whole people, and he is the only elected officer in the government who represents all the people. When presidential power and responsibility comes from the entire electorate of the nation, it is proper and necessary for the Chief Executive to set his judgment, by means of a veto, against that of a congressional majority when, in his opinion, the proposals of that majority are improper or unwise and when the national interest requires a veto. In much the same way that John Marshall clarified the great powers of the Supreme Court, Andrew Jackson made clear the fact that the President is an important legislative officer as well as being the Chief Executive. Jackson was the first President, after the pioneering work of Washington, to explore and to develop the great powers of the highest office in the American government.

Jackson, also like Marshall, defended the power of the central government as against that of the States. On one occasion during his administration South Carolina, suffering from what its people called an injustice, threatened to nullify a tariff law passed by Congress on the ground, as the legislature of South Carolina declared, that the Constitution had not given Congress the power to enact a protective tariff. South Carolina affirmed that under such circumstances a State had the right to declare such a national statute null and void.

In this crisis Jackson announced to the people of the whole nation that he would uphold, by force if necessary, the supremacy of the laws of the United States. He issued a proclamation which was an appeal to his fellow-countrymen in South Carolina to give up their dangerous doctrine in the interests of preserving a united republic and a call to the people of the country to support the government in its intention to enforce the laws of the land. "I consider," said Jackson, "the power to annul a law of the United States, assumed by one State, incompatible with the existence of the Union, contradicted by the letter of the Constitution, unauthorized by its spirit, inconsistent with every principle on which it was founded, and destructive of the great object for which it was formed. . . . Fellow-citizens, the momentous case is before you. On your undivided support of your government depends the great question. . . . It involves—whether our sacred Union will be preserved and the blessing it secures us as one people shall be perpetuated. No one can doubt that the unanimity with which that decision will be expressed will be such as to inspire new confidence in republican institutions."

Jackson received the support he asked for; no State in either the North or the South supported the South Carolina proposal of nullification. Yet in the South, as the years passed, the conviction increased that the best interests of the nation required that the rights of the States be vigorously guarded. The champion of this position was John C. Calhoun of South Carolina.

JOHN C. CALHOUN AND STATES' RIGHTS

For nearly twenty-five years from the beginning of the administration of Andrew Jackson to 1850, John C. Calhoun was the leader of the American group favoring States' rights. Most of these advocates of retaining power in the States came in this period from the South, but the Southerners had many supporters in the North. Calhoun fought until his death for the principle of control by the people of the locality—that is, by the people of a particular State—over that most difficult of all social questions, Negro slavery. Calhoun's life, like that of John Marshall, was influenced by the fact that he had been raised on the frontier.

John C. Calhoun was born in the western part of South Carolina when that region was still a part of the frontier. He came from the same locality which had given Daniel Boone and Andrew Jackson to America. Calhoun's boyhood development was held back by poor health, and as a consequence his father stopped his schooling and put him to work on a farm. For five years, until he was nineteen, young Calhoun plowed the fields in the spring and harvested the crops in the autumn. At nineteen, with health improved, he decided to get an education. The task took him seven years, two years in a preparatory school in Georgia, two at Yale, and three at the Litchfield Law School in Connecticut. He returned to South Carolina to become one of the leading lawyers of the State.

Calhoun was independent in his thinking and forceful in debate; in his own day and ever since he has been recognized as one of the most brilliant Americans of his time. He served as Secretary of War under President James Monroe, was Vice-President under Andrew Jackson, and for many years was Senator from South Carolina. He died in 1850 not long after he had delivered one of his greatest speeches in defense of the interests of the South. His point of view as to the drift of events in America explains why he supported the rights of the State as opposed to those of the central government.

As Calhoun looked out upon the South of his day, he saw an almost wholly agricultural country, a region of one crop, cotton for the most part, but tobacco in some areas. In all the Southern States were large plantations, but the bulk of the people were small farmers making only a few bales of cotton a year. Everywhere in the South, outside the southern Appalachians, Negro slaves provided the principal labor supply. The colored population of the section was very large; in some counties the Negroes outnumbered the whites.

Calhoun had been brought up on the frontier where slaves were few, but throughout his life he was familiar with the institution of slavery. He looked upon it as an institution for which his generation was not responsible. Established in the thirteen colonies early in the seventeenth century, slavery had existed in America for more than 200 years when Calhoun entered the United States Senate from South Carolina. It was an institution that tied the races together and compelled them to work in close coöperation; for a plantation was, in some respects, like a great family. In return for the service they rendered, the planter provided his colored people with houses, clothing, food, and medical attention, and he supported them after they had become too old to work. There were examples of harshness and cruelty in the treatment of slaves, but friendship and genuine affection also frequently characterized the relations between the master and his servants. Calhoun understood how deeply slavery had entered into all aspects of the life of the South, and he was convinced that this ancient institution could not be destroyed without irreparable injury to both races.

Calhoun and his fellow-Southerners watched with mounting apprehension the growth in the North, particularly after 1830, of an abolitionist movement that demanded the immediate freeing of the slaves. Slavery had gradually died out in the Northern States after the Revolution because it was not profitable in that region of growing factories and a diversified agriculture practised on small farms. The North, moreover, was increasing in population, partly because the stream of immigrants from Europe grew steadily larger after 1815. Few immigrants settled in the South because of the difficulties of competition with slave labor. The Irish and Germans, who were most numerous among the newcomers to the North and West, provided labor for the growing factories, helped to dig the canals and build the railroads, and established farms on the frontier in Wisconsin, Iowa, and Missouri.

Calhoun understood the significance for the South of the economic development and the population growth of the North. Down to 1850 the number of States in the Union retaining the institution of slavery remained equal to those depending on free labor. Before 1850, as new States came into the Union, it was common to have them enter in pairs, one from the North and one from the South, with the result that the slave labor interests and the free labor interests retained an equality in voting strength in the United States Senate. So long as this balance of power continued, the South had little to fear from the North. But the position of the South in Congress as a whole was weak because the Northern representation in the House of Representatives was much larger than the Southern on account of the greater population of the Northern States. As Calhoun watched the growth of the abolitionist movement in the North, he foresaw that a day might come when the North, possessing a numerical majority in the American electorate, might attempt to destroy slavery. Such an event Calhoun believed would bring disaster to the South.

The most important problem of the second quarter of the nineteenth century in Calhoun's opinion was therefore to perfect a way in the American democratic system to protect a minority against a majority. Calhoun was unwilling to have the question of slavery settled by the will of a triumphant Northern majority. Slavery, Calhoun insisted, was a Southern institution, a local affair. It should be managed by the communities in which it existed; its destiny should be determined by the men whose lives and fortunes were bound up with it. In short, Calhoun believed that slavery came within the jurisdiction of State governments; it was not a question for the government of the United States to decide. The Senator from South Carolina, therefore, trying to keep the States strong, continued to advocate the theory that a State should have the legal right to declare null and void an act of the central government which in the opinion of the State was contrary to the Constitution.

Calhoun did not want the Southern States to secede from the Union, yet as he neared the end of his life he feared that secession might be attempted because of Southern anxiety and anger at the growth of the abolitionist movement. Calhoun became convinced that his doctrine of States' rights was the only practicable plan to save the Union from the disaster of a separation between the sections. The South Carolinian sensed that slavery was so fundamental to the life of the South that the Southerners would withdraw from the Union before they would permit the institution to be destroyed by a hostile majority in the North. Calhoun insisted that minorities have rights which majorities must respect.

SLAVERY AND THE CENTRAL GOVERNMENT

It proved to be impossible to keep the question of slavery out of national politics. The American frontier was moving westward, and new territories were being carved out of the wilderness with the hope and the expectation that they would become States. Because the government of the United States managed the Territories, the political leaders at Washington had to decide whether slavery should or should not be permitted in any particular Territory. In the earlier years of the westward advance the two sections had entered into an agreement on the matter of slavery in the Territories that was embodied in an act of Congress called the Missouri Compromise. This act established a line across the plains from the Mississippi River to the Rockies and laid down the rule that north of this line in the public domain free labor should be the practice and that south of it owners should be permitted to bring in and use their slaves. Rivalry between the sections for political power in Congress finally brought about repeal of this arrangement.

In 1854 an act of Congress sponsored by Stephen A. Douglas, Senator from Illinois, organized the Territory of Kansas north of the Missouri Compromise line and gave to the people of the Territory the right to decide whether or not they wished to have slavery. The anti-slavery men in the North were angered because it repudiated a compromise agreement that had lasted for more than a quarter of a century, and a determined group of anti-slavery people in the Northern States determined that Kansas should be won for the principle of free labor. Quite naturally the men of the South were on their part enraged at the efforts of their Northern neighbors to exclude the institution of slavery from a region into which the law of the United States permitted it to go. Settlers from both North and South moved into Kansas, most of them going, as pioneers had gone to other frontiers, primarily to take up farms and to found homes. But a considerable group went from the North for the specific purpose of holding Kansas for the principle of free labor. Inevitably on the plains of Kansas men from the North and those from the South clashed. Disorders became serious. Raiding parties on both sides destroyed the property of their opponents.

Houses were burned and men were killed. A member of the national
Congress spoke of "Bleeding Kansas." The conflict on the Kansas
prairies intensified the crisis developing between the North and the
South and prepared the way for the splitting of the Union. The
sections collided because of their efforts to expand into the public
domain.

THE BASIC CAUSE OF SECESSION

The causes which led eleven States of the South to secede from
the Union in the autumn of 1860 and the winter of 1861 are too
many and too complicated to consider here. They may be briefly
summed up, however, without injustice to either side. By 1860 a
vast number of people in the North had become convinced that the
institution of human slavery denied the first principle of American
democracy, that men should be free, and had come to look upon
Negro bondage as a national evil. A radical minority among them
demanded that slavery be ended immediately, but the moderate
majority merely wished to prevent the extension of the institution
in the hope and belief that checking the growth of slavery would
bring about its ultimate defeat and extinction. The anti-slavery men
of the North, in short, wished to purge American democracy of
what they considered to be its greatest evil.

But the men of the South also took their stand on democratic
principles. They demanded the freedom to solve their own difficult
domestic problems in their own way; they refused to permit outsiders to tell them what they might or might not do about slavery.
After the election of Abraham Lincoln to the Presidency in 1860,
Southern leaders asserted that the national government was arrayed
against them and insisted that the election of an anti-slavery man as
President threatened Southern civilization with disaster. They became convinced that the only hope of safety lay in withdrawing
from the Union and founding a separate nation, and as a consequence eleven States seceded and organized the Confederate States
of America.

The act of secession stirred to activity among the people of the
North that loyalty to the nation which had grown strong in part
as a result of the leadership of John Marshall, Daniel Webster, and
Andrew Jackson. They were determined to prevent the break-up

of what they felt to be the greatest democratic nation in the world. They rallied to the support of President Lincoln. He faced the crisis with a single purpose. "I would save the Union," he wrote to a prominent editor in the North in 1862. "I would save it the shortest way under the Constitution. . . . My paramount object in this struggle is to save the Union, and is not either to save or destroy slavery . . . and I intend no modification of my oft-expressed personal wish that all men everywhere could be free."

The conflict which broke out in the spring of 1861 was a struggle on the one hand to set up a new Confederacy limited to the States of the South and on the other to preserve inviolate the old Union which had come into being in the American Revolution.

CHAPTER XIX

THE CIVIL WAR AND AMERICAN CIVILIZATION

The booming of the batteries opening fire on Fort Sumter in Charleston harbor on the morning of April 12, 1861, was the signal for the start of one of the two major wars of the nineteenth century. The other was the long and ultimately unsuccessful struggle of Napoleon to conquer Europe. For the Civil War Americans were responsible; no foreign nation, people, or ideology had any part in bringing about the disaster. It was fought with infinite courage and sacrifice on both sides by Americans; its idealism grew out of the democratic tradition of the Republic; its objectives on either side were to defend an American civilization and particularly American democratic ideals. The South was agrarian; its economic life was founded on cotton, and its crowning achievement was the great plantation. The North was a nation of small farmers, small shopkeepers, and, as the middle of the century approached, more and more small industrialists. In a sense the Civil War was a conflict between an old but vigorous plantation agriculture and a rising industrialism. The people of the South depended largely on Negro slaves to work their fields; in many of their communities the colored population outnumbered that of the whites. Slavery had died out in the North by 1861, but below the Mason-Dixon Line it remained a "peculiar institution" fundamental to the structure of Southern society. To thousands of Northerners slavery seemed to deny the most elementary democratic principle of individual liberty. In answer to the protest of the abolitionist and his demand that American civilization be cleansed of the evil of human bondage, the defender of the South replied that in Southern communities the end of slavery might be the beginning of evils worse than African servitude. Because of this danger he insisted that the solution of this most complex of social problems be left in Southern hands. As the menace of the anti-slavery crusade became greater, an increasing number of Southerners began to doubt the value for their section of remaining in the Union. As a consequence the Civil War became a contest between those who emphasized local loyalties and their kinsmen who were determined to preserve the integrity of the nation.

The conflict that broke out in 1861 found neither side prepared. Much of the Navy of the United States was distributed among foreign ports on commerce protection duty, and many remaining units were either not in commission or laid up for repairs. The Regular Army, of scarcely more than 13,000 men, was for the most part scattered among frontier posts. After the organization of the Confederate States of America in February, 1861, many officers resigned from the Army of the United States and some from the Navy to join the Southern cause.

Because of the smallness of the regular military establishment the war was fought largely by citizen soldiers recruited in the opening years by the volunteer system. In the spring of 1862 the Confederacy resorted to the draft, and the Federal Government followed a few months later. Conscription in the North, however, did not prove effective until 1863. On both sides the draft laws were defective, primarily because of their failure to recognize the full extent of the citizen's obligation to the nation in time of emergency. Both Federal and Confederate acts permitted a man whose name was drawn to gain exemption by hiring a substitute, a practice which because of its manifest injustice impaired the morale both of the forces and of the civilian population. In New York City draft riots, growing out of the charge that the conflict was "a rich man's war and a poor man's fight," terrorized the community for three days in the summer of 1863.

The military policy of the United States before 1861 had produced so few professionally trained officers that on both sides it was necessary to depend heavily for officer personnel upon untrained citizens. In all ranks, including the grade of general, men who had little or no training in the difficult art of war led soldiers on campaign and in battle. Many of these officers in the early years of the struggle were elected by their soldiers, a practice suggesting that Americans in the middle of the nineteenth century had not learned that many of the customs so useful in peace must be temporarily discarded in the emergency of war. Elected and untrained officers failed again and again to develop disciplined and efficient units. In the armies of both sides there was much straggling on marches, sometimes making it impossible for commanders to execute swift maneuvers and to strike hard, unexpected blows. Discipline was so bad in some Federal units that desertion seriously depleted important commands. But the worst consequence of the failure to provide special training for the officers at the outset of the war was the unnecessary loss of life when ignorant leaders tried to handle troops in battle. Men and officers in the 1860's were compelled to get their training in the hard and costly school of actual combat. In the last years of the war both North and South had powerful and trained armies that had learned by fighting and in which the natural leaders had risen to the top. In the spring of 1864 the Army of the Potomac and the Army of Virginia were formidable instruments of war.

The Civil War, like the American Revolution, opened a new era in the history of warfare. In the earlier conflict Americans had pioneered in a people's war with a people's army; in the 1860's for the first time both civil leaders and generals had to adapt to the uses of war the instruments of the new industrialism. The War between the States was the first military struggle in which the railroad was vital to strategy and to the service of supply, and the generals, with no precedents to fall back upon, had to learn how to use and to defend railways. Moreover, an improved rifle, superior to the muzzle-loading musket of the Revolution and the War of 1812, dominated the battlefield and forced a modification of the time-honored close-order tactics. Although close order was not completely abandoned, the basic principles of modern open-order fighting were worked out in the contests of the 1860's.

The major strategy of each side was determined by what it had to accomplish to win the war. The South was engaged in a revolution and was attempting to create a new nation. The Southern armies had merely to hold off the enemy until he gave up the struggle or until some foreign power recognized the Confederacy and intervened. The Federal Government, on the contrary, had to defeat and disperse completely the armed forces of the adversary. The North could not end the war with a treaty of peace; its armies could not be demobilized until the political and military organization of the Confederacy had been annihilated.

If the military task of the South was easier, this fact was counterbalanced by the inferiority of the Confederacy in manpower, in industrial organization, and in financial strength. Sheer weight of superior numbers was a factor of great importance in final victory of the Federals over the gray armies.

From the beginning the strategy of the Confederate President, Jefferson Davis, was defensive. The Appalachian Mountains and the Mississippi River divided the Confederacy into three areas: the east, the west, and the trans-Mississippi region, to list them in the order of their importance. The heart of the Confederacy was the eastern seaboard, and its capital was at Richmond in Virginia. Throughout the war Davis tried to fight off the invading armies both east and west of the mountains, attempting only two major counter-thrusts. These were Lee's invasion of Maryland in 1862, turned back by McClellan at Antietam, and Lee's invasion of Pennsylvania in 1863, halted by Meade at Gettysburg.

The Federal offensive strategy was based on a naval blockade of the Southern ports which, when perfected, isolated the South from the outside world. In 1862 and 1863 military and naval forces cooperated in winning control of the Mississippi, a victory that denied to the Confederacy the resources of Louisiana, Arkansas, and Texas. In these same years the Federal Army of the Potomac had made costly and futile attempts to take the Confederate capital. During the first three years of the war Federal strategy was weakened by lack of a coördinated plan; the Union forces fought important but practically unrelated campaigns east and west of the mountains. Grant, who rose to prominence on the western front where in a perfectly executed campaign he had taken Vicksburg, was given the post of General-in-Chief in the spring of 1864. The genius of Grant lay in his ability to see the war as a whole and to bring its many operations into a single pattern of grand strategy. He organized a gigantic converging attack on the Confederate eastern seaboard. The General-in-Chief sent the Army of the Potomac, under the command of Meade, into a bitter hammering campaign against Lee's Army of Virginia and at the same time ordered Sherman to move out of his base at Chattanooga and strike across the Confederate rear in Georgia. Sherman's brilliant campaign of maneuver, culminating in his capture of Atlanta and his later successful march to Savannah, made inevitable the ultimate defeat of the Confederacy. But Lee gallantly held on in Virginia until in April, 1865, his exhausted and vastly outnumbered army, assailed in front and rear, could stand no longer.

The war of the 1860's saw more pioneering than that in the field of military tactics. The Constitution makes the President the Commander-in-Chief of the Army and the Navy. But the fundamental law does not specify in detail the war powers implicit in the high office of Commander-in-Chief. Two Presidents preceding Lincoln had led the nation through major conflicts; James Madison had directed the War of 1812, and James K. Polk the Mexican War, but neither had realized the powers and possibilities of his office in time of crisis. Lincoln was the first man to explore fully the war powers of the President. He built up and wielded an authority vastly greater than that of any of his predecessors, but he erected the structure of his power within the spirit of the Constitution. One of Lincoln's more important achievements was the pattern of presidential war powers he contributed to constitutional theory and practice. His work provided the essential precedents on which the powers of succeeding war Presidents have rested.

The Civil War, disaster though it was, was the climax of an American age. Before 1861 agriculture was dominant in American economic life, and commerce, foreign and domestic, was its handmaid. The man of the soil, either as small farmer in the North and West or as planter in the South, had prevailed in the councils of the nation; but the years which followed Appomattox belonged increasingly to the men of industry and finance. In the struggle between the sections the trends of the American agricultural-commercial civilization came to a focus. That civilization had produced before 1861 men whose fame transcended the boundaries of the nation: James Fenimore Cooper, Nathaniel Hawthorne, and Herman Melville, novelists; Edgar Allan Poe and Henry Wadsworth Longfellow, poets; and Henry David Thoreau and Ralph Waldo Emerson, philosophers. All of these men made contributions of enduring worth. But the last brilliant and terrible moment of the old agrarian civilization was the War between the States.

This struggle gave to America three men whose stature has grown with the passing years until in the middle period of the twentieth century they have become folk heroes of the American people. The names of two, "Stonewall" Jackson and Robert E. Lee, are united in an enduring partnership; the other, Lincoln, stands alone. These three were not the only Americans to achieve distinction in the War between the States; the list of leaders is long. But these three were carriers in a peculiar sense of the traditions of an old America about to give way to a new age.

THOMAS J. ("STONEWALL") JACKSON

"Stonewall" Jackson, born on January 21, 1824, came from the humble people who inhabited the uplands of western Virginia. He was a poor boy, the orphan of a bankrupt father, and was reared in the home of an uncle near the Ohio River in what is now West Virginia. There were few planters in this country; it was a backwoods region whose inhabitants were for the most part small farmers, a hardy and independent people whose chief interests, outside of their community affairs, were politics and religion. In such surroundings young Thomas Jackson grew up, taking advantage of a little schooling and making a reputation for energy and integrity in the many jobs he held. When he was seventeen, a blacksmith friend told him of an opening in the corps of cadets at the United States Military Academy at West Point, an institution where the Republic educated selected young men at the public expense. Jackson promptly applied for an appointment to his local congressman, and through the support of many friends who valued his quality he won the opportunity to get a military education.

He had to fight his way through West Point, for he was somewhat slow of mind and learning did not come easily. He won no cadet honors. Graduating on the eve of the Mexican War, Lieutenant Jackson saw active service south of the Rio Grande in which he proved to himself and to his fellows that he was at his best when under fire. When peace came, young Jackson left Mexico a field officer. Three years later he resigned from the Army to accept the post of professor of mathematics at the Virginia Military Institute in the Shenandoah Valley, where he remained, a conscientious but not an inspiring teacher, until 1861 took him into the service of the Confederacy.

Before he went to V.M.I. he had made himself a part of one of the oldest and most powerful traditions in the civilization of which he was a part. As the Mexican War was ending Jackson turned to the study of religion. He had no sudden conversion; religion took possession of him with an almost fierce encroachment and dominated his thought and conduct to the end of his life. His was the faith of those stern Puritans who had founded Massachusetts more than two centuries before. On Sundays, when he was a professor at V.M.I., he taught a Negro Sunday school that he and his wife had organized. For Thomas Jackson the essence of religion was duty.

While working at V.M.I. Jackson studied continuously to perfect himself in his chosen military profession, but he had no desire to make war against his fellow-countrymen, and he did what he could in his own small way to avert the crisis. When war came, his knowledge of the military art, his energy, and his leadership took him swiftly into high command. He got his nickname "Stonewall," at Bull Run when his brigade, ever after known as the Stonewall Brigade, stood fast in the midst of disorder and turned the tide of battle. No soldier's nickname was ever less appropriate than that given to Jackson; in independent command he was never a stone wall. He was swift and stealthy by turns, a master of the art of maneuver to confuse and terrify his adversary, a captain who at the proper moment could deliver the annihilating blow. His Shenandoah campaign in 1862 is one of the military masterpieces of all time.

What was the secret of his success? Jackson had the spirit of an ancient Hebrew prophet. He ruled himself and his men with an iron discipline. He demanded and got from every subordinate immediate, complete, and unquestioning obedience. He was hard and just. He lost himself in the one purpose to win the war. "Did you order me to advance over that field, sir?" said an officer to him in the midst of battle. "Yes," said Jackson. "Impossible, sir! My men will be annihilated!" "General ————," said Jackson, "I always endeavor to take care of my wounded and to bury my dead. You have heard my order—obey it."

Beside this story, narrated by an early biographer, should be put another, told by the youngest officer on General Jackson's staff, of an outdoor evening prayer meeting he attended with a general in the Stonewall Brigade. ". . . the camp was there. Bowed head, bent knees, hats off, silence! Stonewall Jackson was kneeling to the Lord of Hosts, in prayer for his people! Not a sound disturbed his voice as it ascended to Heaven in their behalf and, in their faith, the very stars seemed to move softly and to make no noise. When he left, a line of soldiers followed him in escort to the edge of the camp." Beyond that line of pickets many of these men followed him to death.

To Lee, his superior, Jackson gave obedience as complete and as unquestioning as that he exacted from his subordinates. For Jackson the slightest wish of the commander of the Army of Virginia was a command. Once Jackson urged some plans on Lee. "And what does he say of them?" Jackson was asked.

"He says nothing," said Jackson. "But do not understand that I complain of this silence; it is proper that General Lee should observe it. He is wise and prudent. He feels that he bears a fearful responsibility, and he is right in declining a hasty expression of his purpose to a subordinate like me."

"Stonewall" Jackson was mortally wounded at Chancellorsville after his genius and coöperation with Lee had helped to win the victory; he was shot by his own men, who in the excitement of battle mistook him and his staff for an enemy cavalry patrol. On his death-bed his thoughts turned to his chief. "Better," he said, "that ten Jacksons should fall than one Lee." Four words sum up the man—knowledge, energy, loyalty, duty.

ROBERT E. LEE

In Jackson the religion of Puritan America found its greatest warrior. Lee came from a different background and expressed in his life different aspects of that old mid-nineteenth century civilization. He was of a distinguished Virginia family and the son of "Light Horse Harry" Lee, a dashing officer in Washington's army, and as a young man Robert, with the choice of a planter's life or a military career, chose the latter. Like Jackson, he graduated from West Point and distinguished himself in the war with Mexico.

He was doing garrison duty on the Texas frontier when the threat of secession grew menacing in the South. Lee, bound to the nation by ties of family and service, did not believe with many of the Southern leaders in the constitutional right of secession. But, when the crisis came, he took with Calhoun the position that in the American democracy minorities have rights which majorities must respect. He declined the offer of the command of the Union armies and, resigning his commission, chose to be loyal to his section, to his home, to his minority. Believing that oppression threatened his people, he answered the call not of secession, but of revolution, and put himself in the tradition of his father and of Washington, rebels in their day. He fought for liberty and for the principle of self-determination for the South, and he became the leader of a second American war for independence. "We had," he remarked after the Confederacy had passed into history, ". . . sacred principles to maintain and rights to defend for which we were in duty bound to do our best, even if we perished in the attempt."

But Lee personified in his career another American tradition that ran back beyond the opening of the eighteenth century. Englishmen who settled the colonies had brought with them the idea of the gentleman, the aristocrat. The concept of a responsible aristocracy had pervaded American thinking in the eighteenth century, but the tradition did not take firm root on the frontier north of the Ohio and west of the Appalachians and had declined in the older communities of the North; it had survived, however, with much of its eighteenth-century vigor in the Cotton Kingdom. In war Lee fulfilled the romantic dream of what an aristocrat should be. As the commander of the Army of Virginia he became the brilliant soldier, dazzling and overthrowing his enemies by the magic of his strategy. The embodiment of physical courage, he often heard the firing line call out in the midst of battle, "General Lee to the rear," when he advanced too near to the enemy. His mind was ever on the welfare of his men, ill supplied at best by the impoverished Confederate government. He dealt with his officers with the firmness of a commander and the tact of a gentleman. He had the courage to accept responsibility and to confess mistakes. One of these occurred on the third day at Gettysburg when he sent Pickett into that magnificent and futile charge against the well-organized Federal center. The gray line surged forward, closed with the enemy, and then the spent survivors came back, their thinned ranks evidence that the battle, which meant so much to the Confederacy, had been lost. General Lee, hat in hand, rode out to meet his defeated soldiers and said to them as they passed by: "It is all my fault."

The great moment of the gentleman soldier came on the third day at Chancellorsville when his army was driving a superior Federal force in disorder from the field. One of his staff officers has left a picture of the scene on that day at the Chancellorsville house. "General Lee accompanied the troops in person, as they emerged from the fierce combat they had waged in the tangled wilderness, driving the superior forces of the enemy before them across the open ground. He rode into their midst. The troops were pressing forward with all the ardor and enthusiasm of combat. The white smoke of musketry fringed the front line of battle, while the artillery on the hills in the rear shook the earth with its thunder and filled the air with the wild shrieks of the shells that plunged into the masses of the retreating foe. To add greater horror, the Chancellorsville house and the woods surrounding it were wrapped in flames. In the midst of this awful scene General Lee, mounted upon that horse we all remember so well, rode to the front of his advancing battalions. The soldiers with their faces blackened with the smoke of battle, the wounded crawling from the fury of the devouring flames, all seemed possessed with a common impulse. One long, unbroken cheer, in which the feeble cry of those who lay helpless on the earth mingled with the voices of those who still fought, rose high above the roar of battle and hailed the presence of the victorious chief. He sat in the full realization of all that soldiers dream of—triumph; and as I looked on him in the complete fruition of the success which his genius, courage, and confidence in his army had won, I thought that it must have been from such scenes that men in ancient days ascended to the dignity of the gods."

Like Jackson, Lee founded his life fully and frankly on religion, but his was a gentler and more humane Christianity. He prayed in his family and in private. He prayed for victory, and failure did not shake his faith. "I had taken every precaution," he once remarked, "to insure success and counted on it. But the Ruler of the Universe willed it otherwise and sent a storm to disconcert a well-laid plan, and to destroy my hopes." Lee's extraordinary poise was founded on his complete dependence on what he felt to be a Power invisible and eternal. Such dependence kept him humble even in triumph. Lee was an expression of that simple Christianity so important in American life in the first half of the nineteenth century.

Robert E. Lee, while the war was yet in progress, became the leader not only of his army but of the Southern people. In the twentieth century, when the passions of other days have been forgotten, he has emerged as a folk hero for all Americans. His home, Arlington, on the Potomac is maintained by the United States as a national shrine. In his person three important American characteristics were united, the traditions of revolution, of the humane and responsible gentleman, and of religion. He had the balance and the mental power which the ancient Greeks admired, and to these he added the spirit of sacrifice of the first-century Christians. He beheld his army and his nation sink into the dust and displayed no bitterness. After the war when he was president of Washington and Lee College, he once advised a Southern lady as to the rearing of her children. "Madam," he said, "don't bring your sons up to detest the United States Government. Recollect that we form one country now. Abandon your local animosities and make your sons Americans."

ABRAHAM LINCOLN

Lincoln emerged as a public figure in 1858 when he met Senator Stephen A. Douglas in a debate to which all the nation listened. The President died in 1865 just after Lee had surrendered. These seven fateful years were dominated by emotion rather than reason, and Lincoln's outstanding achievement during this passion-ridden time was that in no vital matter did he permit emotion to gain the ascendancy over reason. In 1859, when the overwrought abolitionists of the North were acclaiming John Brown a saint, Lincoln denounced the Brown raid at Harper's Ferry. At his first inaugural, when both Northern and Southern extremists were advocating the letting of a little blood, Lincoln urged the nation not to break the ancient bonds of friendship. In the middle years of the war, when reverse after reverse and a terrible loss of life almost overwhelmed the North with war weariness, the President did not give way to despair but continued to utilize to the full his mental powers to bring victory out of defeat. When the war was over, Lincoln founded his reconstruction policy on the principle that reason rather than hatred should prevail.

Since 1865 Abraham Lincoln has been the greatest of all American heroes, and in the years since his death the Lincoln literature has grown to prodigious proportions; its volume is still augmented with each passing year. He is an intimate yet strangely distant figure; a common man, yet one whose words still carry authority to both humble and great. The basis of his continued influence is to be found not merely in his character and achievements but in the fact that in his career basic traditions of old America found expression.

Lincoln was a nationalist of the school of Alexander Hamilton, John Marshall, and Andrew Jackson who devoted his public life to the realization of that prophecy of Daniel Webster in 1830: "Liberty and Union. One and inseparable. Now and forever." Under the leadership of the man from Springfield, Illinois, the Union was saved; he brought that tradition of nationalism of early nineteenth-century America to its fulfilment.

In addition to his nationalism Lincoln carried forward the democratic tradition that Jefferson had formulated in the Declaration of Independence. The former circuit-riding lawyer was an advocate of equality of rights among men, of manhood suffrage, of equal representation, and of rule by the majority. He gave to America that phrase, as famous as the opening sentences of the Declaration, "government of the people, by the people, and for the people." Not only was Lincoln a democrat in theory and practice, but his career was the fulfilment of the romantic American democratic ideal. He began his life on the wooded frontier of Kentucky and Indiana, from which the hunter-pioneer of the long rifle had not yet disappeared. His family was poor. From such humble beginnings he rose to the White House. But when the farm boy of Pidgeon Creek became a man and seized his opportunity, he was such a leader as no President before him had ever been. Vast armies moved at his command; he struck the shackles from more than a million slaves; he faced and avoided the perils of international war. Here was Aladdin's dream come true. And Lincoln made the picture perfect by never permitting power and success to turn his head. To the end he remained the sincere and humble democrat.

If Lincoln was a nationalist and a democrat, he was also a humanitarian. He early identified himself with the greatest of the humanitarian crusades of the early nineteenth century. He was not a radical abolitionist, but he was an anti-slavery man. "I am naturally anti-slavery," he remarked in 1864. "If slavery is not wrong, nothing is wrong. I cannot remember when I did not so think and feel." Destiny made this kindly and moderate man the emancipator of the slaves; he brought this effort to lift the burdens from a suffering people to its dramatic and complete success. Then, as the war ended, he emerged as the humanitarian of peace who sought to heal the wounds of the defeated enemy. The final phrases of his second inaugural have become part of the enduring literature of his people. "With malice toward none; with charity for all; with firmness in the right as God gives us to see the right, let us strive to finish the work we are in; to bind up the nation's wounds; to care for him who shall have borne the battle, and for his widow, and his orphan, to do all which may achieve a just and lasting peace among ourselves, and with all nations."

In "Stonewall" Jackson, Lee, and Lincoln the old America of the early nineteenth century reached its culmination. The fact that the memories of these leaders of yesterday are revered today suggests that the old ideals for which they lived and fought still have a vitality in a vastly different age from that which these men knew. These men are still bearers of the American tradition.

CHAPTER XX

THE RISE OF AMERICAN INDUSTRIAL CIVILIZATION

For a long time now thousands of Americans each year have journeyed to Washington's home, Mount Vernon, standing on a low elevation beside the quiet Potomac. The charm of the old plantation house is not simply in its association with the Revolutionary leader but in the preservation in the mansion, the outbuildings, and the garden of the atmosphere of an age that did not know the machine. The cooking for the family was done in a fireplace, and the baking in ovens of brick. Fireplaces also heated the house. The family coach suggests the slow travel over unpaved roads of eighteenth-century men. Washington had good books in his library, and the family enjoyed music when the guests included persons who could play on the violin or the harpsichord. No morning newspaper, however, brought accounts of the world happenings of the previous day; for news the family was dependent on visitors, on letters, and on the primitive and inadequate press of the time. The fields lying beside the river were cultivated for the most part with hand tools and the horse-drawn cart and plough. The life at Mount Vernon was unhurried and rich in human associations; this national shrine preserves for us memories of the eighteenth century at its best.

THE ROLE OF SCIENCE

Even in the days when Washington, after his return from the Revolutionary War, was supervising the work of his plantation, science was creating the foundations of a new age. And what was this science? It was the minute, painstaking, and systematic study of Nature and of that energy at the very center of Nature. A hundred years before Washington Sir Isaac Newton in seventeenth-century England had discovered and announced those laws of motion which on the one hand govern the meeting of the wave

and the sand on the ocean beach and on the other hold the stars
and planets in their places in the sky. Eighteenth-century men, trying to grasp the significance of Newton's triumph in predicting
eclipses of the moon and sun, thought of the universe as one great
machine. Then Englishmen, contemporaries of Washington, began
to create crude machines that were driven not by the muscle power
of men or animals but by the energies of Nature that exist in running water or in steam. In the year 1789, when Washington came
to New York to be inaugurated the first President of the United
States, an English craftsman who had made his way to the new
country put together the first American factory. This mill at
Pawtucket, Rhode Island, was a primitive forerunner of the civilization we know.

In the early years of the nineteenth century when the man of
the soil was dominant in American life, Americans made progress in
adapting the machine to the needs of human life. In Europe it was
a period of great scientific advance; the men of the laboratories of
the Old World were pushing rapidly into hitherto unexplored
fields of knowledge. Because the United States was a poor country
and its people were busy with the tasks of conquering a wilderness
as the frontier moved westward toward the Pacific and because
the evolution of American civilization had not reached a point
where great scientific laboratories were possible, Americans made
relatively few contributions to scientific theory before 1850.

If Americans made few additions to the theory of physics,
chemistry, or biology, they were quick to apply scientific knowledge to the practical affairs of life. In an age dominated by commerce and agriculture it was perhaps inevitable that the chief
inventions of the citizens of the Republic should apply to hus-
bandry and transportation. American inventors perfected the plow,
created the cotton-gin, and produced the reaper. The improved
plow made it possible for the pioneers to break the tough sod of
the prairies; the gin transformed the South into the greatest cotton-
producing region in the world; and the reaper, speeding up the
laborious tasks of the harvest, made it possible after the middle of
the century for the husbandman to conquer in a few decades that
vast plains area between the Mississippi and the Rocky Mountains.
At the same time Americans produced a practicable steamboat and

transformed the rivers and lakes of the nation into arteries of commerce. They did not originate the railway, but they took the lead in grappling with the technical problems the solution of which has made the modern railroad possible. By 1868, with the invention of the air brake, most of the basic work had been done.

In this period Americans depended for their sources of power almost wholly on wood, wind, and water. Wood was the fuel for the primitive locomotives and for the steamboats on the lakes and rivers. The ironmasters of the East melted the ore in their blast-furnaces with charcoal. The power of falling water drove the machines in the factories of New England and the Middle States. And before the Civil War wind propelled the ships of that American merchant fleet that carried American commerce into all oceans. The period from the Revolution to the Civil War was an age when wood and iron were, outside of textiles, the most important materials—a time of wooden buildings, wooden ships, and wooden vehicles, and also of iron rails, iron locomotives, and iron machines. The age was epitomized in the Civil War when the Confederates created their most dangerous battle-ships by putting iron armor on wooden hulks.

But in this early period Americans displayed their peculiar genius and made their greatest single contribution to technological advance, the simple device of interchangeable parts. Early inventors of the Republic conceived the idea of fabricating standard machines, guns at first, produced by assembling parts, each of which would fit as well in the finished product as another. The idea was carried over into the construction of houses with the invention of the balloon frame in which timbers of standard sizes took the place of those beams and posts hewed in earlier days especially for a particular building. The principle of standardization and interchangeable parts started American industry on the road to that mass production which in the twentieth century has put American plants in the forefront of the world of manufacturing. After December 7, 1941, Americans turned to their assembly lines to save the nation.

Two inventions of the 1850's were fundamental to the age that appeared after Appomattox. The first of these was a very humble machine, called by its inventor the "stone-breaker," a device capable of crushing the toughest rock, which made possible the firm roadbeds of the post-Appomattox railroads and in later years the modern highway and all concrete construction. The other invention, appearing simultaneously and independently in England and the United States, was a method for making cheap steel. The Bessemer process, as it came to be called, brought in an age of steel—steel rails, steel locomotives, steel ships, steel girders for bridges and for buildings. The period from the Civil War to the first World War became an age of steam and steel. The vast reserves of bituminous coal within the United States became the principal source of power for a swiftly evolving industrial civilization.

The years between 1865 and 1917 saw American civilization transformed by an industrial revolution. The small factories of the 1850's evolved into the great plants that provided the armament and the munitions which made possible the victory over the Central Powers in the first World War. Before 1860 the economic products of America were mostly the raw materials of forests, farms, and mines; after 1900 the nation led the world in the value of its manufactured output. The great corporation appeared, making possible the organization of men, materials, and financial power into gigantic production units.

Basic to the industrial revolution of the last third of the nineteenth century was the rich endowment of the nation in natural resources. Before the middle of the century Americans had made extensive use only of their boundless forests and their millions of acres of rich soil. After 1849 the mines of the western mountains had poured into the stream of commerce vast quantities of gold and silver. It was not, however, until after Appomattox that Americans began fully to sense the possibilities of their reserves of copper, coal, and iron. No nation in the nineteenth-century world had such a wealth of materials on which to found an industrial civilization. Europe had similar resources, but the peoples of that continent were divided among many nations; in the United States, preserved as a single nation by the victory of the Federal Government in the Civil War, it was possible after 1865 to organize industrial development in an area of continental proportions unhampered by the political obstacles of international boundaries. The ultimate realization by the defeated South of the economic benefits flowing from national unity was an important factor in causing the Southern people to return to a complete and enthusiastic loyalty to the nation which the Confederates had once tried to abandon.

The period between 1865 and 1917 was the great epoch in American railroad building, and in these years the nation was covered from east to west and from north to south with a network of steel. The railway made possible the organization of the nation as an economic unit. The "train of cars," as it was called, was the principal mode of transportation in late nineteenth-century America. If the years between 1865 and 1917 were the age of steam and steel, they were also the time when the locomotive, roaring across mountains and plains, was the symbol of national economic power and the instrument making possible national economic unity.

The railroad after Appomattox created the giant city. The strategic location for the manufacturing plant was the junction of two or more railway lines; these brought power to the engines of the factory in the form of coal and carried its manufactured output to the market. Laborers came to live beside the plant. Before 1861 the location of manufacturing establishments had been to a great extent controlled by the distribution of water power, and mill towns had grown up beside dams thrown across rivers. The railway freed the factory from its dependence on the stream, and by 1900 most important American plants were located in cities. By the time of the outbreak of the first World War practically half the population of the United States lived in urban rather than rural surroundings; the dirt farmers had become a minority.

The rise of the new city was as great a revolution as the evolution of the new factories. Into the cities came thousands of young men and women from the farms where labor-saving machinery reduced the necessity for field hands, and to the urban center millions of immigrants from Europe and Asia made their way, seeking opportunities that their homelands did not offer. America became a nation of many stocks and many nationalities and the new city a melting-pot for the peoples of the world. No great nation in the modern world has experienced so vast a friendly invasion of outsiders. Immigrants aggravated the political and social problems of the Republic, but they also enriched American civilization. Many among the newcomers were inferior in mind and morals, but the immigrant flood also gave to the nation leaders in industry, music, art, and science. There were Irish and Germans in the armies that fought the Civil War, but in the divisions mobilized after 1917 to overthrow the Central Powers was the blood of all the countries of Europe and Asia. America had become a new nation.

THE AGE OF POWER

Two developments changed the course of American history about the turn of the century: one a series of outstanding achievements in electrical engineering and the other the perfection of the internal combustion engine. Electrical improvements came first and were stimulated by the pressing needs of the new and rapidly growing cities. Such huge centers of population as grew up at New York, Philadelphia, and Chicago required new means of transportation, and, as a consequence, the electric street railway and later the subway were developed. At the same time electricity made possible the vertical transportation of the elevator, and skyscrapers quickly dominated the skylines of urban America. The needs of the city spurred Alexander Graham Bell to those researches which eventuated in the telephone, while the genius of Thomas A. Edison replaced with electric lights the dim gas-lamps of the middle of the century. Important, however, as were the street railway, the elevator, the telephone, and electrical illumination, these achievements marked but the beginning of an age of electricity to flower in the twentieth century.

The internal combustion engine wrought a revolution after the first World War as far-reaching as that caused by the railroad after Appomattox. Both the airplane and the automobile appeared before 1914, and both accomplished their great transformations after 1918. Within two decades after the Armistice the nation was covered with a network of hard-surfaced highways and the owning of motor cars became almost universal. The new highways multiplied many times the transportation facilities of the nation as the truck, the bus, and the private car became active competitors of the older railroad. No longer was it necessary for industrialists to establish their plants at railway junctions. Factories began to return to the smaller town and even to appear in the open country. City populations began to flee congested streets and to spread out over ever-widening suburban areas. Americans traveled as never before in the history of the nation. Only the occasional family before 1861 journeyed beyond the boundaries of its native State, and then usually to join the westward trek to a new home on the frontier, but in the 1920's and the 1930's Americans in motor-cars explored widely in their country. The result, impossible to measure but none the less real, was a better understanding and a larger tolerance among the people of the North and the South, the East and the West.

In the 1920's citizens of the Republic were so engrossed with the automobile that they were slow to sense the possibilities of flight. For a time the United States fell behind Europe in the commercial use of the plane. But a change came in the 1930's, and American fliers achieved priority in commercial lines across both the Atlantic and the Pacific. The developments in military aviation which have followed September 1, 1939, suggest that the airplane will be as important in tomorrow's peace as it is in today's fighting.

Radio, that greatest triumph of the electrical engineer, has changed the world as much as has the motor-car or the airplane. It has brought voices and music from the far corners of the earth into the privacy of the family circle in the living-room. The most obvious among the social results of the radio has been its success in abolishing the isolation of the lone ranch house on the plains or the cabin high in the mountains; the air waves bring the same symphonies, the same news, and the same discussions to all who take the trouble to listen. In the years between the Civil War and the first World War the opportunities of urban life surpassed those of country life, but the radio and the motion picture have helped to restore the balance. More subtle and, in the long run, probably more important has been the fact that the radio brings to the people hour by hour the news of the world. The globe has grown so small that men and women by their firesides in Boston or in Seattle listen to voices from Buenos Aires, from Turkey, from China, and from Australia. This mid-twentieth century generation knows more of the events in distant lands than the men of a century ago knew of the happenings in the next country. Before 1939 the radio became in the democratic countries an agency for discussion and debate, and the kilocycles carried to the citizens of the Republic the contending points of view of battling interests and of divergent crusades. At the same time, however, in the totalitarian world air waves, burdened with the patterns of party ideologies, beat ceaselessly against the minds of a populace forbidden to listen to anything else. The radio magnified the opportunities both of the dictator and of the democrat. When disaster engulfed the world after September 1, 1939, the radio became an instrument of war used to assail the enemy, to hearten the citizens at home, and to bring together the peoples of the United Nations.

To add to the complexities of the twentieth-century world, the chemists have initiated another transformation. Germany before and during the first World War pioneered among the nations in the creation of materials useful to men that are not found in nature. After 1918 the chemical laboratories of the United States laid the foundations for an industry that put America into the lead and the citizens of the Republic went forward in the middle years of the twentieth century into an age of plastics, of new alloy metals, of medicines hitherto undreamed of, and of fabrics made from the elements of the earth and air. In both the first and the second World Wars chemistry has helped to make more nearly self-sufficient those nations that were cut off from necessary materials from the outside world.

SCIENCE IN THE TWENTIETH CENTURY

To enumerate the advances in technology that have changed the world since the invention of the stone-breaker and the Bessemer process in the 1850's is to suggest the role of science in modern civilization. The twentieth century rests on the laboratory; scientific knowledge, built into machines and materials, has furthered the cause both of democracy and of totalitarianism; it has helped to make men free and to enslave them. But this scientific civilization of the present age is no more immune to decay than was the culture of ancient Rome. It can be lost. It was already declining on the Continent of Europe before the Nazi armies invaded Poland, and this decline has a bearing on the issues involved in the struggle of the 1940's.

Science has two aspects, the knowledge and theory produced by the investigator in the laboratory, and the applications of that knowledge by the technician and the engineer in concrete materials and machines. The knowledge and theory, "pure science" as it is called, is basic. If the advance of pure science is slowed, the change affects not only the engineer but the technological civilization which he has constructed. And pure science cannot live in all worlds; it requires for vigorous life a particular kind of environment.

The investigator in the laboratory must be free to pursue truth wherever his researches lead him. There can be no regions blocked off which he may not enter; he can take orders from no man or group of men as to the particular version of truth he shall find. German anthropologists before September 1, 1939, had discovered, at the command of the Nazi Party, that what they called the Aryan race is superior to all other world stocks. Such "discoveries" are the negation of science. In the same years and at the same command German physicists found that the work of the great Einstein, fundamental to the physics of the twentieth century, was false because the author of the relativity theory was a "non-Aryan." In such an atmosphere in Germany, not many years ago in the vanguard of scientific advance, the contributions to pure science fell off. Some of the scientific figures of earlier and better days lived on and continued to work, but they had difficulty in training up successors among the younger generation whose minds were molded to fit the pattern of party ideology. German engineers and technicians continued to be skillful and ingenious, but pure science languished in an environment in which the principle of individual freedom had been destroyed.

Science rests on morals. If the laboratory investigator must be free, he must also be honest. If he falsifies the observations or measurements he makes in an experiment, he does not produce science. No machines can be built on falsehoods. Honesty is merely another word for responsibility; pure science is the gift to the world of free and responsible individuals. And it requires for its growth mutual trust among men of good-will. For pure science is not and cannot be the work of a single man; each investigator adds his contribution, small or large, to the body of knowledge which represents the accumulated contributions of other men. Science knows no national boundaries; Englishmen, Germans, Frenchmen, Japanese, and American scientists have all coöperated in mutual trust to make possible the science which, in turn, has produced the machines that are blowing the modern world to pieces. It is to be hoped that the time will come soon when scientists from all lands will again work together in harmony for the enrichment of human life.

Those principles on which the work of the scientific investigator rests, the principle of individual freedom and responsibility and that of mutual trust among men of good-will, are none other than the democratic ideals for which American leaders have striven since the founding of the Republic. If they are defeated by a regime founded on might and worshiping force, science is doomed, for the free investigator can make no compromise with slavery. The principles and the moral code on which pure science rests will go far toward providing an adequate foundation for the world of tomorrow.

CHAPTER XXI

AMERICAN DEMOCRACY BETWEEN TWO WARS

When the citizens of the United States in the spring of 1865 relaxed from the strain of war, they did not sense immediately that industrial changes were creating a new civilization. They were for the moment preoccupied with the problems growing out of the recent conflict. They faced the task of reuniting the divided union; of reëstablishing order in communities where government had been destroyed by invasion, battle, and defeat; of assisting a bewildered population of former slaves to become self-reliant members of the community. These problems had to be dealt with in an atmosphere charged with suspicion and hatred, for the war had been long and bloody and one side had been fought to exhaustion. The casualty lists published in the press had plunged a hundred thousand families into mourning. Americans in the reconstruction of the South faced their hardest task in making the ideals of democracy realities in the life of the Republic. They did not achieve the success that Lincoln had hoped for; only a few rose to the spirit of the Second Inaugural.

THE RECONSTRUCTION ERA

This is not an appropriate place to consider the tangled and unseemly story of the attempted reconstruction of the defeated South by the federal government. Suffice it to say that, after a rupture between the President and the Congress, the latter body originated and carried through what proved to be an unfortunate policy. The congressional leaders abandoned magnanimity and embarked upon a course characterized by vindictiveness and hate.

Yet a spirit of humanity rather than rancor governed Congress in the enactment of one of the first reconstruction measures, namely that creating the Freedman's Bureau. Federal agencies were set up in Southern communities to protect, guide, and aid the colored man freed not only from the labor but from the irresponsibility that had been his lot on the plantation. The Bureau was without precedent; never before had the United States attempted so directly to assist the unfortunates among its people. The law creating the Bureau was the forerunner of twentieth-century congressional legislation for the welfare of the unemployed.

But the Bureau was soon turned to political ends. The ex-Confederates, moreover, were unwilling to go as far in social and political reorganization as the congressional leaders desired. Then occurred one of the most extraordinary events in American history. The Congress, overriding the President's veto, abolished the State governments that had been set up in the South after the end of the war, divided the former Confederacy into administrative districts, and put at the head of each a major general. Military power replaced civil power. The United States government treated the defeated States as conquered provinces. No such extreme assertion of authority by the federal government has ever occurred either before or since.

Three amendments to the Constitution came out of reconstruction. The Thirteenth, abolishing involuntary servitude except for crime, completed the work begun in Lincoln's Emancipation Proclamation. The Fourteenth wrote into the Constitution the reconstruction policy of the congressional majority. It disenfranchised Southern leaders who had been prominent in the Confederate effort until such time as they should be pardoned by congressional action; it invalidated all public debts contracted in the struggle for secession; and it guaranteed civil rights to the former slave. The clause having to do with rights became famous; it denied to the States the right "to deprive any person of life, liberty, or property without due process of law." But the amendment had implications for party politics. If a State refused to grant the ex-slave suffrage, its representation in Congress would be reduced. The Fifteenth Amendment laid down the principle that no citizen could be denied the suffrage on account of race, color, or previous condition of servitude. The amendment was in harmony with the highest democratic ideals, but its effect was to ask men who yesterday had been slaves to assume today the full responsibilities of citizenship. One of its purposes, moreover, was to build up political support in the former Confederacy for the congressional majority. The Fourteenth and Fifteenth Amendments created the "Solid South."

The turmoil of the reconstruction period was ended in 1877 when the federal government withdrew the last blue-coated soldiers from the military districts and permitted the natural leaders of the Southern people to assume power and responsibility. The ravages of four years of war in which the Confederates had given prodigally of their wealth and their lives had left their section prostrate. The rehabilitation of the South, beginning after the soldiers left, was a long, slow process. Only in the twentieth century have the consequences of defeat been forgotten in an advance toward a new day.

Since the Civil War Americans of both North and South have confronted the problem of race relations inherited from the seventeenth century when African slaves were first brought to the colonies. In neither section has the treatment of the colored man conformed fully to the ideals set forth in the Declaration of Independence; but in both the difficulties have been canvassed in frank and open discussion. As the years have passed, the contribution of the Negro to the music and art of American civilization has been recognized and the achievements of colored athletes have added to the prestige of the race. Throughout the nation progress has been made in establishing friendly and understanding coöperation between the colored man and the white.

The race question, however, is not the only area of American life in which it has been difficult to make economic and social realities correspond to the ideals of the democratic faith. In fact, the central problem in the history of the American people since 1865 has been to combat evils, and the most difficult have been those arising out of swift changes brought about by the rise of industrialism.

THE EMBATTLED FARMER

When the Civil War ended, most of the vast Plains area that lies east of the Rockies and stretches north from Texas to Montana was still Indian country, the home, among other tribes, of the Cheyennes, the Blackfeet, and the Sioux. Even while the war was being fought the tracks of the first transcontinental railroad were being laid across the grasslands, and in 1869 the Union Pacific and Central Pacific came together to complete the first all-rail route to connect the eastern and western oceans. This railway, and others pushed into the Plains, brought the white man to the homeland of the bison-hunting red men. The Indians fought bitterly before they surrendered, and there were incidents which did little credit to the white man's civilization. In the end the tribes were settled on reservations with the guarantee that the federal government would support them.

Even before the last Indian wars were over, cattlemen were driving herds of young stock northward from the winter breeding grounds in Texas to the ranges of Wyoming. At the same time farmers were pushing westward from the low, well-watered prairies near the Mississippi to the drier grasslands of Nebraska and Dakota. This advance of the husbandmen was speeded by the government's promise of 160 acres of free land to every actual settler, by the reaper now developed into a labor-saving machine of great importance, and by the railroad. The United States, moreover, encouraged railway building across the empty Plains by giving to the companies large blocks of land scattered along the lines, the sale of which to settlers, willing to pay to be near transportation, brought the roads a handsome income. The railroad dominated the economic life of the Plains. It carried to eastern markets the products of the cattlemen and of the crop-raising farmers; it determined the location of the towns; and it brought into a sparsely settled agrarian region not only the necessary manufactured goods but newcomers to swell the population.

The railroad managers of the years immediately following the Civil War looked upon their enterprises as private businesses whose main purpose was to make profits for stockholders. The period was one of uncontrolled speculation that affected even the farmers who settled in the West. Moral standards declined in private and in public life. In 1869 and 1870 the farmers of the agricultural States of the upper Mississippi valley organized in protest against what the husbandman insisted were sharp practices and extortionate rates on the part of many railway companies. An agrarian crusade swept through Illinois, Wisconsin, Minnesota, and neighboring States. The individual farmer was too weak to give battle single-handed to the corporation, so he organized for action and called in the political state to control the new economic giant. Illinois in 1870 and Minnesota in 1871, followed by other States two years later when the Panic of 1873 prostrated the country, passed statutes either regulating directly or setting up commissions to supervise the common carriers. In 1876 the Supreme Court of the United States declared this exercise of police power by the States to be within their constitutional authority.

The "granger laws," as these State enactments were called, intro-duced into American political thought the idea that some private property is "clothed with a public interest" and hence is a proper object of regulation by the political state. They established also another idea: that, in the case of the railroads, the public interest must take precedence over private gain.

The fights of the 1870's between the agrarians and the railway kings were but a prelude to a larger battle. Rapid industrial expan-sion created other forms of "Big Business" than the railroads, while at the same time the fields of the crop-raising farmers were pushed westward into the semi-arid range country until the "nesters," as the cattlemen called them, reached and passed the line where ade-quate rainfall could be depended on. Disaster befell in the late 1880's when droughts, wilting the wheat and corn, reduced or cut off the income on which the husbandman had depended to pay the interest and principal of his mortgage. This last frontier, it should be remembered, like all its predecessors, was founded to a great extent on borrowed money. When debts could not be paid and bankruptcy impended, the money-lender became an ogre to the harassed farmer.

But the issue between agrarian and capitalist that led to the Populist revolt of the 1890's was not so simple as the mere op-position between debtor and creditor. The new industrialism was magnifying inequalities in wealth. Big business had created the millionaire, whose riches were the source of vast political and eco-nomic power. The farmer, moreover, charged that middlemen robbed him of his just return from the products of his fields while, at the same time, the monopolist exacted extortionate prices for the things without which the farm could not exist. James B. Weaver, political leader of the embattled husbandmen of the South and the

West, described in 1892 the national situation as he saw it. "But there is a vast difference," said Weaver, "between the generation which made the heroic struggle for self-government in colonial days, and the third generation which is now engaged in a mad rush for wealth. The first took its stand on the inalienable rights of man and made a fight that shook the world. But the leading spirits of the latter are intrenched behind class laws and revel in special privileges. It will require another revolution to overthrow them. That revolution is upon us even now."

The farmers of the Middle West, brought to the verge of despair by the continued fall in prices of farm products, organized, in the year before Weaver wrote, the People's Party. The platform of the new organization pledged among other things a graduated income tax, government ownership of railways and telegraphs, and certain reforms in political procedures, such as the election of United States senators by popular vote rather than by State legislatures, that were intended to make more effective the working of the democratic process. But the Populists put their chief hope for the remedy of the evils from which they suffered in the depreciation of the currency, and to this end they demanded free silver. Silver was being mined in large quantities, and as the supply increased its market price had fallen. Free silver meant that bullion could be taken by its owner to the mint for coinage into silver dollars which, because of the cheapness of the metal, would be of less value than the old dollar that was tied to gold. In 1896 the Democratic Party, under the leadership of William Jennings Byran of Nebraska, took over the free silver issue from the Populists who at the same time joined in support of Bryan's candidacy for the Presidency. The campaign of 1896 in which Bryan was defeated marked the climax of the Populist revolt. After that event forces only remotely related to politics brought about a steady rise in farm prices over a considerable period of years. Populism disappeared with the advent of better times.

ECONOMIC GROUPS AFTER THE CIVIL WAR

Before 1861 the significant divisions in the United States were those of the sections: the North, the South, and the West. After

1865 the groupings among the American people that became increasingly important were those of the farmers, the wage-earners, and the citizens associated with business and industrial management. Conflicts of interest among these three economic groups were the chief forces underlying American domestic politics between the Civil War and the first World War.

The demand for labor created by the new industries after 1865 drew not only farm boys but a flood of immigrants into the expanding factories. By the end of the nineteenth century the wage-earner group was made up of many nationalities and its members spoke a great variety of languages. A large percentage of workers were newcomers who still cherished the ways and revered the standards of the civilizations from which they had come. Such laborers, moreover, were handicapped by unfamiliarity with American customs and an inability to speak easily, if at all, the language of the country to which they had come. The wage-earner group lacked homogeneity; it had neither common ideas nor a common language. It was, moreover, a somewhat shifting group, for the inflow of immigrants was balanced in part by the return of many of these workers to their homelands after a period in the United States. The inward and outward migrant tides were appreciably affected by the alternating periods of prosperity and depression that disturbed the economic life of the nation between the two wars.

The hard times that followed the panics of 1873 and of 1893 brought acute suffering to the laboring population and led to widespread and destructive strikes, particularly in 1877 and 1894. In the latter year organized bands of despairing men who could find no employment moved across the country toward the national capital to present in person to the legislators and the President their grievances and their demands. The attempt to influence the federal government failed, and the conditions that had produced the "armies" remained essentially unchanged.

In the 1870's and 1880's an effort was made to unite and organize the workers of the nation in one great fraternal order that took the name Knights of Labor. In the local units or chapters of this society skilled workers of many trades sat down in the meetings with men who had no special skills. For a few years in the early 1880's the

Knights grew rapidly, only to decline sharply in membership and power in the latter years of the decade. By 1900 the order had practically ceased to exist. There were many reasons for the failure of the Knights. Its national leadership was not effective and the conflicting interests of its many dissimilar trades and occupations often proved to be an embarrassment in time of attempted action. At the end of the 1880's, moreover, certain trade-unions that were affiliated with the Knights withdrew to found the American Federation of Labor. But behind these causes lay two other factors impeding the organization of American labor. These were the confusion of nationalities and languages that made it impossible to weld the wage-earners into a single whole, and the opportunities of an expanding industrialism that permitted the strong men, who would naturally have become leaders, to rise to managerial positions and sometimes to become the heads of great enterprises. Such a man was Andrew Carnegie, who rose from the position of bobbin boy in a cotton factory and, later, that of a railway telegrapher to become the steel king of the end of the century.

The decade of the 1890's was the period when the foundations of the American Federation of Labor were laid, and 1900 found that organization firmly established on a trade-union basis. After 1900 leaders of the small but growing Socialist Party tried to persuade American labor to put its faith in political action, but the A. F. of L. stoutly maintained its policy of limiting its action to trade union negotiations and contracts to improve the job. When the United States entered the first World War, trade-unionism was dominant in American labor. Before 1917, however, the A. F. of L. contained unions of the industrial type that were later to become the foundation of the Congress of Industrial Organization.

THE PROGRESSIVE ERA, 1901-1917

In 1901 Vice-President Theodore Roosevelt became President when William McKinley was assassinated while attending the Pan-American Exposition at Buffalo, New York. During the Roosevelt administration there gradually took form a concerted effort for political and economic reform that came to be called the Progressive Movement. The climax of this crusade to make the public interest paramount in American economic life came on the eve of war in the administration of Woodrow Wilson. Wilson in 1913, when he was still President-elect, set forth the problems and expressed the mood and the objectives of the early twentieth-century Progressives. "We have come," said Wilson, "upon a very different age from that which preceded us. . . . Yesterday, and ever since history began, men were related to one another as individuals. . . . Today, the everyday relationships of men are largely with great impersonal concerns, with organizations, not with other individual men. . . . You never saw a corporation, any more than you ever saw a government. Many a workingman today never saw the body of men who are conducting the industry in which he is employed. And they never saw him. . . . So, what we have to discuss is, not wrongs which individuals intentionally do—I do not believe there are a great many of those—but the wrongs of a system. . . . American industry is not as free as once it was free; American enterprise is not free; the man with only a little capital is finding it harder to get into the field, more and more impossible to compete with the big fellow. Why? Because the laws of this country do not prevent the strong from crushing the weak. . . . But we are coming now to realize that life is so complicated that we are not dealing with old conditions, and that the law has to step in and create new conditions under which we may live, the conditions that will make it tolerable for us to live. . . . We are upon the eve of a great reconstruction."

Wilson was the only one of many men in high positions who attempted, during the Progressive Era, to revamp government to enable it to deal effectively and in the interest of all the people with the complex problems of an industrial age. "Combinations in industry," said ex-President Theodore Roosevelt in 1910, "are the result of an imperative economic law which cannot be repealed by political legislation. An effort prohibiting all combination has substantially failed. The way out lies, not in attempting to prevent such combinations, but in completely controlling them in the interest of the public welfare. . . . Moreover, I believe that the natural resources [of the nation] must be used for the benefit of all our people, and not monopolized for the benefit of the few. . . . Conservation is a great moral issue, for it involves the patriotic duty of insuring the safety and continuance of the nation."

What did the Progressive Era accomplish in the field of economic legislation? The Progressives had two precedents from which to advance. In 1887, in the administration of Grover Cleveland, the federal government had created the Interstate Commerce Commission, charged with a limited responsibility for regulating the railroads. Three years later, in the administration of Benjamin Harrison, Congress had enacted the Sherman Anti-Trust Law, which declared combinations in restraint of trade to be illegal. Neither the I.C.C. nor the Sherman Act, however, became important before 1900. Federal statutes written by Progressive majorities in the Congress after 1901 greatly strengthened the power of the national government to supervise and control not only the railroads but all agencies of transportation and communication engaged in interstate trade. Other laws, revising the Sherman Act and creating new government agencies, laid the foundation for national regulation of business, financial, and industrial enterprises.

Another issue faced Americans as the twentieth century opened. Since the Civil War political bosses had become increasingly powerful in the organizations of the national political parties. Too frequently the boss was a center of corruption and was an instrument used by special interests to gain favors that were against the public interest. The problem of the Progressive Era was to make democracy work—to see to it that the actions of the governments of the cities, the States, and the nation conformed to the public will. The rallying cry of the age was to take the government out of the hands of the boss and the special interests and put it into the hands of the people. And what was accomplished between 1901 and 1917? Following a demand first made by the Populists, the election of United States senators was taken from the control of the State legislatures and put in the hands of the people. Experiments were made in several States with devices permitting the voters to initiate legislation and to pass on bills by referendum vote. More important was the widespread adoption of the direct primary, a method of nominating candidates for public office that was aimed directly at the control of the political boss over the party machinery. And finally, in 1920, the Nineteenth Amendment doubled the size of the electorate by making suffrage universal. The Progressives sought to cure the ills of political democracy by giving the nation more democracy. "I believe," said Woodrow Wilson in 1913, "as I believe in nothing else in the average integrity and the average intelligence of the American people. . . . This great American people is at bottom, just, virtuous, and hopeful; the roots of its being are in the soil of what is lovely, pure, and of good report."

THE FIRST WORLD WAR

The outbreak of war in Europe in August, 1914, took the American people by surprise; the citizens of the Republic had in general little understanding of the diplomatic background of the struggle. It was at first the almost universal conviction in the United States that the war was a European affair. President Wilson, asking the nation to be neutral in thought as well as deed, pushed forward aggressively in the years of neutrality the Progressive program of social and political reform.

Events, particularly the German campaign of unrestricted submarine warfare, however, transformed for America the face of the conflict. In the spring of 1917 the Imperial German Government broke its pledge to Wilson to give up the unrestricted use of the submarine, and the United States became a belligerent. For the generation that fought the first World War the conflict was an effort to overthrow militarism and an attempt to win a peace in which it would be possible for democratic nations to carry on without having to face the continual threat of armed autocracy. The Progressive crusade for social and political reform in the domestic scene expanded for Americans into a crusade for the world triumph of the democratic principle.

CHAPTER XXII

THE EXPANSION OF THE UNITED STATES BEYOND THE SEAS *

Pearl Harbor and the campaign that followed made clear that the Japanese plan of expansion included important units among the Pacific possessions of the United States. On December 7, 1941, the Japanese government was probably more aware of the location and characteristics of American holdings in the Pacific than was the average citizen of the Republic. Americans east of the Rocky Mountains have been slow to realize the importance and the problems either of the Pacific or of Asia. The fact that the thirteen original colonies stemmed from England long tended to direct American attention eastward across the Atlantic. The habit of paying more heed to the politics and development of Europe than to those of any other region was firmly fixed in American thinking by the preëminence of that continent in nineteenth- and early twentieth-century world affairs. As a result of this focusing of attention on Atlantic nations, the average American voter has had only vague notions concerning the characteristics of American commitments and responsibilities in the Pacific or the politics of eastern Asia. On December 7, 1941, however, the American people discovered that Asia as well as Europe was of primary importance to the Republic not only in some distant future but in an immediate and critical present.

THE PURCHASE AND DEVELOPMENT OF ALASKA

Alaska, huge in size and rich in resources of food and minerals, encloses much of the Pacific Ocean on the north. In its more northern part Alaska is separated from the mainland of Siberia only by the narrow Bering Strait, and its southern coastline, indented by many harbors, is extended westward toward Japan by the long line

* The author is indebted to James H. Stone of Yale University for assistance in preparing this material.

of the Aleutian Islands. In recent years Alaska has been developed into one of the two most important bastions defending the continent of North America on the west.

Secretary of State William H. Seward negotiated with Russia in 1867 the treaty by which Alaska was purchased from that nation. How did Russia come into possession of this large territory in North America? In the eighteenth century when American colonists on the Atlantic seaboard were slowly pushing westward toward the Appalachian Mountains, a Russian frontier moved eastward across Siberia to the Pacific. Leaping the Bering Strait and the Bering Sea, aggressive adventurers established Russian power on the southern coast of Alaska. Sitka became a Russian frontier outpost and commercial center. From here Russian traders in the early nineteenth century pushed as far south as northern California, but Russia made no serious effort to hold what is now the Pacific Northwest of the United States. After the middle of the century changing conditions in Europe caused the Russian government to worry about its ability to retain permanently so distant an outpost as Alaska. British power was moving westward across what is now the Dominion of Canada, and the British fleet was superior to that of Russia. Fear of the possible loss of Alaska to Britain was one of the reasons that made Russia willing to sell the region to the United States.

Most Americans in 1867 considered Secretary Seward's purchase of Alaska a piece of folly, and down to the end of the century the United States did little to develop the region. In the twentieth century, however, the population has increased and the rich resources of the country have been utilized. In the administration of Franklin D. Roosevelt a government-supported colonization plan caused a number of farm families to go to Alaska. At the same time base facilities for naval and air forces were established on the southern Alaskan coast, for Alaska is on the Great Circle route from Chicago to Tokyo. Alaska is a strong point of vital importance for any hostilities in the north Pacific.

POSSESSIONS IN THE PACIFIC AND THE ATLANTIC

The second bastion defending the western coast of North America is that isolated archipelago called the Hawaiian Islands.

They lie in the midst of the Pacific and have long been known as the crossroads of that ocean because they are the focus of many trade routes. Their original population was made up of brown-skinned Polynesians, an attractive, courageous, and musical people about as far advanced, when the whites found them, as the American forest Indians. Today the population of the Islands is a mixture of native Hawaiians, Chinese, Japanese, Americans, and other nationalities.

In the western Pacific, a little north of the Equator and not far from the coast of China, lie the Philippines, discovered in the sixteenth century by that prince of navigators, Magellan, whose expedition, sailing for Spain, was the first to make the trip around the world. Magellan's bones lie buried in the Philippines, for the natives killed him when he was resting and refreshing his men in one of the harbors of the region. His discovery and later Spanish occupation added the Philippines to the once great Spanish Empire.

The western Pacific is crowded with islands. On December 7, 1941, the United States possessed a number that served as stepping-stones between the Hawaiian Islands and the far sides of the Pacific. There was tiny Midway to the northwest of Hawaii and Wake west and south of Midway. About half-way between Wake and the Philippines is Guam, larger than Wake. Before December 7, American planes hopped from one to another of these islands on their way from Honolulu to Manila. But there was another line of islands of importance to America on December 7, 1941, connecting Honolulu with New Zealand in the southwestern Pacific. About half-way between the Hawaiian and the New Zealand groups lies the small tropical Tutuila, one of a group known as the Samoan Islands. Tutuila with its fine harbor, Pagopago, belongs to the United States, while the rest of the Samoans are under the control of New Zealand. The Samoan people, who are also Polynesians and cousins to the native Hawaiians, live mainly by producing cocoanut meat which is dried and sold in the American market. Between Pagopago and Honolulu are several tiny uninhabited islands that are possessions of the United States. Some of these are stepping-stones on the air lane that extends from the Hawaiian Islands to Samoa and from there to New Zealand and Australia.

The United States has possessions in the Atlantic as well as in the

Pacific, the most important being the West Indian island of Puerto Rico whose Spanish-speaking people are for the most part descendants of the Spaniards who conquered and occupied the region in the sixteenth century. The United States controls also the Virgin Islands, purchased in 1916 from Denmark, which lie to the east of Puerto Rico. The Virgin Islanders are, for the most part, Negroes. In this group the harbor of Saint Thomas is an important anchorage. In addition to these islands, the United States possesses that narrow strip of land stretching across the Isthmus of Panama from the Atlantic to the Pacific called the Canal Zone; the central axis of this bit of tropical territory is the vitally important Panama Canal.

ORIGINS OF AMERICAN EXPANSION IN THE PACIFIC

The roots of American expansion in the Pacific run far back into the past. The Revolutionary War which made the United States an independent nation also brought to an end the profitable sea trade which American colonials had enjoyed within the British Empire, because the new United States was outside the Empire and was excluded from its trade exchanges. American sea traders sought markets elsewhere and, before the end of the eighteenth century, had opened routes for sailing ships to China. In the first half of the nineteenth century the China trade, centering mostly in the city of Canton, became so profitable that it brought much wealth to New York and New England. In the 1840's American shipbuilders created in the clipper ships, built primarily for the China trade, the greatest sailing ships the world has ever seen.

But other ships flying the Stars and Stripes also plied the Pacific in the first half of the nineteenth century. These were the sturdy, snub-nosed whalers that put out from Nantucket Island and from ports along the eastern and southern shores of New England and not only hunted whales in the oceans about both the North Pole and the South Pole but also cruised endlessly in the Pacific. These seafaring men from New England were so much at home in the Pacific that in Nantucket, on the shore of the Atlantic, the club of the whale captains was called the Pacific Club and the local bank the Pacific Bank.

Americans of the early nineteenth century who were engaged in the sea trade or in the whale fishery came to know well the scattered islands of the broad Pacific Ocean. The whaler, in particular, paused at many islands to take on food and water. Early in the century the Hawaiian group became an important stopping place for ships sailing from the western coast of North America to China and enterprising Americans established trading posts in Hawaii to serve the needs of the vessels which paused for water, food, and repairs in the harbors of the islands. Missionaries followed the sailors and the storekeepers. By the middle of the century a small but important American population had appeared in Hawaii. They established sugar and pineapple plantations as well as shops, and they became increasingly important in Hawaiian politics.

But American seamen also became interested in Japan, a nation that down to 1854 had been isolated from contacts with the outside world by the deliberate policy of its government and people. No Japanese ships sailed abroad, and no foreign vessels were permitted to tie up for trade at Japanese ports. These nineteenth-century Japanese were farmers, fishermen, and craftsmen. They knew nothing about steam-engines or the manufacturing of goods by machines in factories, yet they made by hand a great variety of useful and beautiful articles. The native religion of Japan was Shinto, a belief that the Japanese Emperors are descended from the chief of all deities, the Sun Goddess, and that the Japanese are her peculiar people destined to lead the world in civilization. Storms sweeping across the Pacific sometimes wrecked American whalers or merchant ships on the Japanese coast, where the natives almost invariably dealt with the survivors harshly and cruelly. The United States had no way to protect the unfortunate sailors cast up on Nipponese shores because the policy of Japanese isolation kept all foreigners, including diplomats, excluded. American sea captains, moreover, desired to be allowed to put into Japanese harbors for water and provisions.

Finally an American naval expedition commanded by Commodore Matthew C. Perry forced its way without a fight into Japanese waters. The steam warships and heavy cannon of the Americans overawed the Japanese, armed only with primitive and outmoded weapons. When Perry demanded a parley with a high-ranking official, the American naval officer was met by a Japanese prince near the shore of the sea under the guns of the American fleet. The Commodore delivered a message from the President of the United States addressed to the Japanese Emperor which declared that the American officer had come to treat for "friendship, commerce, a supply of coal and provisions, and protection for our shipwrecked people." The treaty which Perry signed in the name of the United States in 1854 opened the doors of Japan to the commerce of the world. Since this event, less than a hundred years ago, the Japanese have adopted the policy of getting from other nations what they feel will be of advantage to them. They have studied the machines and the methods of Europe and America. Their emergence as a world power has been one of the marvels of modern history. But they are still, at bottom, the inscrutable Orientals that Perry found. Shinto is still their national religion, teaching their soldiers that the highest glory is to die for that divine descendant of the Sun Goddess, the Emperor, and impressing upon the Japanese people the idea that Japanese civilization leads the world.

ORIGINS OF AMERICAN EXPANSION IN THE CARIBBEAN

The background for American expansion into the Caribbean Sea is European imperialism in the nineteenth century. While American whalers were searching the Pacific for the black, spouting sea-monsters and American merchant captains were developing the China trade, European nations were dividing the continent of Africa among themselves. France, Belgium, and Britain were the most important nations that conquered and organized colonies in the Dark Continent. In the same century, moreover, France and Britain were active in extending their power not only in southern and eastern Asia but over the islands of the Pacific. In the middle years of the century British subjects began making their homes in Australia and New Zealand and the history of those important dominions began. In the latter half of the nineteenth century European nations were developing empires throughout the world. Germany, not fully organized as a nation until 1870, was a late comer in this imperial rivalry.

In a late nineteenth-century world that emphasized imperialism many Americans also began thinking of expansion, and responsible officers at Washington asked the question whether European expansion would extend to the western hemisphere. A series of events gave American statesmen some concern. A French corporation, known as the De Lesseps Company, completed the Suez Canal in 1867 and so opened a new water route to Asia. A short time later Britain, by establishing a protectorate over Egypt, through the territory of which country the Suez Canal ran, made it clear that the Canal was part of the lifeline connecting the British Isles with Britain's colonies and possessions in Asia and the Pacific. Then the De Lesseps Company entered into an agreement with Colombia to excavate a canal across the Isthmus of Panama. The news of this arrangement shocked Americans, and the commencement of actual digging by the French concern was a force in stimulating Americans to build up a powerful fleet. The new Navy was intended to prevent European expansion from extending to the western hemisphere.

In the spring and summer of 1898 the United States fought a fifteen-week war with Spain, one of the two European powers that still had important possessions in the Americas. Of the somewhat complex causes of the conflict three were of particular importance. A rebellion that had broken out in the old Spanish colony of Cuba had led to measures of repression on the part of the Spanish military authorities in the island that outraged Americans because of their brutality. The news of the sufferings of prisoners in the Cuban concentration camps had made sensational headlines in the American press for months before the outbreak of the war. A second cause for the war was the presence of small but growing American economic interests in Cuba, the greatest sugar-producing region in the world. Finally, in the spring of 1898 the battleship *Maine*, stationed at Havana to protect citizens of the United States, was mysteriously blown up and sunk, an event which provided the final push toward war. In the diplomatic crisis following the tragedy of the *Maine*, Spain expressed a willingness to change for the better the conditions in Cuba and to grant most of the Cuban demands, but the United States refused to trust the word of the Spanish government. On the recommendation of President William McKinley Congress declared war.

The conflict opened when Admiral George Dewey, commanding an American squadron in Asiatic waters, sought out the Spanish naval force whose mission was to defend the Philippines. The Americans found the Spaniards in Manila Bay. Forcing his way into the harbor, the American commander fought and completely destroyed his adversary. While Dewey remained at Manila, the United States hurried a small army across the broad Pacific. This force joined with Philippine insurgents in defeating the Spanish army there and in overthrowing Spanish power in the archipelago.

The second campaign of the war was fought in the Caribbean. Spain sent a fleet across the Atlantic to defend Cuba, but Admiral Cervera's warships were no match for the naval power the United States concentrated in the waters off its southeastern coast. Admiral Sampson of the American Navy bottled up Cervera in the enclosed harbor of Santiago on the southern shore of Cuba, and an American army, aided by Cuban rebels, then advanced against Santiago. When the city was about to fall, the commander of the Spanish forces in Cuba ordered Cervera to make a dash for the open sea. The admiral obeyed in a gallant but futile daylight attempt to gain freedom. When the battle of the fleets had ended, not a single Spanish ship remained afloat. The fall of Santiago was the signal for an invasion of Puerto Rico. General Nelson A. Miles landed an army on this island and was getting his campaign well under way when he was stopped by the armistice that concluded the fighting. With two fleets destroyed Spain could not continue. Never in the history of war has sea power proved more decisive.

THE RESULTS OF THE SPANISH-AMERICAN WAR

The treaty of peace that followed the war with Spain gave to the United States possessions scattered half-way around the world. The easternmost was the island of Puerto Rico. Cuba passed under American control with the guarantee—later carried into effect—that the colony should become an independent nation. In the Pacific the United States acquired Guam and the Philippines.

While the treaty negotiations were in progess there was considerable uncertainty as to what to do about the somewhat unexpected problem of the Philippines. They were far away and were inhabited by several different tribes of dark-skinned peoples. A group of American political leaders, among whom was Theodore Roosevelt, had discussed the desirability of getting the Philippines even before the outbreak of the war with Spain, but many Americans were strongly opposed to the taking over of this distant, tropical, and relatively undeveloped region. President McKinley, after much deliberation, finally decided to add the archipelago to the possessions and the responsibilities of the United States. He was persuaded that the natives were not yet ready to maintain a government that could defend the islands from predatory powers. He also believed that Manila in American hands would be a base for the development of commercial interests in China. The treaty of peace provided for a payment to Spain for the region. The decision to take the Philippines was one of the most momentous in recent American history. It carried American policy and power across the Pacific; it created an American outpost farther west than Japan; it took the United States into the politics of Asia and ultimately caused China and the American Republic to draw closer together; and it placed the United States athwart the imperial ambitions of what later became an expanding Japanese Empire.

THE NAVY AND THE PANAMA CANAL

The steel navy that won the Spanish-American War was new. The *Oregon*, one of its most famous vessels, was completed on the eve of the conflict at a shipyard on the Pacific coast and hurried under full steam around Cape Horn to join the Atlantic Fleet, reaching the Caribbean just in time to participate in the decisive engagement at Santiago. During the weeks while the *Oregon* was making her historic run American citizens were fearful that a Spanish fleet would appear off the Atlantic coast in such strength as to defeat the naval forces of the United States. The cruise of the *Oregon* focused American attention on the need for a canal joining the two oceans.

The acquisition of possessions so far separated as Puerto Rico and the Philippines created for the United States a new problem of defense. It became obvious to all thinking citizens not only that the Navy must be enlarged but that it must be given greater freedom to maneuver by means of a Panama Canal which would permit warships to be easily transferred from one ocean to the other.

Realization of the magnitude of the new strategic problems of the United States resulted in the annexation in 1898 of Hawaii and in the following year of the island of Tutuila in the Samoan group. The United States had for some years followed a policy of friendship for the local Polynesian chieftains of Tutuila and from them had acquired rights to establish a coaling station in the harbor of Pagopago. For ten years before 1899 the United States joined with Great Britain and Germany in maintaining a protectorate over the Samoans, but in the year following the Spanish War this arrangement was dissolved and the American Republic took over full control of Tutuila. Pagopago became a naval station in the southwestern Pacific.

Five years after the annexation of Tutuila war broke out in eastern Asia between Russia and Japan, and after several months of fighting Nippon was victorious on land and sea. The nations of the world were surprised and impressed. Japan had not only created a fleet which defeated and sank the Russian naval force in Asiatic waters, but the Japanese raised some of the sunken warships and added them to their naval strength. The victory of Japan in the Russo-Japanese War elevated the Island Empire to a world power of the first rank, and the new Japanese Navy emphasized to Americans the need of increasing their own naval forces.

In the early years of the twentieth century the American fleet was enlarged and improved, while at the same time plans were made for the digging of the Canal. The negotiations between the United States and Colombia over the building of the Canal, however, did not go smoothly; the Colombian government held out for more money than the first proposed treaty stipulated, whereupon a rebellion in Panama created a new nation whose independence was immediately recognized by the Washington government. From the Republic of Panama the United States acquired the Canal Zone and the right to build the great waterway. But the cost of obtaining these rights was more than that set forth in dollars and cents. The circumstances of the Panama revolution and the swift recognition of the rebel government by the United States sent a wave of fear and anger throughout Latin America. South

Americans thought they saw their powerful northern neighbor using its strength to force its policies on a weaker nation. Later the United States recognized the injury that had been done to Colombia by paying to that nation $25,000,000. In 1914 the Canal was opened, and it has since been the cornerstone of the naval defense of the United States.

THE PROBLEM OF COLONIES AND AMERICAN DEMOCRACY

At the end of the nineteenth century many Americans opposed the acquisition of overseas possessions on the ground that for the United States to establish a permanent rule over weaker peoples of a different race and of less developed civilization was to deny the democratic principle that men should be free and should govern themselves. The necessity of reconciling the ideals of democracy with the fact of overseas possessions has played an important part in the development of the American policies for the administration of outlying dependencies. These policies have not always been above criticism. But almost everywhere the United States has attempted to introduce into its dependencies education, modern hygiene, improved communications, and a measure of political democracy. Cuba, after a period of aid, was established as an independent nation. Filipinos were not only trained in self-government but, several years before Pearl Harbor, were guaranteed independence in the middle 1940's. President Roosevelt repeated the pledge of independence after the Japanese had invaded the islands. Puerto Rico, the Hawaiian Islands, and Alaska all have legislative assemblies elected by the people. The American policy for the smaller islands, such as Guam and Tutuila, has been to govern them through administrators appointed by the Navy Department. In Tutuila the United States has sought to preserve the native life and to protect the native people from exploitation by outsiders. In spite of blunders and occasional lapses into selfishness, the general drift of American policy in the administration of its dependencies has been toward the establishment of the principles and the strengthening of the institutions on which the life of the Republic is founded. The effective and sustained coöperation between Filipinos and Americans in the defense of islands against the Japanese invader suggests the Philippine attitude toward the policies of the United States.

THE UNITED STATES AND CHINA IN THE EARLY TWENTIETH CENTURY

The name China brought to the minds of most Americans in 1900 only vague ideas of a nation made up of some 300 millions of people who, though they had been highly civilized for more than a thousand years, had fallen hopelessly behind the nations of the West. As a matter of fact, China, though nominally ruled at the end of the century by an Emperor or Empress, was a nation in little more than name. The Chinese of the north could not understand the spoken language of those of the south, and the many provinces of China were virtually independent of one another. The Chinese man was bound by ties of loyalty to his family more than to his nation.

Japan, after having made a beginning in learning to use the tools and weapons of Europe, struck China in 1895 and defeated the Chinese armies. As a result of this victory Nippon acquired a colony, Korea, which was renamed Chosen. The weakness of China attracted the attention of the powers of Europe, and as the nineteenth century drew to a close, Russia, France, Italy, and Great Britain began to consider the possibility of dividing China among themselves. In 1900 an organization of Chinese patriots who called themselves Boxers attacked the "foreign devils" who were oppressing their land, with the result that a joint army composed of the soldiers of many nations marched on Pekin, the capital, to rescue the Europeans and Americans who were being besieged in that city by the Boxers. The fate of China hung in the balance. There was an American detachment in that international expedition, partly for the purpose of protecting Americans and partly because the United States was opposed to the break-up of China. The American policy with respect to the vast Asiatic nation was called the "open door," a phrase which meant that the United States proposed that all nations be permitted to trade on a footing of equality with the Chinese people.

The Boxer expedition marks the beginning of a period of friendship between the United States and the Chinese nation that has lasted now for nearly half a century. The powers that joined in the Boxer expedition exacted from defeated China a heavy indemnity, but very soon after the affair the United States set aside a considerable part of its share to bring Chinese students to the United States to study in American schools and universities. Many of the leaders of present-day China got their training for national service in the United States. In particular, they took back home a knowledge of science and modern engineering methods. They have played a leading role in the great task of modernizing that ancient civilization.

American commercial interests, such as the Standard Oil Company, went into China, but McKinley's hopes of a vastly increased trade in China that had helped to bring about the decision to take the Philippines never materialized. When compared with those of Britain, American commercial investments in China remained small. Commerce was not, however, the only bond tending to hold together the Chinese and American peoples. Many churches, colleges, and universities in the United States established in China during the first third of the twentieth century schools, hospitals, and colleges which sought to bring to China the best ideals of Western civilization. These hospitals and institutions of learning have made a remarkable contribution to Chinese life and one much appreciated by the Chinese government and people. Christianity became an important religion in China. Its present significance in that nation is suggested by the fact that Generalissimo Chiang Kai-Shek, head of the Chinese government, and his wife, Madame Chiang, are active Christians.

The twentieth century has seen China begin to emerge from an antiquated empire into a modern nation, a transformation stimulated in part by the growing friendship between Americans and Chinese. The modernization of China disturbed Japan. If the more than 300 million people of China should follow the example of Japan and acquire the science and industries of Western civilization, the new power of the Empire of the Rising Sun would inevitably become relatively less important. The Japanese, moreover, desired to develop China as a source of raw materials and as a market for Japanese manufactured goods; the Japanese policy was to make China an economic dependency. In 1931 Japan began an armed aggression against the Chinese which continued for many years and finally grew into a larger out-thrust against the peoples of southeastern Asia, the East Indies, and Australia and New Zealand. Much of China was overrun by Japanese armies, but the nation was not conquered. On December 7, 1941, when the Japanese moved against the possessions of the United States, the Chinese and Americans became allies. Then the average American slowly began to understand that the second World War broke out in Asia in 1931 and that the Chinese, who refused to bow to the conqueror, had been fighting, for a decade, not only their own battles but those of the Republic of the West.

CHAPTER XXIII

EVOLUTION OF THE MONROE DOCTRINE *

The Monroe Doctrine is the name of the most famous policy of the United States with respect to foreign affairs and is fundamental to the world outlook of the American Republic. It is old. President James Monroe announced it in its original form in 1823 in a message to Congress. Since his day it has undergone modification and development, but through all changes its central idea has remained the same. The core of the Doctrine, as accepted by the people of the United States, is the concept of security for the Republic; for more than a century the government of the United States has taken the position that imperialistic adventures or other aggressions in the western hemisphere by non-American nations constitute a threat to the peace and the well-being of the Federal Republic. The Monroe Doctrine is the public affirmation of this position.

THE ANNOUNCEMENT OF THE DOCTRINE IN 1823

James Monroe, Virginia planter and experienced diplomat, served as President for eight years from 1817 to 1825. Before he became chief executive the revolt of the Spanish colonies in Central and South America had begun, and during his administration the independence movement south of the Rio Grande achieved its final triumph. Citizens of the North American Republic were sympathetic with the revolting colonists of the Spanish Empire, and Simon Bolivar, the greatest of the leaders of the rebellion against Spain, became the hero of the western hemisphere. The United States watched with approval the establishment of a republican form of government in most of the former Spanish colonies. Even though it turned out that many Latin American nations were republics in name only and were, too often, controlled by military

* The author is indebted to James H. Stone of Yale University for assistance in preparing this material.

294

dictators, the new states had at least avoided setting up the European type of monarchy. The one exception was Brazil, where for a time a member of the royal family of Portugal reigned, but even here the monarchial system disappeared about the end of the first quarter of the nineteenth century. President Monroe shared the general American satisfaction over the break-up of Spanish power and the liquidation of European power in the larger part of the western hemisphere.

As Monroe came to office, certain developments among the nations of Europe caused some anxiety in the State Department at Washington. While the armies of the revolting Spanish colonies were winning independence, a few of the more powerful European countries joined in what they called the Holy Alliance. The monarchs of these nations were disturbed by the growth of democratic principles on the Continent of Europe, which led to demands that the people be represented in parliaments. Because the Holy Alliance attempted to maintain wherever possible absolute and monarchial forms of government, Americans became fearful that the new combination of European states would intervene in Central or South America for the purpose of restoring the rebellious colonies to Spain.

While these events were occurring in Europe, the attention of Monroe and Adams was diverted to what was in those days a very remote part of the North American continent. Russia possessed Alaska and was making moves to extend the sphere of its commercial interests southward to what is now the Pacific coast of the United States. This threat of a Russian advance into what is now California and the menace of the Holy Alliance provided the immediate background for the announcement of the Monroe Doctrine.

On December 2, 1823, President James Monroe included in his annual message to Congress two warnings that, when taken together, have been called the Monroe Doctrine. In the first of these, which was obviously directed at Russia, Monroe declared that the American continents were no longer to be looked upon as areas in which European powers could establish colonies. The announcement included South as well as North America. The second half of the Doctrine, aimed at the Holy Alliance, announced that the

United States would consider any attempt to extend the European
type of absolute or monarchial political systems to the New World
as dangerous to American peace and safety. Monroe qualified his
Doctrine by saying that no attempt would be made to interfere
with European colonies already established in the New World, but
added that the United States would protect any independent western nation from oppression or control by European powers.

The Monroe Doctrine, then, was announced to defend American peace and safety, and this defense was to be undertaken by
preventing any European nation from creating a new colonial
empire in the New World and by guaranteeing the preservation of
the republican form of government in the western hemisphere.
Monroe added that the United States had no desire or intention to
interfere in issues that were peculiarly European.

Of all the European nations, only England greeted the Doctrine
with anything less than complete opposition. England, because of
her growing trade with Latin America, had suggested that some
such protectorate of the former Spanish colonies be established by
joint Anglo-American action, but the United States had refused
such a joint declaration. England was powerful in international
affairs; the United States, not yet a half-century old, was still relatively unimportant. Secretary of State John Quincy Adams declined to put the United States in a position where it would seem
to be, to use his language, "a cockboat in the wake of a British man-
of-war." As a result of this refusal by Adams the Monroe Doctrine
became the statement of policy of a single nation; the United States
assumed full responsibility for its announcement and for its enforcement.

DEVELOPMENT OF THE DOCTRINE TO THE TWENTIETH CENTURY

In 1823, when Monroe wrote his message, the American people
were on the march westward in that great advance which brought
the national boundary to the Pacific in 1848. During this period, in
which Europe suffered no major wars, England and France were
the principal nations interested in the affairs of the western hemisphere. For nearly twenty years after Monroe's message the Doc-

trine was seldom mentioned. Then, in 1845, President Polk revived it. In this year the Republic of Texas, after nine years of independence, was annexed to the United States in spite of quiet British efforts to prevent the union. England, naturally, desired to keep this important cotton-producing region as much as possible under English influence. Other reasons influenced President Polk in reaffirming the Monroe Doctrine. He looked westward to the Pacific coast, about which the average American citizen knew so little, and invoked the Doctrine to prevent what he took to be British meddling in the affairs of California, then a part of Mexico. Polk was mistaken about the relations between England and California, but his revival of the Doctrine provided a background for the negotiations with Britain that finally divided the territory of Oregon and established the present international boundary between our country and Canada. The Monroe Doctrine, then, played a small part in the expansion movement of the middle of the nineteenth century.

Part of that expansion, however, was the result of the successful outcome of the war against Mexico, from which nation the United States acquired that vast Southwest extending from New Mexico to California. The Mexican War and its results in loss of territory to a Latin American state worried the nations of Central and South America that had recently escaped from the control of Spain and Portugal. Some Latin Americans began to fear that the United States intended to use the Monroe Doctrine as a cloak for further expansion southward.

The War of 1861 between the North and South helped to make clear what could happen in the western hemisphere if the United States should become weak or were broken into two or more nations. While that conflict was still in its early stages, the Emperor of France began interfering in the disturbed internal affairs of Mexico, where a President had been elected to whom the more conservative Mexican classes were opposed. French troops aided in setting up an Austrian prince, named Maximilian, as Emperor of Mexico. The United States could do nothing while the Civil War raged, but, when that conflict ended with the Union still intact, Secretary of State Seward dispatched some sharp notes to France at the same time that a considerable force of veterans of the Civil

War was assembled near the Rio Grande. In 1867 France withdrew her soldiers from Mexico; Maximilian's empire crumbled, and the former prince died before a Mexican firing squad. The retirement of France from this venture in the western hemisphere tended to strengthen the doctrine that Monroe had announced in 1823.

In 1894, a long-standing dispute over borders between British Guiana in South America and Venezuela flared up. In a friendly attempt to assist the two parties and at the invitation of Venezuela the United States government suggested that the dispute be arbitrated. In instructing the American Ambassador to England to propose arbitration, the American government maintained that any attempt by England to settle the border dispute by force would involve the transfer of territory in the western hemisphere to a foreign power and that such a change could not be allowed under the Monroe Doctrine. England's reply denied the appropriateness of the Doctrine in the situation and refused arbitration. Thoroughly aroused, President Cleveland recommended to Congress that an American commission be appointed to determine a boundary for the territories in question, which the United States would then support by military action if necessary. At this point, England, wishing to retain the friendship of the United States, agreed to arbitrate. England at the moment was beginning the establishment of the colony that became British South Africa and did not wish to incur the hostility of the American government. The importance of this episode in the development of the Doctrine is that it brought about British recognition of the Monroe Doctrine. After the Venezuela affair Britain drew closer to the United States and adopted the policy of not interfering with the development of American power in the Caribbean.

THE ROOSEVELT COROLLARY

Since the first announcement of the Monroe Doctrine, no European power had tried to establish new colonies in the western hemisphere. In fact, the reverse had been true. Spain had lost all of her territory in the New World except the Caribbean islands; England had retreated in North America above the 49th parallel, the western part of the boundary between the United States and

Canada; and Russia had sold Alaska in 1867 to the United States. Tentative efforts by Germany to purchase footholds in the western hemisphere had not been successful. In one of its primary aspects, namely, further European colonization in the western hemisphere, the Doctrine seemed to have become obsolete, having no occasion to operate. Furthermore, direct attempts by European powers to influence the course of political development in the western hemisphere had tended to subside as colonial interests were reduced. Thus the necessity to apply the Doctrine in another of its aspects, that prohibiting the disruption of republican forms of government, had become less as time went on.

Actually, only one reason remained for forceful action by European powers to interfere with the self-development of Western nations. This cause was economic. Many of the less stable Latin American countries were periodically unable to meet their financial obligations to European investors, and by revolution and default they occasionally tried to escape, if they could, from their debts. Following international custom, it was usual for the injured creditor powers, in extreme cases, to support demands for payment of obligations with naval or military force and in some instances to take over and operate the agencies in the defaulting nations for collecting duties and taxes. As long as no territorial demands were made and occupation or management of the state under pressure was only temporary, the United States made in the nineteenth century little objection to this form of debt-collection. The imperialist expansion of European nations became more marked, however, as the twentieth century opened. The United States, moreover, with possessions acquired from Spain extending from Puerto Rico to the Philippines, began to build up a fleet and to work out a plan for naval defense founded on a proposed Panama Canal. Under such circumstances American leaders began to doubt the wisdom of permitting European powers to use fleets or soldiers to collect debts owed by such Caribbean countries as the Dominican Republic or Venezuela. Such attempts might give to a non-American power a foothold that could later be developed into some sort of military base.

The alternative that lay between allowing foreign powers to coerce Latin American nations and permitting Latin American countries to default debts with impunity was the adoption by the United States of responsibility for the financial behavior of the unstable nations in the Caribbean region. President Theodore Roosevelt took up in the first decade of the twentieth century this challenge to look out for the financial good behavior of South American countries, and his practice of taking action that would prevent European nations from using force in the western hemisphere came to be known as the Roosevelt Corollary to the Monroe Doctrine. Under the Roosevelt Corollary the United States assumed the role of policeman of the Caribbean. Roosevelt's reasoning was to the effect that constant interference by Europe with Western affairs, even for legitimate purposes, constituted a possible threat to American safety as defined by the Doctrine. He therefore demanded that the United States act as a buffer between Latin America and Europe. Carrying out this policy, the Federal Republic took charge of customs in the Dominican Republic in 1905. The Navy was held in readiness in case that nation should seek to escape her obligations by a revolution. On the whole, however, Roosevelt's actual practice in carrying his policy into effect was moderate. Subsequent Presidents, however, were more firm. Under Taft the United States went about setting in order the finances of other Central American states, controlling customs and negotiating loans. The United States took sides in a revolt of 1909 in Nicaragua, and in 1912 Marines entered the capital of that nation to restore and maintain order.

The policy of intervention in the affairs of neighboring unstable nations was continued under President Wilson, but in a setting that was somewhat changed. The first World War began in 1914 and in the next two years Imperial Germany achieved such successes as to suggest the possibility of a German victory. The Panama Canal was completed and opened in 1914 in the midst of the world conflict. President Wilson never lost sight of the threat to the interests of the United States that would be created by ultimate German success in Europe. He saw also the dangers inherent in chronic revolutions in nations that were close neighbors to the United States and to the Panama Canal, so essential to the defense not only of the Federal Republic but of the western hemisphere. The Wilson policy was twofold. He tried to support constitutional government in neighboring nations against efforts of ambitious chieftains to set up military dictatorships. In pursuit of this policy he intervened in 1914 in a long and bloody revolution in Mexico against the power of a dictator who had made himself leader of that nation by the murder of its constitutional President and by the use of armed force. There was no permanent occupation by Americans of Mexican soil; Wilson made it abundantly clear that he opposed merely the Mexican dictator and that he desired to assist the Mexican people in setting up a government which they would control. American troops entered Mexico again in 1916 in pursuit of a revolutionary leader, Pancho Villa, who had made a raid into New Mexico. Wilson's policy in Mexico probably aided in bringing to an end in 1920 a ten-year period of revolution and disorder in the country and in the establishment of constitutional government.

The Wilson policy with respect to Haiti and Santo Domingo was somewhat different. When the Negro republic of Haiti was threatened with chaos in 1915 as a result of bloody domestic strife, President Wilson sent Marines into the country to restore and maintain order. In the following year the United States established a protectorate over the Dominican Republic, neighbor to Haiti on the east. President Wilson made these two moves to enforce peace in the Caribbean in the years when Germany seemed to be winning the war in Europe. The President was supporting the Monroe Doctrine as the traditional defense policy of the American Republic by taking preventive measures which would reduce the possibility of the establishment of German power in the Caribbean in the event of a defeat on the part of the Allies. He was making sure that no non-American power should have an excuse to get a footing and possible naval base on the big island east of Cuba.

ABANDONMENT OF THE ROOSEVELT COROLLARY, 1918-1929

The Monroe Doctrine under the Roosevelt Corollary meant, when carried to its extreme implications, that the United States assumed the responsibility for good conduct in international affairs of all nations in the western hemisphere, with the exception of Canada and the European colonies in Central and South America. To make effective this assumption of responsibility it would have been necessary for the United States to have acquired that position of international power called hegemony over the western hemisphere. To such an extension of power the Latin Americans naturally objected strenuously. They had been suspicious for a long time that the Monroe Doctrine, while protective, might be used by the United States to dominate and perhaps to swallow up the smaller southern nations. When during the first part of the twentieth century the American policy in the Caribbean seemed to justify their fears, they exerted increasing pressure against the Doctrine. Opposition to the United States was strengthened by the fact that some South American countries, particularly Argentina, were bound by trade exchanges to Europe rather than to the United States, a nation that tended to compete with them on world markets.

It was not until just before the first World War that recognition of this hostility toward the United States began to penetrate the minds of Americans, who hitherto had believed that their protective attitude was welcome in South America. With the growing understanding that Latin Americans feared the "Colossus of the North" and proudly insisted that they were able to take care of themselves, the attitude of the United States toward the Monroe Doctrine began to change. Two simultaneous movements transformed the Doctrine from the interpretation given it by Theodore Roosevelt, which emphasized the control of the United States over Western affairs, to that given it by Presidents Hoover and Franklin D. Roosevelt, which emphasized coöperation and the "good neighbor" attitude. On the one hand, interest in using the Doctrine as a weapon for control began to diminish in the 1920's; on the other hand, the idea of Pan-Americanism rose to prominence in the same period.

The change in the Doctrine is linked with the withdrawal of the United States from European affairs after the first World War. Fearing that membership in the League of Nations would draw America into the confusion of European politics and possibly into future war, the United States abandoned the Wilson policy of taking a place in world affairs and fell back upon the principle of isolation. This withdrawal began as early as the Peace Conferences at Versailles, when President Wilson himself proposed the amendment (Article 21) to the Covenant of the League of Nations which was to keep problems covered by the Monroe Doctrine from coming before the League for discussion and was to preserve the right of the United States to determine how the Doctrine should be interpreted and when it should be invoked.

Although the United States, after the war, renounced the plan for international coöperation represented by the League of Nations, it did not repudiate the principle of settling international conflict peacefully and coöperatively. The League was considered by Wilson and his supporters to be an extension of the principles which were implied by the Monroe Doctrine, particularly those which insisted upon the right of self-development of nations, exclusive of foreign control or interference. While the League was repudiated by the United States, the interest of American citizens in self-determination and in the mechanisms for ensuring justice in international dealings continued through the 1920's.

This feeling of good-will softened the interpretation of the Monroe Doctrine. Secretary of State Charles Evans Hughes, in 1923, announced the first retreat from the "big stick" policy of Roosevelt when the Secretary publicly assured the Latin American nations that the Doctrine did not mean that a protectorate would be established over any of them. Hughes still insisted that the United States had a right to intervene in Western affairs when circumstances should warrant action to protect American peace and safety, but henceforth such action should not be taken under the protective wing of the Monroe Doctrine. This reassurance of peaceful intentions was marred somewhat in 1926 when the United States sent Marines to occupy Nicaragua.

The change in the interpretation of the Doctrine continued, however, and reached its climax in 1929, when a bulletin of the State Department redefined Monroe's famous announcement. The Hoover administration declared in effect through this pronouncement of the State Department that the so-called Roosevelt Corollary was invalid, that the Monroe Doctrine does not extend to purely inter-American affairs, and that the true purpose of the Doctrine is to prevent European interference in the western hemisphere. The State Department document, however, reaffirmed the right of intervention in unstable nations but separated this right from any connection with the Monroe Doctrine.

The continued narrowing-down of the Monroe Doctrine allayed somewhat the fears of the Latin American nations. Nevertheless, as long as the United States, under whatever pretext, insisted upon the right of intervention, the small southern nations could not be free from anxiety. The final step, the denial of the right to intervene, came in 1933. The policy of intervention declined as the idea of the solidarity of the western hemisphere grew in importance. The concept of hemispheric unity is called Pan-Americanism.

The first Pan-American conference of the independent nations of North and South America was held in 1890. Subsequent conferences met in 1902, 1906, and 1910; after which the series was interrupted by the World War. During this period Latin American fears of the United States were great, and protests against the policy of intervention were made at the meetings. In 1933 the Pan-American Conference held its seventh meeting, and a non-intervention pact intended to prevent the interference by one nation with external and internal affairs of another was brought forward. Secretary of State Hull, acting under the declared intention of President Roosevelt to carry out the good neighbor policy, accepted the non-intervention pact, which was ratified unanimously by the Senate in June, 1934. In the same year the Platt Amendment, which since 1902 had allowed the United States to intervene in Cuban affairs, was abrogated. Troops that had occupied Haiti up until that time were withdrawn, and for the first time in twenty years no armed forces of the United States interfered with the activities of any Latin American country. Furthermore, the United States had agreed that such intervention would not be undertaken again. Pan-Americanism, in terms of the Monroe Doctrine, meant that henceforth all nations in the western hemisphere were considered to be equals; inter-American affairs were to be conducted with all due regard to this equality and were to emphasize coöperation among the American nations.

The non-intervention pact was elaborated further in 1937, and mechanisms for peaceful settlement of questions arising under it were set up. In 1938, after the European crisis at Munich, the Pan-

American nations met at Lima in Peru and there drew up a convention which announced their unity of spirit and intentions and agreed that in case of any danger to one of them consultation would take place. Two years later, after the fall of Holland, Belgium, and France, the American nations met at Havana in one of the most momentous international conferences in the history of the Americas. As in the days of President Monroe, when the United States had faced a hostile Holy Alliance of European powers, the American nations assembled at Havana confronted the Axis, triumphant on the Continent of Europe. Holland and France, now overrun by Germany, had colonies in the West Indies and in South America. What would happen to these possessions? The Havana Conference asserted that no European colony in the New World could be transferred from one nation to another nation and authorized any American state to take steps for its own defense or for that of the continent. If it appeared that the colonial territories in the western hemisphere were about to fall into hostile hands, an Inter-American Commission of Territorial Administration was provided by the Havana Conference to take over and defend the threatened colony. The conference had particularly in mind French and Dutch Guiana in South America and the French and Dutch islands in the West Indies. Another step of American unification of purpose and action occurred at Rio de Janeiro in January, 1942, when the nations of the western hemisphere moved toward the common policy of breaking off relations with the Axis powers.

The Pan-American movement that flowered in the decade of the 1930's was supported by economic and cultural, as well as political, measures. Exchanges of artists and musicians, and such affairs as the Pan-American Music Festival, have attempted to bring greater mutual sympathy and understanding among the American nations. In the economic realm, Secretary of State Hull, beginning in 1933 when he proposed reciprocal trade agreements at the Pan-American Conference, has negotiated tariff schedules which give Latin American countries most-favored-nation privileges, and those favors have been granted in turn to the United States by many southern nations. Those whose products are tropical have been thus brought closer in an economic sense to the United States, but it has not been possible to make such arrangements with the temperate-zone countries such as Argentina, a nation whose products of meat, hides, and wheat compete with the output of American farms and ranches. In 1939 the Inter-American Financial and Economic Advisory Committee was set up in Washington, D. C., to assist the planning of economic coöperation. The Pan-American movement, so important for the region south of the Rio Grande, was extended in 1940 to include Canada, when the United States and the Dominion formed a joint council for defense. Previously, reciprocal trade agreements had helped to unite American and Canadian interests. Now war has brought complete coöperation.

In these later years the Monroe Doctrine has been extended, in effect, to aggressions in the western hemisphere by Asiatic nations as well as by those of Europe. It still remains the cornerstone of the foreign policy of the United States and still affirms that the defense of the Republic requires the prevention of aggression of any kind by Europeans or Asiatics in the New World. But the nations of North and South America have also adopted this principle as fundamental to their foreign policies. For the first time in history the free nations of two neighboring continents have presented a united front of opposition to interference in the affairs of a hemisphere by nations from any other part of the world.

CHAPTER XXIV

THE UNITED STATES SINCE 1918

When the order to cease fire on November 11, 1918, brought the first silence in four years to the Western Front, the American Army in France and the people at home felt that the end of an era had come. President Wilson had called the war a crusade; he had addressed the soldiers as crusaders; and they had triumphed after fighting in the Argonne one of the hardest and bloodiest campaigns in American history. It was inevitable that Americans should think of the war in terms of reform, for in 1917 they had passed from a campaign for the achievement of social justice at home to an attempt to guarantee the principles of democracy throughout the world. Now the crusade was over; it had achieved its objective; the armies of the Allies had destroyed the monster called German militarism. November 11, 1918, was a climax. But, as the event proved, it was not the end of an era.

THE LEAGUE OF NATIONS

When President Wilson brought to the peace table in 1919 a proposal that the nations of the world be organized into a League of Nations, he made himself the spokesman of a movement for an organized world, which had appeared in the United States even before the entry of that country into the conflict. After some hesitation on the part of European powers the Covenant of the League was introduced into the Treaty of Versailles, but not until after the American President had guaranteed to the French Premier that the United States would come to the aid of France in the event of another German attack. The idea of a world organized for peace was at first well received by the American people, and in many circles the American entry into the League was taken for granted. The event, however, turned out otherwise. The Senate of the United States declined to accept the Wilson guarantee to

France and then refused to ratify a treaty containing the League
Covenant. When the United States signed separate peace treaties
with the defeated Central Powers, the American Republic formally
embarked upon an international policy of isolation. That the majority of the American people came to accept the Senate's negative
of the League there can be no doubt. After 1920, neither of the two
principal parties made adherence to the Covenant a leading issue.

There is no space here to probe fully the question as to why
America rejected the League. Among many factors two only can
be considered. The first was the fact that isolation had been the
normal American policy since the close of the War of 1812. In the
nineteenth century the citizens of the Republic had conquered the
Western wilderness, had destroyed slavery in a bloody war, and
had transformed the United States into the leading industrial nation
in the world. For a hundred years before 1919 Americans had been
busy with the tasks of peace as these came to hand within the
boundaries of their own country. Europe and Asia seemed far
away. Americans after 1919 were not prepared to reverse so old a
tradition and to undertake international commitments and responsibilities that would limit the freedom of action of the nation. They
were in the 1920's a powerful and victorious people; they were
protected on the east and west by broad oceans; they felt secure.
This sense of security was the second factor leading to the rejection
of the League. Americans believed they did not need the League.

The absence from the councils of the League of a state so powerful in both an economic and strategic sense as the United States was
from the beginning a source of weakness for that organization.
Whether American adherence to the League would have prevented
its ultimate decline and collapse is mere speculation; the record
discloses that the influences making for international rivalries
finally prevailed over those furthering international coöperation.
The post-Versailles epoch saw the triumph of nationalism and the
appeal to force instead of witnessing the flowering of the League
and the supremacy of rational discussion.

AMERICAN NATIONALISM BETWEEN TWO WARS

The first World War greatly stimulated the growth of the sentiment of American nationalism. After 1919 American citizens were

more conscious than their nineteenth-century forebears had been of their nation as a member of a society of nations and of the fact that events in Europe or Asia might be of importance for their country. The conflict had taken more than 2,000,000 American soldiers to France alone; many had passed through England; some had seen service in Italy and in the Army of Occupation that held the Rhine for many months after the Armistice. The American press put a greater emphasis on foreign news than in the pre-1914 days. And a widespread movement in the public schools of the United States emphasized the importance of giving the pupils some knowledge of the world beyond the national boundaries. The average citizen, in spite of (or perhaps because of) his larger knowledge of world affairs, tended to think in terms of American nationalism. The inability of the victorious Allies to pay to the United States the war debts incurred in defeating Germany was a potent factor in causing the American man-in-the-street to develop an attitude of suspicious aloofness toward other nations. The factors making such payments difficult or sometimes impossible were not widely appreciated.

The new nationalistic emphasis expressed itself in three quite different policies laid down by the Congress. The United States returned almost immediately after the war to a high protective tariff, a policy which the Republic had followed since the Civil War until 1913, when the Underwood Tariff had been established on the principle of providing revenue for the government rather than reducing foreign competition in American markets. After the war, however, both major political parties supported the policy of economic nationalism that is expressed in a high protective tariff. The second manifestation of the spirit of nationalism had to do with the rank of the United States in the society of nations, particularly as that position was expressed in the size of navies. The United States, while not demanding that it be accorded the position of the leading power on the sea, insisted that it would not take second place. Very soon after the war American policy crystallized into the demand for naval parity with Great Britain and naval superiority to any other nation. The third manifestation of nationalism emphasized the idea of America for Americans, and had to do with immigration. The outbreak of the World War in Europe in 1914

stopped the flow of emigrants from that continent to the New
World. After the Armistice the United States was threatened with
a deluge of unhappy Europeans seeking to escape from the miseries
that followed in the wake of war. American labor became frightened at the prospect of hundreds of thousands of foreigners com-
peting with native workmen for jobs. Other Americans were
doubtful whether the country could assimilate and Americanize
hordes of newcomers, speaking many different languages and
bringing with them customs as different as those of the Armenians
from the Near East and the Finns from the Baltic Sea. The Congress in the Immigration Law of 1924 laid down the principle of
drastic limitation on the number of non-Americans who would be
permitted to make permanent homes in the United States and provided for a rigorous selective control over those who were permitted to enter. All Asiatics were excluded on the ground that they
could not be assimilated. The protective tariff, the demand for naval
parity, the policy of restrictive immigration, all announced to the
world the developed nationalism of the United States.

AMERICAN INTERNATIONALISM BETWEEN
TWO WARS

The refusal of the United States to accept membership in the
League and the intensification of American nationalist sentiment
did not mean that the citizens of the Republic were not interested
in other peoples and were not anxious to further the cause of international peace. In the 1920's the humanitarian urge, a traditional
aspect of American civilization, caused the citizens of the Republic
to raise vast sums to alleviate sufferings in other lands. Funds raised
in the United States were poured into the Near East to relieve the
persons in that region left destitute by the conflict. When in 1923
an earthquake rocked the mainland of Japan and threw down much
of the great city of Tokyo, the American people hurried generous
aid to the stricken Japanese.

During these years Americans pinned their hope for world peace
to the policy of disarmament. The government of the United
States urged the reduction of navies by international agreement
and of its own volition reduced its regular army to a size scarcely

greater than that permitted to defeated and disarmed Germany. In the end the treaties for the limitation of navies failed, but before the failure came the United States had taken the lead in a world-wide movement to outlaw war. The Kellogg-Briand Peace Pact of the late 1920's involved a pledge on the part of each ratifying nation that it would give up aggressive war as an instrument of national policy. Today this pact of yesterday seems completely unrealistic, but it serves to remind us that the fixed purpose of the American people was to further peace among the nations.

THE GROWTH OF NATIONALISM THROUGHOUT THE WORLD

The development of American nationalism after 1918 was not an isolated phenomenon; the same sentiment appeared on all the continents. European countries moved toward the economic nationalism of protective tariffs or other types of trade restrictions. The new nations that came out of the war, such as Poland, Czechoslovakia, and Yugoslavia, pursued vigorously their respective policies of economic organization and political development. Canada, Australia, New Zealand, and British South Africa refused longer to be thought of as colonies and in a great conference in 1926 in London were recognized by Britain as equal partners in that new organization known as the British Commonwealth of Nations. Nowhere was nationalism more important than in Asia. In Japan it led to increased emphasis on worship of the Emperor as the divine descendant of the Sun Goddess, the original creator of the Japanese people. The idea of nationalism made its way slowly among the more than 300 millions of China, where the science, the learning, and the religion of Western civilization were modifying customs sometimes thousands of years old. Nationalist sentiment stirred the people of ancient India. This spirit of nationalism emphasized the fact that the human race living on the globe was divided into a large number of great and small rival groups.

THE DEPRESSION AND AMERICAN CONSTITUTIONAL CHANGE

The first World War was a disaster that involved not only great loss of life but destruction of property and disorganization of the processes of production beyond the possibility of the ordinary man to comprehend. The result was economic suffering, which came first to Europe and, after 1929, to the United States. In the 1930's life in Europe and in the United States was disrupted by a depression of catastrophic proportions that on every hand brought political and economic alterations of vast importance. The depression made clearer than ever before the economic maladjustments among the nations of the world in the post-Versailles decades. The countries possessed of limited or inadequate resources were driven by adversity to desperate measures, embedded in which were the seeds of war. In the darkest days of the depression the first steps toward September 1, 1939, were taken.

The depression provided the background for a very important constitutional change in the United States. As hard times slowed down or closed the factories and demoralized the business of the nation, the number of unemployed mounted into the millions. Farmers, unable to sell their wheat or cotton abroad, faced bankruptcy on a nation-wide scale. Americans of other generations had gone through financial panics and economic dislocations, but none was on a scale equal to what came to be called the Great Depression. The specter of hunger haunted the family of the man who walked the streets day after day in a vain attempt to find a job. The depression was the worst disaster that had befallen the American people since the Civil War. There were some despairing ones who began to doubt whether American democratic institutions could withstand the impact of so great a degree of adversity. There was, however, no revolution.

In the depths of the depression a large majority of Americans turned to Washington for help and for direction. Congress put on the statute books measures regulating finance, business, industry, labor, and agriculture. Some of these were pioneering acts exploring areas of federal regulation hitherto unentered. They naturally aroused vigorous political controversy. A failure of such far-reaching enactments to have stirred up political debate and conflict would have been evidence that the democratic process had disappeared from American life. The very intensity of the disputes over the new economic policies emanating from Washington was proof that traditional American political methods had suffered no paralysis. For a time the controversy focused popular attention on the Supreme Court of the United States, for to that body fell the task of deciding whether the Constitution had given to the federal government power to regulate directly the economic life of the nation. At first the Court opposed the new tendencies and rejected some of the earlier laws moving in the new direction. After it had overturned by unanimous decision the new federal device for regulating industry known as the National Recovery Administration, NRA, no effort was made to set up on so grand a scale a similar governmental agency. In the end the policy of the Court changed and the highest judicial tribunal announced in effect that in its opinion the Constitution provided the national government with power to regulate directly such businesses or industries as had interstate significance. This new position of the Supreme Court completed the movement toward centralization of political power in the national government begun by the first pioneering acts seeking to end the depression. It was the most momentous constitutional change since the Civil War. That conflict had decided on the field of battle that no State has a right to secede from the Union. In the midst of the disaster of the 1930's it was determined that the time had come when the government of the United States should take the lead in regulating the economic life of a nation grown to continental proportions and become the seat of the greatest industrial organization in the world.

The Objective of a Balanced Economy

As American citizens looked out across the nation in the midst of hard times they beheld a topsy-turvy world. Though factories could produce enough for all, men went ragged; though farmers were raising a surplus of wheat that lay in elevators because it could not be sold abroad, American families went hungry; though there was work that desperately needed doing, millions were unemployed. That gigantic and infinitely complicated machine called American industry had been thrown out of gear. In spite of the poverty and suffering over the nation, it was clear that American farms and factories could produce, if properly managed, all and more than was necessary for life. Before the depression, Americans by the use of science had harnessed the forces of Nature and had employed this natural energy to transform the vast resources of the nation into consumers' goods. Secretary of Agriculture Henry A. Wallace set forth in the midst of economic disaster his view of the cause of the calamities under which the nation suffered. "The pioneers," said Wallace, referring to earlier generations who had occupied the old thirteen colonies and had pushed the frontier across the continent to the Pacific, "lived in a scarcity economy. The first obligation of life was to produce enough of the necessities to go around. . . . It marks the difference between the pioneer era and our era. . . . For now, the fifth and sixth generation beyond those old pioneers, we have come to a time of abundance, instead of penury. But because we have not learned how to live with abundance, men go hungry and ragged."

But the practical question was how to make possible more goods for all. The general policy worked out by the national government involved the application to the problems of the depression of a very old American idea. Alexander Hamilton, Secretary of the Treasury under President Washington, had introduced into American political life before the end of the eighteenth century the concept of a balanced economy. In a famous report to the Congress Hamilton had declared that the three important phases of American economic life showed a lack of balance. Two, agriculture and commerce, were well developed, but the third, manufacturing, was lagging behind, for, as Hamilton had pointed out, practically all American manufacturing at the time was done by hand. The Secretary urged a protective tariff to stimulate the building-up of American industry. The idea had appeared again in national politics when John C. Calhoun of South Carolina insisted in the 1830's that Southern agriculture was suffering and that the national objective must be a balance of well-being among commerce, manufacturing (now too much favored by tariffs in Calhoun's opinion), and agriculture. The old ideal reappeared in the depression. "Therefore," said Secretary Wallace in 1936, "the job is to establish good relations between town and country, with adequate incentives for both industry and agriculture to work toward a balanced abundance." "What we seek," added President Franklin D. Roosevelt, "is balance in our economic system—balance between the wage-earner, the employer, and the consumer."

The federal government strove to achieve the objective of a balanced economy with experiments on a nation-wide scale in agricultural management, with other experiments in wage and hour legislation, and with the guarantee to wage-earners of the right of collective bargaining.

The Objective of Security for the Individual

Throughout American history the social and political thinking of the citizens of the Republic has emphasized the importance of the individual. The individual man must be free; he must assume responsibility for furthering the well-being of that great coöperative enterprise known throughout the world as the United States of America. The foundation of American thought has been from the beginning that the political state is an instrument in the hands of its citizens, not only for the creation of a better civilization but for the assisting of individuals to realize fully their powers and possibilities. The chief expression of this ideal is the American public school system extending from grammar school through the university, an educational organization giving to individual Americans opportunities to be found in no other great nation in the world. The high school and the State university are living embodiments of the ideal that the prime function of the political state is to guarantee freedom to the individual citizen and to assist him in the development of his abilities so that he may use that freedom with a sense of responsibility toward his fellows and for the common interest of the community.

In the depression, when the complicated industrial machine failed for a time to function efficiently, Americans began to give thought to the problems of those unable to find employment in the emergency and of those other older people who had passed beyond the age of productive work. Out of these dark years came a gigantic insurance plan to which both individuals and government contributed and which provides assistance for the temporarily unemployed and an income for those who have left behind the active years of life. The public school system has freed the American from the slavery of ignorance; social security is freeing him from the slavery of fear born of temporary unemployment or of the prospect of permanent dependence on others.

National Planning

The depression also gave an impetus to the idea that the political state should make long-range plans, particularly for the management and utilization of the natural resources of the nation. President Theodore Roosevelt in the first decade of the twentieth century had introduced this principle into the political thought of the United States in his long and vigorous advocacy of conservation. He had emphasized the importance of conserving forests and mineral resources and had instituted the policy of setting aside wooded areas as national forests. The sufferings of the depression period compelled a more thorough consideration of the whole problem of national planning. A National Planning Board, now called the National Resources Planning Board, was established in 1934.

In its report of December 1, 1934, this board called attention to what it spoke of as the "planless tradition" in American history. "The traditional American attitude toward land," said the report, "has been to develop and exploit it as rapidly as possible. . . . This . . . was the natural attitude of a new Nation . . . confronted with an apparently illimitable array of resources. This attitude contributed to a rapid expansion and development, but at the same time produced a planless, crazy-quilt pattern of land use, destroyed or impaired a large proportion of the Nation's irreplaceable resources, and wrecked the hopes, aspirations, and the very lives of untold thousands of people."

The national government took steps to remedy the worst aspects of the situation. Federal authorities achieved two great advances in this field. The planless tradition had been responsible for the destruction of fertility in thousands of acres of soil; it had increased the boundaries of that area in the dry plains of the Southwest known as the dust bowl. The first important achievement of federal planning was the formulation and the putting into operation of a variety of plans adapted to the needs of different localities for the preservation of the fertility and often of the soil itself in those broad agricultural regions whence comes the food of the nation. The second accomplishment had to do with waterways. The westward march of the frontier in the nineteenth century had resulted in stripping the forest covering from most of the land of the United States where agriculture was possible. It became clear in the twentieth century that one of the results of this deforestation was an increase in the volume and the destructiveness of floods, particularly in the rivers of the East and in those of the Mississippi valley. One of the most important achievements of national planning has been the study of the problems of and the formulation of programs for flood-control.

THE DEPRESSION IN EUROPE

The depression that settled down on Europe in the 1930's caused the decline on that continent of the practice of political democracy. Hard times in the 1920's had been an important influence making for the overthrow of a liberal government in Italy and the setting-up of Benito Mussolini's Fascist dictatorship. In the 1930's suffering in Germany was a factor of great significance in enabling Adolf Hitler to overthrow the German Republic, created after the first World War, and to set up his Nazi absolutism. In Japan also an early twentieth-century inclination to imitate the liberal parliamentary governments of England and France was halted by the rising power of the Army, possessed of boundless prestige after its defeat of China in 1893 and of Russia in 1905. By the end of the 1930's the Japanese armed forces had created a military autocracy that determined the domestic and foreign policies of the nation. Even in the French Republic men of high position and wide influence moved quietly and without causing alarm toward a position where in time of crisis they could repudiate democracy and set up such a regime as Vichy, pledged to collaboration with totalitarianism. In Europe in the 1930's the men who, with the French patriots of 1789, believed in French revolutionary principles of liberty, fraternity, and equality retreated before totalitarian mass movements.

For the doctrine that the political state exists for the free individual and is an instrument in his hands for the betterment of society the German Nazis set up the doctrine that the individual exists for the state and must not only become the slave of the state but must accept external control of his most private affairs. And to this was added that other tenet, namely, the superiority of the Aryan race, and its corollary, the persecution, even to extermination, of non-Aryan peoples. The symbol of this new race worship and religion of the state became the concentration camp.

When hard times brought economic suffering to the entire Continent of Europe, the different nations not only tried to make the most of the resources they possessed but attempted to make themselves as independent as possible of one another. Ideas of economic nationalism controlled the policies of the powers of Europe as they built tariff walls or established other trade restrictions to protect their peoples from foreigners. Economic self-sufficiency became the ideal that every country strove to realize as far as circumstances permitted.

In such a world Nazi Germany rearmed and reoccupied the Rhineland; Japan invaded North China; and Italy attacked the independent kingdom of Ethiopia. These early tentative outward thrusts suggested the events to come. But few men in Britain or the United States were able to read aright the danger signals hoisted aloft by the leaders of the powers that had substituted autocracy for the rule of the people. The dictators were organizing their battalions to seize the wealth of the world. The average American citizen, still lulled by his sense of national security, paid little heed. To him Germany, Italy, and Japan seemed far away.

THE HOUR OF DESTINY

There were many reasons why the men of the democracies slumbered in the latter half of the 1930's while a hurricane gathered on the horizon. Each nation was preoccupied with its own pressing domestic problems. There was also a general failure to comprehend the power and the deadliness of the military weapons being forged to overthrow the might and to seize the wealth of France, the British Commonwealth of Nations, and the United States. In every threatened nation were thousands who refused to believe that the gathering storm would break against their particular country. But perhaps most important of all the many causes for the blindness of the democracies had to do with education. Men and women whose fathers and grandfathers for many generations had been trained to believe that the goal of a life is to develop the free, responsible, and humane individual could not understand how any people could long accept the slavery, the cruelty, and the worship of force involved in Nazism. Such a tyranny, dragging in the dust the dignity of men, seemed to our people to belong to some vanished age, an evil dream that must soon pass away. Because of a blindness born of the standards of their own culture the men of the democracies could not see the quality of the danger that threatened them.

As a result of their failure of yesterday to understand the movement of world forces the democracies today fight for their very existence. The enslavement of Poland, Holland, Norway, and Greece provide a preview of a possible world. If the democracies fail, their people know now that they may expect no mercy. Defeat means the death of civilization as we know it.

In 1776 Americans thought they could establish liberty by throwing off the yoke of colonial subordination. Their descendants who fought in the first World War were persuaded that the world could be made safe for democracy merely by winning the victory on the field of battle; peace seemed to the generation of 1917 the panacea that would solve all problems. We have learned in the school of hard experience the magnitude of that mistake.

We now know that winning the war is only the first problem, and that beyond military victory lies the long, hard task of winning the peace. We cannot yet see in detail the outline of tomorrow. But the most simple among us can understand and appreciate the elementary ideas of freedom and brotherhood that must underlie the world which is to arise out of the travail and the carnage of our time. We fight that we and other men may be free and that we may have fellowship one with another.

There are moments of destiny for individuals and for nations. The changes of history give opportunity now to one people and now to another. The twentieth century has seen the American Republic become not only an industrial giant but emerge as a world leader in science, in learning, and in the arts. As the American people worked their way out of the depression they saw opening before them a brilliant age of constructive achievement. Then came September 1, 1939, and after that December 7, 1941. Americans, as they laid aside plans for future peaceful progress, realized that the task of the moment was to hold fast to and to conserve ancient values. Western civilization is threatened with disaster. It can sink back into barbarism, as once the light went out in ancient Greece and Rome. If the civilization we know—those standards of value and that religious outlook which give meaning and significance to our lives—is to be saved, America must save it. For the United States the moment of destiny has come.

PART IV

The Armed Forces

by

Second Army Board

CHAPTER XXV

BASIC FACTORS IN ORGANIZATION

The present chapter is calculated to draw a broad picture of the organization of armed forces. It is easy to state in so many words that military organization must be flexible, that it must be abreast of the times, that it must have an objective, that the means at hand must be constantly kept in mind, and that the nature of the human material is important. Not so simple, however, is the application of these principles. Somebody is always liable to forget something. You remember the saying:

> For want of a nail the shoe was lost;
> For want of a shoe the horse was lost;
> For want of a horse the rider was lost;
> For want of a rider the battle was lost;
> For want of a battle the kingdom was lost;
> All for the want of a horseshoe nail.

Keep in mind the word *flexibility*. Without it an organization becomes a deadweight for any commander. At the battle of Arbela, Alexander the Great, with an army of about 40,000 Greeks, was faced with a host of over a million Persians. The two sides lined up. Alexander was able to make a shift over to the left. The Persians tried to shift, too, but they were poorly organized and were thrown into hopeless confusion, with a gap left in their lines. Through this went the forces of Alexander. The Persian defeat was a rout. Alexander succeeded because his organization was flexible.

Keep in mind that an organization must be abreast of the times. Military history is full of examples where self-satisfaction with what a people possessed has brought disaster. Did you ever hear of Genghis Khan? He could be called the Hitler of his day. Galloping from the heart of Asia, he and his Mongol hordes overran almost the entire continent. The people in the cities with strong walls around thought they were safe. They said, "He cannot get this far; if he does we can hold him off." But he came anyway and took their cities by direct assault in spite of all they could do. He had one effective means of taking cities. He would place the prisoners that he had taken from the last city in front of his army so that they would absorb the missiles thrown by the defenders; then he would assault the town.

Do not forget that military organization must have an object. You have heard of the Swiss. In fact, Switzerland is one of the few countries of Europe that Hitler has not already invaded. Perhaps he remembers what happened to the Austrians who tried to invade the country 500 years ago. The Swiss had one object: to keep their freedom. They knew they could not keep free by simply talking about it, they knew they would have to fight, so they built up an organization based on the conception that every man must fight when an emergency arose. They knew who would threaten their freedom, they knew that when the enemy came they would be men on horses. Therefore, the Swiss armed themselves with pikes, or long spears, and long-handled axes. When the Austrians came, the Swiss waited until the enemy were caught in a defile and attacked them there. The horses could not charge. Their riders could not use their weapons. The Swiss slaughtered the Austrians, and after two such attempts the Austrians gave up.

Today the Swiss still have one object: to keep their freedom. Well do they know who the enemy is and they know what he has: an army that has overrun Europe. They know too, that the enemy has dive-bombers which could blast them from any position they took. But should Hitler invade Switzerland, he would find that every tunnel had been mined and blown up. His communication with Italy would be destroyed through Switzerland, not to mention the losses he would sustain in fighting such a people.

Means at hand will determine organization to a large extent. The clever commander is one who uses means to the best advantage. General Pershing knew that the rifle was a weapon with which many, if not most, Americans were familiar. He knew, too, the American character, which is one of independence. Pressure was placed on him to send machine-gunners to France and to incorporate them in the Allied Armies. But he stood his ground. He insisted on an American Army armed with a traditional American weapon.

But Pershing had to get an army together in a hurry. While America during the first World War was already an industrial nation, he could not wait while factories were converted. In this present war our national leaders became aware of the true situation much sooner. Why do they insist on more and more industrial effort in the manufacture of planes, ships, guns? Because if an industrial effort is applied to their manufacture, it may well tip the scale. Our leaders are insisting that we use all the means available.

We must keep in mind, too, the importance of the human material. This involves the factor of leadership and the moulding of men. Colonel Merch B. Stewart, one-time commandant at West Point, told a story in this connection that we could all take to heart. Colonel Stewart was asked by a civil engineer during a discussion: "The Army is all right and it must be an interesting profession, but what do you build? When an engineer completes a bridge or a dam he can see that he has built something—that he has made something—that something exists in the world which was not there before." Colonel Stewart replied, "The Army does build something; it builds men."

Man has always found that organization was necessary if he expected to accomplish his aims. The family, the clan, the state, and the nation are but organizations that men have formed to gain security and accomplish good for all. The efforts of any organization were successful only when directed toward a common goal; this called for a leader who had the confidence of the group. The duties and responsibilities of the leader continued to increase as communities and cities grew into states and nations.

The organization of armies parallels, in general, the organization of other activities of mankind. From the earliest times, men have found that they must defend their homes and their institutions to prevent their destruction in an unfriendly world, and they were quick to utilize the means by which they accomplished other goals for defense purposes. A leader was essential to armed effort; even today savage tribes trust a leader or chief to lead them in war. If the forces are large, it becomes necessary to employ sub-leaders, or sub-chiefs; and the basic elements of military organization are born.

In the development of a community certain individuals have always demonstrated an inventive capacity; inventions took the form of mechanical means by which an individual found ways to accomplish a task at hand quicker and better, or with less labor on his part, or to create an element which nature denied him, or to add to his amusement or pleasure. More important, inventions were not retained solely for the use of individuals but were copied or employed by other men so that people benefited as a whole.

About 150 years ago a new system of dividing up jobs began to be adopted in many countries. A number of inventions relating to the processing of cotton and its manufacture into finished products became almost universally adopted, and this led to the factory system of manufacture. Inventions followed in other fields. New factories sprang up, until at the beginning of the present century the factory system of manufacture had been firmly established, not only in our own country but in the principal countries throughout the world.

This factory system meant that each individual had only a small part in the completion of a finished product instead of, as formerly, the making of an entire article. For example, take the construction of furniture. Under the old system, a cabinet-maker himself completed a bed, table, or chair, from the selection of the lumber to the final finishing. But under the factory system, one man buys the lumber, other persons process it in kilns or otherwise, and still others plane it, shape it, glue it, and finish it. The advantage of such a system is: the organization of the factory permits so many more articles to be made.

The success of the factory system, or mass production as we most often call it today, lies in organization, and in a new word which now makes itself more and more important: discipline. Organization means all the finished parts must come together at a certain point at the same time, in order that the factory can turn out finished articles properly assembled. But good organization is not enough. Care must be taken to see that parts are correctly fashioned, so that they will fit other parts when all are assembled. Precautions must be observed to be sure that some parts are not made or some operations not completed behind others, and this involves discipline: the obedience to instructions or orders; care in operation of machines; constant alertness to prevent accidents or break-downs; frequent inspection to see that workers are not placed in the wrong jobs.

In most activities, discipline is obtained not through making the individual afraid but through a kind of leadership that causes men to *desire* to do the right thing. The discipline of fear is confined for the most part to the prison or institution, for which we are thankful. The successful enterprise is the one that is based on the desire of men to coöperate, to produce, to participate in the success of the whole. Fortunate indeed is it that this condition exists. Imagine a bank or any other organized endeavor where one man had to be hired to watch every other man.

Returning to military organization, the defense of a clan, city, state, or nation always has been essential to its progress, even its life. Hence men included in their other inventions new tools and machines for making war, in order that they would possess an advantage over those who might attack them. Constant effort was made to improve these tools and machines (or as we call them, weapons). Consider your rifle as you aim it in the direction of a target; you know that it will fire; you know that it will project a bullet in the direction of that target and if you are aiming correctly you will hit that target. From your modern rifle it is a far cry to the weapon soldiers were forced to use only 300 years ago. The soldier of the Thirty Years' War even had to have his powder mixed on the battlefield; his piece was discharged with what is called a matchlock, the idea being that the match was put in contact with a powder train in the piece to discharge it. The match resembled a piece of rope; it burned like a piece of punk with which we used to light firecrackers. In a rainstorm the match went out. In any case it was often necessary to wave the match around one's head to keep it lit. Sometimes a soldier, getting low on powder, would forget and go back to where it was stored to replenish his supply, waving the match, and you can imagine what would happen when the lighted match came in contact with the whole store of powder.

With improvement in, and multiplication of, types of weapons, it was found necessary to introduce into military organization *specialization*, with the result that different groups in the military organization, or the *Army*, as it came to be called, would use or operate different weapons. This complicated the picture, but it added power to the whole. Coupled with the improvement of weapons, men found ways of defense against them. Other men devised new weapons and new ways which would overcome the accepted types of defenses.

Military history is full of examples to show how this process has operated. In 1346 there took place in France the battle of Crécy, between the French and the English. The French placed their trust in heavy-armored knights who were supposed to charge in a mass and run down such foot-soldiers as they did not kill. Until that time, this method had worked on numerous occasions. The man in armor seemed almost as invincible as a tank did at one time. But the English were armed with the longbow. As the French horsemen approached, they were met by a storm of arrows which penetrated the joints in their armor and brought down their horses. Soon the battlefield was a shambles. The French knight had met his match in the English peasant armed with the longbow. But a bow and arrow as a weapon was nothing new. The novelty was that the English employed a more powerful bow, used it in a different way, relied on it when all Europe's eyes were blinded to the possibility that horsemen could suffer defeat by foot-soldiers. And the French would not give up their ideas even after Crécy. Only ten years later their armored horsemen suffered another bloody defeat at the hands of the English bowmen.

It is not necessary, however, to go back to medieval history to find this conflict between the old type of arms and the new. During the war of 1914-1918, the machine-gun came into its own in virtually all armies. It seemed at the time that the use of the machine-gun had opened a type of warfare where neither side could advance, but was forced to dig trenches and to remain in them in order to get away from the deadly fire. But the ingenuity of man was not dead. The increasing use of artillery fire and the invention of the tank overcame to a great degree the invincibility of the machine-gun.

Naturally, the increasing use of different types of arms has had a great influence on organization of all armed units, but the basic principles have remained the same. The importance of the leader remains. His responsibilities have been multiplied. The wide adoption of the factory system of manufacture has been applied to the making of arms as well as other articles. Mass production has insured a sufficient number of arms so that the size of armies has increased to what would formerly have seemed unbelievable figures. It has become necessary for the leader to surround himself with a small host of assistants (his staff); sub-leaders, or *commanders* of units, with commanders under them. How this is accomplished will be covered in a later chapter.

The development of our present-day armies, however, has not been solely due to the availability of an increasing number of arms, either in quantity or variety. Men have a tendency to carry into the organization of armed forces those principles they practise or profess to practise during peaceful years, and in times of revolution or violent upheaval the organization or reorganization of the armed forces has often been one of the first changes accomplished.

It is not intended here to go into the causes or even the events of the French Revolution. But the principles of the Revolution were translated into the armies of France, and as such have a genuine importance for anyone who is trying to understand modern armies, not so much because of the effect on France, but because other nations were forced to adopt the French way in order to resist successfully Napoleonic aggression.

Prior to the French Revolution, the head of each of the European countries regarded his domain as the personal property of the ruling house. Areas, together with their inhabitants, were considered to be the legitimate spoils of war, diplomacy, intrigue, or marriage. In order to further or protect his interests, the reigning monarch was forced to employ an army. This army was made up largely of hired soldiers, employed much as masons, carpenters, or mechanics would be employed, and they often were not of the nationality of the monarch who employed them. True, there were notable exceptions, such as the volunteer armies of Frederick the Great and Gustavus Adolphus, but mercenaries were the general rule. Soldiers were often hired for a particular campaign. Small princes even found that the furnishing of soldiers to a monarch was a ready means of paying a debt, as witness the sending of the Hessians to America to serve under the English King during our own Revolution.

One of the principles of the French Revolution was that of the "Nation in Arms." This meant a large army made up of conscripted citizens, young, willing, and eager, rather than a small professional army, whose members served mainly for hire. Moreover, it meant that the position of the officers would depend on merit rather than birth. The French armies that were organized under these principles were able to drive back from the frontiers of France the best armies of Europe. Later, under Napoleon, the same type of armies conquered a large part of the Continent of Europe. And it was not until the enemies of Napoleon adopted methods similar to the French that they were able to bring about his downfall.

The idea that the whole nation must participate in armed conflict has persisted since the French Revolution. The idea that only the specially qualified can be included in the actual armed forces stems from the fact that people have found that efficiency, be it on a farm, in a factory, in a school, or even within the nation as a whole, is possible only if the specially qualified occupy the key positions. As we study more about the organization of the Army in later lectures, it will become apparent that every individual in the Army occupies a key position in the organization that is necessary for an Army such as ours to function. And there can be no doubt that he occupies a most important position in our whole national structure.

Mention was made previously in this chapter of the word *discipline*. It was brought out that discipline is necessary in every organized effort. It was also observed that in general discipline is obtained because men realize the purpose of an effort, whatever it may be, and they desire to do their best.

In the military organization, discipline is doubly important. In the factory, a man who did not do his best might slow down production, but in an Army the penalty that will be exacted for an individual's slipping will quite likely be the lives of others, not to mention the safety of the nation itself. All of us are familiar with the material on this subject in the *Soldier's Handbook*. It is needless to review it here. It need only be mentioned that if everyone in an organization is doing his best, if he is making every reasonable effort to improve his knowledge and his skill, and if he is carrying out his part to the best of his ability, that organization, if soundly founded, will click. Such a concept of discipline must be self-imposed.

Every American is familiar with some sort of light car: Chevrolet, Ford, or Plymouth, according to inclination. Each runs. Each will accomplish the same things. Each will carry an individual to another place in a hurry. And each is dependable.

The chief reason that one can depend on the light car for long trips is that for any particular make the parts are interchangeable, so that a broken or worn part does not spell an end to the car's usefulness. Even a short interruption is scarcely necessary. A new part is quickly obtained, and the driver is again on his way.

This leads one to the comparison of the light car with the military organization. Like the light car, organization must be simple, it must be adequate, it must be calculated to respond to the slightest wish of the leader. Its parts must be capable of replacement, must be capable of improvement.

But after all, a car is an inanimate object. Military organizations are made up of men, not machined parts. Therefore, the establishment of a military organization is an art rather than a science. Men possess virtues, but too they are filled with shortcomings, and the military organization must, if successful, take all this into consideration. "The arms of the era determine the organization best adapted to utilize them." But in the long run the skill of the organizer determines the organization that will best utilize existing arms and at the same time employ to the utmost the capabilities of those operating them. The foresight of the organizer will insure that the organization is flexible, that its units are interchangeable.

So important is this whole subject of organization that changes and advances are not entrusted to one man or even to a group of men. As has been pointed out, new equipment and changes in organization go hand in hand. Moreover, deficiencies in existing equipment and organization are under constant test by the field forces. Recommendations for changes may come from the field forces themselves, or they may come from officers who constantly study the subject, or they may come from a study of foreign armies, especially those which prove successful. Certain units and service schools, like the Infantry, Cavalry, Field Artillery, Coast Artillery, Armored Force, Signal Corps, and Corps of Engineers Schools, are designated to make tests to insure that the new is desirable. And through the whole process, care is exercised to make certain that the adoption and servicing of a new weapon does not impart a rigidity to the whole organization or any of its parts.

Every one of you has heard the saying of the famous Confederate general, Bedford Forrest. When asked by an admirer the reasons for his success on the battlefield, the General replied, "Well, I reckon I gets there fustest with the mostest men." What he meant was that at the point of contact with the enemy he was stronger than they, although almost invariably Forrest was weaker on the whole battlefield. Forrest was a natural soldier. As such, he was able to marshal his forces, principally cavalry and artillery, so that when he struck, it was a real blow. No small part of his success was due to his organization; due to the certainty that his soldiers knew their parts and played them; due to the fact that his artillery and riflemen worked hand in hand; and due most of all perhaps to the assurance that his forces could adapt themselves to the mission at hand. At the battle of Brice's Crossroads, Forrest defeated a much larger force. During the engagement he directed his artillery to move right up to the front line. His artillery commander replied, "General, we might lose our guns." Forrest admitted that such might happen, but he wanted his guns up there. So, up to the front lines they went and, by employing direct fire at close range, played a big part in the final victory. The Union forces did not expect guns to be so used; when the guns were in position it was too late to do anything about it. Moreover, in the organization of Forrest's forces, there never was any question about who the leader was. They still tell the story about the Confederate soldier who wanted a furlough to go home and harvest his corn. Because of impending operations, his first request was refused. The soldier tried again, this time accompanying his application with a long explanation. Again a furlough was refused. But this soldier was hard to discourage and for the third time he applied. This was too much. Forrest said to his adjutant, "Let me answer this," so, taking the application he wrote across the face: "I told you twicet goddamit no." The soldier did not put in a fourth request.

On the other hand, American military history contains many examples of how poor organization contributed to or was almost solely responsible for military disaster. Let us consider for a moment the following. On the eve of the War of 1812 Congress attempted to raise a volunteer army. The attempt failed. So Congress had to ask the governors of the States to have 80,000 troops ready to march at a moment's notice. The whole story of the War of 1812 could be told by showing how this policy failed to function. One example will suffice. On October 11, 1812, General Van Rensselaer had collected at Lewiston, New York, about 2500 militia. It was planned to take the heights of Queenstown across the river in Canada, because this point could serve as a base from which an invasion could be launched into New York. The scheme called for sending 600 of the best troops first to seize the heights, after which the rest were supposed to follow. At the last minute it was found that there were not enough boats; only 225 men actually could get across. But they took the heights and bravely withstood charge after charge by the British to retake them. Overpowered at last, nearly all were either killed or captured. But where were the rest of the troops, over 2000 men, that were back across the river? They just stayed there. Orders, entreaties, threats were all tried. Still they would not move. They claimed that under their constitutional rights they did not have to invade a foreign country!

Up to this point, we have concerned ourselves with the basic factors of the military organization itself. Equally important is the organization of the whole nation itself. Today we hear the talk of *Total War*. Under this concept of war every activity of a whole people is directed toward the winning of the war. The Army is only a part of the war services; so is the Navy. In the broadest sense, every individual in the warring nation fits somewhere into the organization for war. Farms are organized to produce the needed foodstuffs; factories are converted so that they can manufacture engines of destruction; the very life of a nation is converted.

It was mentioned earlier that at one time a ruler had a hired army. Unless this army came through a district, the fighting that it did had little effect on the people who were bakers, shopkeepers, wheelwrights, or washerwomen; life went on much the same. When the idea of the "Nation in Arms" was thrust upon Europe by the French Revolution and Napoleon, people had more of a personal interest in warfare because the sons of bakers, shopkeepers, and so on were conscripted into the army. Still, unless the invading armies came close, war annoyed rather than disrupted civilian life. But with the advent of total war, the organization behind the lines became part of the military power of a nation. No longer could civilians expect security. To win, a nation must now wreak destruction wherever it could; to win, it must now organize not only armed forces, but the very life of a nation; every activity that could count in the scale must be directed toward winning the war.

Now all this organizing and disciplining of the lives of all the people in a nation is not a pleasant thing to think about. Most nations do not want to do it. Certainly the United States does not. But what we want to do cannot dictate our actions in the present-day world. Whether we wish it or not, the United States must organize all of its resources for the common defense.

To sum up, the organization that is flexible and is abreast of the times, whether it be a squad or the whole armed force of the nation, is built on solid ground. Leadership will insure that all the means at hand are used, and that the human element is applied to its utmost advantage. Emphasis has been placed throughout the training of our entire Army on leadership. More even than leadership in the high command has the stress been placed on leadership of small units. One asks, "Why has this been the case?" Because those in charge of directing our training know, both from personal experience and from the study of history, that the greatest leader that ever lived cannot hope for battle success unless every part of his military team clicks. The subordinate leader must insure to the higher commander that every element is doing its part. But in the final analysis every man is a leader; he must lead himself. With a full appreciation of his duties and his position, this will follow.

No doubt you are interested in knowing what this course is going to be like. It will consist of twelve assignments,* one to be studied each week. These assignments are to be studied concur-

* Chapters XXVIII and XXIX of this book were combined in one lecture assignment.

rently with those you are having on geography, American history, the meaning of the Constitution, and the events in the world which forced the United States into its present position in international affairs.

The course which we are starting on organization of the armed forces will cover: the part the United States Navy plays in defense; the organization of the Navy and the way it operates; military aviation; the organization of a division; branches of the service; how the square, triangular, Cavalry and Armored divisions are formed; how divisions and separate units are combined to form corps and armies, combat teams and task forces; what staff work means and how it operates; the duties from private to general; observations on foreign armies, especially the German, with a discussion of their proven methods; and how propaganda is organized and used as a weapon of war. This seems like a big order. But when the course is completed it is expected that every last member of the Second Army will know more than just his particular job; he will appreciate the importance of everyone else's job, not only in the Second Army, but in the whole defense scheme. When this course is finished, it is expected that you will know something about what a sailor does on a ship; how a big warship is operated; how an air task force is formed, and what it is expected to do; why the sky always seemed full of Blue planes on the Louisiana maneuvers; how the Army Commander spends his day; how your chow gets to you (or maybe why it *doesn't* sometimes); how German units work; the way you distinguish between truth, propaganda, and pure, unadulterated BUNK.

CHAPTER XXVI

THE PART THE NAVY PLAYS IN
UNITED STATES DEFENSE *

"History is geography in motion," said the late great Newton D. Baker, Secretary of War during the Wilson administration. Let us consider a map of the world. While the land masses do not move in a physical sense (except perhaps during an earthquake), their relative importance to the members of the human race undergoes constant change. Because people learn to use new things, part of the world become vital to their standard of living. Our grandfathers did not have nearly the material interest in the world that we do; our children will have more. New means of communication and travel tend to reduce distances, making every one of us closer and closer to the rest of the world, whether we wish it or not.

Consider for a moment the distance between the Americas and Europe and Asia. On the map it appears as so many inches. Put a scale on the map and we read that it is 3036 miles from New York to Liverpool, and that Yokohama, Japan, is 4768 miles distant from San Francisco. What difference does that make? What we want to know is how long it takes to cover these distances.

When Sir Francis Drake (the first Englishman to make a trip around the world) crossed the Pacific, the journey occupied over three months. For modern steamships the trip is a matter only of weeks or even days. Clipper planes reduce the travel time even more. Europe is scarcely farther from us than the next county was from our grandfathers.

Keeping in mind that geography represents something that is moving, and that the continents tend to move closer together in a

* The sources used in the preparation of this lecture have intentionally been confined to published reports, analyses, and news items, which have appeared in publications with a national circulation. In short, *all* the sources are readily available to anyone. This procedure insures that no information is disseminated that is not common knowledge.

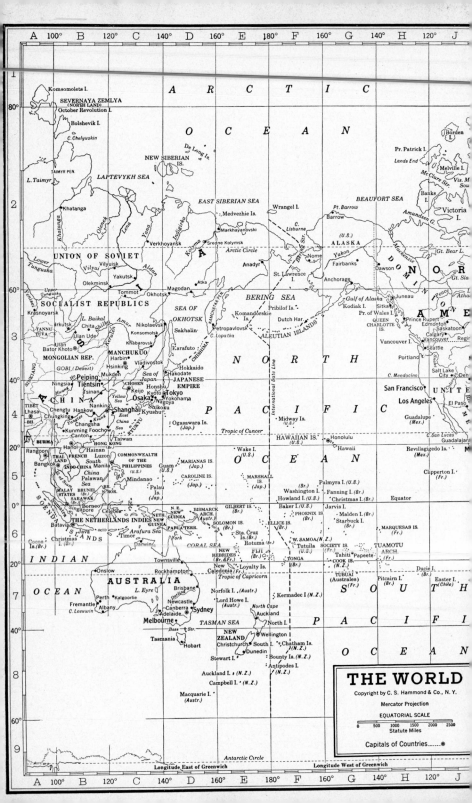

THE WORLD

Copyright by C. S. Hammond & Co., N. Y.

Mercator Projection

EQUATORIAL SCALE

Statute Miles

0   500   1000   1500   2000   2500

Capitals of Countries......⊙

Longitude East of Greenwich   Longitude West of Greenwich

Antarctic Circle

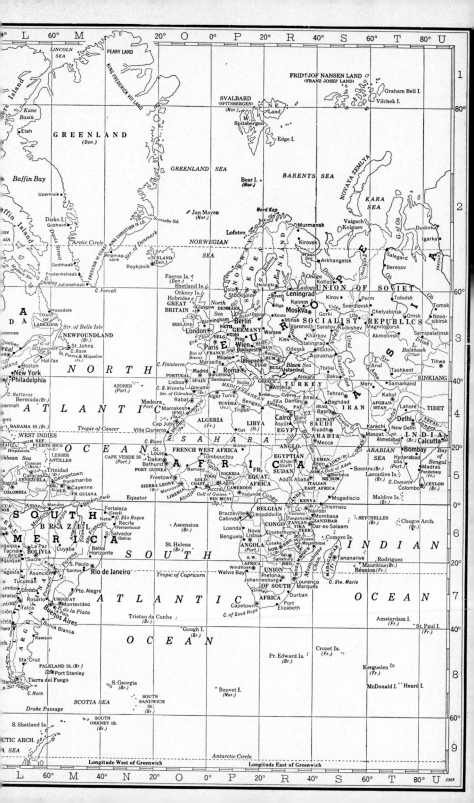

time sense, one concludes that we are more than ever a part of the world, whether or not we wish to be. Many people have tried to show that the oceans that surround the Americas represent such an obstacle that invasion of this continent is well-nigh impossible. Too often is it forgotten that history has more often proved that oceans are highways. How did the colonists reach these shores? By sea. How did the British spread all over the world, transplanting their civilization to the corners of the earth? By sea. If one looks at the map a bit more carefully, it immediately becomes apparent that the United States is surrounded by broad routes leading directly to the American continent, rather than by impassable barriers. Moreover, there are routes leading to our flanks; consider the distance from Africa to South America—so apparent from the map.

Obviously, our nation must defend, if not control, the sea routes leading to the North American continent. On maneuvers you frequently went into bivouac; you used roads, trails, or other approaches to arrive there. Upon arrival, everyone could not just go off to sleep; it was necessary to establish outposts on the approaches, both to give warning and to hold off an enemy in case of attack until the main group was able to wake up and take up a position. Our nation, secure for the time being on this continent, has designated and organized a force to defend the approaches thereto. This force we call the Navy.

Now a navy is not something that is thought about and organized on a moment's notice. True, we might convert a number of liners, freighters, fishing boats, etc., but the building of modern warships is bound to take time—lots of time. Moreover, the correct *type* of ship must be constructed, depending on the task we wish to assign to our Navy. In short, for what do we expect to use our Navy?

The whole plan for the use of the Navy is based on certain general principles. These general principles simmer down to what sailors call *sea power*. This term means the power to control, or dispute the control of, a portion of the high seas or the oceans of the world. It rests upon all elements of the national power, but more particularly upon fighting ships and aircraft, merchant marine, and bases.[1]

It remained for an American naval officer, Admiral Alfred Thayer Mahan, to point out to the world the real meaning of sea power. In a book, *Influence of Sea Power on History*, he showed how often in the past sea power had been the determining factor in war. Moreover, he showed how a navy that was prepared to take the offensive would seize sea power from an enemy. His works were read by naval men around the world—the navies of Britain and Germany, especially the latter, being greatly influenced by Mahan's teachings. It was he who first pointed out the importance of the capital ship.

The term *ships* covers several types. At the base of the structure is the *capital ship* or the *battle-ship* or the *ship of the line* (all are different names for the same thing). Every ingenuity of man is called into play to make the battle-ship the strongest thing afloat. It has heavy armor, the biggest guns; in short, it is a floating machine or fort capable of delivering or withstanding the heaviest blows. Just the presence of battle-ships in a Navy, just the threat that they constitute, is ofttimes of vital importance not only in the relative sea power of different nations, but in world politics and international relations.

A modern addition to navies is the aircraft carrier. Carriers have one principal weakness: they are vulnerable to attack. Therefore they carry fighter planes to drive off hostile aircraft. For protection against surface craft they have bombers and torpedo planes. But these are in general insufficient, so for real protection, carriers are employed with other warships. Moreover, carriers carry reconnaissance aircraft, which permits the surface ships which they are accompanying to find the location of an enemy force. The mission of carriers is to launch planes which will bomb or torpedo enemy vessels at distances greater than the range of naval guns on surface ships. The Japanese have employed them with great boldness in attack. The American Navy has used them skillfully in daring raids on Japanese-held islands where important installations have been bombed. Tremendous developments in the numbers and fighting capacities of ship-borne aircraft may be expected.

Lighter than the battle-ship is a vessel of war called a *cruiser*. Lighter-armored and with smaller guns, this ship is built for speed rather than power. It is employed to make contact with an enemy, for scouting, and for raiding.

The *destroyer* is built almost entirely for speed. It acts as the eyes and ears of a fleet on the surface, besides being used for scouting, patrolling, convoy work, and for any other task where it is not desired to risk larger ships.

Since the battle-ship is the mainstay of a fleet, every effort must be made to insure that battle-ships are not lost except on missions which involve the very safety of the nation itself. The building of battle-ships is a matter of years; they are irreplaceable in time of war. If a nation loses its capital ships, its standing as a sea power is immeasurably reduced. The loss of the *Prince of Wales* and the *Repulse* off the coast of Malaya is an example of the disaster to sea power that results when capital ships are risked in a mission for which they are not eminently suited. When Japanese aviation, apparently land-based, destroyed these two great vessels, they demolished the weight of British sea power in the Indian Ocean and opened the way for control by lighter Japanese naval units off the Malayan and Burman coasts. By the loss of these two capital ships, British sea power in the Indian Ocean was tragically affected. This was the most startling instance in the war exposing the vulnerability of "floating forts" to attack by land-based aviation.

The story of the present conflict includes one of the epic naval fights of all time, the engagement culminating in the sinking of the *Bismarck*. It is especially interesting because it involved capital ships and aircraft.

On May 22, 1941, a German capital ship, identified as the *Bismarck*, was observed leaving Bergen, Norway, accompanied by a cruiser. Moving rapidly by a route which took her to the north of Iceland, the *Bismarck* was met off the coast of Greenland by two British capital ships, the twenty-two-year-old *Hood* and the new *Prince of Wales*, with accompanying lighter craft. In the engagement that followed, a shot from the *Bismarck* apparently caused an explosion in the powder hold of the *Hood*. The ship blew up, with the loss of almost her entire crew. The other British battle-ship, the *Prince of Wales*, and the *Bismarck* were both somewhat damaged.

In the fog and the mist the *Bismarck* was able to draw off toward the south. Contact was maintained by the British for a time, but eventually lost. Now the *Bismarck* was a new ship. Every German ingenuity had been called upon to make her the most powerful thing afloat. No stretch of the imagination is needed to picture the consternation which followed in the headlines of the press of the world. Here was a ship at large that could possibly if not probably sink any single unit of the British Navy.

But by this time the British ships were converging from all directions of the compass: from the north, from the British Isles, and even from the Mediterranean. In the meantime, the fleeing *Bismarck* had been located by the British with an American-built flying boat, a type called a Catalina. From the deck of an aircraft carrier of the Mediterranean force, the *Ark Royal*, an airplane was dispatched that launched a torpedo at the *Bismarck*. Luckily this torpedo damaged the *Bismarck's* steering mechanism. Two battleships, the *King George V* and the *Rodney*, now approached the *Bismarck* and started pouring big shells into her. Badly damaged and well-nigh helpless, the huge ship was finally sunk by a torpedo from a cruiser.[2]

Altogether the *Bismarck* had suffered hits by seven torpedoes, twenty 14- to 16-inch shells, and 300 8-inch shells. She had caused a loss to the British Navy of a twenty-two-year-old capital ship, but this represented only one-sixteenth of the British strength, while the loss of the *Bismarck* meant that Germany had lost one-quarter of her capital ships.

Many experts have drawn conclusions from this engagement. Perhaps it was demonstrated that a single big ship when loose in the oceans can act somewhat like a panzer force on land. At any rate her presence will force an entire fleet to stop what it is doing and hunt her down. On the other hand, it was shown that one loose ship, no matter what her size, is scarcely a challenge to a nation's sea power.[3]

Without the help of the airplane it is doubtful whether the *Bismarck* could have been found, let alone sunk. Moreover, without the airplanes from the aircraft carrier, *Ark Royal*, the *Bismarck's* steering gear would not have been damaged, setting the big ship up for the kill. This does not mean, however, that the airplane has superseded the battle-ship. The engagement did prove that air power for a fleet was vital; but planes need bases. In the open ocean these bases are supplied by the carrier. The airplane enhances the power of the capital ship; the carrier brings the airplane close enough, and on its part the capital ship provides protection for the carrier.[4]

The true reason why Germany risked the *Bismarck* probably will not be told fully until after the war, if then. It gives "experts" something to write about, at least. She must have been on an important mission. As for the British, they risked their capital ships, but little could they afford to do otherwise; their hands were forced.

Returning for a moment to a consideration of our own Navy and the ships that help make our own sea power, let's not neglect one more important thing: the men. It has been said the personal is to the physical as three is to one. These huge floating battle machines do not run themselves. Ships are fought because of the spirit of the men inside them, from the captain on the bridge to the men deep down in the hold. The personnel of a ship must not only be trained down to the last man, but the personnel must have a fighting spirit—the same spirit that made the Americans cross the Delaware, or fight at Bunker Hill or at Chancellorsville or at Cold Harbor, or in the Meuse-Argonne. Proud indeed are the sailors in the American Navy of the tales told about their forebears on the sea. At Annapolis they display Perry's old flag with the motto for all to see: "Don't give up the ship." It calls to mind how Lawrence in the *Chesapeake,* with a green, drunk, and mutinous crew, was attacked on June 1, 1813, by the *Shannon,* one of the best and strongest ships in the British Navy. The *Chesapeake* was soon helpless. Lawrence was twice wounded, but, as he was carried below, he cried out the immortal words: "Don't give up the ship." [5] Proud too are sailors, as well as all Americans, of Farragut at Mobile Bay on August 5, 1864. The defenses of Mobile consisted of three forts and a triple line of torpedoes or mines. As Farragut attacked the defenses, his leading ship struck a torpedo and sank. The ships following stopped and began to head back; the rear ships came on. Soon it looked as though there would be hopeless confusion. Seeing this, Farragut shouted, "Damn the torpedoes! Full speed ahead!"

and headed his flagship at full speed for the line of torpedoes. Strange to say, the other ships all followed and all passed safely into the bay. But every man thought each moment was his last. This spirit does not die. During the last struggle, on May 4, 1917, United States Destroyer Division 8 arrived in Queenstown, Ireland, and reported for duty. When asked when he would be ready for sea, Commander Taussig replied, "We are ready now, sir; that is, as soon as we finish refueling." Such is the spirit of the American Navy.

What is our Navy supposed to do today? The answer is ready on the lips of all: "Protect the United States." Since that is an undebatable point, the divergence of opinion will be on how this is to be done.

One way would be, let us suppose, for our Navy simply to occupy harbors on either coast, wait for an enemy to come, and when he did, go out to meet him. If we had to defend just a small island, this plan might work, but it would be comparable to a football team's waiting under its own goal-posts throughout the game, not doing anything until the opponents were about to make a touchdown. Consider the length of the coastline of the United States. Employment of our Navy as was outlined would just invite attack. More important, such a short-sighted policy would have permitted Japan or Germany to establish bases in this hemisphere to serve as jumping-off places.

So, if our naval policy is a realistic one, it must insure (a) that no unfriendly powers establish bases on this side of the world, (b) that we have bases at sufficient distance from our coast so our Navy will not be tied to the mainland, and (c) that our ships are so built that they can operate a long way from home, since we cannot set up bases wherever in the world we might like. Moreover, we must have more ships than the other fellow; we must have more powerful ships than he. In short, our whole Navy must be the best. There is no use having second-best ships; they are just like the horse that comes in second—he does not even get a cheer. Maybe we can get some satisfaction from an athletic contest if we lose; we say that anyway our side played a good game. But naval warfare is played for keeps. There is no second chance. You either win or you are licked, and if you are licked, you are through.

Glancing again at the map, we see that the picture of our coast-line resolves itself into two coastlines, joined together by a canal. As long as the canal is open, a fleet may pass from one ocean to another, so that it can be employed against a power attacking from either direction. The only joker here is that, if Germany could get the French fleet, she and Japan might attack at the same time, or the Panama Canal might for some unforeseen reason be closed. If all our ships were gathered together, our fleet might be stronger than one of the attackers, but how about the line of seacoast that would be undefended? The answer to this is to have a Navy so strong, that, even when it is divided into two fleets, it will have superiority in both oceans. This means having a *two-ocean navy*. It also means having sufficiently strong land-based aviation so that control of the air may be maintained at all approaches to the points of attack.

On September 14, 1940, our government laid down a new naval policy calling for the organization and maintenance of a Navy capable of "major operations in both the Atlantic and Pacific."[6] This meant that in *each* ocean the United States would strive to keep a naval force that would protect her from any foreseen or unforeseen threat. In line with this policy, three fleets have been designated: the Pacific Fleet, the Asiatic Fleet, and the Atlantic Fleet.[7] Briefly, a fleet is analogous to an army; it is a naval force containing all the elements necessary for independent action within a given area. It is commanded by a full admiral.

Of course, as has already been brought out, a considerable amount of time must pass before the desire for ships for a "two-ocean Navy" can be translated into the ships themselves, actually sailing the seas. We cannot have a "two-ocean Navy" by simply wishing for it. Although in the War of 1812, we sent Perry up to Lake Erie and told him to build his own ships after he got there, he was faced by an enemy who also had to build his own ships. The building of a modern naval force takes years. Our government, fully alive to realities, has undertaken a tremendous building program.

Toward the close of the year 1941 we had seventeen battle-ships or capital ships. By 1946, or possibly sooner, we shall have thirty-two. Our number of aircraft carriers (now seven) will be increased almost threefold. Cruiser strength will be more than doubled. Likewise for destroyers and submarines. More important, the ships to be added to our Navy will be of the very newest type. Here is the table showing planned increases:

	1941	1946 or earlier
Battle-ships	17	32
Aircraft carriers	7	18
Cruisers	37	91
Destroyers	171	364
Submarines	113	185[8]

So much for fighting ships. Two other elements of sea power, *merchant marine* and *bases*, will now be discussed.

A merchant marine is essential to sea power. Broadly speaking, *merchant marine* means every ship that flies the flag of a nation that is not part of its actual naval forces. In order to control the sea routes, which is after all what we want from sea power, troops and supplies must be moved to various points. A merchant marine, too, is a training ground for sailors, and it also serves as a reservoir from which naval auxiliary craft can be drawn. Even by last summer there were 143 ships in our Navy that had been former ocean liners, freighters, tankers, trawlers, and pleasure yachts.[9]

In the past our people have not always been aware of the value of a merchant marine, although before the Civil War American ships occupied a major place in the carrying trade of the world. After the War of 1812, Americans were quick to realize the value of speed. So well did they apply their ideas in the building of ships that the carrying of mail and passengers across the Atlantic fell almost entirely into American hands. Then largely because of the California gold rush, a new demand was created for big and fast ships that could reach California in the shortest time. The ships built for this purpose were the famous "clippers." It was but a step to start service to the Far East, the clipper supplying the demand for speed.

But from the Civil War on, there was a decline in American shipping. During that war, many American-owned vessels were sold to British owners. At the completion of the Civil War, American mind and energy were more concerned with developing the continent. It was the day of "Go west, young man!" Most shipping under the American flag was confined to the Great Lakes.

The World War in 1914 found the United States almost dead as a maritime power. True, there were American ships that sailed the seas, but the total of United States tonnage formed only a small part of the world total.

But when we entered the war, we saw the importance of shipping and merchant marine. How could we attack the enemy unless our troops reached him in ships? We saw that we would have to depend on other nations, especially England. Suddenly we realized how the U-boat was playing havoc with the shipping of Great Britain. From January to June, 1917, German submarines sank nearly 4,000,000 tons of Allied shipping. If we were going to win we saw that we must do two things: reduce losses from U-boats and build more ships. Consequently, the United States embarked on the greatest shipbuilding program in history, and the American and British Navies started a U-boat campaign that reduced losses by half.

The war ended before the completion of the United States building program. It would seem that we might now become a maritime power with all the World War ships that we had. But the United States fell off again in merchant marine, this time for two reasons: other nations used government money to make up shipping losses for owners, and American ships cost more to operate because of the higher wages and better living conditions required for the crews.

But now our government is wide awake to the necessity of a merchant marine. As early as 1936 a Maritime Commission was set up. The President urged an emergency merchant fleet last January. The current shipbuilding program contemplates an expenditure of almost ten billion dollars for shipbuilding. Besides fighting and private vessels (the latter can be taken over by the government if it is so desired), it is expected that there will be built 500 high-quality cargo and passenger ships by 1948. In addition, within two years we should complete 200 emergency cargo ships, slow but suitable for convoy work; and 212 lend-lease ships.[10] Yet even these are yesterday's figures. Faced by the threat of German submarine attacks in the western Atlantic, and also by the necessity for carrying the war to the enemy, the United States government has tremendously enlarged its previously announced shipbuilding program. Already mass production methods never before seen in the marine world are being employed in new American shipyards whose designers have undertaken to challenge the impossible—and are succeeding.

The subject of bases has more than a passing interest for those in the Army. Bases must be defended. The Army is fitted for this task. Therefore, an efficient Army, capable of organizing task forces, is a necessary adjunct to sea power.

Bases are essential for both surface ships and aircraft. A ship is a machine, and a most complicated one. It must be refueled and refitted, not to mention repair of possible damage incurred in conflict with an enemy. And, while aircraft can be dispatched from a carrier, the vulnerability of carriers, especially in narrow waters, means that too much reliance cannot be placed on them; besides, they too need bases.

It should be observed, before we proceed, that in many cases land forces can attack a nation's sea power, either by capturing existing bases or by seizing land on which bases could be established. If we consider the map of Europe for a moment, this becomes plain. Britain is denied bases in Norway, as well as other places on the European Continent, because the Germans are there, and they got there mainly by the use of well-organized land forces. A German thrust through Spain to Gibraltar would result in the loss of a most important base to England, unless the thrust could be halted. Likewise, a German surprise thrust across the Atlantic to South America would injure the United States.

And we must not forget air power. If air bases can be set up sufficiently close, air power can harass a naval base to such an extent that it may become useless as a ship base. For example, the British use of Scapa Flow, one of their greatest bases, is severely restricted because it is too near to the source of German air power.

The location of American bases is tied in with the whole defense scheme of the nation. The remainder of this chapter will be devoted to a consideration of America's position in the world, and how her sea power can be used to defend her.

Let us make an estimate of the enemy. There is one on each side of the United States: Germany on the east and Japan on the west.

In October, the President of the United States said: "We know that we could not defend ourselves in Long Island Sound or San Francisco Bay. That would be too late. It is the American policy to defend ourselves wherever such defense becomes necessary under the complex conditions of modern warfare." At the same time, while announcing that it was our duty to extend more assistance to Britain and Russia, he remarked that Hitler has offered a challenge which we shall not tolerate.[11]

For present purposes, let us make our own estimate of the situation. The President has clearly stated our mission: to defend ourselves, not along our coasts, but at whatever distance, and by whatever means, circumstances demand. Consider the potential threats to the United States. From the east, Hitler has three routes of approach to this hemisphere: by way of Iceland and Greenland and Newfoundland; by way of Spain, the Azores, and Bermuda or Newfoundland; and by way of Dakar and Brazil. Considering the physical possibility of Germany's being able to use any of these routes, remember that twice, in the case of Norway and Crete, she attacked over water, that she has crushed eight European nations by military force, and that the mere threat of military persuasion has drawn several others into her orbit. Now as long as Hitler is fighting a major contest on the European Continent, or if he should suffer defeat, our problem in the Atlantic would be solved. To that end, we help Britain and Russia by every material means. But we cannot rely on others for a thing so vital as defense, hence in the end we must put our final trust in our own right arms. And to conclude, the means by which the reach of our good right arm is extended into the Atlantic is the possession of a number of bases, both ship and aircraft, at a sufficient distance from the shores of the United States so that any possible enemy will be met and defeated at a great distance from those shores; moreover, if *we* have the bases, Germany cannot seize them, provided we defend them.

To this end, in September of 1940, by a trade of destroyers with Britain, we acquired rights to build bases in Newfoundland and Bermuda, besides a number of islands in the Caribbean. From the map it is apparent that this deal constituted a first step in establishing bases on all possible routes of approach. To close the northern route, our government early last summer occupied Iceland to prevent its falling into Germany's hands. On the middle route there still remain the Azores; there has been some urging to seize them. To the south lies Dakar.

Germany's intentions with respect to Dakar must be inferred, but it is known that a railroad is being pushed across the Sahara from the Mediterranean toward that point.[12] While the harbor at Dakar would be a commercial rather than a military base because of its size, it is only 1700 miles from Brazil [13] and could easily serve as a jumping-off station for commercial exploitation of South America. And the Nazi pattern has repeatedly shown that commercial activity is followed by military.

So there still remains a weak spot in our Atlantic armor. Attempts have been made to strengthen it. Under the urging of Uruguay it was proposed that the United States be granted the right to build bases on the South American coast, especially at the mouth of the Rio de la Plata. But Argentina refused her assent.[14] The mouth of this river seems from the map to be, and is, off the direct route of approach, but its seizure by a strong unfriendly power would be a serious threat to the United States. Uruguay has one cruiser, three gunboats, and an army of 6000 men with which to defend this vital spot. This would be like one of our company baseball teams playing the New York Yankees.

But in general in the Atlantic we shall be a sea power. We have or shall have ships with the necessary aircraft, a merchant marine, and bases. We are already able to dispute control of the Atlantic with anyone. When our program is completed, our position will be so strong it will not permit even a dispute.

On the other side of the American continent there is another enemy—a nation that assumed an increasingly unfriendly stand, culminating in final treacherous attack: Japan. It will not be out of place here to outline briefly the reasons for her unfriendly attitude, since without a bit of such knowledge Japan's likely intentions cannot be understood.

Up until 1932, relations between the United States and Japan were friendly. Japan had silk to sell; we had cotton. You know how American women consider silk stockings—they would probably go hungry rather than do without; the Japanese needed cotton for their textile mills, and a large amount was purchased from the United States. The trouble started when the Depression hit (undoubtedly you all remember it!). American women were too broke to buy many silk stockings; this hit the Japanese silk-raising industry, and they had to buy less of our cotton. In Japan, the group which claimed it could lead Mr. Japanese Common Man out of depression and to a more abundant life was the militarists —including the Army and the Navy. Now our Army and Navy is responsible to the people. But in Japan, the Army and the Navy were responsible only to the Emperor. In other words, they could go off on a glorified raid into the territory of another nation, and could be called on the carpet not by the people's elected representatives, but only by the Emperor, and his hands were tied by tradition. So the Japanese militarists, especially the Army, went into Manchuria, brought on the China incident, were successful for a time, and finally bogged down. All the time these Army militarists kept up a propaganda by pamphlets and controlled press trying to convince Mr. Japanese Common Man that his position was getting better. But high casualty lists do not convince one that good times are here. Rationing of practically every item of normal use does not mean a more abundant life. All the fine promises of the militarists, especially those in the Army, had failed of fulfilment. Now the naval militarists had never looked with too much favor on the thrust to the mainland. They believed in the use of force to improve Japan's position just as much as the officials in the Army, but they wanted expansion to take place toward the south, eventually into the East Indies, with their fabulous wealth. (Remember, the East Indies were what Columbus was looking for when he bumped into America.) The struggle for control of trade with them has been the cause of innumerable bickerings and wars. But with the British and Dutch in control, the United States has hitherto been able to get what she wanted from that region; these two nations would sell to the buyer who had the money, and we had enough. But the whole Japanese militaristic scheme is to exploit, and to use this exploitation as a basis for further military power. When Japan looked south, we were vitally affected; our supply of rubber, our quinine, and our hemp, just to mention three articles, come from that region.

Our policy was not and never has been to prevent a peaceful Japan from having the same access to materials that we had. We surely indicated that in our own sales to Japan. In our international trade relations we did not follow a "dog in the manger" policy, but it became increasingly necessary for us to make sure that no other people would follow such a policy where it vitally affected us. You can readily note how vitally we are affected by enemy control of the islands off southern Asia. It has affected our economy, by denying us natural rubber. It even affects our health, by denying us quinine.

With that background, suppose that we make an estimate of the situation in the Pacific, even though it must be a very sketchy estimate. Obviously, if the United States could be reduced to an impotent state, the way for permanent Japanese militaristic control to the south of Asia would be assured. Japan by herself did not seem powerful enough to attack the United States and Britain single-handed. But with Britain's power inhibited by her war needs elsewhere, and with Japan's surprise attack upon Pearl Harbor, the road was open for the opportunistic Japanese to move toward those regions of vast wealth and resources that have been developed by other nations. To how great an extent Japan can consolidate her gains will depend upon how deeply the United States will be involved with Germany on the other side of the world. Certainly it is Germany's hope that we will tangle most intimately and desperately across the wide wastes of the Pacific with Japan. Certainly the Japanese hope that we will seek to crush Hitler first. Both hope that we will so divide our Navy that it will not have full striking power in either ocean.

With commendable foresight—and remember, in a realistic world we must deal with realities—the United States, as has already been observed, is building a Navy that can operate in both oceans. It is a race against time. It is a race to hold and to seize and to regain bases. The map inserted in Chapter VIII at page 102 shows our Pacific position better than a thousand words.

Bases on the mainland at Seattle, San Francisco, and San Diego will permit our ships to defend the actual coastline, if worst comes to worst; moreover, they will permit repair, in a comparatively quiet atmosphere, of possible damage to any ships which may be operating from our mid-Pacific bases. Better still, in Hawaii, and in Alaska at Sitka, Kodiak, and Dutch Harbor, we have, or are building, bases that will permit our naval combat units (including aircraft) to operate far from our shores; and of course it follows that these points are denied to Japan.[15]

The base at Manila, which was a bastion on the flank of a Japanese thrust to the south and a threat to any attempt for an ambitious eastward push, has been lost. But certainly as a base for ultimate operations against Japan and for severing the dangerously extended line of Japanese communications, a foothold on the Philippines will have to be secured again. There a people whose loyalty to the United States—which is a loyalty to their own interests—cannot be questioned will form an enormous and effective fifth column against the Japanese that have occupied their islands. They wait only for the time when America is prepared to strike.

The part that *bases* play in the broad picture of war affects the soldier vitally because Army task forces are necessary to defend the bases or to retake them if they are lost. Already Army units are occupying some. As danger threatens, others will undoubtedly be occupied or forces increased in those bases where American troops are already stationed.

What any part of the Army is doing concerns us all. And the activities of the Navy tremendously affect our land operations of the present and the future.

REFERENCE NOTES

[1] See *Encyclopedia Britannica* (1941), Vol. XX, p. 249, for a discussion of sea power.

[2] See *Life*, Vol. X, No. 23 (June 9, 1941), p. 53, for an account of the sinking.

[3] H. W. Hale, "The Lesson of the Bismarck," *New Republic*, Vol. 104, No. 22, p. 782.

[4] *Time*, Vol. 37, No. 23 (June 9, 1941), p. 43.

[5] United States Navy Recruiting Service, *Outstanding Events in United States Naval History* (NRB, 1940).

[6] *Newsweek*, Vol. 16, No. 12 (Sept. 23, 1940), p. 35.

[7] *Newsweek*, Vol. 17, No. 3 (Jan. 20, 1941), p. 34.

[8] *Newsweek*, Vol. 18, No. 17 (Oct. 27, 1941), pp. 31-32.

9 R. L. Pepperburg, in *Christian Science Monitor Magazine*, May 31, 1941, p. 3.

10 S. C. Davis, in *The Atlantic Monthly*, Vol. 168, No. 1 (July, 1941), p. 97.

11 *Vital Speeches*, Vol. 8, No. 2 (Nov. 1, 1941), p. 34.

12 *Life*, Vol. 11, No. 20 (Nov. 17, 1941), p. 132.

13 W. V. Pratt, "The Bases That Flank Dakar," *Newsweek*, Vol. 18, No. 9 (Sept. 1, 1941), p. 19.

14 *Newsweek*, Vol. 18, No. 2 (July 14, 1941), p. 16.

15 Corey Ford, "Alaska Gets Hot," *Collier's*, Vol. 108, No. 22 (Nov. 29, 1941), p. 23.

CHAPTER XXVII

ORGANIZATION OF AN ARMY AND ITS BRANCHES

In a previous chapter we took up the basic principles of organization. You will recall that they were: an organization must be flexible, it must be abreast of the times, it must have an object, the means at hand must be employed, and the human material must be taken into account.

Today we are going to cover the organization of our own Army. Now we could proceed in two routine ways. One way would be to start at the top—with the War Department—and work down. Another way would be to start with the squad and build up. We are going to approach the subject in neither way. While it might be a good plan to start with the squad, work through the platoon, company, etc., it seems that that plan would be like the man who goes swimming by first inserting a toe into the pool, followed by a gingerly testing with the leg, gradually getting wet all over. That is a painful way to swim; and it's a painful way to explain organization. We are going to leap in all at once, and the first thing that we shall consider will be a division.

THE DIVISION

What is a division? To most of us it is something that has become a part of our very lives, whether we are in one or not. We wear a shoulder patch telling the world that we are members of such and such a division. But how has it come about that they have a division for each of us to be in, or at least to work with? Is the answer that some one sat down one night over a couple of beers and thought that it would be a good idea to have divisions? Or did some past hero come out at reveille one morning and remark to his adjutant, "Maybe what the country needs is a good five-cent cigar, but what the Army needs is divisions"?

No divisions were born of necessity and cleverness in war. They were at first, and still are for that matter, a direct means of applying the principles of organization that we have already covered. And a division did not, like Topsy, just happen. The organization represents a long, slow process in organizing men for war. Well, then, if they did not always have divisions in armies, what did they have? And, what, after all, is a division?

Do you remember in a previous chapter that we mentioned hired soldiers? And undoubtedly you remember that a king in any particular nation hired an army, some of whose members might belong to the same nationality as the monarch but not necessarily. The Germans, the Swiss, and the Irish were especially good mercenaries. True, the tendency was for the various armies to contain more and more individuals of the same nationality as the monarch, but the principle of hiring soldiers persisted.

As a rule, the king did not hire individual soldiers. About 600 years ago he hired them by units which were called companies. The deal was made with an individual called the captain; this worthy received the pay for the whole company and distributed it; he was charged with the discipline of his company; he was charged with provisioning and even such medical care as the times permitted. The captain's men looked to him for everything; he was responsible for his company—it was his. He dickered with various monarchs and princes in order to receive the best pay for his men.

Now, some kings got tired of hiring mercenaries and tried to make themselves independent of foreign captains who had only their own selfish interests at heart. So efforts were made in some nations to organize companies of men who belonged to the same nation as the king. These companies, however, when organized followed the same organization as the mercenary companies; the captain was just as important an individual. The main difference was that the captain now, and hence all his men, possessed a loyalty to a monarch instead of just to their pocketbooks.

But we are supposed to be talking about fighting men. Fighting men had to be organized or grouped some way in order to wage war. The earlier forms of organization of higher units provided for an arrangement by which a number of companies were grouped under the captain of one of them for a particular action.

This senior captain was referred to as a captain-general. This grouping of companies soon became well established. In France the groups were called battalions. In Spain they were called *tercios*.

It is interesting to see how these armies operated. Let us take the Spanish. *Tercio* means "third," and that is exactly what the Spaniards meant. They organized an army so that it was divided into thirds; one *tercio*, or one third, was the van which was to engage the enemy initially; the next *tercio* or third would correspond to our main body; and the third *tercio* or third would be the rear. If everything went well, the three thirds or three *tercios* would line up for battle; one would be the right wing, one the center, and one the left wing. This sounds something like divisions, but was not. Why? Because each of the wings was made up of infantry. Artillery was employed separately by an artillery commander or by the commander-in-chief himself. If there was cavalry, it was employed by itself on the flanks.

This seems like a stiff organization, and it was. There was, however, an idea of advance guards and rear guards. A contemporary of Joan of Arc wrote a military text as early as 1465 about their duties (he called the advance guard the "discoverers of the country"). But it was not until the Seven Years' War (in the latter half of the eighteenth century) that anyone succeeded in marching an army in several columns with an advance guard for each.

It is realized that in this discussion up to the present point we have indicated that there was a stiffness in all armies. This was not always true. Frederick the Great, Gustavus Adolphus, Prince Eugene, Marlborough, Turenne, and Condé were all superb soldiers, and they did, it is true, bring a flexibility to the battlefield that has been the admiration of succeeding generations. But if one looks a bit closer, he is forced to the conclusion that their flexibility was the result of their genius and not of their organization. At any rate, their armies continued to fight in the formal fashion with a right wing, a left wing, and a center. Moreover their artillery was used in most cases as something separate from the infantry or the cavalry.

That brings us then to the division. Let's answer the question what a division was and is and get it over with. It is a fighting unit in which several regiments are grouped. But more important, the

unit contains not only regiments of troops which can close with
the enemy, such as infantry, cavalry, or armored units, but it also
contains artillery. And this should be firmly fixed in mind. The
Spanish *tercio* was not a division because it contained only infantry.
A division is capable of waging a battle all by itself, and as it
wages a battle as part of a larger force it fights a little battle all
by itself.

The division was born during the French Revolution. The
people of France had overthrown the noble or governing class,
they had killed their King; they were ready, they thought, to em-
bark on a new life of liberty, equality, and fraternity. However,
the reigning monarchs of other European countries looked with suspicion on the French experiment. They feared that the new ideas
would spread to their territories and that they might lose their
heads. The best way to prevent such a happening would be to
stamp out the new ideas in France. So they gathered their armies
and marched them toward the French frontier.

Now these armies were deemed the best in Europe. And in
France the old army had been broken up. Most of the officers who
had belonged to the noble class had fled the country in fear of
the guillotine and the mobs. The French had enthusiasm but lacked
a means of meeting the invader, who now numbered some 300,000
men. Enthusiasm might help, but it alone could not win battles.

Good ground was necessary for the old way of fighting a battle.
The commander himself must see what was going on so that he
could use his cavalry and artillery. If the French had attempted
to organize under the old principles, there is no telling what would
have happened. Remember, their army was new and was made up
of many recruits. Many of their officers were green, including
officers of high rank. But the French created the division, which
was, as we mentioned before, a grouping of a number of regiments
into a permanent organization with—and this was most important
—artillery. This plan permitted the French to meet the various
parts of the foreign armies on rough ground. There was no waiting while a battle line had to be formed; there was no scurrying
of aides and messengers to bring up artillery. It was there. Moreover, it became easy to march in several columns. Suppose one was
attacked, it had its artillery. Each part of the French Army was

capable of carrying on a sustained action by itself. It was not necessary to mass the whole force before opening combat.

Napoleon improved the organization, but he fully appreciated
the value of the division and built his army around it. If he desired
he could combine several; and he did on most occasions. And
while we do not want to question the brilliance of the campaigns
of Napoleon, or the fact that he employed great masses of artillery,
we must remark that he owed no small part of his success to the
divisional organization.

Is a division the same thing today? It is, except that more complicated war has made the division a more complicated unit. It
still remains a grouping of regiments composed of troops that can
close with the enemy.

It naturally was found that artillery was not enough to insure
the advance of the regiments. Artillery could assist the regiments
only *by fire*. In many cases something besides fire was necessary.
There were streams to be crossed, roads to be repaired, enemy obstacles to be removed. Therefore, engineers were included in the
division. And from time to time other types of troops have been
assigned to divisions. The principles, however, have remained the
same.

ORGANIZATIONS BELOW THE DIVISION IN SIZE

During this discussion we have not yet considered brigades and
regiments. Originally a brigade was a grouping of several regiments for battlefield flexibility and to make command easier. It
was not like a division because it contained only soldiers of one
branch. It remains the same today.

While the regiment, too, contains soldiers from a single branch,
it represents something more. You remember that we mentioned
companies, especially mercenary companies. Now the Germans
were especially active as mercenaries. A young man would go off
to the wars to make his fortune somewhat as a young man today
might go off to work in the oil fields. The would-be mercenary
could not just go off by himself, however; he had to join some
one's company. There were a large number of German mercenary
companies, both cavalry and infantry; and in the employ of a

certain monarch it was observed that several companies would be from the same district. If these companies were put into the line together, they would fight better. As this became the practice, it was natural for these companies to combine into a permanent organization, if for nothing more than to further their bargaining power. Gradually, it became the custom to group a number of companies, not only for a particular war, but permanently into an organization known as a regiment. A permanent leader was installed; he was called a colonel. Notably, however, the regiment did not include men from different branches. Infantry regiments and cavalry regiments remained distinct and separate, and neither included artillery. It was something like masons and carpenters wanting to belong to different unions.

In Spain, too, one finds the beginning of a regimental organization. Remember the *tercio*. Now, many Germans served in the Spanish armies, and they began to look on the *tercio* as they did on a regiment. Moreover, soldiers who were not mercenaries saw the advantage of the regimental organization. France and England in time formed regiments. The important thing about the regiment in all countries is the tradition that is built around its organization. The regiment was a permanent home to the soldier. It might sustain frightful losses, but its spirit was something that did not die. It might have four or twenty companies, but it was still a regiment. No one but a soldier can appreciate what a regiment means.

When permanent regiments were established about 300 to 350 years ago, the number of companies varied greatly; some regiments had thirty companies, some only ten. So an organization known as a battalion came into general use. This was a group of companies, comprising about 800 men. It became customary to estimate the strength of a command by the number of battalions, a practice which is still used.

This was the case with the infantry. The cavalry regiment was divided into squadrons. However, the squadron was about the size of a troop of American cavalry and has remained that way in European armies. In the American tradition the squadron is about half the size of a battalion of infantry.

But you remember that we said that organization must be flexible, that it will change according to the times and the arms available. We in our own time, just within the past few years, have witnessed the inauguration of a new organization: the *combat team*. A combat team is a grouping of a basic unit such as a regiment of infantry or a brigade of cavalry with an appropriate amount of artillery, engineers, and medical units. The big point of a combat team is that these attached units train with the basic unit, so that all the commanders know each other and know what the other one is likely to do; the enlisted men and the officers of all the units become used to working together. Then when combat is imminent, or even before, the combat team marches as a unit, goes into the battle as a unit, and in the battle functions as a team because it has practised as one. It carries the principles of the division down to smaller units. General Marshall recently summed up a combat team as follows: "It is a team of many parts, the decisive element of which remains the same little-advertised, hard-bitten foot soldier with his artillery support."

A task force, as the name implies, is one created to perform a specific task. But the force is not organized on the spot. The Germans are the ones who conceived the idea of task forces. What the German High Command does first (after getting its orders from Hitler) is to decide what the task is. Let us suppose that the Germans have decided to grab off an island in the Atlantic. Conduct of the task force is not left to depend on coöperation between army, navy and air forces, which will vary with the whims of commanders in each instance, but is controlled by issuing mission orders to all the branches involved and appointing a supreme commander to carry them out. He may be an army, navy, or air officer, but after he is appointed, any unit which becomes a part of the task force is subject to his orders, whether the units are from his branch or not. Then decision is made as to what the task force should consist of. Suppose that to seize an island in the Atlantic it is found that six destroyers and a number of transports are needed. These come from the navy. A determined number of airplanes come from the air forces. And the army furnishes the required number of divisions, or other units in the proportion required for the particular task to be accomplished. Then the elements of a task force train together, and train in view of their mission. For example, the infantry in General Rommel's task force, which was formed for duty in Libya, trained in heavy clothing to accustom themselves to heat; they trained along the seashore to accustom themselves to operating over sandy country. They were composed of units especially developed for the operations they were to undertake. So far as ordinary tables of organization were concerned, they threw away the books.

WHAT IS AN ARMY?

As for an army, we must fix in our minds what an army means. Just the word *army* means two things. Used one way, the expression alludes to all the land forces of the United States as distinguished from the sea forces, the Navy. But the word *army* also means something else: an *army*, or more properly, a *field army*. This force is a combat unit, but instead of consisting of a number of regiments, as was the case of the division, it is made up of a number of divisions. In order to simplify the army commander's task, especially if his army is large, divisions are usually grouped into corps. The corps is a unit which consists of two or more divisions.

You remember that the division was made up of a number of regiments that could close with the enemy, and forces like artillery and engineers that would help their divisions in their tasks. For example, a corps has a cavalry regiment, half horse and half mechanized. This regiment can be used to seek out an enemy, to guard the flanks, to serve any number of purposes so that the divisions will not have to fritter away their strength doing these essential things. Both the army and the corps usually have extra artillery with which they can support a division which has tough going. They have engineer troops for special missions such as building a big pontoon bridge.

A field army may have five different kinds of divisions. Though all seem different, there is one striking similarity. All are made up of regiments that can close with an enemy, together with troops which can help them to do it, artillery and engineers.

Above the field army, there is an organization known as General Headquarters, better known by the letters *GHQ*. General

Headquarters has a number of troops known as the "GHQ Reserve" with which it can reinforce the various field armies for special missions, or which can be used to fill out task forces. Armored forces, tank battalions, and recently tank destroyer battalions, and special air forces are examples of GHQ troops. When these GHQ troops complete their mission or task, they are drawn back into GHQ Reserve.

If you pored over the organization tables of a division you would see that there are numerous other units in a division besides combat units, such as quartermaster and medical units, M.P. companies (we all know about these), ordnance companies, headquarters companies, etc., etc. These are concerned with administration, supply, and evacuation. Before taking up the duties of such units, we must understand what these terms mean and, more important, we must understand something else: the difference between tactical organization and administrative organization, and the difference between the expressions *tactical units* and *administrative units*.

First, you *must* know what *tactics*, TACTICS, means. Briefly, it is movement of troops on or up to the battlefield to win battles; it is the disposing and maneuvering of individuals and units for battle in accordance with the strategy adopted by the high command. What, then, is *strategy*, STRATEGY? The term applies to the big picture; it is used in direction of campaigns, the planning of operations, and the fighting of battles to win wars. A tactical unit, then, is one that can be moved or used as a unit on the battlefield, or during operations that are leading up to a battle. A squad, a platoon, a troop or company, a battalion or squadron, a regiment, a brigade, a division, a corps, an army—all are tactical units, because they are units that the commander employs to win his part of a particular battle. Each unit has a commander responsible to the next higher one for the movement and the employment of the unit in the engagement. In this connection, it is interesting to note that our Field Service Regulations specify that the battalion is the basic tactical unit, and for this reason higher commanders think in terms of the employment of battalions, although the battalion is itself composed of a number of smaller units (companies, platoons, squads, etc.), and the battalion, likewise, is itself a part of larger units (regiments, brigades, divisions, etc.). In modern war, however, the squad, which is the smallest organized unit, has high importance as a tactical unit.

We talk of "good tactics" or "poor tactics." *Good tactics* means that the commander has moved and employed his tactical units in such a way that full use is made of their power. For example, it probably would be poor tactics if a corporal attacked a machine-gun with his squad head on; he might lose all his men. It might be good tactics if he worked his squad around in rear of the machine-gun and captured it.

On maneuvers you constantly heard the expressions *the tactical situation* and *the tactical plan*, or simply the *situation* and the *plan*. All the term *tactical situation* means is this: the location of the various tactical units at any particular time. Of course, consideration is given to the size of the units. The situation of a platoon would show where each squad was; the situation of a division would show where each brigade, regiment, or combat team was. The *tactical plan* shows what the commander expects to do with each of his units to accomplish his mission. The tactical plan of an army might take several days to fulfil, while that of a platoon might take only a few minutes.

To repeat: a tactical unit is a fighting unit that can be moved on the battlefield to further the wishes of the commander—to permit him to accomplish his tactical plan.

You hear so often in the Army the word *administrative*, AD-MINISTRATIVE. You hear, too, of administrative units. What is an administrative unit? You get a new pair of shoes, eat Spam sandwiches on maneuvers, draw gas for a truck, send your laundry, have a tooth pulled, get a furlough, have accurate records kept of your service, buy a package of cigarettes or a couple of beers, and last, but not least, get paid. This is not actual fighting, so it is all called administration. Good administration means that everything arrives on time and in sufficient quantity for the combat troops.

Every combat unit is a tactical unit, but in order to cut down paper work only half are administrative. An army, a division, a regiment, and a company are administrative units besides being tactical units, because their commanders handle administrative matters. This does not mean, however, that the commanders of the

in-between units are not concerned with good administration, because only by such can units be ready for combat. However, the
in-between commanders are relieved of the details and therefore
the squad, platoon, battalion, and brigade have little to do directly
with administrative detail.

Each of the administrative units has an organization to carry
on the details of all this administration. In the regiment there is a
headquarters company, troop, or battery, and in a division there
are similar and larger organizations. Now do not get the idea that
because these organizations are concerned mostly with administrative matters that life in them is any less dangerous than in the
front line, because the delivery of supplies in a combat area must
be carried out if the combat troops are to be successful. Do not
think that these administrative troops can simply find a hole and
hide. They can't; and often their work is more exhausting and
hazardous than operations in the front line itself.

Later in this course, you will have a lecture on staff work, what
it means and how it operates. At that time you will understand
more fully this whole administrative picture.

THE ARMS

The remainder of this discussion will be devoted to branches of
the service. Now you are already familiar to a certain extent with
this subject. You know that the purpose of present-day branches
is to permit men to specialize, in order that the whole team can
function better and win. This idea of specialization was touched
upon in the first lecture; it is unnecessary to review it here.

At the beginning let us discuss the meaning of *arms* and *services*.
It is the duty of the Arms to engage and overcome the enemy;
it is the job of the Services to help the Arms in their combat
missions by relieving them of any mental concern or diversion
of energy over problems of supply, administrative duties, or
evacuation.

The Arms are: Infantry, Cavalry, Field Artillery, Coast Artillery Corps, Air Corps, Corps of Engineers, and Signal Corps. Some
troops of the Chemical Warfare Service also have combat functions. The other subdivisions, such as the Quartermaster Corps,

Medical Corps, Ordnance Department, and so on, are the Services. Recently the tank, which in our Field Service Regulations has no official place, has developed as a special arm distinct from those mentioned above, and hence will be so treated in the present discussion. In field forces tanks are usually grouped into the Armored Division, which is a special armored team of tanks, infantry, cavalry, and field artillery, with the necessary services to sustain it, all motorized and fighting from armored vehicles.

The Infantry

An understanding of the role played by modern infantry begins with an understanding that *principles remain though methods change.* The Infantry is the arm which must close with the enemy and defeat him, or which must hold the ground that the enemy is trying to occupy. Infantry is an old branch. For over 400 years, or since the invention of firearms, it has been employed in war to deliver fire and to close with the enemy with cold steel and annihilate him.

The principal weapons of the Infantry are still the rifle and bayonet, but the number of men so armed has steadily decreased. An increasing number of automatic arms has been included in the infantry organization, besides weapons which have artillery effect, like small cannon and mortars.

But the Infantry must still fight at close range; it must close with the enemy. By a combination of fire and movement, and sometimes by shock action in the form of the bayonet, it is the arm which in the end will occupy the enemy's position. Of course, in days past Infantry fought in a mass. Increased use of fire has forced Infantry to adopt open formations, to utilize all available cover, to avoid any open area. But this simply means that more and more reliance must be placed on the small unit, on sub-leaders, and on the individual soldier. The individual has increasingly become a thinking, planning tactical unit.

Hence the necessity of thorough training, not only for the men carrying or operating weapons, but for everyone connected with the Infantry.

Regardless of the amount of transportation used, the Infantry remain foot troops. Motor transportation can bring Infantry near the battlefield more quickly, but on the field itself they must fight as foot soldiers. *The ability to march long and well is more important today than ever.*

One more point should be mentioned in connection with the Infantry: its power to dig in. When the Infantry has seized ground, the enemy will, if he possibly can, try to retake it. In order to prevent recapture, the foot soldier must dig in. As it takes an Infantry battalion about nine hours of hard work to prepare a reasonably effective position, one sees at once the importance of the pick and shovel. "An ounce of sweat may save a quart of blood."

The Cavalry

The Cavalry, like the Infantry, is an old branch. It owes its origin, as we know it, to the mounted knight in armor of the Middle Ages. Of course, ever since the first man tamed the first horse, there have undoubtedly been men who rode to war on horses, but it has only been in our civilization that gunpowder has been effective in wars; in our civilization the Cavalry has been forced to contend with firearms, and, too, it has been the only Cavalry that has had firearms to use.

Cavalry at one time represented the method of war of the wealthy class. When every man had to arm himself, only the rich could afford horses. But during the Thirty Years' War, about 300 years ago, two important innovations were made. First, infantry men were mounted on horses which could take them quickly over the battlefield to a point where they could dismount and attack as Infantry. These mounted infantrymen were called dragoons. Secondly, the Swedish King, Gustavus Adolphus, began to make ordinary soldiers into an organized cavalry. Through many ups and downs the idea of a mounted soldier who could fight on foot has persisted. It remained for Americans such as Jeb Stuart and Bedford Forrest in our own Civil War to get the full value of the mounted man, who could fight either mounted or dismounted and who could bring to the battlefield mobility combined with fire power.

Most of what we said about the Infantry applies to the modern

American Cavalry. And then it has one more thing: a higher degree of battlefield mobility. But its organizations are only about half the strength of similar Infantry organizations, hence they are not capable of a sustained attack or defense like the Infantry.

The foregoing remarks apply to horse cavalry. The addition of scout cars, automatic arms, motors for transportation, and so on have not changed the backbone of the Cavalry: the trooper with his horse. More important, to you who are in other branches, remember this: that the Cavalry does have battlefield mobility far superior to foot troops, so if you are ever opposed by Cavalry, WATCH YOUR FLANKS.

The Field Artillery

Coming to the Field Artillery, it has and has had in the past one principal mission: to utilize its fire to beat down the enemy, so that our forces can close with him and complete his destruction. The history of the development of artillery is most interesting. Of course, artillery, as we know it today, dates from the introduction of gunpowder. When it was found that a projectile could be thrown from a tube by the explosion of a charge of powder, armies were eager to employ this means to help them win.

A new note, however, was struck in all armies by the development of the artillery branch. We have already remarked that armies were formerly made up partly if not largely by mercenaries. But the making of cannon was an expensive proposition, so it became the custom for a king to organize his artillery on a more permanent basis. At first, cannon were largely used for siege work and in order to hasten the battering of walls. Some of the cannon used about 300 to 400 years ago were huge; some of the larger pieces required the efforts of thirty-five horses to move them. But men saw that if artillery was to be employed on the battlefield the weight of the pieces had to be made less, so experiment and effort were made in this direction, until guns were lightened and could readily be moved.

It was another step to employ artillery on the battlefield as a mobile unit, but with the short ranges of the artillery it was necessary to move it in order to make it effective against an enemy. In the nineteenth century two most important inventions came into general use; the rifled cannon, which increased range and accuracy, and the invention of indirect laying. This latter meant that the artillery could remain out of sight and by using observers and mathematical calculation could fire at troops which could not see the artillery. Moreover, the improvement in powder and steels made artillery capable of ranges which had formerly not even been dreamed of. So it is no longer necessary to move artillery physically about the battlefield; its fire can be shifted from one place to another where it will do the most good. Whether troops belong to infantry divisions, cavalry divisions, or armored divisions, they are going to be affected by artillery. Their own artillery is on call to help them by laying heavy fire on enemy installations which otherwise could be captured only by heavy casualties; it will knock out the enemy artillery; and it will deliver fire on rear areas through which enemy supports and reserves may be advancing. On the other hand, troops must know that the enemy also will have artillery. It can fire on troops that cannot see it. Therefore, our troops must know what cover means.

At present, our light artillery, that is, the artillery that is part of a division, is in a state of change. A "howitzer" is being substituted for the "gun."

The Coast Artillery

As for the Coast Artillery Corps, much that has been said about the Field Artillery applies here. The point for the soldier to remember is that in general the bigger guns are manned by the Coast Artillery. As the name implies, the Coast Artillery is charged with the operation of coast-defense guns. Since these guns may have to engage battle-ships or other warships which have big guns, the coast-defense guns must be big. Furthermore, they must have sufficient range to engage the enemy ships at a distance. These big guns are sometimes permanently installed around crucial points such as harbors; sometimes they are mounted on railway carriages so they can be shifted to threatened points. The Coast Artillery is also charged with mining harbors and other crucial points.

A comparatively recent task assigned to the Coast Artillery is anti-aircraft defense. This is possibly more interesting to the mem-

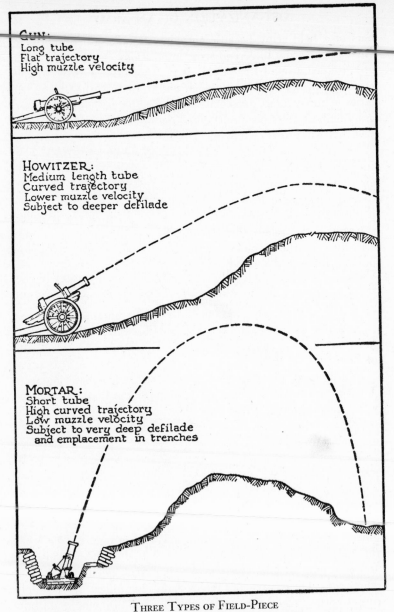

GUN:
Long tube
Flat trajectory
High muzzle velocity

HOWITZER:
Medium length tube
Curved trajectory
Lower muzzle velocity
Subject to deeper defilade

MORTAR:
Short tube
High curved trajectory
Low muzzle velocity
Subject to very deep defilade
and emplacement in trenches

THREE TYPES OF FIELD-PIECE

The sketches show the influence of the barrel length on the muzzle
velocity and trajectory of the projectile

bers of a field army because anti-aircraft units are properly included in an army to defend army installations. Besides, these units are grouped around large cities or in other crucial areas, to keep attacking planes high up in the air and to destroy them. The batteries of anti-aircraft guns must detect and hit targets that fly several hundred miles per hour. They must also be highly mobile so that they can protect a moving army.

The anti-aircraft forces are being equipped with a more powerful gun. The shells have time fuses which are set to burst in the air around the enemy's airplanes, so that it is not necessary actually to hit an airplane to destroy it. A so-called "mechanical brain" automatically computes the right direction for pointing the guns and transmits it electrically to dials for each gun. In order to aim properly then, all the members of the crew have to do is keep two pointers on each dial together.

Powerful searchlights help illuminate targets at night. Sound locators tell from which direction aircraft is approaching. Observers in a larger circle give warning to the whole anti-aircraft defense.

Now this seems to lead up to the Air Forces, *but they are going to be covered in a separate section*, so we shall go on to the Corps of Engineers.

In a division, the Engineers are known as Combat Engineers. This is the first arm discussed whose principal job is to work rather than to fight. While they are equipped to fight as infantry, modern war has made their work so essential that they are used as combat troops only if absolutely necessary.

All armies are committed to the use of mechanized and motorized equipment, but unless the roads and bridges are kept in good condition, this equipment may become a liability rather than an asset. Moreover, the breaking-up or demolition of roads and bridges can delay an enemy, as we all saw on maneuvers. The Engineers are specialists in these things. They not only do the work themselves but show the other troops how to do it. They construct and give help to others in constructing road blocks, or in their demolition. They install and remove anti-tank mines. They supply tools to other troops for special jobs. Besides surveying and drafting jobs, Engineers make and reproduce maps for the other troops. They pump, filter, and chlorinate water for the other troops.

Most of their activities are carried out under the most difficult and hazardous conditions. Throwing a foot-bridge across a river in the face of enemy fire, or waiting until the last possible moment before blowing up a bridge in the face of an advancing enemy are not recommended for the curing of nervous disorders. This foregoing applies to Engineers as combat troops. Their function as a service will be discussed in the next chapter.

The Signal Corps

The Signal Corps provides and maintains communication. Signal Corps units are not attached to units below the division, but the Signal Corps does have an interest in lower units in that it supervises the training of Communications personnel and supplies material for signal purposes. Of course, the development of radio and wire communication has made the Signal Corps mean to most of us a number of men with ear-phones, or a truck going by in a cloud of dust with a wire trailing after. But in old armies signals were just as important to transmit commands. We have already mentioned the Spanish *tercio*. One of the highest-paid individuals in the *tercio* was the band leader who trained the trumpeters to blow the proper signals. More important, he was supposed, with his superior musical ear, to interpret the calls of the enemy, so that the Spanish commander would know what the enemy was going to do.

Today signal communication is more important than ever. Well-trained Signal Corps and other communications personnel are essential in combat. Commands and orders must get through.

The Armored Division

The Armored division is built up around regiments of tanks in the same fashion that the Infantry division is built around regiments of riflemen and the Cavalry division around regiments of troopers. Its outstanding feature is power; its mission is to overrun, crush, or knife through the enemy lines.

Today the tank is a weapon as basic as a rifle or a cannon. In order to understand the Armored force we must understand what a tank can and cannot do.

It has crushing power, ability to move over varied terrain, high fire power, protection for its crew, and speed. On the other hand, it is comparatively blind under fire and some types of bad ground, such as heavy timber or swamp, will stop or slow it; delivery of accurate fire while moving is extremely difficult; and its armor can be penetrated by modern anti-tank guns. Do not by any means be contemptuous of the power of a tank, but keep in mind that it is not invulnerable. It is not a guarantee of victory in war; it must be used at the right time in the right place to gain results. Later in the course you will have two discussions on German tactical methods. At that time you will learn a great deal more about tanks and their employment.

In this chapter we have made only the briefest mention of the Services. At the beginning of the next chapter we shall take them up: the Adjutant General's Department, the Inspector General's Department, the Judge Advocate General's Department, the Quartermaster Corps, the Medical Department, Engineers, Chemical Warfare Service, and last but not least, the Finance Department, which always manages to find enough money to pay us at the end of the month. Also in the next lecture we shall discuss the duties of soldiers in our Army from private to lieutenant general.

CHAPTER XXVIII

THE SERVICES

In the last lecture we gave general consideration to the subject of the Arms and the combat units of the Army. Before going into the subject of the duties from private through general, we will spend a little time on the services—the units of the Army concerned with non-combat duties. A brief general explanation of their nature and their duties will assist in an understanding of the operation of the Army as a whole.

We cannot accurately call the services non-combat units because, with the exception of the Medical Department, they are all armed and will fight when it is necessary. As a matter of fact, the primary job of one of the services, the Chemical Warfare Service, is that of combat. On the whole, however, we find that the principal mission of the Services is, as the name implies, to service the individuals and organizations in the Army. It is to keep the troops supplied, quartered, healthy, and on record. In other words, the primary mission is to make for a going concern in the operations of war.

The Adjutant General's Department

Without taking the services in any order that would tend to indicate their relative importance one to another, we shall begin with the Adjutant General's Department.

The soldier is somewhat familiar with the duties of his battalion and regimental adjutants. In a sense they are a sort of managerial secretaries. That is a fairly sound indication of the duties of the Adjutant General's Department. But instead of belonging to the Infantry, Artillery, Cavalry, or some other branch, like the adjutants, personnel of this department belong to a branch of their own: the Adjutant General's Department. Actually they constitute the adjutant's offices of division and higher headquarters. They comprise what may familiarly be called the "Paper Work Department" because they keep the records, publish the orders, handle the incoming and outgoing official correspondence, and even run the Army Post Office. Your promotions, transfers, and discharges, not to mention your pay, are all a matter of their records—and they have plenty of them. The Adjutant General's Office in Washington, for instance, has some 660,000,000 records of 35,000,000 soldiers who have served in the army since 1776. Its World War No. 1 files alone contain the names of 50,328 Smiths, 40,101 Johnsons, and 28,902 Browns.[1]

The Inspector General's Department

The Inspector General's Department, as the name indicates, does the inspecting. It is true that all of your unit commanders inspect, but their operations are limited within the regiments, divisions, or field armies to which they are assigned. *This* department inspects all of the units. It functions in somewhat the same way as an auditor functions when called in by a business concern. It makes an impartial inspection of all units—their administration, training, mess, funds, property, and sanitary conditions—which serves as a check-up on the efficiency of the organizations and brings to light any deficiencies that exist in the command as a whole. Its purpose is not to criticize but to improve the efficiency of the command by pointing out errors and tendencies that otherwise might have been overlooked and to see that standards of uniformity are maintained in those matters that require uniform practices.

The Judge Advocate General's Department

Large business firms have legal departments, and many individuals have lawyers. The Army, too, follows this practice and has its lawyers in what is called the Judge Advocate General's Department. This department furnishes legal advice and interprets civil and military law when needed, exercises general supervision over courts martial and boards of inquiry, and reviews such of the cases of these courts and boards as may require review.

The Quartermaster Corps

Another of the services, the Quartermaster Corps, undoubtedly affects all Army personnel more of the time than any other branch; and it does this without interruption from the beginning of one's military career right to the end. It builds the barracks or furnishes the tents in which the soldiers live, and it supplies the coal to keep their quarters heated; it transports men and equipment by truck, train, or boat and supplies the gas and oil for their vehicles after they arrive at their destination; it feeds and clothes the Army, does its laundry, delouses the soldier if necessary, and even buries him if that time should come. This covers a broad subject in a few words, but those few words cover plenty of territory, whether one is at a camp in the United States or in an overseas theater of operations.

The Medical Department

The Medical Department contains the doctors, dentists, nurses, veterinarians, and what you might call sanitary engineers. This department is divided into six corps, one for each of the above—medical, dental, nurse, veterinary, and sanitary corps, and the Medical Administrative Corps, which does the administrative work for the others. Together they constitute the one purely non-combat branch of the services in the field, inasmuch as they are not armed for combat purposes. They take care of your health, first by preventive steps such as vaccination, inoculation, and advice on sanitation, and second by positive steps such as treatment and hospitalization when you are sick or wounded. One of their most difficult tasks, and one which we are apt to underestimate, is that of withdrawing casualties from the battlefield to areas in the rear where they can be properly treated. This is called *evacuation*, EVACUATION. The battalion aid stations and division collecting stations and clearing stations are set up in the field by the Medical Department for the purpose of giving first aid and such other treatment as may be necessary (and is possible to administer) before the casualty is sent back to the Army evacuation hospitals to be given further treatment. There is no job in the Army that is more strenuous than that of the litter-bearers. Day or night, rain or snow, through gassed and shelled areas—their work goes on, with the result that the casualty rate among these unarmed, non-combat troops is the highest of that of any of the Services. They answer the call for "stretcher-bearers" from wherever it comes with a devotion to duty second to none.

The Ordnance Department

The Ordnance Department is responsible for the design, manu-facture, supply, and maintenance of all arms, ammunition, tanks, fire-control instruments, and other similar equipment used by the Army. In the field the Ordnance men are responsible for the sup-ply, maintenance, and repair of the same items. In other words, their function with respect to ordnance equipment and supplies is similar to that of the Quartermaster with respect to Quartermaster equipment and supplies. As in the case of the Quartermaster Corps, we feel as though we were slighting them with so few words in outline of their many duties and responsibilities. The briefness of this description, however, cannot detract from the importance of the Ordnance Department, the branch that develops, furnishes, and maintains the weapons with which we fight.

The Chemical Warfare Service

We have covered the Medical Department as the only purely non-combat branch of the Services. Now we shall consider a branch of the Services that is more of an Arm than it is a Service, one that is more combatant than non-combatant—the Chemical Warfare Service. The duties of chemical officers in divisions are chiefly defensive, inasmuch as they supervise the instruction in defense against chemicals by means of gas masks, gas-proof shelters and methods of decontaminating gassed areas and materials. But they also advise their commanding officers on offensive means. The Chemical Warfare Service as a whole is interested in the use of chemicals—that is, gas, smoke, and incendiaries—as weapons. Consequently it supervises the development and manufacture of gas and smoke in this country and then supplies those agents to chemical and other units in the field. International treaties and fear of the employment of gas by their enemies have restricted the use of gas by belligerents in the present war, but the employment of smoke and incendiaries is general in all armies. The smoke candles and pots and the incendiaries are supplied to the Air Corps and to the ground forces by the Chemical Warfare Service; if poisonous gases should ever be used against us, it will be the Chemical Warfare Service that will meet this threat blow for blow.

The Corps of Chaplains

Believing that one of the keystones of democracy is religious freedom—the right to worship as we please—the Army has included a branch to encourage it, the Corps of Chaplains. There is one chaplain for approximately every 1200 men, and his denomination usually is the one to which most of the men in an outfit belong, whether Protestant, Catholic, or Jew. The chaplains are the ministers, priests, and rabbis of the Army, but they minister to all the men in their organization who wish it, regardless of their creed. They are the moral "leaning posts" of the troops—conducting religious services, visiting the sick, advising the troubled, and otherwise entering into matters that concern the mental and spiritual welfare of those in our Army.

The Finance Department

A century or more ago, men in the Army received a part of their compensation on the basis of the amount of material they captured. It was a European custom. After a battle was over, all the captured material was gathered and appraised, and the money value of that material was distributed to the soldiers in proportion to their rank. That distribution represented a sort of bonus for winning. If they lost the battle or didn't capture anything, they were lucky if they received any pay. However, the high officers got the lion's share under this system. After the Battle of Waterloo, for instance, Wellington received some $300,000 as his share, whereas his captains each received about $450, his corporals about $10 and his enlisted men probably enough to buy them a couple of beers.[2] Today every soldier receives a definite amount of pay; the Finance Department sees that he gets it. It pays him a stipulated amount, according to his grade, rank, and length of service, near the first of every month, month in and month out, win or lose. It also pays for the clothes he wears, the food he eats, and the things he uses. In other words, it spends the Army's money where it should be spent, and keeps the books to prove it.

These few paragraphs have only roughed in very sketchily the basic duties of those elements of the Army team that are known as the Services. For further information you are urged to turn to the Field Manuals, which will impress you with the considerable degree of organization and the complexity of duties required to service the American soldier at his home station, while enroute from place to place, and in battle areas.

REFERENCE NOTES

[1] War Department, *The New Army of the United States* (Washington, D. C., 1941), p. 101.
[2] "Waterloo Army Prize Money," *London Gazette*, June 21, 1817.

CHAPTER XXIX

DUTIES FROM PRIVATE THROUGH GENERAL

"Essentially nothing," says General de Gaulle, "lends itself better to the taste for sport than a military career. There is no single warlike action which is not a collective test and does not demand the concerted action of well-trained teams." [1]

The army is a team composed of smaller teams just as, in reality, a baseball team is composed of three smaller teams, the battery, the infield, and the outfield; and a football team has a team of linemen and one of backfield men. These teams-within-teams play in the same game as one unit—yet the part each group plays differs widely from that of the other group. The success of a football team depends upon the concerted action of the line and the backfield, and the concerted action of the line and the backfield depends upon the complete coöperation of every man in that line and in that backfield.

When we consider the varied duties of individuals in the Army, let us think along these lines by considering each one a member of a team and see how the primary duty of every man in the Army, as in football, is to subordinate his interests to those of his organization—to those of his team. And when we use the term *subordinate* let us, in the words of the Spanish General Mirando, "never confuse subordination, which is the self-denying virtue of a soldier, with submission, the low state of a serf." [2] When a quarterback gives the ball to another backfield man, then runs interference for him and blocks a prospective tackler, the ball-carrier may make a touchdown and may get most of the glory for it. Now would you say that the quarterback was submissive? Certainly not! Instead of going after the glory himself, he gave the ball to another man who, perhaps, was more likely to make the touchdown or at least gain ground substantially. He subordinated his interests to those of the team, and, as a result, the team had a better opportunity to win the game. The crowds may not have noticed it, but if he

378

hadn't blocked that tackler, the touchdown would not have been made. He coöperated for the good of the whole. What about the center who originally passed the ball to the backfield? And the guards and tackles? They may never get a chance to make a touchdown—but they make it possible for ball-carriers to do so. And what is just as important, any one of them, by *not* doing his part, may cause the play to fail and the game to be lost.

We mention how varied the duties of football players are. Certainly the duties of a rifleman in an infantry regiment are totally different from those of a truck-driver in a quartermaster regiment, just as the job of a center is totally different from that of a quarterback. Yet all of them—rifleman, quarterback, truck-driver, and center—have one thing in common; they "do duty for duty's sake and not for the benefit it may bring them." [3] They place the good of the team ahead of their own good, and no one is to say who is the more important—the man who carries the ball or the man who gives it to him; the man who does the shooting or the man who brings him the ammunition to shoot. They must coöperate. One cannot live without the other. Each man on the football team and each man in the Army has a job to do, and in neither case can one man fail to do his part and still expect his team, or his army, to win. Let us not forget that this applies to defense workers in our factories also.

Passing up football for a while, let's take a look at your duties as soldiers. You may be a clerk, an artificer, radio operator, Number 6 man on a 155-mm. howitzer, horseshoer, tuba-player, postal clerk, litter-bearer, or almost anything. We cannot cover all these duties in this discussion, and it is not necessary that we do so. Each one of you knows the duties connected with your own particular job anyway; if you don't, it's high time to get hep to yourself. So, rather than attempt to touch each specialty, let us make a general analysis of the duties that pertain to each rank.

A private, for example, *must know his job;* he must be alert and ready to act on his own initiative, must have a sense of responsibility, a devotion to duty, and must be courteous, considerate, fair-minded, and reliable in his dealings with others. It sounds like a pretty big order, doesn't it? Well, it may be—but, nevertheless, that is what is expected of him. And if he gives less, he's not carrying his load on the team, he is a liability to others, he is not fulfilling his comradeship with his friends and associates.

What about corporals? What do they do? They have to *be* everything that privates are, *do* everything that privates can do— *and more*. They not only have to look after themselves but after the men in their squads. They are responsible for how the squad performs and for the condition of the area it occupies. They must be "aggressive, bold, resourceful" and capable of great physical exertion. They must be morally prepared to rise to the emergency or the opportunity of the moment. It is up to the corporals to maintain discipline in their squads and assist the sergeants in matters that involve their squads. A corporal unwilling or unable to give more of himself to his work than he requires of any man in his squad is incompetent for the responsibility he accepted.

Next in line come the sergeants—section and platoon. The senior sergeant in the platoon is the platoon sergeant and is second in command and principal assistant to the platoon leader. The section sergeants and the squad corporals are his subordinates; and he supervises and controls them in order to enforce the platoon leader's orders. He keeps the platoon leader informed of shortages and deficiencies. If three canteens and one first-aid packet are missing and one rifle is unserviceable, he reports the fact to the platoon leader so that replacements can be secured and the platoon won't suffer when it goes into the field or, more important, when it goes into combat. And he'd better see to it that the area is neat and clean so that the platoon leader and company commander don't get "skinned" for it. In battle he directs and leads his section or platoon. And we mean LEADS—exemplifying the spirit and initiative of the leader, the soldier that other soldiers would emulate.

The supply sergeant is just what his name implies. He is the man who has the things you need, and he has them all arranged efficiently where he can find them when you need them. Not only that, but when he pulls them out they are not covered with rust or full of moth-holes. It is his job to protect and preserve this equipment. He knows what you have and what you will need later; and if your unit pulls out all of a sudden, it is his job to know everything that must be brought along. The supplies are ready to go, and he knows just what trucks are required and ready to carry them. Repairs are also among his responsibilities; he trains and supervises the armorer-artificer—the company mechanic—so he is the man to see about that broken tent-pole, or canteen-cup handle, or damaged gas mask.

The mess sergeant is another whose designation is descriptive of his responsibilities. He is generally a cook or has had experience as a cook, and he is responsible directly to the company, battery, or troop commander or to the mess officer for all matters pertaining to the mess. He is the man who prepares menus and then, if they are approved, draws or buys the rations necessary to put them into effect. He has to know the financial condition of the mess in order to do this, so that is another of his jobs—keeping a daily financial statement. If the mess hall, the tables, the benches, or the utensils are dirty, in fact if they are not spotlessly clean—it is probably his fault, because he has charge of the KP's. Furthermore, if you are not properly dressed when you go to mess, he is the one to correct you, because the kitchen and the mess hall are his domain and he has strict orders on the subject of what you shall wear and how you shall act while eating.

Next comes the Top Kick—the first sergeant. It has been said that system is what *you* have and red tape is what *the other fellow* has. Well, call it what you may, in the Army it has its beginnings in the job of the first sergeant. He is the administrative assistant of the company commander and has to look after all the details of the morning report, duty roster, sick report, outgoing communications, field desks, and everything connected with the paper work. He is by no means a paper soldier only; he is the Number One non-com in the company, and when all the officers are absent he is in command of the company. "He is the strong right arm of the company commander and the ambassador of the company in the orderly room. His loyalty to the company commander must be complete and his devotion to the company be beyond question." [4] Anyone who thinks that that is an easy job should try it. The first sergeant's standard of conduct and measure of *loyalty and ability as a soldier* at his station and on the field of battle should be exemplary at all times. His responsibility is unending, twenty-four hours a day.

There are three other grades of sergeant ranking respectively below, with, and above the first sergeant. Proceeding in order of rank from bottom to top, they are staff, technical, and master sergeants. A *master sergeant* is often a brigade or regimental sergeant major, but, aside from that it is difficult to generalize about his duties. A *staff sergeant* may be a mess sergeant, radio operator, battalion sergeant major, or any one of a number of things. The same applies to a *technical sergeant*, who may be motor transportation sergeant, supply sergeant, or radio technician, just to mention a few of the possibilities. Master sergeants likewise may have various other assignments, such as chief of the enlisted personnel of a staff section. The important things to remember are that the men in these grades must all have specialized knowledge in their particular fields and that they, along with the first sergeant, are the ranking non-coms.

The importance of the highest standard of conduct and ability among non-commissioned officers cannot be overestimated. Good N.C.O.'s working as a team are essential to the esprit de corps of the unit, to its proper training, and to its effectiveness in combat. "A corps of first-rate non-coms usually means a first-rate outfit." [5]

It is possible for an inefficient N.C.O. to fool his officers or company commander part of the time, but he cannot bluff or fool the men in the ranks for long. They note his weaknesses or neglect and take his measure with unerring eyes. He is constantly under their observation. His respect for his uniform when off duty, his sense of obligation toward the members of his unit and to his company officers, his ability to do a soldier's work exceptionally well, his capacity to evoke teamwork—all such matters are being daily measured by observing eyes. No duty of a company commander calls for greater skill and judgment of character than his selection of non-commissioned officers.

Next in rank comes the warrant officer, and again it is difficult to define his duties *in a general way*. Band leaders are usually warrant officers but not all warrant officers are band leaders. Most of them perform primarily administrative duties comparable to technical and master sergeants in division and higher headquarters. They outrank all enlisted men.

In dealing with the subject of officers, we find that rank determines seniority and responsibility of command and that is just about all it does determine. It is true that as a rule we find certain ranks in certain positions, but it is the position that determines the duties and not the rank. A second lieutenant, for instance, may be a platoon commander, mess officer, staff officer, aide to a general, or any one of a number of things. Most often we find second lieutenants as platoon commanders, and in that capacity they are responsible to the company commander in the same manner and for the same reasons that the sergeants are responsible to the platoon commander. If the platoon doesn't function as it should, if it is not up to standard and if its area isn't in shape, it's the funeral of the platoon commander, and if he doesn't know it he will soon find out.

A first lieutenant may be company administrative officer and, at the same time, second in command of the company. Under the company commander he is usually the officer who supervises the mess, supply, and the paper work done in the company. As a matter of fact, in the field he actually runs the mess and supply service of the company.

We have had to follow several steps in order to arrive at this point, but now we hit "The Skipper"—the company, battery, or troop commander. His assignment calls for the rank of captain, and his responsibilities are considerably greater than those of his subordinates. Everything connected with the company—its welfare, training, mess, supply, and the selection of non-commissioned officers—is his responsibility. He even is financially responsible for all the property that is issued to the company and has to pay for any unnecessary losses, whether it is your fault or his. Records, reports, rosters, company funds, memorandum receipts, losses, grumbles, complaints, food, entertainment, equipment, training, advice, and a multitude of other things are all a part of his daily life. He may delegate some of these jobs, but they are still his responsibilities, all of them, twenty-four hours a day. His job seems to include everything from advising the lovelorn to assuring the success of his company on the battlefield. And his personal, friendly relationship with his men as an adviser may have much to do with later success on the battlefield.

We must pause at the figure of the company commander, because he must be all things to the men whose training and welfare are entrusted to his care. No other position of command calls for greater devotion to duty, the unending, daily living of a life of duty and of responsibility. Wherever a fault may be found within his organization, he must accept it as his fault; wherever a failure, he is accountable to his superiors and, indeed, to his own men for that failure. His leadership is measured even by the a.w.o.l. and venereal reports; his training capacity by performance on the firing range and in field exercises; his disciplinary control by the perfection of close-order drill, the immaculate standards of barracks and company area, the prompt execution of orders, the coördination and coöperation of the company units; his recognized moral superiority as a leader by the desire of the men of his company to conduct themselves at all times in a manner indicating respect for the uniform and the service. Such are the standards of the ideal company commander—unlimited devotion to duty and to his men, seasoned with a sense of humor and an understanding of human nature. These are the principles and standards of leadership. To develop and attain such capacities and stature, constant and unrelenting effort at self-improvement is the obligation of the officer who aspires to do his full duty to his country and to the men entrusted to his care and command. Any lesser aspiration is itself a mark of the disqualification of an officer.

Going up in rank from this position, we meet majors and lieutenant colonels, colonels, brigadier generals, major generals, lieutenant generals, and generals; commanding battalions, regiments, brigades, divisions, army corps, armies, and groups of armies. Their responsibilities are enlarged in proportion to the size of their organizations, although some have less administrative work—paper work—than others, battalion and brigade commanders for instance. We may call any of them "The Old Man," but what we have said about "The Skipper" applies to them—every one of them—although their relations to the men are inevitably less intimate. They are the coaches and captains of the teams and of the teams-within-teams. Full coöperation with them will assure the big success that is vital to everyone. We shall cover the duties of most of these leaders in the next chapter, in which we briefly discuss the duties of their staffs. In this chapter, however, let us confine ourselves to a glance at the big picture from a general officer's position.

The story is told about General Sherman sleeping alongside the road, stretched out with his hat pulled down over his eyes and his head propped against a tree. You can picture him there, a bearded, rumpled figure in his wrinkled, dust-covered clothes. Long columns of tough, hardened soldiers trudged past him. Many of the soldiers recognized him, and it is safe to say that their respect for him was rapidly decreasing. Perhaps there were others who thought it, but there was one who said: "There's The Old Man sleeping last night's drunk off." General Sherman heard the remark and replied in loud, clear tones: "You are wrong. I spent the whole night working to make it easy for you today. Now it's my turn to take it easy!" [6] He could have said: "Did you get up all right this morning without being surprised by the enemy in your sleep, have breakfast and enough to eat? Did you receive your mail? Did you move off on schedule? Did you take any wrong roads? Did the enemy catch you unaware? Have you enough ammunition to protect you when you meet the enemy? Did anything go wrong that could reasonably have been avoided by planning? Well, while you slept I worked to make those things possible—so you can't begrudge me a little sleep now, can you?" This same point is well and briefly illustrated by a sign that hung at one time on the wall of a factory. It read: "No person in this plant is permitted to work more than forty hours per week, except the boss —and he *has* to!" *That* boss is your commander.

Let's see how this operates on a maneuver. It may be merely one phase of a maneuver which may be scheduled to be concluded sometime before noon. It is now 4:00 A.M. You have been moving into position during the night and may have reached assembly areas in time to catch twenty winks. How about the General? What has he been doing? He has been moving too, reviewing plans prepared by his staff. He has been constantly in touch with the situation—yours and the enemy's, so that at any time he will be in a position to make instant decisions. His staff has been getting as much information for him as they can. Your commanders of lower echelons have been keeping him advised of their movements and the enemy situation to their front—information that is based on what you have given them. The plan is to attack at daybreak. That had already been decided, and orders had been issued, but does that mean that they will not have to be changed? Certainly not. In combat, unusual events are the usual thing. In this maneuver, two divisions that were supposed to have arrived on line have not arrived. It would be suicidal to attack without their support. The orders must be modified. How did the march go last night? Were there any accidents? How many and how serious were they? Has word been received yet whether or not we will have the support of that bombardment squadron? Dawn arrives and we don't attack. The "enemy" does, and pushes us back. The command post must now be moved. (The next phase of the maneuvers starts the day after tomorrow. We will be thirty miles away. Thereafter the maneuver area will be further south. That means we must change the location of the railhead. The Governor is due to arrive at 11:30—that's four hours away now. He wants to see what a maneuver is like.) Those two divisions are coming up now, but it will be three hours before their help can be effective. Better commit our reserves. The maneuver is terminated, so get the reports ready for the critique at 4:30 this afternoon. The press? Sure! Show them in. There are twenty of them, asking scores of questions. That's over, and there is correspondence to answer. All the professional, civic, and social clubs of Squeedunk are going to have a joint meeting—will the General be the speaker of the evening? The War Department wants comments on the effectiveness of the newly organized tank destroyer units, on the proposed chigger-bite remedy, and on the present size of the Class C ration. Refer those letters to the proper sections for report. The town of Never, now off limits, claims that it has cleaned up and expects to be put back on limits. The mayor says he wants to be sensible about it, but if necessary he will appeal directly to the War Department, or even to the President, certainly to his congressman. The Governor arrives, which means that some members of the staff are called together for introductions, and everyone goes to lunch. Let's see those notes for the critique. What do the umpires have to say? How about the radio broadcast at 5:30? It will be a coast-to-coast hookup, and a five-minute speech must be written. Call in the Public Relations Officer. The radio men will arrive at 3:00 for a rehearsal. The next phase of the maneuvers must be considered. Is the Chief of Staff ready to make a preliminary report? The newsreel photographers are outside and want a few shots of the

General driving a jeep. There is not much time in which to study the notes for the critique. The radio men arrive, and there is the rehearsal; then the critique, then a meeting with all the general officers, then one with the staff to check the plans for the next phase of the maneuvers, then the broadcast, then supper, perhaps a quick inspection trip to the hospital and a tour of the bivouac areas, and then to bed. No, not yet! Must quickly glance through those staff reports and the newspapers and check up on what has happened at headquarters since supper. The general's aide tries to shield him from much interruption—well-intentioned callers, newspapermen that want "exclusive" interviews, the stream of telephone calls. It's midnight, and rest is necessary, so some of these matters will have to wait until morning—if they can. Moreover, he must take a reconnaissance flight by plane with the chief of staff and G-3 in the morning. But it's important to rest. The General, who must make the final decisions and commitments, needs to keep his head fresh and clear and as free as possible from details. To bed with him! And may his sleep be sound and refreshing!

Do the highly specialized members of the staff take care of most of the details that have been mentioned in this description of a general's day on maneuvers? Yes, many of them, as you will learn in the following lecture. But the final decisions rest with the general, the final responsibility is his; and these problems of his own and of his staff are always pressing at the back of his mind, no matter how much he rightly endeavors to avoid details, no matter how much his staff—if it is an effective staff—tries to save him from minor problems of planning and preparation.

This day for a general that we have described is a non-combat day, although it is during a maneuver period. It is much less complicated by the unpredictable; less serious, and far less strenuous than a day when bullets are real. A day in real combat might involve decisions vital to thousands of lives and to the course of a campaign, perhaps even to the outcome of a war. It would include the messing-up of well-made plans by bombs that actually explode, by casualties among staff officers upon whose technical advice the general relies, by increased difficulties with supply, and so forth. And there would be the emotional wear and tear to which the coolly calculating mind of the general must remain immune. How-

ever, under those conditions there would be fewer visits by distinguished civilians, and, we are very sure, not many radio broadcast rehearsals.

You wonder how this concerns you? Well, even the hoped-for
untroubled sleep of your commanding general is of importance to
you. The gap between you and a general officer seems tremendous,
yet every decision of his affects you, is made on your account and
as a result of what you have done or seen or can do. He is the
coach and director of the big team in which you think you are
insignificant. But you are wrong about that. The general's success
and the success of the team depend directly—not indirectly—on
the positive and negative acts of every one of you. Neither of you,
general or private soldier, can act or not act without having it in
some way affect the other. Coöperation between you means unity.
We may alter a certain quotation to say: "Show me a just cause
and a unified army, and I will show you victory."

We have the just cause, and by our mutual coöperation, fully
given to the limit of our lives, we have the unity by which victory
will be won.

> It ain't the guns or armament, or the money they can pay,
> It's the close coöperation that makes them win the day;
> It ain't the individual, nor the army as a whole,
> But the everlastin' teamwork of every bloomin' soul.[7]

REFERENCE NOTES

[1] Gen. Charles de Gaulle, "Toward a Professional Army," *The Cavalry
Journal*, Washington, D. C., Nov.-Dec., 1941.
[2] Gen. Abel Mirando, "Algunas Palabras a los Jovenes Oficiales," con-
densed and translated from *Revista Militar* by Col. F. M. Barrows in *The Cavalry Journal*, Nov.-Dec., 1941.
[3] Same.
[4] "Company Duties: A Check List," *The Infantry Journal*, Vol. XLIX, pp.
24-35 (Dec., 1941).
[5] Same.
[6] The Infantry School Mailing List, *Men of War* (The Infantry School,
Fort Benning, Georgia, 1939), Vol. XVII, pp. 91-93.
[7] J. Mason Knox, "Coöperation," *The Cavalry Journal*, Nov.-Dec., 1941.

CHAPTER XXX

WHAT STAFF WORK MEANS AND HOW IT OPERATES

THE FUNCTIONS OF A STAFF

In the press we read, "His gravest mistake was in not recognizing the preparations the Axis was making for a push. This may have been a matter of bad reconnaissance, *bad staff work*, or a dozen other things, . . ." [1] In a magazine we see a picture of some Army officers in Iceland with the caption, "*Staff Officers* of an infantry regiment pose for a group portrait in their leather mittens and fur caps." [2] Over the radio we hear a news commentator say, "I asked a *staff officer* about that today. He gave me some figures." [3] Now, what is the importance of staffs and staff officers that merits these references?

We have a United States Military Academy at West Point for a thorough, fundamental training of Army officers, and we have R.O.T.C. units at many colleges. We have service schools at Fort Benning, Fort Sill, and Fort Riley for further schooling in the Infantry, Artillery, and Cavalry, and similar schools for the other Arms and Services. We know their excellent reputations for maintaining the highest standards of military education. Why, then, do we also have a Battalion Commander and Staff Course at Fort Benning and a Command and General Staff School at Fort Leavenworth for officers who already have been graduated from other schools? And why do the British have a Staff College, and the Germans a General Staff School, for officers who have graduated from the Royal Military College and the Kriegsakadamie (War Academy), respectively? The answer must be that the importance of staff work is sufficiently great and their duties are sufficiently complex to warrant the existence of special staff schools and special training.

The foregoing is an indication of the importance that is attached to staffs by the press and by those in charge of military training, but it doesn't tell us what they are, or why they are necessary or important.

The Staff Officers' Field Manual gives the following definition: "The staff of a unit consists of the officers who assist the commander in the exercise of his command." [4] That staffs assist commanders is certainly no revelation and is a statement that is accurate and simple enough. So simple, in fact, that it is deceiving, for it fails to indicate the countless activities that are involved in rendering that assistance to the commander.

The teachings of the Command and General Staff School build an explanation of the functions of a staff around the following seven words: a staff ". . . advises . . . foresees . . . prepares . . . co-ordinates . . . informs [the School uses the word *enunciates*] . . . supervises . . . (and) serves."

a. "It ADVISES the commander, furnishing him with full information on which to base his plans and decisions, in such digested shape as will relieve him from the fatiguing [and time-consuming] study of details."

b. "It FORESEES the needs of the command in all that relates to personnel, operations, intelligence, and supply."

c. "It PREPARES strategical, tactical, and training PLANS in accordance with the commander's decision."

d. "It COÖRDINATES the agencies within the division—the various services and technical agencies—where there is duplication, or competition."

e. "It INFORMS (enunciates) . . . (as to) all policies, decisions, and basic plans of the commander; and coördinates expeditiously their execution by supplementary plans, decisions, and orders.

f. "It SUPERVISES to see that orders and instructions are carried through to conclusion."

g. "Finally, . . . it SERVES the troops in all things which will increase their combat efficiency. One of the fundamental doctrines of the British Staff College is that 'the red tab of the British general staff officer is a badge of servitude.'" [5]

Please note one significant point: every definition or explanation we find treats the staff in its relation to the needs or desires of the commander. The commander alone stands responsible for whatever acts are done by him or in his name, and he cannot delegate that responsibility to his staff. History will credit him with his victories or condemn him for his failures, whether these victories or failures are due to his own act or to the acts or advice of his staff. A commander, especially of large units where it is physically impossible for him to keep his fingers on everything at one time, is reliant on his staff—just as a football coach relies on his end, line, and backfield coaches, or an airplane pilot relies on the mechanic for the mechanical condition of his plane, on the meteorologist for information on flying conditions, and on the navigator for the course he follows. It is the commander's responsibility to surround himself with an able staff. Failures that arise as a result of the incompetence of one of his staff officers will be the failures of the commander and are apt to affect the welfare or the very existence of the entire command. And successes similarly are reflected. "For, as Ludendorff was the brain of Hindenburg, so if in a less degree, he himself owed much to certain brilliant assistants . . . artillery tactics devised by Col. Bruchmuller . . . combined tactics drawn up by Captain Geyer . . . strategical brains of Lt. Col. Hoffman . . . and of Lt. Col. Wetzell. . . ." [6] It is doubtful that any recent general ever attained greatness without the aid of an able staff, and conversely it is doubtful if any general with a consistently poor staff ever attained greatness.

Thus far we have referred to commanders and staffs of large units. This is likely to give us the mistaken impression that staffs serve only in higher headquarters and that there is no need for them in headquarters of smaller units. Actually, there are staffs, or men who perform certain duties of staff officers, in all units, including the squad.

In order to reduce the subject to its simplest terms, let us take a machine-gun section, and for the purpose of this discussion let us assume that it is operating alone. There we have a section leader and two machine-guns (each with a corporal, gunner, assistant gunner, and ammunition carriers). At the outset we are faced with four fundamental problems that must be solved in order to put those guns into action—personnel, intelligence, operations, and supply. First of all, we must have men capable of operating the guns. It would be ridiculous for us to take those guns into the field without troops to operate them, or with troops who were unfit for combat. Consequently, as section leader, we look to the squad corporals to report the strength of their squads and the condition of their men, thus solving our first problem—personnel. Next we need something at which to fire the guns—a target. For that reason we require information of the enemy—where it is, how big it is, what kind of a target, etc.—and we have an observer probably equipped with field-glasses, searching the ground ahead of us for any indication of hostile troops. He spots some hostile infantry deployed in the woods about 500 yards to our front, estimates them to represent about one company, and judges from their actions that they are not aware of our presence. He transmits that information to the section leader. Now we have located the enemy—our target—which solves the second problem, information of the enemy and of enemy terrain—intelligence. What is our next problem? A location for the machine-guns, a position from which to fire them and from which we will have maximum cover from the enemy, but still can see the enemy and fire on him without any intervening obstacles. In other words, a position with a good field of fire in front of it. Another consideration is the manner in which we will employ our guns; i.e., the direction from which we wish to deliver our fire, because it may be advisable to maneuver into a position on the enemy flank, so that we can deliver flanking fire; and we must determine the rate of fire—how fast the guns should be fired. Some one has to work that out—the plan of attack, the operation of the machine-gun section to best advantage. In this case, the deductions would be made by the section leader, who would then cause the guns to be put into position. That solves the third problem, operations. Thus far we have the men, a target, and a good position for the guns, but we can't fire our guns without ammunition. The ammunition carriers know that and made sure before leaving bivouac that they had sufficient ammunition in the boxes for that purpose. They run up to the guns with the ammunition, thus solving the fourth problem—supply. Each one has done his part in the solution of the four problems—personnel, intelligence, operations, and supply—and through their coöperation, the guns are now in action.

Responsibilities don't cease there, however. It is a continuing process. One of the machine-gunners is hit by enemy fire and becomes a casualty. The assistant gunner takes his place, and the ammunition carrier takes the place of the assistant gunner. This action is automatic, but who takes the place of the last ammunition carrier? The section leader is advised of this shortage so that he can request a replacement (personnel). The observer finds that the enemy is emplacing a machine-gun on its right flank, so he immediately notifies the section leader (intelligence). This means that the section leader must shift the fire of one of his machine-guns to the new target, the enemy machine-gun (operations). The firing continues, consuming ammunition all of the time. The ammunition carriers bring up more ammunition, and, when the supply is getting low, they tell the section leader about it (supply). It is not likely that the section leader can keep an eye on his men and know at all times how each one is, also keep an eye on the enemy, observe his movements, and calculate all enemy capabilities, devise plans for employing his weapons in different ways to meet any possible situation and keep track of his ammunition—all at one time. Consequently, he has his own "personnel officer" (the corporal), his own "intelligence officer" (the observer), his own "operations officer" (himself), and his "supply officer" (ammunition carrier).

A demonstration such as we have just given illustrates the four questions that confront us as commanders in the accomplishment of our mission: (1) Have we troops capable of doing the job? (Personnel); (2) What can the enemy do to stop us? (Intelligence); (3) What can we do to stop the enemy? (Operations); and (4) Have we enough ammunition, weapons, food, etc., to see us through the job? (Supply).

In units as small as sections the commander can answer most of these questions himself, but he nevertheless is reliant on the advice of those under him; and we find that those who advise the commander can do so in addition to other duties. In the case of companies or similar units, however, we find that the commander has a full-time adviser in a first lieutenant who is the second in command and who serves as a full-time staff officer. As the units grow larger the task becomes more complicated. The number of troops involved becomes greater; the units themselves contain a variety of weapons; the area they cover is larger; and altogether the situation is more complex. Here we find that not only is it impossible for the commander to keep in touch with everything, but that his advisers must devote themselves exclusively to the task of assisting the commanders. They haven't the time to devote to any other duties. Consequently in the case of battalions and squadrons, we find full-time advisers whom we call staff officers.

The one full-time "staff" officer of the company (or similar unit) is not sufficient to serve a battalion or squadron. Here it is necessary to have from three to five officers. One of them, like the lieutenant in the company, is the second in command, but he might also be the operations officer and is the coördinator of the staff. He is the executive officer, and as such he coördinates the work of the adjutant (personnel officer) and the intelligence officer. Except in the case of separate battalions, the commanders are not particularly concerned with supply and do not need a supply officer. Their supplies are handled directly by the regiment. Separate battalions, such as a tank destroyer battalion, an engineer battalion in a triangular division, or a signal battalion (in other words, battalions that are not a part of any regiment), must handle their own supplies, however, and consequently must have full-time supply officers. In all battalions we also find the start of what we might call a special staff. It is composed of part-time staff officers who have other jobs to do—officers such as the motor transport officer and the commanders of machine-gun and weapons units. They serve as special advisers to the commander on matters pertaining to the technical aspects of their jobs.

The regiment offers further complications. It is still larger and comprises a variety of communications, service, medical, heavy weapons, and perhaps anti-tank units. The task of feeding, training, supplying, and otherwise caring for the needs of the troops involves considerably more work. The problem of supply becomes more acute, and, with the exception of separate battalions, we find for the first time the need of a full-time supply officer. In fact, it is the first time that we find an officer for each of the four jobs already mentioned—personnel, intelligence, operations, and supply —who performs exclusively the duties relative to his section. We find also the addition of other special staff officers such as the medical and communications officers.

In the interest of brevity we don't refer to these officers each time as personnel officer, or operations officer, partly for the same reason that we find it more simple to say O.D. instead of olive drab, or K.P. instead of kitchen police. Using the letter S to denote "staff," we refer to the four staff officers as S-1, S-2, S-3, and S-4. They are the personnel, intelligence, operations, and supply officers, respectively.

In all headquarters we find that the operations officer is also the training officer. We sometimes refer to him as the operations officer, sometimes as the training officer or even P & T (plans and training) officer, but he is one and the same man and is the S-3. He is interested in the operations of the troops on maneuvers or in combat, after he has observed and advised on their training, much the same as a football coach is interested in the operation of his team in the game on Saturday after coaching them during the week.

Bearing in mind that the training officer is also the operations officer, we can use a memory device to aid in recalling the duties of the various staff officers. That device is the word PITS—P-I-T-S —Personnel, Intelligence, Training, Supply—S-1, S-2, S-3, S-4. Here, with the addition of the executive officer to act as coördinator, we have a staff.

The next higher unit is the brigade, and here we find the same staff set-up, with two notable exceptions: (1) Except in the case of separate brigades, the staff is usually smaller than that of a regiment because it is not ordinarily burdened with the details of supply. (2) The executive officer is not the second in command of the brigade. We have found that the executive officer of a regiment or a battalion is the second in command of that regiment or battalion, but the second in command of the brigade is the next ranking officer in that brigade, probably the senior regimental commander. The brigade executive officer is the head of the brigade staff and exercises no function of command other than that over the brigade staff officers and enlisted personnel assigned to the staff.

This brings us to a point in connection with staff officers in general. Staff officers have no command authority in their own right except over the personnel in their own sections. (This applies to staff officers who are not regimental or battalion executive

officers, or special staff officers who are also unit commanders.)
They are advisers to the commander and issue orders only in his
name and as a result of his wish or intention.

A division staff is essentially the same as that of lower units, but,
in the same progression, it is greatly increased in size. Instead of an
executive, there is a chief of staff. Instead of six or eight officers,
there are twenty-five or thirty, and they are formally divided into
two groups: the general and special staffs. We say "formally
divided" inasmuch as here we find some full-time special staff
officers as well as full-time general staff officers. The general staff
consists of the G-1, G-2, G-3, and G-4 and their assistants. The
letter G (denoting "general") is used in divisions and higher units,
and corresponds to the S used in brigades and lower units; consequently in recalling their duties our memory device "PITS" still
applies: personnel, intelligence, training, and supply. The special
staff, as we have outlined before, is composed of officers who are
advisers to the commanding general in their separate fields, in fields
of a more technical nature such as ordnance, finance, law, medicine, engineering, religion, etc. Some of them, such as the medical,
engineer, and artillery officers, are part-time special staff officers
because they also command the medical, engineer, and artillery
units in the division. Others, such as the ordnance, finance, adjutant general (the division adjutant) and judge advocate (the
lawyer), are full-time special staff officers. This list is by no means
complete, but it is doubtful that, as a result of studying this chapter
alone, we could remember all the special staff officers, anyway.

For the purposes of this discussion, there is no need of covering
staffs of larger units in any detail. Those of army corps, armies
and of General Headquarters (G.H.Q.) are amplified division
staffs. We shall cover this subject simply by saying that each staff
is larger and more complex than the previous one, and that on the
general staffs of army corps and higher units we may find, for
the first time, a deputy chief of staff, and a secretary of the general
staff; and on the special staffs we may find additional officers such
as the anti-aircraft officer, coast artillery officer, officer in charge
of civil affairs, and many others.

INDIVIDUAL DUTIES OF STAFF OFFICERS

So far we have touched on the duties of staff officers in general, on the composition of staffs, and slightly on the individual duties of staff officers. We are going into a little more detail with respect to their individual duties, but first let us take one more look at the seven words that generalize the duties of staffs: they ADVISE, FORESEE, PREPARE, COÖRDINATE, INFORM, SUPERVISE, AND SERVE.

The individual duties of staff officers are so numerous that a listing of them is tedious: The Staff Officer's Field Manual, for example, begins to enumerate the duties of G-1 (S-1) as follows: ". . . the planning for and supervision of activities concerning— (1) Procurement, classification, reclassification, pay, promotion, transfer, retirement, and discharge of all personnel. . . . (3) Decorations, citations, honors, and awards. (4) Leaves of absence and furloughs. . . . (9) Strength reports . . . casualty reports, prisoner of war reports, station lists, . . ." [7] etc., etc. And tersely and briefly as these duties are described, the manual requires twenty pages to cover the duties of staff officers.

Fully aware that we are omitting numerous essential duties of these officers, let us skim over the top and hit the most important of these duties. For example, in the case of G-1 we can say that they include the planning for and supervision of activities concerning the welfare of the men; their pay, promotion, recreation, decorations, and punishment—and let it go at that. Approaching the subject of G-2 in the same manner, we can say that his primary job is to keep the commander (and others concerned) constantly informed of the enemy situation and prevent the enemy from being informed of our situation. His duty is to collect all the information of the enemy and enemy terrain, evaluate it—that is, sift it out in order to determine its degree of usefulness—and pass it on to everyone concerned. At the same time, by supervising methods such as the use of codes, censorship, and secrecy, it is his duty to prevent the enemy from obtaining information from us. We call this "counter-intelligence." The G-3 supervises and advises with respect to the training of the troops through training directives,

schools, selection of training sites, etc., and then he supervises the
actual employment of the troops in the field. He makes a continuous study of the tactical situation and develops various plans of
action that can be put into effect to meet any emergency. G-4 is
concerned principally with supply and evacuation. He supervises
activities with respect to hospitalization and the procurement, stor-
age, and distribution of supplies, as well as the construction of the
roads, docks, and utilities necessary to accomplish this.

These duties of individual general staff officers may seem separate and independent—personnel, intelligence, training, and supply—but actually they are closely related. One of the gravest mistakes that a staff officer can make is to consider himself locked
up in a water-tight compartment; to develop a "that's-your-prob-
lem" attitude. Staff officers are absolutely dependent on one another. They are separate lobes in the commander's brain, so to
speak, and coöperation must be their middle names. They must
work together; they cannot work apart. They must be interchangeable [8] in the event that one of them becomes a casualty and,
to give an apt description by means of an awkward sentence, each
staff officer should know *as much* about the *other* staff officers'
jobs as they do and *more* about *his own job* than they do. Each
must know the duties and limitations of the other, in order that he
may know what information or help may reasonably be expected
from the other, so he won't make unreasonable requests. Before
G-3 can devise a tactical plan, he must know what sort of an
obstacle the enemy will present. This means that he must work
with G-2, the man who has the information of the enemy. On the
other hand, G-2, in order to secure some information about the
enemy, may require patrols to be sent out for that purpose. But it
is up to G-3 to furnish the patrols or raiding parties, consequently
G-2 must work closely with G-3. G-4 has the job of procuring
rations, but G-1 is the man who has the up-to-date figures on the
strength of the command, so G-4 has to work with G-1 in order
to find out how many men he must provide with food and where
they are to be found.

Each has the task of planning how his part of the job may best be
accomplished, and in doing so he consults other members of the
staff. But what happens when there is a conflict in opinion? For

instance, G-4 decides that Dusty Pike is an ideal road up which to move his supplies, but he finds that G-3 has chosen the same road for the movement of troops. And G-2 has it all figured out how he can use that flight of observation planes for aërial reconnaissance and photographing, but the artillery officer and G-3 had planned to use them for command missions and observation of artillery fire. All of them can support their decisions with ample reasons, each one firmly convinced that his use of the road, or the planes, is in the best interests of the command as a whole. Obviously, some executive decision must be made. It is true that we have a commanding officer, but he makes basic decisions, decides upon broad plans and determines policies on a large scale. He should not be troubled with problems every time they arise. Then, too, he may be out on reconnaissance at the time and not available for a decision. Some one has to weigh the relative merits and make a decision, and that man is the chief of staff (or in smaller units, the executive officer). He is the one who is closest to the commander and the most conversant with his policies. He is the one in front of whom the commander "thinks out loud." A general officer, comparing a commander to the president of a large manufacturing company, once gave the following illustration: "The president has a brother —an uncle to all the rest of the family—perhaps ten years younger than he. This brother has also been up and down and around in the business world to a considerable extent. He is at a very effective age—old enough to have developed horse sense and to have acquired experience—yet still young enough to be capable of high-pressure leg work in an emergency (as, for instance, to clinch that contract for a big sales order). He is the General Manager and Chief Executive of the business. He is responsible that details are worked out and executed. He coördinates things. He sees to it that 'The Old Man's' broad policies and basic decisions are developed into detailed plans, workable to the last degree. Finally, he sees that these plans are executed. He is the Executive or Chief of Staff of the company." [9] And there we have the executive officer or chief of staff of a unit. It is through him that the recommendations of the staff are transmitted to the commander, and it is through him that the orders and wishes of the commander are transmitted to the staff or to the appropriate persons. He "is the principal assistant to the commander" and "the principal coördinating agency of the command" [10] and of the staff. The Chief of Staff and his assistants, the G-1, G-2, G-3, and G-4, must be sufficiently well informed of the commander's plans and intentions that they can devise plans and put them into effect in his name in order to meet some emergency that may arise in his absence.

As an illustration of the need of staffs, let us go back to the day when staffs did not exist and see how they were conspicuous by their absence.[11] In the times that we are about to discuss, commanders had aides who performed some of the duties that staff officers now perform, but they did not have actual staffs as we recognize them today.

At the battle of Chickamauga in 1863, Rosecrans, a Union general, was on the defensive. An aide reported to him that there was a gap of 600 yards in the front line where Brannan's division should have been. Rosecrans could not understand how this had happened, but he knew that there had been some orders pulling Brannan out. These orders were supposed to have been rescinded, but it appeared from this information that they had not been. Consequently, he ordered Wood's division on the right to move over to the left and close the gap. Actually, Brannan's division was still there, concealed in the timber and thick underbrush where the aide could not see it. Wood was puzzled by the order; however, saying, "I'm glad it's in writing this time," [12] he obeyed and pulled out of position in order to close the gap. Ordinarily this mistake would have been discovered and corrected in short order, but in this case there was a disastrous coincidence. Wood moved out at just the time that Longstreet, of the Confederates, had planned to attack. The result was that Longstreet attacked, found the hole left by Wood, and swept the entire right wing of Rosecrans' army from the field. Would this have happened if Rosecrans had had a general staff? Probably not, because he would have had a G-3 with the accurate information, and Rosecrans would not have had to rely on his memory.

Another illustration comes from McClellan's campaign in the Peninsula in 1862 against the Confederate forces under Lee. His army outnumbered Lee's army, but he was not aware of it.[13] The only information he had was what he received from Pinkerton's

Secret Service, which told him that Lee's army was much larger than his own. For that reason, instead of attacking boldly and taking advantage of his superior numbers, McClellan proceeded cautiously, awaiting reinforcements.[14] What he needed rather than reinforcements was a good G-2.

For a third illustration we can study the activities of Florence Nightingale with the British in the Crimea in 1854. There was a deplorable condition in the British medical service at that time, due to an incompetently administered medical bureau, lacking in every need. The sick and wounded were mistreated, there was a lack of medical supplies, and 45 per cent of the patients died within six months. The commanding general apparently had little control over this wretched situation.[15] Is it likely that such a condition could exist today? Again the answer is, probably not. The G-4, working with the army surgeon, would have been conversant with the situation from the beginning, would have anticipated the needs in so far as facilities and supplies were concerned, and would have kept the commander constantly informed. Where corrections were necessary, he would have drafted orders to be given in the name of the commander to accomplish them. Supplies and hospitalization are a part of his job. Sick and wounded soldiers needed a Florence Nightingale in 1854 to make their plight known to the world. Today efficient staff machinery plans for them as thoroughly as for every other army activity.

The comparison of a commander and his staff with the officers of a large manufacturing concern is a good one, and an analogy of this sort invites more attention. Let us suppose that the president of the Doo-Dad Manufacturing Company decides that he wants to add another item to those that the firm already manufactures—it is a sure-fire, double-action, supercharged, ball-bearing mouse-trap. It is the greatest thing he has seen, it has been recommended by his staff of experts, and he wants to "put it over" in a big way. It is a big task and will necessitate the construction of a new wing to the plant building. He calls in his general manager (his executive officer, or chief of staff) and informs him of his decision. The general manager (or perhaps the president himself) then calls in his staff of managers. The personnel manager (his G-1) must hire the laborers, mechanics, and helpers who are going to operate the machines in the new plant. He will probably promote an assistant foreman from some part of the present shop to be the foreman of the new shop. How about the sales manager? He has been scouring the market to find out what is needed to make the new product appeal to the public. He is the G-2. He knows that there is a Simplex mouse-trap on the market, but it is only single-action, and it is difficult to set. However, and this is important, the Simplex Company is working on a new mouse-trap that they can get on the market within two months. This new trap will offer stiff competition for the Doo-Dad mouse-trap. Next comes the production manager (the G-3). He has to build the thing. G-1 will hire the workmen, but G-3 must supervise their instruction. He has to set up a production line and make sure that it turns out an article that will capture the market that G-2 said existed, and it must be done now, before the marketing of the new Simplex mouse-trap that is reported on its way. A new wing must be built onto the plant, and he needs machinery. That is where the purchasing agent comes into the picture. He has to procure the wood and the steel that go into the mouse-trap. He is the G-4. These four men, even with their assistants, aren't enough for the job, however. A contractor must be engaged to build the plant; he is an engineer. Another must be engaged to install the machines and machine tools; he is the ordnance officer. Contracts must be drawn for the purchase of materials, so the head of the legal department must be consulted; he is the judge advocate. The interoffice communication set-up must be expanded, so in comes the signal officer; and so on down the line.

It wasn't due to any stroke of luck that the president of the Doo-Dad Manufacturing Company had a capable staff of managers at his beck and call. They were carefully selected over a period of time and were experts in their fields, and the president knew that he could rely both on their recommendations and on their ability to carry out his orders. The commander of a military unit is no different in this respect, and his use of his staff officers is very similar to the use that the company president made of his managers. In his book *My Experiences in the World War*, General Pershing said, "It required no genius to see that coördination and direction of the combat branches and the numerous services of large forces could be secured only through the medium of a well-constituted general staff, and I determined to construct it on the sound basis of actual experience in war of our own and other armies." [16] Results bore out his opinion.

Let us suppose that a division commander, after thoughtful consideration of all the facts, decides that he wants to capture the town of Nohow. He tells his chief of staff (the general manager) about it. In other words, he issues his directive and states the essential elements of information that he wants. The chief of staff (or the general himself) calls the staff together. What information can he get from G-1 (the personnel manager)? Well, he can get some extremely vital information, for instance: the strength of the division at that time is 17,946; the health of the command is excellent—that epidemic of dysentery has entirely disappeared; the morale of the troops is good, couldn't be better. They have never liked the Nohowans anyway, and the series of successes in the past few days have filled them with confidence. Such an operation as the general contemplates will probably result in approximately 200 dead and 1000 wounded, so he will institute steps in advance to procure replacements. Now for G-2 (the sales manager). What can he offer? It would probably be something like the following: The civilians in Nohow are unfriendly to our forces; there is a force estimated as a division, reinforced by a regiment of cavalry defending Nohow; other enemy troops cannot reinforce them before tomorrow night; Alibi Creek is unfordable due to the heavy rains in the past three weeks; the enemy forces have been in that locality for six days and have heavily fortified their position; for that reason their greatest capability is defense. Next we come to G-3 (the production manager) and find that he has recommendations to make. To the east of Nohow is some high ground and woods and a good road-net affording a favorable approach. He recommends that the main attack be launched *to* the west *from* there, and a secondary attack be launched from the south. He must consult the special staff in order to complete his plans: the engineer officer concerning the construction of pontoon bridges across Alibi Creek; the quartermaster officer for the use of additional trucks to carry the troops who are to make the main attack; the artillery officer relative to artillery support, etc. We have yet to draw G-4 into the picture.

He says that the units have already drawn enough rations and ammunition to last them until tomorrow night, and that there is more ammunition at the distributing point at Perkfield. The Jerkville road can be used as the main supply road, and gasoline and additional rations can be drawn at Elbow Creek Church and Bruce's Corners, respectively. The commanding general, after considering all these recommendations, decides to adopt them and states that the attack will be launched at daybreak. Then things start humming. Immediately the staff issues a warning order and each member works out the details in connection with his own section. G-3 incorporates all of the contributions in one field order. Their work does not cease there, however, for then they must follow up the field order to make sure that it is being carried out, and they must keep themselves constantly informed of the situation as it develops. They continually devise new plans and new estimates to fit the ever-changing situation—plans that, when approved, can be put into effect instantly to meet an emergency, whether the commander is there or not.

Few generals have had a greater reputation for being masters of their own minds and for having more confidence in their own judgment than did Field Marshal Viscount Allenby in World War No. 1. He took the criticism that was directed at him as a result of his failures in France as though they were the result of his own failings; and later he took the praises that were heaped on him for his successes in the Near East. He might have deserved those criticisms and those praises in his own right, but it must be remembered that at all times he had a staff to advise him and to carry out his orders. In referring to Allenby's attack on Beersheba, General Sir Archibald Wavell said, "Thanks to the care with which the previous reconnaissance had been done and to the extremely able staff work, a complicated and difficult movement was made without a hitch, over a roadless and almost featureless country. It was probably the biggest night march which has ever taken place in war, made entirely across country, and the credit for its success belongs to Brigadier General W. H. Bartholomew of Chetwode's staff. . . . It was a fine success, well-earned by the skill of the staff and the dash of the troops." [17] There is no denying the greatness of Allenby, but at the same time it would be hard to deny that his

CHAPTER XXXI

MILITARY AVIATION

The thought of flying has possessed the imagination of man probably from the time that he first began to develop an imagination. There is the myth of Icarus, which was a favorite among the ancient Greeks. The legendary youth Icarus, son of Dædalus, sought to fly with his father from Crete to Sicily; and he attached to his shoulders, with the aid of beeswax, two great feathered wings. But Icarus ignored his father's sage advice concerning high altitudes. Zestfully he spiraled upward until the growing heat of the "molten sun" melted the wax, loosened the feathers, and sent him plunging down to death. Dædalus winged through the central zone to safety.

Perhaps the most versatile genius of all time was the great Florentine Italian, Leonardo da Vinci. Da Vinci was a painter, a sculptor, a scientist, an architect, a military engineer of great renown. He painted the famous "Mona Lisa," he built fortifications for the Duke of Florence, he designed battering rams to demolish fortifications. His great dream was to build an instrument that would fly; but science was not far enough advanced in his time. There was no internal combustion engine in the fifteenth century.

Leaders in the early development of the airplane that did fly were Americans and Frenchmen. One reason why there are so many French terms commonly used in aviation (which is itself a derivative from the French) is due to French pioneer developments. Some of the most important flights by Americans—notably by the Wright brothers—were made in France.

We all have heard of the town of Kitty Hawk, North Carolina, where on December 17, 1903, the Wright brothers made their first weird contraption fly, and, after months of experimentation, finally flew for half an hour a distance of twenty-four and a half miles. Some of us remember the Frenchman, Blériot, who startled the world in 1909 by flying a "crate" successfully over the English Channel.

United States Army officers were among the first to realize the potentialities of the airplane in warfare; but our Army experiments were severely handicapped by lack of funds.

It was in France and in Germany, therefore, that the development of the airplane for military uses proceeded the most rapidly, but even in those countries the combat potentialities of the plane were not appreciated until World War No. 1 was well under way. Had Germany had effective air reconnaissance in September, 1914, the Battle of the Marne might have resulted in a different conclusion—and with it a different conclusion to the history of that war.

First military aviation in World War No. 1 was for purposes of observation. In the earliest period of the war pilots carried pistols as sole armament. Machine guns were soon mounted and later were synchronized to fire through the propellers. Bombing missions were a comparatively late development. These were all short-range operations, and only light loads could be carried. The machine-gun was the chief anti-aircraft weapon until the later stages of the war when the ancestors of the present anti-air weapons were employed to throw high-explosive shells at attacking planes, with indifferent results. The German bombing attacks on London were carried out by lighter-than-air craft, the Zeppelins.

The Germans and French led in the military development of aircraft in the first World War, with the British rapidly catching up. American production was late, due mainly to the late entry of America into the war. Nearly all American fliers on the Western Front were outfitted with French and British planes. The first 100 per cent American planes were not completed in time for action.

All of this was very new—and the wonders of modern military aviation are still very new. Only thirty years elapsed between the time when Blériot triumphantly flew one way across the Channel and the time when Hitler loosed his tremendous air armadas with their vast bomb loads over the cities of England and Scotland in World War No. 2.

In the years that followed the first modern World War, tremendous developments had taken place.

The honor of making the first trans-Atlantic flight goes to the United States Navy. Three Navy flying boats started from Newfoundland to fly to Portugal, making a refueling stop at the Azores en route. The flight was completed on May 27, 1919, by Lieutenant Commander A. C. Read, piloting the NC-4.

The first *non-stop* trans-Atlantic flight, however, was made later that year by two intrepid British aviators, Alcock and Brown. They flew a Vickers plane from St. Johns, Newfoundland, to Ireland—a distance of 1,936 miles.

Eight years, during which many more historic flights were made, passed before Lindbergh made his famous solo trip to Paris in 1927, flying 3,313 miles. A few weeks later, the United States Army took on the flight from Oakland, California, to Honolulu over 2,400 miles of ocean in twenty-five hours and thirty minutes, a flight duplicated from Honolulu to Oakland by Amelia Earhart in January, 1935, in eighteen hours and sixteen minutes.

Just as the English Channel became a ditch after Blériot's flight in 1909, so America's broad oceans were shrinking.

One of the most magnificent of all flying feats, never since duplicated by a solo flier, was Wiley Post's single-handed around-the-world flight, from New York to New York, in 1933—15,600 miles in seven days and eighteen hours.

In 1938, Howard Hughes and his crew of four swung around the globe from New York to New York in the amazing time of three days and nineteen hours.

Neither oceans nor mountains were any longer the barriers they had formerly been. The flying arm of military powers had been given not only wings, but speed and endurance. Today at elevations of 30,000 feet and more, fighter planes engage bombers in the sub-stratosphere, and huge planes may bomb cities from such elevations that the planes cannot be seen with the naked eye and are extremely difficult to locate even with the aid of high-powered glasses.

CLASSES OF MILITARY AIRPLANES

The military airplanes of the United States Army may be considered in five major classifications:

(1) Training airplanes
(2) Cargo airplanes
(3) Bombardment airplanes
(4) Pursuit airplanes
(5) Observation airplanes

Training airplanes are subdivided into three sub-classifications:

(1) Primary trainers—PT
(2) Basic trainers—BT
(3) Advanced trainers—AT

The primary trainer, which is known as PT, plus the number that gives further description of the type, is for primary flight training. A student commences his preliminary flying experience in this airplane. The basic trainer, described as BT, is the final step before flying the service airplanes. All student pilots pass through these two stages of preliminary training before they are given their intensive training with service planes.

Cargo airplanes are used for passengers and cargo carrying and are commonly called transports. The use of similar planes for transport purposes has been widely engaged in by the Germans in their offensive operations. These planes are also used to carry parachute troops and air-borne troops. We will discuss that use in more detail later.

The bombardment planes are divided into four classifications. There are the heavy bombers, such as the B-17, or Flying Fortress, and the B-24; the mediums, such as the B-26, capable of carrying two 2,000-pound bombs, and the B-25; and there are the light bombardment planes such as the A-20 and dive-bombers such as the A-24.

You will note that two classes are named the B planes, the B standing for bombardment; whereas the third class of light bombardment planes and dive-bombers are described as A planes, the A being taken from the word *attack*.

The present heavy bombers are powered with four engines. You have heard of the great feats of our "Flying Fortresses." The medium and light bombers are two-engined craft, and the dive bombers have a single engine. All are used to attack enemy personnel and matériel with bombs.

Types of Pursuit Planes

There are two types of pursuit planes—the fighter and the interceptor, the latter also being a fighter. The fighter carries the greater amount of gasoline and can go as an accompanying airplane on short bombardment missions. On such missions its purpose is to engage enemy interceptor or fighter planes undertaking to attack the bombardment formation accompanied by its protector fighter forces. Pursuit planes are identified by the letter P, .with a model number, for example P-40. Such planes, manned by American pilots, have had a most destructive effect upon the Japanese bombers and fighters in Burma.

The interceptor is a fast-climbing, speedy fighter whose principal mission is to intercept and destroy hostile aircraft attempting to penetrate over our lines or territory. The interceptor carries a heavy load of ammunition and a correspondingly light load of gasoline. It must get into the air very rapidly and work fast to break up enemy bomber formations and destroy enemy craft before they succeed in unloading their bombs over their targets. The British Spitfires have been a fine example of that type of operation. It may be remembered that Winston Churchill was speaking of the British fighter and interceptor personnel when he said, "Never in the field of human conflict was so much owed by so many to so few." These were the types of planes that smashed the daylight attacks of the German Luftwaffe over England in September, 1940, forcing the Germans to take up night bombing operations as a necessity for the first time in the war.

Observation Planes

A tremendous change in observation aircraft is about to come, and the old designation O may not be painted upon the planes. The observation fliers of the immediate future will use converted pursuit and bombardment craft. These will be lightly armored, and speed will be heavily stressed. The new observation-pursuit type will be known as P-39-L, while the heavier ship will bear the title A-20-C.

These machines are designed for sortie missions and not for lengthy reconnaissance. They will speed to the point of observation and hasten back, attempting to outrun enemy pursuit in the process.

The medium observation squadron will be equipped with:

Six bimotor, multi-place, high-performance airplanes
Six single-motor, single-place, high-performance airplanes
Six liaison airplanes

The light observation squadron will be equipped with:

Six single-place, single-motored, high-performance airplanes
Twelve liaison airplanes

Medium observation squadrons will operate with armies, corps, and armored and cavalry divisions. Light observation squadrons will operate with infantry divisions.

The new observation planes will be lightly armed and not suitable for pursuit or bombardment action.

The liaison airplane is unarmed and is intended exclusively for operation behind our own lines at very low altitudes. It keeps the commander informed as to the disposition of his own troops, carries messages, acts as an elevated observation post for artillery, and from the advantage of its elevation can be used to observe forward for a limited distance. The Cub airplanes were so employed in Louisiana during the maneuvers of the Second and Third Armies in September, 1941. Such planes can be usefully employed for personal reconnaissance by division commanders.

Airplane Armament

The type of armament of a plane naturally depends upon its mission.

Modern pursuit craft are both armed and armored. They are armed with cannon (37-mm. or 20-mm.), machine-guns (.50-cal. and .30-cal.), and some of these even with one 500- or 600-lb. bomb. They are armored with bullet-proof glass and heavy armor for the protection of the pilots, and self-sealing gasoline tanks.

The bombardment airplanes are armored in the same fashion as the pursuit planes, but to a greater extent. They are larger all around, and carry more weapons—more machine-guns and more bombs. The weights of the bombs range from 100 to 2,000 pounds, and the number of them carried depends upon the size of the plane, the size of the airfield, and the amount of gas that must be carried.

It is the total weight of the airplane that counts. Gasoline has weight, consequently the more gasoline it carries, the smaller is the bomb load that it can carry. At the same time, the greater the load, the longer is the runway for the take-off.

The bombs may be equipped with either instantaneous or delayed fuses. This means, simply, that the bomb will explode the instant it strikes the target, or it will wait until it has burrowed down a bit, then explode. The first type is more effective against personnel; the second is more effective against matériel such as ships, where the bomb explodes under water, causing a water-hammer blow against the thin under side of the ship, or against airplane runways and roads where the bomb explodes underground, creating a much larger crater.

ORGANIZATION OF THE ARMY AIR FORCES

The recent War Department reorganization removed anchors from the flying men and brought forth the Army Air Forces. This is under the direction of the Commanding General, Army Air Forces, who is advised by a special council. Immediately beneath him is the Chief of the Air Staff and Deputy Chief. The air Staff has six sections, and the first four are familiar enough—A-1, A-2, A-3 and A-4. In addition to these there are a Plans Section and an Air Inspector.

Then come the special Staff Directors—Director of Military Requirements, Director of Technical Services, Public Relations Officer, Director of Personnel, Air Surgeon, Air Judge Advocate, Budget Officer, and Director of Management Control.

These are in turn broken down again. Take the Director of Technical Services for an example. He commands the Director of Communications, the Director of Weather, the Director of Traffic Control and Regulations, the Director of Photography, and the Director of Technical Inspection.

The Air Forces are organized into combat groupings, the 1st, 2nd, 3rd, 4th, Iceland, Panama, Hawaiian Air Forces, etc. These Air Forces are further subdivided into commands according to type as:

Interceptor Command
Bomber Command
Ground-Air Support Command
Air Base Command

These commands are subdivided into groups and squadrons for tactical and administrative control.

An interceptor command has assigned to it varying numbers of pursuit groups. A pursuit group will have a headquarters squadron and three pursuit squadrons. A pursuit squadron consists of two flights of eight airplanes each, and one flight of nine airplanes. A bomber command has varying numbers of bombardment groups assigned. These groups are heavy, medium, light, and dive bombardment groups.

Each heavy and medium bombardment group consists of a headquarters squadron and three bombardment squadrons, and one reconnaissance squadron. Each heavy bombardment squadron has two flights of four heavy four-motored airplanes each. The headquarters squadron has three heavy four-motored airplanes, giving the group a total of twenty-seven heavy airplanes. The combat crew for one of these airplanes consists of pilot, co-pilot, navigator, bombardier, aërial engineer gunner, assistant aërial gunner, and two radio operator gunners. In addition, the navigator and bombardier are trained gunners.

A medium bombardment group has assigned a headquarters squadron, two bombardment squadrons, and one reconnaissance squadron. Each bombardment squadron has two flights of four medium airplanes each and one flight of five medium airplanes. The headquarters squadron has five medium airplanes, making the total for the group forty-four airplanes. Each airplane carries a crew of seven.

A light bombardment group has a headquarters squadron and four bombardment squadrons. A dive bombardment group also has a headquarters squadron and four bombardment squadrons.

Observation units only are assigned as basic units of a Ground-Air Support Command. Bomber units, transport and glider units for parachute and air-borne troops, and in some cases even pursuit aviation, when serving in support of ground forces, will be *attached* to the Ground-Air Support Command.

The function of observation is to secure information for the ground troops. Observation airplanes are not equipped for action against ground personnel or matériel. They are very lightly armed, are not armored, and carry no bombs. Liaison airplanes carry no armament. Light bombardment squadrons are equipped with thirteen airplanes, dive bombardment squadrons with eighteen airplanes.

Under the Commanding General, Army Air Forces, are the technical duties of developing, servicing, supplying, procuring, setting up training schools, making technical inspections, etc.

The Air Service Command operates repair depots, supply depots, and the air transports that carry supplies to the tactical units.

The Ferrying Command ferries American aircraft from the factories to the using personnel, whether this personnel be American or Allied personnel. Now civilian services are also being utilized.

The Flying Training Command and *Technical Training Command* are in charge of all the training schools. These commands are responsible for training the thousands of pilots, observers, bombardiers, navigators, gunners, airplane mechanics, armorers, radio technicians, photographers, and other highly trained technicians whose services are required.

The Matériel Command is charged with the development and procurement of Air Corps equipment. This equipment takes in a wide range. Airplanes, instruments, flying clothing, parachutes, airplane engines, tools, cameras—in fact everything, except guns and radios, that goes into providing and equipping air fleets.

The Technical Inspection Division provides the inspection service that insures a high standard of safety in air operations.

The Flight Surgeon's Division provides for the specialized medical examination of flying personnel.

Formation of an Air Task Force

The formation of air task forces follows the same procedure as the formation of ground task forces. The air forces are organized to support the ground forces. An air task force will contain the various components in such strength as the situation requires and will permit in order to accomplish the objective. The formation would comprise pursuit, bombardment, and observation aircraft. The strength available and the forces needed elsewhere have to be considered.

Parachute Troops and Air-borne Troops

The movement of parachute troops and air-borne troops from an airdrome to their objective is an air corps function. The troops are carried in air transports. As transports are highly vulnerable to hostile air attack, all such movements must be heavily protected by pursuit aircraft. Parachute troops may be dropped in any open terrain. Air-borne troops can be landed only where there are suitable airplane landing areas held by our forces. The task of holding such areas is normally accomplished by parachute troops. Bombardment aviation, particularly dive bombers, may be used to support the actions of both parachute troops and air-borne troops.

HOW AVIATION HELPS THE GROUND FORCES

The air forces assist the ground forces in many different ways: by observation aviation, which gives the ground troops vital information of strength, location, and disposition of hostile forces; by pursuit aviation which intercepts and destroys the hostile aircraft attempting to penetrate our lines; and by bombardment, which attacks and destroys hostile troops and matériel.

Here are some examples of how the air-ground team has operated. In the invasion of Norway, German dive-bombers neutralized a Norwegian airdrome. Air-borne troops landed in sufficient numbers to overpower the Norwegian ground troops in the vicinity and permitted the immediate landing of sea-borne forces. This surprise resulted in an almost bloodless victory.

The taking of a great fort in Belgium was accomplished by the Germans in the following manner: Dive-bombers blasted craters inside the fort. Glider troops landed gliders inside, took refuge in the craters, and with machine-guns prevented the operation of the fort guns. Reinforcing troops took the fort easily.

In France a path was blasted by dive-bombers for the advancing ground forces, both armored and infantry. The movement of reinforcements by the French was scattered by dive-bombers. After the break-through was accomplished, the retreating French were pounded by bombs which were being dropped *alongside* the road, so that the road would not be damaged for the pursuing Germans. Low-flying planes machine-gunned troops and civilians alike to induce panic. French armored attacks were broken by dive-bombers.

In all this work the coördination of the air-ground team was almost perfect. The air would answer ground calls to break obstacles which were unduly hampering or holding up the advance. The air did not displace artillery but supplemented artillery, and came into action rapidly. IT MUST BE NOTED THAT IN ALL THESE OPERATIONS THE GERMANS HAD AIR SUPERIORITY.

The successful evacuation of the British forces from Dunkirk was accomplished only because, at terrible cost, the British Air Force established local air superiority over the area and prevented the Germans from completely destroying the broken British forces.

HOW AVIATION PLAYS THE PRINCIPAL ROLE IN A TASK FORCE (CRETE)

Crete is an example of how aviation can play the principal role in a task force. In Crete, the Germans attacked the British airdromes with superior air forces. The British aircraft were destroyed or forced to flee to Africa to escape destruction. Parachute troops were dropped in such large numbers that they soon controlled the airdrome. Large forces of air-borne troops were landed with light guns and mortars and immediately deployed against the British and Greeks. A steady stream of reinforcements arrived by air until by sheer weight of forces they overwhelmed the defending garrisons. In this type of operation, large quantities of transport airplanes are required. They can transport personnel, equipment up to 105-mm. howitzers and supplies, including food, ammunition, and, if necessary, even water. All except the heavier equipment can be dropped where needed by parachute. Tests conducted in our Army have demonstrated the feasibility of this type of operation. Again it must be noted, *the attacking force must have air superiority*. If the British had had air equality in Crete and dispersed airdromes, or available areas to place dispersed airdromes, the Germans would not have succeeded in their mission.

MILITARY AVIATION ON SEPARATE MISSIONS

In the present war, military operations do not always involve the contact of hostile ground troops. Sometimes the action is entirely an air action on one side against hostile forces or installations. An example is the air war being waged across the English Channel. English observation aircraft locate important hostile installations or manufacturing centers. Photographs are made. These photographs form the basis of an "objective folder." These "objective folders" contain all available data about prospective targets for bombardment airplanes. When in the opinion of the British Air Command the target is ripe for bombing, and its importance sufficient to bring it high on the priorities list, a bombardment mission is dispatched against it. The mission may be either a day or night mission. All personnel participating in the mission are thoroughly informed concerning the objective. They learn its location in detail, what it is, what anti-aircraft defenses surround it and are located on the way to it, and what air resistance may be encountered. Detailed plans for the attack are made, and then at the appointed time the bombers depart on the mission. Upon completion of the mission each member of the combat crew who returns gives his observations in detail to an intelligence officer. If possible a picture of the target is taken after the attack has passed. This often indicates the success or failure of the mission.

An outstanding example of air operations directed at definite objectives was the attack on Hickam Field by Japanese bombers on Sunday, December 7, 1941. It was obvious that detailed plans had been made for this attack, that every plane had a definitely located objective.

The bombing of industrial centers by bombardment aircraft stops or slows down the manufacturing or processing of supplies vital to combatant forces. The bombing of railroad bridges and highway bridges delays the delivery of vital supplies to combatant forces. The action of the British Air Force against the German industrial areas is undoubtedly having an important effect on the widespread front.

LAND-BASED AVIATION VERSUS SEA POWER

It has been demonstrated in the present war that sea power, unprotected by air power, venturing into or being caught in the range of strong land-based bombardment aircraft will suffer severe damage and loss. The British are unable to base at Scapa Flow due to hostile air action. The damage inflicted on the British in the early part of the war forced the abandonment of this base. American and Dutch aircraft operating in the narrow waters around and within the Dutch East Indies and the region of the Malay Archipelago have struck telling blows against the Japanese fleet units and transports.

Another example is the tragic disaster that overtook the British battle-ship *Prince of Wales* and the heavy cruiser *Repulse*. Unprotected by air, they were destroyed by Japanese bombers and torpedo planes, which were free of all opposition except the anti-aircraft guns on board the two vessels. The value of anti-aircraft artillery is great, but alone it is often not enough. Air power must be used to protect surface vessels whenever that is possible, recent experience has shown.

To operate land-based aviation it is imperative that adequate land bases be supplied. Until about 1935 aviation could operate out of practically any cow-pasture. The airplanes were relatively simple, they did not weigh much, and their landing speed was low. The present airplanes are fast; many land at speeds in excess of 110 miles per hour and glide at 150 miles per hour. The bombers are heavy. All of them are complicated machines. Air bases are as necessary for modern air fleets as navy bases are for sea fleets. Aircraft may operate from any smooth, hard surface with sufficient width and breadth to provide runways; but repairs in the field are as difficult for aircraft as repairs at sea are for navy vessels. Surface fleets operating within range of powerful, well-maintained land-based air fleets are always in serious danger of heavy losses. The air bases provide maintenance for the airplanes which cannot be accomplished on fields provided only with runways, often tem-

porarily laid steel runways. The bases also furnish vital supplies
for aircraft.

THE PARTS PLAYED BY THOSE WHO FLY AND THE
PARTS PLAYED BY THOSE ON THE GROUND

Combat crews range in size from one, in *interceptor* aircraft, to
eight or more in *heavy bombers*. The one man in the interceptor is
the pilot, navigator, radio operator, engineer, and gunner combined. He aims his guns by aiming the plane. In the case of the
bomber, however, there are one or more men for each of these
jobs, and the guns can be aimed separately. In between these two
extremes there are crews of varying sizes: *two-place liaison planes;
three-place observation planes* carrying as a third man a gunner
who relieves the observer of this responsibility; *dive-bombers* carrying a crew of two, the gunner keeping the enemy off the tail so
that the pilot may carry out his mission; *light bombers* carrying a
bombardier in addition to the pilot and gunner; and *medium bombers* carrying a crew similar to that of heavy bombers.

For every hour that an airplane is in the air, many man-hours of
skilled labor must be expended by highly-trained ground crews.
Daily inspections, pre-flight inspections, and 25-, 50-, and 100-hour
inspections must be performed by the ground crew. These inspections are detailed. In addition to the airplane, its instruments, engines, and propellers, they include the radio and armament as well.
Adjustments and repairs are made as soon as an inspection indicates the need. The crew to inspect an airplane includes airplane
mechanics, armorers, radio mechanics, and propeller, electrical,
instrument, and carburetor specialists.

In addition to these services, repairs may require metal workers,
welders, and machinists. The bombsight requires the expert service
of a bombsight specialist. These men keep the complicated mechanisms of the modern American airplane in first class operating
condition. Without their skilled labors, flying a battle plane would
be a hazardous stunt. The relatively low casualty rate in the present emergency, compared to the high rates of the former war is
a tribute to their skill and devotion to duty.

In addition to those who work directly on the airplane or its equipment, there are tasks for others which increase safety and the efficiency of aërial activity. There is the weather forecaster who keeps a running record of the weather all over the United States and our possessions and outposts and tells what weather may be expected at any place along a designated route and what may reasonably be expected in a following period; the photographer who develops aërial pictures, titles them, and prepares them for study by intelligence officers; the parachute rigger who gives the combat crewmen a chance if the ship fails or the fortune of battle goes against them; the radio operators who are in contact with ships in the air and in emergencies provide a radio beacon to guide the ships to safe landings; the Link trainer specialists who teach pilots to fly by instrument in bad weather; and the technical clerks who assist in making available the latest technical information to the mechanics who operate the technical maintenance system for the unit. Without the services of these men the aircraft must remain on the ground.

GROUND PRECAUTIONS FROM THE POINT OF VIEW OF THE MAN IN THE AIR AND OF THE MAN ON THE GROUND

On bulletin boards and in company day rooms throughout the Army, silhouettes of Allied and enemy planes may now be studied by the soldiers. The careful study of types and how they look in the air is necessary not only for the personnel in the Air Forces, but for ground forces as well. The ability of men in all units to identify friendly and enemy planes not only leads to better security measures on their part but prevents the unfortunate experience of friendly troops firing upon their own planes or those of their Allies. Army orders emphasize that the use of photographs, silhouette charts, training films, and film strips in identification of enemy aircraft must be stressed in all commands.

One of the most important things for the ground soldiers to know is what the airman is able to see from the air. This of course depends on his altitude. From practically any altitude he can see the movement of motor vehicles on roads. When motor vehicles move on dusty roads, observation aircraft are drawn from long distances

to see what is going on. Motor vehicles, troops, and dumps in
heavy woods are normally well concealed. Too many troops make
the mistake of spreading sheets or other eye-catching articles near
the edge of woods. Such articles often betray the location of forces
in the woods. They act as panels. Trucks should be well in the
woods and drawn under heavy trees or brush or camouflaged.
Troops attempting to conceal themselves in thin woods should not
move when aircraft fly over, as any movement catches the eye
quickly. Olive drab uniforms fade quickly from sight, but khaki
is easily seen from the air. The color of pyramidal tents is readily
seen, and where these tents must be erected they should be camouflaged. The most serious offense against safety from air attack
committed by the ground soldier is massing of motor transportation on roads. This should never be done, as dive-bombers can
wreck trucks and the roads at each end of a line of motor vehicles
so massed and then proceed to wreck the entire convoy, killing,
wounding or dispersing the personnel with it.

At night, unless the moon is shining brightly, an air observer
can see little without the use of flares. Flares illuminate but a relatively small area. The observer must catch something which causes
him to believe there is a subject below worth seeing before he
ignites a flare. Columns of troops in open country without roads
have been located at night because, despite orders to the contrary,
troops insisted on smoking. A match here, there, and further along
the line indicates to the trained observer that a column is below.
He shoots a flare and soon has the information he seeks. Flash-
lights in the hands of officers have betrayed movements at night,
and of course automobile and truck headlights are quickly spotted.
Panel stations have betrayed the locations of command posts.
Panels should never be displayed except on call and then only if
there are no enemy aircraft in sight. Trucks and cars improperly
concealed have betrayed command posts. Roads through thin
woods are easily found and photographed. Mosquito bars have betrayed locations. Remember, movement and any color not blending
with the background betrays locations in daylight; lights betray
locations at night.

What we have said here about the conditions of insecurity that
are noted from the air should remind all of you who were in the

August and September, 1941, maneuvers of the failure of ground troops to take proper precautions. The air task force commanders of both the Second and Third Armies were confident that their operations would have created havoc in your ranks and would have destroyed vast quantities of your equipment as well as innumerable lives.

During the maneuvers neither side had command of the air. The air forces were approximately even in strength. Therefore it was natural that the Blues thought that the Red airplanes were always over their heads and the Reds thought the Blue planes were always over *their* heads. So far as bombardment missions were concerned, neither side could watch its own aviation. So far as fighters were concerned, there were not enough pursuit planes on either side to prevent the enemy from accomplishing his mission in most instances. However, that also is a *practical example*. One does not always have air superiority at every part of a front. While general air superiority might be held by one side, local superiority may from time to time be enjoyed by a weaker enemy. That has undoubtedly been the case on the Russian front, 1,000 miles long. You may have air equality with an opposing force and nevertheless receive very severe punishment. At the same time you are giving similar punishment to the enemy. You cannot, therefore, as ground forces, take a short-sighted view of the air condition on your part of the front.

It is quite possible that soldiers reading this chapter will have just such experiences on the battlefields on which they will serve —times when an enemy may have local superiority, times when equality of air forces might make you feel that you are getting the worst of it from the air, even when you are giving as good as you are getting—perhaps more. It is essential for you to understand these matters for the sake of your own judgment, so that your courage is not affected by conditions that are just as disadvantageous for the enemy that is facing you. Your capacity to "take it" better than he can may well determine in more than one field of battle who the victor will be. Your strict cultivation of the most careful habits of dispersion and of concealment, even when engaged in an advance, will have much to do with your success in battle—or whether you will survive the day. Your prompt digging of slit trenches—2 x 2 x 6—may have everything to do with your success or failure in battle.

We mention this particularly as *the cultivation of good habits*. It is too frequently remarked that once bombs start falling the soldiers will quickly learn better habits. That doesn't follow at all. They may learn to run quickly to cover, but that doesn't mean that they will have cultivated the habit of using cover and concealment and dispersion and still be in hand and under command to conduct their operations. It is one thing to learn to get away from a severe air attack. It is another thing to learn how to protect yourself from such an attack and still be under the control of your officers and still be pursuing your mission as integrated units. That requires the cultivation of good habits, no matter at what expense of hard, sweating effort.

CHAPTER XXXII

ORGANIZATION AND DUTIES IN THE UNITED STATES NAVY AND THE MARINE CORPS

The basic fighting unit of the Army is the soldier—a man whose business is waging war with the aid of certain weapons. All the training of the Army enlisted man—all his duties, his drills, and his maneuvers—are directed toward making him a more efficient fighter. On the other hand, the Navy enlisted man is not primarily a warrior in the same sense that he expects to fight hand to hand. Rather, he is a specialist whose existence is dedicated completely to making the warship an efficient battle machine. All his training, his duties, his drills, and his customs are predicated on this function.

This is the fundamental distinction between the soldier and the sailor. It is a key to understanding a great many things about the Navy enlisted man—from the kind of pants he wears to the way he thinks in a gun turret under fire.

There are now (1942) more than 300,000 men in the Navy, in addition to some 65,000 Marines and almost 25,000 Coast Guardsmen who are serving with the Navy for the duration of the war. These numbers will be greatly increased during the coming months as men are added to man the new ships of our two-ocean Navy.

The typical Navy recruit comes, oddly enough, from the Middle West—perhaps from Indiana or Iowa, far from blue water. His average age is nineteen; his average education, three years of high school. Enlisting at a recruiting station is only the first step in a long and careful training process he must undergo before actually joining the crew of a man-of-war. First comes a rigid physical examination. All phases of the applicant's life are then investigated, including the references which have been required of him. His fingerprints are checked at criminal bureaus. He takes an intelligence test and is assigned a mark.

If found acceptable in all these regards, he is sworn in and sent to a training station to go through an intensive eight-weeks course which thoroughly acquaints him with his new life before he so much as sets foot aboard a ship.

To safeguard against his introducing a communicable disease, the recruit must spend his first three weeks of training in the detention unit, a section isolated from the rest of the training station. These first three weeks are the hardest period in a sailor's naval career. He is granted no leave and is plunged abruptly into a new and bewildering life. Because there is not much room aboard any warship, he must learn to live out of two canvas bags and a tin box called a "ditty box." He learns to roll his clothing just so, and to lay it out in a precise formation for weekly inspection. He finds out that cleanliness in the Navy means hospital cleanliness. He is taught to salute, to respect authority, and to say "Aye, aye, sir," instead of "Yes, sir" or "Okay."

One of the first things a recruit learns is to recognize the uniform and insignia of his service. The sailor's uniform is completely different from a soldier's because he has a completely different job. It is important that the individual soldier be invisible to the enemy, so he wears khaki. But it doesn't matter whether the individual sailor is seen or not, so he wears blue in winter and white in summer, although he, too, has a khaki outfit which is sometimes substituted for his white.

The uniform of the Navy enlisted man is designed to combine utility with tradition. It has bell-bottomed trousers because they are more easily rolled up when the decks must be swabbed. It has an open neck for greater comfort and freedom. Its square, bib-like collar in back is a holdover from the days when sailors customarily wore the long, greasy pigtails that earned them the nickname "Jack Tar."

The force to which a sailor is attached aboard ship is indicated by the color of the strip running around the shoulder seam of his blouse. If it is white, he is in the seaman branch; if red, in the engineering branch. The slanting stripes on his sleeve are his service stripes, better known as "hash marks"—one for each four years of service. A seaman's rating is shown by the stripes on his cuff, one for a third-class seaman, two for a second-class, and three for a first-class. As in the Army, chevrons indicate the non-coms, or petty officers, one chevron for a third-class petty officer, two for a second-class, and three for a first-class.

In addition, Navy enlisted men wear sleeve insignia to show what kind of work they do. As there are nearly forty such insignia, we cannot review them all. Sights for a gun-pointer, a torpedo for a torpedoman, crossed quills for a yeoman, a crescent for a cook, sparks for a radioman, and crossed anchors for a bo's'n's mate are only a few. These insignia also appear with the chevrons of a petty officer's arm badge.

Although all petty officers below the rank of chief wear enlisted men's uniforms with their badges on the sleeve, the chief petty officer is entitled to wear a double-breasted uniform similar to that of a commissioned officer.

As he moves out of the detention unit into the "main side" of the training station, the recruit (who is now known as "Boots" because of the leggings he wears) is becoming well grounded in the fundamentals of infantry drill. He acquires the knack of handling a rifle and learns how to pull an oar. He learns semaphore signaling and "marlinspike seamanship," which includes nautical terminology, rope-splicing, knot-tying, and the elements of sailing. Finally, he learns what his life aboard a modern man-of-war will be like—what his duties, both general and specific, will be and how to carry them out.

Either at the conclusion of this basic training period or at some future period in his service, the enlisted man may take specialized courses at one of the Navy service schools. These vary in length; some are held on shore and others afloat. About 80 per cent of Navy personnel complete trade-school courses at some time in their careers, thus becoming specialists, which entitles them to increased pay. To give an idea of the diversified kinds of instruction available, the Navy has schools for:

Machinists	Fire controlmen
Woodworkers	Gyrocompass electricians
Electricians	Motion-picture technicians
Ordnancemen	Torpedomen
Clerical personnel	Aërographers
Musicians	Aviators
Hospital corpsmen	Deep-sea divers
Cooks and bakers	Dental technicians

Parachute materialmen	Radiomen
Pharmacist mates	Submarine personnel
Photographers	Metalsmiths

Their study, furthermore, does not stop with the completion of their service school training, but continues aboard ship.

After a man is assigned to duty on board a warship, his further advancement is determined by his own ability. There are eight grades of seamen and non-commissioned officers, ranking progressively as follows: third-, second-, and first-class non-rated men; third-, second-, and first-class petty officers; acting chief petty officers; and chief petty officer. The latter corresponds roughly to a top sergeant in the army. Pay ranges from $21 a month for third-class seamen to $126 for chief petty officers. Although it takes many years to attain this top pay, all men who have become expert at some specialty or have more than a few months' service earn more than base pay.

If a chief petty officer shows particular qualifications, he may be promoted to warrant officer, a rank just above non-commissioned officers and just below commissioned officers. Warrant officers may, upon fulfilling the proper requirements and passing a satisfactory examination, obtain commissions in the line of the Navy.

So much for the training of the Navy enlisted man, and the opportunities which the service offers him. But what of his life on shipboard?

OPERATION OF A BATTLE-SHIP

Picture a modern man-of-war. It is a collection of complicated machines and weapons all packed tightly together in a steel shell. There is very little room in which to move, and almost none in which to live. Everywhere the sailor turns are pipes, air ducts, electric cables, and big valves. He gets used to ducking every time he goes through a door, and used to sleeping wherever he can find two hooks to sling his hammock.

Naturally, if as many as 1600 men are to remain healthy while living so closely together, every inch of the ship must be kept scrupulously clean. If they are to move about the decks and the narrow passageways, nearly every step must be according to careful regulations. If they are to carry out their widely varying duties in perfect coördination in any contingency, they must be drilled to perfection. Thus the restricted space of a ship, together with the necessity of its functioning at top efficiency at all times, dictate most of the duties, drills, and customs that constitute the sailor's daily routine.

The efficient operation of the ship is the responsibility of its officers, recognizable to the recruit by their plain blue double-breasted uniforms with circular gold stripes around the sleeves. An ensign, he discovers, has a single gold stripe; a lieutenant, junior grade, one full-width plus one half-width stripe; a full lieutenant, two full stripes; a lieutenant commander, two and a half; a commander, three; and a captain, four full stripes. He learns, furthermore, that an ensign in the Navy corresponds in rank with a second lieutenant in the Army; a Navy lieutenant, junior grade, with an Army first lieutenant; a Navy full lieutenant with an Army captain; a lieutenant commander with a major; a commander with a lieutenant colonel; and a captain in the Navy with a colonel in the Army. The Navy rear admiral, vice admiral, and full admiral are the equivalent, respectively, of a major general, lieutenant general, and full general in the Army. They are distinguished by very wide gold sleeve stripes, and by two, three, or four stars on their shoulder-straps.

Commissioned officers of the line are usually graduates of the United States Naval Academy or, in wartime, of shorter and more intensive courses which lead to a reserve commission. Although the majority of the appointments to the Naval Academy are made by members of Congress, the law also authorizes the appointment of 100 enlisted men each year. Upon graduation from the Academy or from shorter emergency courses, the cadet enters the service of the Navy as an ensign.

Aboard ship, however, officers are distinguished not so much by their rank as by their official duties. A ship at sea must of necessity be a wholly self-contained unit. In addition to its direct war functions, it must contain all the facilities of any isolated community of human beings. Its administration strikingly resembles that of a municipality, with the various functions assigned to the equivalent of city commissioners.

At the head of any ship is the captain or commanding officer. It should be noted that he is not necessarily a captain in rank, but is a captain by courtesy since he is in command of the ship. On the smaller vessels the commanding officer is usually of a lower rank. The captain has complete authority over all members of the ship's company. His is the ultimate and final responsibility for the safety and well-being of the vessel and those aboard.

OPERATING DEPARTMENTS

The commanding officer does not, however, see to the execution of his orders himself. His orders are transmitted through the executive officer, the line officer next in rank. The executive is the direct representative of the captain of the ship and is responsible for seeing to it that all the captain's orders are carried out. The routine operation of the ship and coördination of the various departments come directly under the executive.

There are six of these departments: Gunnery, Navigation, Engineer, Construction, Medical, and Supply.

Gunnery Department

This includes all the men who fire the guns and care for them, the aviation men who are responsible for the catapult planes, and the Marines on board. The gunnery officer, who has one of the most responsible positions aboard a war vessel, is responsible for drilling the men with guns; for the armament and the ammunition in the store-rooms; and for the safety precautions in connection with the latter.

Engineering Department

The engineer officer of the ship is responsible for everything pertaining to the engines which drive the ship through the seas; all machinery, except radio and signal apparatus, comes under his supervision.

Navigation Department

The Navigation Department, headed by the navigating officer, is responsible for all the work of finding the position of the ship and for all the apparatus used in navigation. He prepares the weather reports, which are sent to Washington. In time of battle he assists the commanding officer in handling the ship. The navigator usually has such additional duties as being in charge of the ship's library, courts martial, and the various courses of training and education for the crew.

Construction Department

The Construction Department is in charge of the first lieutenant, who is responsible for seeing that the ship is properly kept up, clean, trim, and neat in appearance, and in good order. The first lieutenant is in charge of any construction and repairs which are made aboard. In battle he has the responsibility of repairing at once any damage caused by enemy fire.

Medical Department; Supply Department

The Medical Department, under the medical officer, requires no explanation.

The Supply Department is under the supply officer. Personnel, accounts, and purchasing, the mess and the ship's store, the paymasters, the storekeepers, the cooks, the bakers, and the stewards all come under his control.

Each of these departments is subdivided according to the different types of jobs to be done. Thus, for example, the engineering department would include, among other divisions, a boiler division, the engine-room division, and the electrical division, each under a division officer.

The departmental heads and the assistant division officers are primarily concerned with the maintenance and preparation for battle of the various departments of the ship. The actual routine, day-in and day-out operations of the ship are supervised by the watch officers. There is at all times one officer responsible for the operation of the ship, the officer of the deck. Regardless of his rank, as long as he holds this title all other persons aboard the ship who are subject to the commanding officer are also under his order, save, of course, the executive. While he is on duty the officer of the deck is responsible for the safety of the ship and her efficient operation. In case of emergency or change of course he reports to the commanding officer.

The officer of the deck is assisted by other, junior officers, the number varying according to the size of the ship and responsibilities involved.

THE MARINES

A unit of Marines, which is stationed aboard all larger ships and on some smaller ones, man certain units of broadside and anti-aircraft guns, help police the ship, function in ship ceremonies, and may help regular Navy men in taking watches. On battle-ships and aircraft carriers, for example, there are units of approximately 100 Marines.

Although their duties in conjunction with the fleet constitute the most important of the Marines' functions, they perform valuable land duties as well. They have their own bases as well as training stations, and their officers may come either from Annapolis or from civilian colleges, or may work their way up from the ranks after passing stiff examinations. Their ranks correspond throughout with those in the Army.

Marines act as military police in guarding United States naval bases, docks, storehouses, and ammunition dumps, both in this country and abroad. They also protect American legations in countries where trouble is expected. In addition there is the Fleet Marine Force, which consists of infantry, artillery, tanks, signal corps, engineering and chemical troops, and an air force—all highly trained and practised in executing landing operations on hostile shores.

A DAY ABOARD SHIP

The typical day aboard ship begins, as in the Army, with reveille —which is sounded over the ship's amplifying system at 5:30 A.M.

Then comes the bo's'n's mate with his "Up all bunks" or "Rise and shine," which means business. There is no more sleep after that. All hands wash and dress.

At 6:00 A.M. a bo's'n's mate passes the word to "pipe all sweepers" and all hands turn to. They scrub and wash down the main deck and shine the ports and brasswork. These jobs done, the guncovers are removed and the gun screens rolled up. At 7:30 A.M. the meal pennant, better known as the "bean rag," is hoisted and breakfast is ready.

Breakfast is followed by muster and reports to the executive. At 7:50 A.M. the guard of the day is called, the bugler sounds the call to colors, the band plays the national anthem, and the colors are hoisted.

All hands not detailed to special jobs muster on deck at 8:15, when the division officers outline the plan of the day and detail working parties. At 8:30 sick call is piped for those requiring special medical attention, while all others clean their quarters. The rest of the morning is taken up with various classes and drills which we shall examine in more detail in a few moments.

When the meal pennant has been hauled down after the noonday meal, a bo's'n pipes the sweepers to clean the mess, the living compartments, and "topside." At this time bedding may be aired. The band gives a twenty-minute concert on the main deck at 12:40.

Promptly at 4:00 P.M. all bluejackets not on special duty may knock off work. At 5:30 the meal pennant is again hoisted and the crew piped for supper. At 6:00 the anchor watch, which changes every two hours, is mustered. In peacetime, motion pictures are usually shown on deck in the evening, or other entertainments are held. Now, of course, the ship must be on the alert and no lights shown.

Taps is sounded by the bugler on the quarterdeck at 9:00. A bo's'n's mate of the watch passes the word to turn in and pipe down. At 10:00 all lights go out and everyone must be in.

Of course the daily routine on a smaller ship, such as a destroyer or a submarine, differs considerably from that outlined here, and life is generally much more informal. The same principles, however, hold true there too.

Actually, the schedule outlined above would scarcely be recognized by a bluejacket, because the Navy tells and writes time differently from anyone else. There is no such thing as A.M. or P.M. They count all hours straight through from one to twenty-four, starting at midnight. Thus, one o'clock in the afternoon is 13 o'clock, 2 P.M. is 14 o'clock and so on. When it is 9:30 P.M. in the Army it is 21:30 o'clock in the Navy.

DRILLS

No warship is at peak efficiency unless every man on board knows exactly what to do in every conceivable emergency. To this end, a good deal of the working time aboard a Navy vessel is spent in endless drills until each man can do his particular specialized task by habit alone. Each man's station and duties have been worked out long in advance, in the light of centuries of experience, and these orders are posted on "bills," which are lists showing where each member of the ship's company is to be in a given emergency.

Some of the important drills are as follows: First is the fire-drill, emphasizing the necessity of getting fire extinguishers to any portion of the ship in a few seconds' time. In the man-overboard drill, the men practise throwing lines and buoys and then rowing out in boats to rescue a dummy representing a drowning man. In a collision drill, the most important thing is to close the water-tight hatches in the section of the collision. Still another drill is the abandon-ship drill, in which boats are loaded with provisions and lowered away.

All other drills, however, are incidental to the battle drill. The basic, ultimate purpose of a warship is to win a battle, which may be decided in the space of a half-hour. All the training and practice of a sailor, which may take years, is preparation for this essential moment.

In battle drills, all the ordinary work on the ship stops. Loose gear is tied down, and most of the inflammable paints and oils, as well as most of the wooden furniture and fixtures (which would splinter dangerously if hit) are thrown overboard. All ordinary electric light bulbs are taken out and the electric circuits cut off. The battle circuits are thrown in so that all the emergency signal systems and gunfire-control apparatus are working. Special blue battle lights, invisible a few hundred feet away, are turned on below decks. Ammunition is brought up on elevators from the hold to the gun turrets.

Fire-hoses are tested and the first-aid kits are prepared. Life-preservers are brought up. All unnecessary steam and water systems are cut off. Gunners stuff cotton in their ears. The captain and his assisting officers are ready to direct operations from the armored conning tower. In the fire-control plotting room, far down, men at complex machines stand ready to assemble the information needed to train the guns and to relay the ranges to the turrets and gun compartments. The gun crews stand ready to load the guns. This is the moment for which all the rest of the sailor's life is preparatory. He is at his station, an indispensable cog in making his ship a completely efficient and powerful weapon.

NAVY TRADITIONS

In the course of centuries many traditions, customs, and courtesies have grown up in the Navy which are distinctive and unlike those of any other service. Naval ceremony starts with the moment a visitor steps on the deck of the ship. He turns and salutes the quarterdeck at the stern of the ship. The quarterdeck on the modern battleship is no longer distinguishable from other portions of the ship's deck. But in the past it was the raised portion of the stern of the ship, held sacred for the use of the captain.

If the visitor is a senior officer or otherwise important, he will be met on deck by two rows of seamen who will salute as he passes through them. The members of the greeting party are known as "side boys," and their number varies in accordance with the person being honored. In the case of a formal visit a salute is fired with guns, the band plays a special march, and the Marine Guard is drawn up at attention.

The captain is not only the most important but also the most isolated man aboard ship. By ancient tradition he dines alone and in general sees little of the subordinate officers, except in connection with official duties. The senior officers of the ship generally mess together, while the junior officers have a mess of their own.

Warrant officers, petty officers, and the various divisions of enlisted men also have their own messes.

As in the Army the salute is the recognized means of greeting members of the service. Ships also salute each other by firing guns, manning the rails, and turning out the band and Marine Guard to play as they pass each other on formal occasions.

The landlubber, suddenly put on a man-of-war, would be unable to understand not only the time of day but most of the rest of the speech as well. Sailors have their own language. All brass fittings are "brightwork," and the ship's hospital is "sick bay." The storekeeper in charge of uniforms is called "Jack of the Dust," dating from the time when he was in charge of the ship's supply of flour too. Time off to go ashore is called "liberty." Sailors have "leaves" too, but there is no such thing as a furlough in the Navy. "Scuttlebutt" is their name for a drinking fountain.

KINDS OF NAVAL VESSELS

Naval vessels, of course, vary widely in size and duties, from the great battle-ships to the tiny torpedo boats that skitter along our coasts. These variations may at first seem confusing, but they are based upon the very logical principle of specialization according to the duties they have to perform.

A number of different characteristics are desirable in fighting ships. They must have offensive power, which means big guns. They must have defensive strength, which means heavy armor. They must have high speed, which means large engines. They must have great cruising range, which means large fuel tanks. They must be maneuverable, which means a size easily handled.

Some of these desirable characteristics are mutually exclusive. For example, it is impossible to make a ship large enough to carry heavy guns and heavy armor which is at the same time highly maneuverable. It is also impossible to build a ship with great hitting and defensive power which is light enough to have a very high speed. Therefore, the ships of the fleet are divided up into a number of different types, each of them emphasizing one or more of the desirable characteristics.

The largest and most important ships of the fleet are the battle-ships. These have maximum hitting power in big guns and maximum defensive strength in heavy armor. They obtain these things by sacrificing speed and maneuverability. They carry a large main battery of guns from twelve-inch to sixteen-inch in size, as well as a considerable number of anti-aircraft and small rapid-fire guns. Their complements are from 1100 to more than 1600 men. Besides their armor they have additional protection against torpedo attack in the form of "blisters" along the sides under water. The blisters are long empty compartments, the outer walls of which are designed to explode a torpedo before it can reach the main part of the hull. In addition, the hulls are divided up inside into a large number of small compartments which may be made completely water-tight by closing electrically operated doors. These are used when a vessel is hit to isolate the portion torn open and prevent water from filling the rest of the ship.

The next largest type of warship in service with the American fleet is the cruiser. These are armed with a large number of guns and anti-aircraft rapid-fire guns, are very fast, and, compared to a battle-ship, lightly armored.

They work in close coöperation with destroyers, the smallest service fighting vessel to serve with the fleet. Destroyers have no armor whatever, being very fast and highly maneuverable. Their principal weapon is the torpedo, although they carry dual-purpose guns which may be used to fire either at surface vessels or at aircraft.

In a category by themselves are the aircraft carriers. They are of different sizes, ranging from the huge *Lexington* and *Saratoga* to the smaller *Ranger*. These vessels have flat, wide upper decks with the superstructure removed, enabling planes to land and take off. The carriers are lightly armored and of moderately high speed. As a rule, their gun-power is light, since they are intended to be protected by the other vessels of the fleet.

Carriers are equipped with fighter, scout, observation, dive-bomber, and light bomber aircraft. The heavy patrol bombers are shore-based at strategic points. In addition battle-ships and cruisers carry a small complement of planes which are launched by catapult.

Finally among combat vessels come the submarines, which range in size from less than 500 tons to 2000 or more tons. Because of the extra danger of their work, crews of submarines receive additional pay.

A large number of the vessels in the United States Navy do not, of course, have combat duties. The fleet train, as it is called, is made up of all the services which feed, fuel, and repair the fleet. It includes tankers, store ships, ammunition ships, transports, minesweepers, hospital ships, destroyer tenders, submarine tenders, seaplane tenders, and so forth.

In addition, there are a large number of smaller naval vessels connected with coastal defense. These include motor torpedo boats, minelayers, submarine chasers, and patrol boats of various sorts.

Battle-ships, cruisers, destroyers, submarines, and carriers are all grouped into divisions; the number of ships in a division varies with the type. The smaller vessels—the destroyers and submarines —are grouped into squadrons of several divisions each. All the vessels of each type with a major fleet form a distinct unit and have a separate commander.

FLEET ORGANIZATION

We have, at the present time, three major fleets: the Atlantic Fleet, the Pacific Fleet, and the Asiatic Fleet.

In addition to the three principal fleets, there are smaller organizations known as task forces. These are independent forces organized for special duties. They vary widely in composition, being extremely flexible so that they may be especially adapted to the task at hand. There is no regular number of task forces, since they have no continuing organization.

When any sort of an organized naval force puts to sea, whether it be a task force of half a dozen vessels or a great fleet of half a hundred, the general organization remains the same. The largest vessels, usually battle-ships, go in the center of the formation. The lighter vessels on the outer fringe protect the large ships from torpedo attack, which the big ships are too heavy to avoid by maneuvering. Ahead of the main body of heavy ships will be found an attack force, which usually consists of cruisers and a destroyer escort and is intended to block any enemy vessels which may crash through the outer lines. Behind the main body is a rear guard, also of cruisers, which prevents the enemy from crashing in from the rear. Also, there will usually be a force of destroyers and battleships called a support force, which is so placed as to reinforce any part of the battle line that is threatened by attack.

Outside of all these bodies is the inner screen of light cruisers and destroyers. Outside of that, perhaps forty or sixty miles from the main body, will be an outer screen of destroyers and possibly submarines. These screens are to protect the heavier ships from torpedo attack and, at the same time, to discover the whereabouts of the enemy and, if an opportunitiy offers, to deliver a torpedo attack against his ships. To further safeguard the fleet on long cruises a scouting force of cruisers is centered along the course of the fleet. This force proceeds far enough ahead of the main body so that it will meet in daylight any enemy groups close enough to the fleet to steam to the attack during the hours of darkness.

DUTIES OF THE NAVY

All these various tasks the Navy has to perform in wartime. Warships have, in general, three major duties: to defeat the enemy fleet in battle, to protect our shipping against attack, and to attack and destroy enemy shipping.

To defeat the enemy in battle is the major job of a battle fleet. It is to this end that the immense organization of the Navy is devoted. It is for this task that officers and men are trained for many years and upon their success in carrying out this duty depends victory or defeat for the Navy.

The circumstances in which the fleet comes into battle vary so greatly that it is impossible to lay down more than the most general rules of combat. The principal aim, of course, is to maneuver the enemy into a position where a superior force of your own ships is able to attack and destroy an inferior force of the enemy before he is able to escape or send reinforcements. At the same time you seek to avoid having any of your detached forces caught by the main body of the enemy's fleet. To prevent the enemy from escaping and to force him to change course, harassing tactics by aircraft and destroyers are used. Air attacks also force the enemy vessels to move in zigzag courses and otherwise slow them up so that our own heavy ships are able to overtake the enemy and force him into action.

On the other hand, if an inferior force of our own should be caught by the enemy, we would seek to retreat under cover of a smoke-screen; we would drop mines in the rear of our ships so that anyone pursuing would have to make a detour around them; and our light vessels would counter-attack with torpedoes to slow up the enemy pursuit.

For convoying, our own lighter vessels—cruisers, destroyers, and armed merchantmen—are employed. Convoys are organized with the merchant ships in exact formation under a covering screen of light vessels.

The attack against convoys comes either from enemy surface vessels which have eluded our own warships or from submarines or aircraft. Every attempt is made to hunt down and capture surface raiders before they can do any damage. The oceans are wide, and inevitably some raiders escape detection. When they attack a convoy it is up to the convoy vessels to fight them off while the merchant shipping makes its escape.

Submarine attacks are met by elaborate sound-detection devices which can hear the approach of a submarine under water. Surface vessels rush to the spot where the submarine is believed to be and launch depth-bombs overboard to destroy the undersea raider.

The problem of protecting convoys against aircraft is a comparatively new one. To some extent it can be solved by mounting anti-aircraft guns in large numbers on both the convoying vessels and the merchant ships themselves. However, it appears that the only really successful defense against air attack consists of a counter-attack by plane. For this reason there is a growing tendency to transform merchantmen into auxiliary aircraft carriers. These carry a number of fighter planes which may be launched into the air to attack enemy bombers. When the attack occurs within range of shore, shore-based planes can assist in driving away hostile air raiders.

In attacking enemy shipping the situation is, of course, reversed. We ourselves would employ submarines, bombers, and surface raiders for this purpose. Fast, well-armed cruisers are the best for surface raiding, since they are able to break through the defense of enemy warships protecting the convoy.

The ultimate duty of the Navy is to coöperate with Army and Marine forces in landing on the enemy's shores. This maneuver, to be successful, calls for the utmost in coöperation of all forces to be used—land, sea and air.

To explain how such a joint maneuver works, let us begin at the top. First of all, there should be a unified command for the special task. Whether this command shall be headed by Army or Navy depends on the particular factors involved. If the major portion of the problem concerns the Navy, it is reasonable to assume that a naval officer would be placed in charge. If the Army is to bear the brunt of the task, the whole task probably would be directed by an Army officer. If air operations were most important, a Navy air commander or Army air commander probably would be named.

Plans for such a unified command have already been worked out between the two services. These plans have been tested in maneuvers in the Hawaii area and elsewhere. Also, in the Louisiana Army maneuvers, Navy and Marine Corps airmen coöperated with Army land and air forces.

Almost any landing on an enemy shore presupposes that there will be opposition from the enemy. In the Philippines, the opposition was supplied by American and Philippine troops against a far superior Japanese invading force. It is more than probable that, before this war is over, the Japanese will find themselves on the defensive against an adequate Allied invading force.

Now for the problems of the actual landing: First of all, the Navy must clear the waters near the invasion point of hostile naval craft. This means that there must be naval superiority on the sea, beneath the sea, and in the air. If the invasion point is within flying range of our own shores or air bases, air superiority will be attained by Army, Navy, and Marine Corps planes fighting as a single unit. If no air bases are near enough to the invasion point, air superiority must be attained by carrier-based planes, the handicap being that the carriers must endeavor to stay out of range of the enemy's shore-based bombers.

Once the fleet landing force is near enough, the landing point is placed under heavy fire from ships and planes, clearing the im-

mediate sector of defending forces. Then the landing parties set
out by boat.

In almost all cases, this initial landing force will be made up of
the "soldiers of the sea," the Marines. They have been especially
trained for the job. They are provided with special equipment for
just such a task. Each Marine knows exactly what he is to do.

A heavy covering fire is provided by fleet and planes as the
Marines board landing boats especially built to land on shallow
beaches and in heavy surf. Some of these boats might carry light
artillery and tanks. Many types of these boats are armored to protect the landing parties against shore fire.

When a beach-head has been gained, the landing force at once
sets to work to fortify it against the enemy and to push the enemy
back as far as possible. The landing force is seldom meant to occupy
the interior. Its principal purpose is to gain a foothold on enemy
territory as a basis for more extensive operations to be undertaken
by the Army.

Once a sufficient area has been cleared of the enemy, with protection from the sea and the air, Army transports are moved in
under convoy, with all the technical equipment needed to carry
out an invasion in force.

With the beginning of extensive land operations, the Navy's job
is by no means ended. Supply lines for the land forces must be kept
open against enemy craft, and supplies and reinforcements for the
enemy must not be allowed to land. In addition, if the land operations are not paramount, and the Marine force is not needed by
the Navy, the Marines may be assigned by the President to the
Army, in which case they form a part of the Army force as needed.

This was done in the American Revolution, the Mexican War,
the Spanish-American War, and in the World War, where the
Marines formed a part of the Second Division of the American
Expeditionary Force.

The foregoing description of a joint Army-Navy landing operation is, of course, general. The specific task at hand would dictate
the exact procedure to be followed. In any case, however, the prime
necessity is for coöperation—complete coöperation in every detail
—if the landing is to be carried out successfully.

The Navy is now battling on two fronts—at home and abroad.

At home officials are winning the war of production, rushing to completion ships which will practically double the size of our Navy, making it the greatest and most powerful the world has ever seen. Abroad our ships are engaged from the East Indies to the North Atlantic. Long weeks of patrol alternate with brief periods of furious battle. In the Atlantic the problem is to keep open the supply lines to the British Isles. In the Pacific we are still in the preliminary stages of a long campaign which can culminate only in the defeat of the Japanese fleet. The war at sea will be long and arduous. The Navy faces it with grim confidence.

CHAPTER XXXIII

THE JAPANESE ARMY

Two months before the attack by Japan upon Pearl Harbor, the curriculum of the Second Army Educational Program included a chapter on the Imperial Japanese Army. The timeliness of the subject was emphasized by the bombs that fell on December 7, 1941.

American soldiers today have an especial interest in the Empire of Japan, the Imperial Army, and the type of foe that will be met in the Japanese soldier. It is the purpose of this discussion briefly to cover that field.

Several things we have definitely learned—the Japanese may suddenly resort to desperate measures, they plan and are effective in employing the element of surprise, their staff work is good, their best troops are aggressive, and they have a conception of honor very different from what we have in the West. Moreover, they have systematically studied the habits of the white Western races and attempt, sometimes successfully, to exploit habits and tendencies that we, on our part, must not permit to become habitual. No one is better aware of the complacency and carelessness of Western peoples than the Japanese.

It behooves us, therefore, to understand this tricky enemy, so that we may take his measure.

POSITION OF THE ARMY AND NAVY IN JAPAN

Before taking up the organization of the Japanese Army and its tactical methods, we should consider the position of the Japanese armed forces in the nation itself, because it is very different from the American idea of an army's relationship to government or to a nation. It will be necessary, too, to outline the traditions and motive forces that govern the conduct and influence the minds of the personnel of the Japanese armed forces. Western peoples are not the only ones having mental habits that fit into grooves.

Therefore, when you consider the Japanese, it is necessary to drop or discard a lot of preconceived ideas. This is certainly true when you come to study their political activities and the relationships of their generals, admirals, and junior officers with their government. We have an hereditary Western conception of civilized political activities, which in substantial measure we inherited from the English settlers on this continent. That is why we periodically are shocked by the strange political ideas that absorb the German people, who are inexperienced with the traditions of civil liberties and constitutionalism that we take for granted, and who have no such heritage in their background. In the case of the Japanese, the chasm that divides our conceptions is far greater, even though superficially it appears that they have a form of government with some institutions that have been copied from Western models. The copying is only a veneer. It covers an atmosphere, a way of thinking, and a system of relationships that are entirely antagonistic to our ideas of government and of the determination of the destinies of peoples. This is not said for the purpose of creating a prejudice, but for the purpose of clearing the decks for a comprehension of the subject of our study. It is important that we have this comprehension. Then the Japanese can neither shock us nor surprise us. And it will save us from harboring impractical ideas.

Japan is a comparatively recent addition to the family of nations. In 1854 Commodore Perry sailed to Japan with a flotilla of American vessels and, by a mild display of force and more persuasion, caused the Japanese to realize that it would be to their advantage to carry on trade with the world after the fashion of Occidental countries. Until then—only eighty-eight years ago—the Island Empire had persisted in a policy that excluded all foreigners. All intercourse with the outside world, except for one ship a year permitted the Dutch, was prohibited. Even shipwrecked sailors were mistreated. For over 200 years this policy had persisted. The last people who had tried to open trade were the Portuguese. (The members of one such expedition had had their ears cut off and were sent back with the message from the Japanese: "Think no more of us, as if we were no longer of the world.")

During this period the government of Japan was military in character. There was an emperor, although he did not rule for himself but was under the power of an individual called the *shogun*,

SHOGUN, who actually governed the country and whose office was hereditary. The first of that line of shoguns had reached his high position by armed force; succeeding shoguns used force to maintain their positions. The country was divided up into large domains, each of which had its lord. Each lord possessed a private little army of warriors known as *samurai*, SAMURAI, who were not permitted to engage in business or to marry outside their class. More important, the samurai had to do the bidding of their lord under any circumstances, even if it meant the sacrifice of life; the samurai warrior dared to cause his lord no embarrassment whatever. If he did, he was supposed to (and he invariably did) commit *seppuku*, SEPPUKU, or *hara-kiri*, a form of heroic suicide.

(To commit seppuku, the principal sits on the floor with sword in hand. By drawing his sword across his belly, he disembowels himself, and to do a good job must fall forward on his face. Needless to say, it is a painful form of death. It is still the popular method in the military caste of atoning for failure or disgrace.)

The whole set of rules for samurai conduct was known as the Samurai Code, or as *Bushido*—the Way of the Warrior. It is important to keep in mind this code, because when Japan later became a member of the family of nations and built an Army along Western lines, the Samurai Code was carried into the new army, the Emperor replacing the old-time lord as the object of the warrior's or soldier's devotion.

The transition of Japan from a nation that would not have anything at all to do with foreigners to a world power was not accomplished all at once, even though eighty-eight years are but a small time in history. When she resumed relations with the world, many leading Japanese individuals saw that Western methods must be adopted or copied if Japan was to survive. First the shogun was overthrown, and the Emperor in person became for the time being the actual head of the state. Young men were sent to various countries to learn the Western way. French methods of army organization were studied, but since it was thought that the Prussians (or Germans) had the most efficient army, Japan's army was modeled after the Prussian. For similar reasons, her navy followed the British pattern. Conscription was adopted, and, most important, the Japanese leaders saw to it that the common man was conscripted, not just the samurai. Of course the warrior class did not approve of that. They were soon denied the privilege of carrying two swords; they were permitted to marry commoners; and although they had been pensioned, these pensions were steadily reduced. In many sections of the country they rebelled against the new order, but the conscript army, made up not of warriors but of Japanese peasants, was able to quell the rebellious samurai.

Now you might think the samurai would give up and cease to be a factor in the nation's life. But on the contrary, they accepted after a time the new order and, realizing that they could not beat the movement, they joined it. More important, they entered the army and the navy in large numbers and mostly as officers, until they completely dominated both. In addition, they brought with them the principles of the old Samurai Code, remodeled now around a fanatical loyalty to the Emperor. This loyalty is difficult for Americans to understand. It is not so much a loyalty to what the Emperor actually wants or desires himself as it is a loyalty to what the military class thinks he ought to want or desire.

The Japanese adopted a constitution, but by its terms the army and the navy were made directly responsible only to the Emperor. Later decrees prescribed that the Minister of War (who corresponds to our Secretary of War) and the Minister of the Navy (who corresponds to our Secretary of the Navy) must be high-ranking army and navy officers on the active list. And while the constitution provided for a law-making body called the Diet, this body could exercise *no real control over the army and the navy*.

And so the history of Japan during the past fifty or sixty years has been a story of how the military forces, always expressing, be it noted, a devout loyalty to the Emperor, have on their own responsibility injected Japan into schemes of conquest, wars, incidents, and now perhaps even national suicide. During this period the armed forces have not always had smooth sailing. There have been many attempts by liberal-minded Japanese statesmen to put the military forces in their proper place, but in the long run these attempts have come to naught for several reasons.

First, there has been the internal composition of the army itself. After World War No. 1, a commoner became Premier of Japan. With the world giving lip-service if not actual adherence to the

idea of democracy, it seemed natural, perhaps, for the Japanese to
initiate some changes in their army. In accordance with this desire
to imitate whatever seems practical, new regulations were issued,
which permitted selected non-commissioned officers to receive
commissions. By 1927, 30 per cent of Japanese officers had come
from families which did not have a samurai background. One might
deduce that these so-called young officers that were not of privi-
leged classes would welcome civilian control of the army; but they,
even more than the old-line officers, came under the influence of
extremely radical military elements. Actually the N.C.O.'s as well
as the officers of the regular army were not chosen from the *heimin*
(common people) but from the samurai, although large numbers
of them came from impoverished samurai families. Reserve commissions only were given to heimin. Because they came from families of poor or moderate means, they were the most outspoken
group of all in demanding that the army do something, even to
originating a kind of national socialism or fascism, independent
of civilian control. They demanded that the army, independent of
civilian wishes, carry on a program of Japanese expansion on the
mainland of Asia.

Next there was corruption among Japanese civilians and politicians who were mixed up with the big business concerns. Universal suffrage became a reality in 1926, but the Japanese voters
were susceptible to bribery; they simply sold their votes to the
highest bidder. They had had no experience with self-government.
(Probably the selling of votes did not weigh too heavily on the
conscience of a people who, when the wolf growls at the door,
readily sell their daughters into a life of prostitution—a common
practice among the peasantry of Japan.) At any rate, the big
businessmen freely used money in the elections to name members
of the Diet, which they thus were able to control. Moreover, they
did not hesitate to bribe even cabinet members themselves. When
these conditions became generally known, the radical groups in
the army could readily say, "We told you so, we intend to reform
all this."

And then there is the practice of political assassination, and the
secret societies that adopted assassination as a creed. Many army
officers, especially the "young officers," belonged to these societies.

There has been something in the taking of the life of a highly placed official which has appealed to the Japanese mind. Political assassination was freely used to rid the Japanese government of some of its most able and level-headed statesmen. This dirty work was actually accomplished by the "youth movement" in the Japanese Army. It was highly popular among youth throughout the country, thousands of whom wrote letters in blood appealing for clemency for the young assassins.

But one asks, "Couldn't some one in Japan do something about such a situation?" The answer is, "No." Because no matter what the army or the navy does (the Army even staged a rebellion in 1936) the Ministers of War and of the Navy must be—let me repeat, MUST BE—*a high-ranking general and admiral on the active list;* and these officers are not responsible to anyone but the Emperor, who occupies a sacred position. None but the Sacred Emperor can touch these Ministers of War and of the Navy—and he usually accepts the officers first recommended by these services. Any appointments he makes to these posts are made from officers recommended from the services. The Imperial Household Minister, usually a retired field marshal or fleet admiral, makes the nominations. This important personage, the Household Minister, nominates ALL cabinet officers. What has the Diet, the Japanese Parliament, to do with that? Nothing whatsoever. The theory of parliamentary government does not go very far in Japan.

So when the Japanese armed forces made their attack on Pearl Harbor and the East Indies, including the Malay Archipelago and the Philippines, it was not necessary for the army and navy leaders to talk it over with anyone but themselves. (By this time even the Premier was an army general.)

Does this imply that the Japanese people might resent the pretensions of their militaristic leaders or not be entirely loyal to the enterprises of their army and navy? Let us not fool ourselves. Nothing could be further from the truth. The minds of the Japanese people had long been prepared for any and every adventure of war. From their earliest days in history until today they have been led to feel that the outside world was a bitter, jealous, and antagonistic one, that would destroy them if it could. Bushido, the warlike code of the samurai, was and is as generally respected among Japanese as the Ten Commandments are among peoples of the West.

The Japanese militarists, from the years of arrows, spears, and armor to the era of bombs from planes, have dreamed of conquest and of a destiny to rule the world. The propaganda has been as continuous as the cultivation of the rice fields. The army and navy have planned the westward and southward movement of the Flag of the Rising Sun for decades and generations. The entanglement of Great Britain in the present desperate struggle with Germany and Italy, and America's necessary preoccupation with affairs in the Atlantic as well as the Pacific presented the Japanese militarists with the opportunity for which they had prayed to their gods. For this gigantic gamble with the very life itself of Japan the militarists were ready, their plans carefully prepared—and the Japanese people psychologically prepared as well.

To the Japanese, the army and the navy are the agencies which will make the nation great, fulfill Japan's destiny, drive the white man out of Asia, make the fortunes of the hard-working Japanese peasant better, and carry out the dictates of that divinity which is the Emperor. It is scarcely possible for the American mind to grasp this, particularly this emperor-worship that is related to the army and the navy. But it is the very foundation of Japanese morale. The great majority of the Japanese believe profoundly that the Emperor is god; that the army and the navy are the instruments of god and, as such, partake of certain divine attributes.

HOW GOOD IS THE JAPANESE ARMY?

So, then, if the army is so much a part of Japanese life, what kind of an army is it? Is it any good? It believes it is working for the Japanese god; does it think it possesses any miraculous powers?

The backbone of the Imperial Japanese Army is the Japanese peasant. According to our Army's standards, large numbers of their fighting men would not be considered fit for active service. The average height of the Japanese is 5 feet 3½ inches; his legs are extremely short; he is not at all prepossessing to Western eyes. He has, however, a stamina that has been developed by centuries of hard labor under the hardest of farming conditions. He has been accustomed to short rations from birth. He has a high regard for his duties as a soldier. He accepts the idea of death with greater stoicism than Western races. His teachings imbue him with great confidence.

In the technical arms, such as artillery and engineers, he does not display much initiative. He is not readily adaptable to changing conditions, especially if they tend to be unfavorable over a period of time. The Japanese peasant-soldier hates to be away from home for long periods, the strong family tie causing him to become homesick. But to show homesickness would be disgraceful; if captured he may commit suicide rather than betray his weakness. This soldier—who comes into the army as a simple peasant—is capable of almost unbelievable arrogance and brutality when he has the upper hand. His treatment of the conquered portions of China has done much to unite the people of China in bitter and unending hatred of the Japanese soldier. Despite his discipline and code of behavior, he may have lapses into savagery and disorder and go completely out of hand. No army in history ever committed greater outrages against a helpless people than the Japanese in the sack and rape of Nanking in 1937, in which neither age nor sex was spared in day after day of horror. At Port Arthur in 1894 the Japanese troops indulged in similar excesses against the Chinese. Apparently these periods of going berserk are tolerated by the junior officers, are overlooked by the higher command. Perhaps they are considered as a reward to the troops on the one hand, a warning lesson in frightfulness to the conquered on the other hand.

High casualty lists apparently have little effect on this soldier, if he is numbered among the survivors. Once he is committed to an attack, no consideration of personal safety will bring about a let-up. It may be said that the only efficient way to stop a Japanese advance is to kill or wound the entire group. When it is reasonable for them to retire because of heavy losses, they are just as likely to charge again. On the other hand, they are skillful in flanking operations, experienced in infiltration methods, and adept in the use of camouflage. You will note that pictures of Japanese troops in jungle operations show camouflage over their helmets and often over their shoulders.

One physical characteristic has hindered the development of the

Japanese soldier, and this is particularly interesting to the American doughboy or trooper who puts his trust in the rifle. Because of the conformation of the Japanese eye, the Japanese soldier is rarely a good marksman. The fold of the upper lid covers the eye in such a way that the angle of vision is reduced. Consequently, while Japanese infantry is the basic arm of the combat team, their infantry is not regarded as a source of fire but of shock. Infantry is a shock force, a force for close bodily contact with the bayonet.

It must not be inferred from this that the Japanese infantry is incapable of laying down fire. But the basis of employment is not a rifle squad, but light machine-gun section of ten men. They are also proficient with mortars. The company is made up of four platoons, three light machine-gun platoons and one mortar platoon. But most infantry soldiers carry the rifle, of Mauser action, similar to our Springfield, with the bayonet. Some Japanese infantrymen may be armed with the "Tommy-gun." The ambition of the Japanese infantry is to come to close quarters. Their training puts emphasis on coming to grips with the enemy.

The Japanese cavalryman is issued a straight sword, forty-eight inches in length, a lance, and a carbine. It is not contemplated that he will simply act as a mounted infantryman but will many times be employed mounted, closing in with the sword or lance. Such action has been successful against ill-equipped Chinese troops. It would be disastrous against straight-shooting American riflemen and machine-gunners.

ARMY ORGANIZATION AND TACTICS

The Japanese Army is organized into battalions, regiments, and divisions, as the United States Army is. The divisional artillery, however, is not generally attached to smaller units but is employed under the direction of the division commander. The services in the division are approximately the same as the American, except that signal communication is arranged by the engineers. The Japanese communication agencies are not as complete as they are in the American division, most reliance being placed on buzzer phones and flags. Recent reports, however, indicate radio communication between dive-bombers and commanders of small units. A Japanese division contains only two companies of engineers, who have purely technical duties; the tasks performed by the American Combat Engineers are undertaken in the Japanese division by pioneer detachments in the infantry companies.

The Japanese have another organization of comparatively recent origin: the independent brigade. This unit consists of two infantry regiments, one cavalry regiment, one pack artillery regiment, one engineer company, and one so-called gendarme company—an outfit that combines the duties of military police and counter-intelligence. The whole is commanded by a major general. Moreover, for special operations it is customary to attach additional infantry strength to independent brigades, so that they often contain as many as twelve battalions, or the infantry strength of a division.

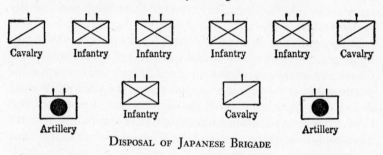

Cavalry   Infantry   Infantry   Infantry   Infantry   Cavalry

Artillery   Infantry   Cavalry   Artillery

DISPOSAL OF JAPANESE BRIGADE

These independent brigades have borne the brunt of much of the fighting in China and Manchukuo. To judge from the number of times and the regularity with which they have been employed, it may be that the Japanese Army is working toward an organization based on independent brigades rather than the division. At any rate, their use is an application of the principle of flexibility. It is maintained that the independent brigade permits easier supply, that it is more mobile, that it is more adaptable to difficult country. And the Japanese have had plenty of experience with difficult country in China (and with difficult people there, too). Difficult and unyielding also have been the Russians in the North, where Japanese "incidents" have not been very successful.

The independent brigade depends for success upon a heavy concentration of the fire of automatic weapons and the use of cavalry. The brigade has often been observed advancing behind a screen of one troop of cavalry. When contact is made, the brigade may be disposed as shown in the diagram on page 453.

If more battalions are present as part of the brigade, the same principles apply. Note that the artillery is disposed so that it can cover each flank as well as the center of the line. Note, too, that the reserve squadron of cavalry is placed so that it can be readily employed, especially for pursuit. Small tanks may be attached and may accompany the infantry attack.

The Japanese do not preach the doctrine of defense. Perhaps it is inconceivable to the Japanese mind that their troops will ever be placed on the defensive. Their wars have all been wars of aggression, initiated by surprise attacks. When they are driven to defense, it is probable that they will employ extremely active defense measures. Moreover, it is probable that they will use any weapon which offers itself, including gas.

Japan signed but did not ratify the Geneva Protocol in 1925 prohibiting the use of gas in war. She has used gas in her campaign in China. For a while there was some uncertainty as to whether the Japanese had employed that weapon against the Chinese. As early as 1938, the Chinese protested the Japanese use of gas. Since that time it has been established on unimpeachable authority that the Japanese have employed gas in their Chinese operations, bringing it into play when hard pressed.

With a soldiery so instilled with the spirit of shock and the attack as the Japanese, it is only to be expected that they will run into situations where their attacks will be directly against a strong position. This has happened. When it has, the Japanese have sustained frightful casualties. Stress on shock action can be costly. In the Chinese War, up until May, 1939, it is estimated that 200,000 Japanese were killed in China, and 500,000 so severely wounded that they were incapable of further active service. Incidentally, the last official casualty list, published in December, 1937, gave 150,000 as killed alone.

It would be a mistake to think that Japanese divisions are uniformly good. There is no such thing as uniformity of excellent soldier material as there is in the United States, where from all sections of the country and all walks of life we draw manpower worthy of being designated as shock troops of the highest order.

The bulk of the Japanese troops are peasants of very limited literacy. Their acquaintance with machine equipment and motors is made after they have been conscripted. Their average technical knowledge until that time is very near the point of zero. Their capacity for imaginative thinking under conditions where they run against a skillful, determined, and well-armed enemy is very limited.

The Battle of Bataan has demonstrated the severe check that can be administered to greatly superior numbers of picked Japanese troops when they encounter an opponent who is cynical of Japanese claims of superiority as soldiers in battle and is prepared to follow the bullet with the bayonet. The American soldiers there and the American-trained Filipinos, vastly outnumbered as they were and with negligible air support, were but a sample of the opposition that the Japanese are to meet when they encounter the intelligent, vigorous, and determined American forces destined to face them in the future with at least equal desire to come to close quarters. The fighting spirit and ability of the outgunned, outnumbered, outplaned defenders on the Bataan Peninsula went far to destroy the myth of superiority of the Japanese as warriors which the Japanese have so carefully cherished among their own people and propagandized to the outside world. It meant much to Japanese prestige quickly to dispose of, eliminate, annihilate General MacArthur's forces. In spite of the ultimate outcome of that battle of many weeks, the Japanese failed in their essential mission —a speedy victory. And they discovered an opponent who, no matter how desperate his plight and apparently hopeless his chance of relief, could laugh between his shots and curses.

THE INTELLIGENCE SERVICE

Something must be said about the Japanese intelligence service. In outlining to you how this service works, it is not intended that you peer behind every bush on your way back to quarters to see if there is a lurking Japanese spy in hiding. It is intended, however, that members of our armed forces be made familiar with some Japanese methods.

The Japanese espionage or spy or intelligence organization does not confine itself to the gathering only of military information, but seeks out any information that can be used in trade or business or otherwise. The Japanese are notorious collectors of all details. A Japanese himself, however, makes a poor spy almost anywhere in the world unless he poses as a member of a Japanese colony. His racial characteristics give him away. But the Japanese are past masters in utilizing others for their purposes. That is being done on a large scale in the Far East today.

The Japanese intelligence organization contains persons with a samurai background who have, in one way or another, disgraced themselves. They are called *ronins*, RONINS, or outcast samurai.

This term *ronin* is old in Japan. You remember that when we were talking earlier in this lecture about the samurai, we remarked that in the old days these warriors owed absolute devotion to their lord. But sometimes an accident would happen to one of these lords, and when it did, his samurai warriors could not simply go off and hire out to another lord. They became lordless samurai or ronins. If their lord had died because of the action of another, they would seek revenge. When revenge was accomplished, they might simply march off and become bandits or they might commit suicide.

The following story illustrates the point. There were once two lords who had a bitter quarrel. One drew his sword on the other in the sacred precincts of the castle where the shogun lived. This was considered such a breach of etiquette that the lord who had lost his temper was forced by tradition and his own conscience to commit seppuku, which he did, so the story goes, in the best form. This lord had forty-seven samurai, but when he died they became lordless warriors, or ronins. They vowed revenge. Two years later they were able to catch their deceased lord's enemy off guard and run him through (remember they each carried two swords). Then the whole forty-seven went out and committed seppuku themselves.

The Japanese think this a wonderful story of heroism. The incident has been the subject of books, poems, plays, and bedtime stories to Japanese children. It has been an inspiration to many Japanese soldiers that American troops will meet in battle.

In the modern application, the samurai loyalty is to the Emperor.

If an officer is cashiered from the army for some escapade, he could take his own life because he had caused his Emperor embarrassment; but he is given a chance as a ronin to gain back his position and caste by some conspicuous deed or service to the Emperor. In the Japanese intelligence service, with its attendant danger, he may accomplish this.

These Japanese intelligence agents are entirely unprincipled and are guided by the most compelling motives. Bribery is only one means they employ. That is an undependable means, however, because if a person can be bribed by them he can be bribed by others. They have found that the most effective means of gaining information is by the use of dope—heroin is one of the principal drugs so employed—so that the person who is gathering the information for them and Japan is bound to them by the invisible but 100 per cent effective bond between the drug addict and his supplier. For many years the Japanese have been methodically accumulating all sorts of information, sifting it out, analyzing it, preparing themselves for the attack upon the United States and Britain.

It may be expected that in any planned attack, including one of surprise, the Japanese intelligence will have secured all possible information. Too, it seems to be especially efficient in determining profitable air targets.

THE JAPANESE IN THE AIR

Military observers in past years have voiced a considerable difference of opinion as to the efficiency of Japanese bombing, but the best opinion now seems to be that it has proved accurate and methodical, and that its objects are definite and not vague. The Japanese employ torpedo planes on a considerable scale against war vessels. They practise dive-bombing with ability and follow it in most cases with high-altitude bombing. They can be expected at any time to launch strafing attacks against ground troops and installations. Moreover, the Japanese pilot as well as the entire airplane crew will rise to great heights of personal bravery to insure success in the attack. However, the remarkable success of the American flyers in Burma indicates again the mettle of an opponent prepared, trained, and eager to meet the Japanese in combat and shoot them out of the skies.

FURTHER CHARACTERISTICS OF ARMY OPERATIONS

The operations of all armies show under study certain well-defined characteristics. If, during the American Revolution, a British officer had been trying to tell a newly arrived British commander what he could expect from the Americans, mention undoubtedly would have been made of the American practice of fighting in open formation, the American reliance on the rifle, and the American habit of picking off the gaudily dressed British officers by well-aimed individual fire. The Japanese operations which have been studied and the statements of their officers indicate that the Japanese troops have certain well-defined characteristics. (However, no one should blindly say that the Japanese are not capable of any other kind of fighting. We must never expect an enemy to remain in a groove comfortable and easy for us to anticipate.)

We have already discussed some Japanese characteristics, especially their reliance on the offensive and shock action. Now we shall mention a few more.

Training in the United States Army has stressed the ability of troops to march well over long distances. Can the Japanese march? Many observers have reported that Japanese troops on the march present an unkempt appearance and that the infantry seems to "straggle" rather than march. But a study of Japanese operations shows that thirty- to forty-mile marches are not uncommon for foot troops and that Japanese forces reach their destination after long marches ready to fight. We must expect, therefore, to meet an extremely mobile enemy, often in terrain that does not permit extensive motor transportation or under conditions that make motor transportation inadvisable or impossible. The implication is obvious.

When analyzed by professional soldiers, Japanese tactics are not brilliant. But neither were Grant's before the defenses of Richmond during the closing days of the Civil War. Opposed by one of the greatest soldiers and tacticians this continent has ever produced, Robert E. Lee, Grant's tactics could be summed up in his immortal words: "I shall fight it out on this line if it takes all summer."

Not brilliant tactics, but they worked. Japanese tactics work, or at least have worked, and as soldiers that is what we have to measure. In the fighting on the Malay Peninsula, Japanese tactics of infiltration were exceptionally successful and merit close study and understanding.

Compared to other nations the Japanese may seem weak in arms, especially in artillery. But huge sums have been spent on mechanization, aviation, and motorization. And the Japanese have been most successful in maintaining secrecy. Only since Pearl Harbor has the extent of Japanese modernization of their arms been appreciated, so closely had the Japanese preserved the secrecy of their preparations. The *whole* of Japanese industry has been geared to the war machine since 1938. On March 16 of that year, the Diet or legislative body completed the surrender of its powers by the passage of the National Mobilization Law. In general this bill provided for the drafting of all subjects of the Empire for mobilization enterprises; for a rigid control of materials and communication facilities: for a dictatorship over business; for the dictating of employee conditions and wages; and for the settling of labor disputes by government order. By subsequent reinforcing legislation and decrees, the government, which you realize was firmly in the hands of the militarists, have geared the whole of Japan to a war economy—*a total war economy*—perhaps even more complete than that of Germany. Naturally, production is limited by the size of the Japanese industrial machine.

As for actual operations, the Japanese may be expected to attack at night or during bad weather, when they think the enemy is off guard. Terrain is considered no obstacle—let it be repeated, *terrain is considered no obstacle*. Training in night fighting is stressed in all schooling. They appreciate the importance of secrecy and surprise in all their operations; it can be expected that in any attack some device will be employed to conceal their true intentions. And in this connection, do not forget what we mentioned about the Japanese intelligence sections.

The Japanese are especially well schooled in landing operations. It is said that all of their shock divisions have had such training. The places where landings may be attempted are carefully reconnoitered both by aircraft and intelligence agents. The day of land-

ing is carefully picked, so that advantage can be taken of the tides.
If possible, periods of rain and storm are chosen. The operation
itself usually takes place just before dawn. Possibly during the
night especially trained swimmers have made their way to shore
and filtered in as advance units. The transports have been pushed
up during the night. Men take their places in landing craft and
push rapidly for shore. They try to ground on the beach at fifty-
yard intervals. Military patrol craft give close support while air
and naval units assist the operation. When landing is made and a
beach-head established, the troops move inland as rapidly as possible. They waste no time in deriving the fullest benefits from surprise action.

The Japanese regard the meeting engagement as being the type
of combat best suited to decisive results. It is contemplated that
bold, independent action on the part of subordinate commanders
will gain and keep the initiative and permit them to seize the most
favorable terrain. Of course, such employment may result in piece-
meal attacks and failure, but the Japanese do not allow this greatly
to influence them. Their subordinate commanders, the "youth
movement," are resourceful, capable, and daring and show great
initiative. But that such attacks may result in heavy losses when
opposed by keen and courageous troops was again demonstrated
by our men and their Filipino comrades on Bataan Peninsula.

The Japanese fully appreciate the advantage of getting on their
enemy's flanks. If possible they will strive to outflank a defensive
position. If they are prevented from doing this, they quite likely
will attack head on, even though they sustain frightful losses. As
we have previously noted, they have confidence that when they
close in they will overcome their enemy. However, you may recall
the very true saying of the prizefighting ring: "A good big man is
better than a good little man." That's where we come into the
picture.

JAPAN IN PREVIOUS WARS

It is always interesting to inquire into the moral capacity of a
people to wage war, especially if it is an all-out war. Have the
Japanese ever really defeated a first-class power? Let us conduct

a little review of past Japanese wars on which their confidence
and propaganda are based.

In the sixteenth century, before Japan had closed herself to foreigners, she was ruled *for* the Emperor by a would-be Napoleon
called Hideyoshi, HIDEYOSHI. He had dreams of Asiatic conquest as extensive as the plans of Japanese militarists today. He had
been able to unify Japan, so he figured that his next step would be
to take over China. Accordingly, he sent a message to the Chinese
Emperor demanding submission. The answer was peculiarly Chinese. The Emperor sent an envoy to Hideyoshi, accompanied by
a fitting number of retainers. The envoy bore a most imposing
document all rolled up in a scroll. Hideyoshi was almost too
pleased for words. A magnificent ceremony was arranged, and at
the proper time, with appropriate fanfare, the envoy made his
appearance and delivered the scroll. Imagine Hideyoshi's surprise
when the scroll was unrolled and it was read therein that the
Chinese Emperor was pleased to appoint Hideyoshi "King of
Japan." Hideyoshi was furious. He raised an army and embarked
for Korea as a first step in the conquest of China. He won a battle,
slaughtered 55,000 people, cut off their ears, and sent the ears
back to Japan to impress the people with his deeds. But the Koreans
organized a navy, with ships with iron prows and, it is said, with
iron sides and tops as well. They were called "turtle ships." When
the Japanese ships would approach, the Koreans would run; when
the Japanese closed in for the kill, the Koreans would turn and
ram the Japanese ships. In a short time Hideyoshi was isolated. He
ravaged the country but was soon forced to return to Japan. Thus
ended Japan's first invasion of China.

Japan tackled China again in 1894-1895. This time the Chinese
armed forces, such as they were, received a sound thrashing, accompanied by great slaughter, but the Chinese were beaten more because of graft, inefficiency, and corruption than because of the
efforts of the Japanese. As a matter of history, Japan could have
accomplished as much as she did without a war, but it was engi-
neered by her militarist leaders to make Japanese political parties
unite behind a militaristic program.

The Russo-Japanese War in 1904-1905 has been thought of by
many people as a resounding Japanese victory. True, the Japanese

Navy by a surprise attack before a declaration of war (a forerunner of Pearl Harbor) was able fatally to cripple the Russian Asiatic Fleet. True, too, is the fact that at Tsushima the Japanese Admiral Togo destroyed the exhausted and badly handled Russian European Fleet, which had sailed halfway around the world and ran into a trap. True also are the Japanese victories on land, culminating in the successful siege of Port Arthur and the capture of Mukden. But did the Japanese actually invade Russia? Did their commanders dictate a peace in the Russian capital? The truth is that the Japanese Army commander in Manchuria told the Japanese statesmen back home that Japan's army had shot its bolt; that peace must be made; that the statesmen should try to get all they could from Russia, but that the Japanese Army was incapable of further effort. The badly led Russian armies were defeated but never destroyed. When President Theodore Roosevelt proposed that the belligerents meet at Portsmouth, New Hampshire, in the United States, the Japanese were only too eager. The war had been like the football game in which a team made a lot of first downs, but could not make the touchdowns.

Of course, the Japanese people had thought all along that they were great victors. Their newspapers had painted the Japanese exploits in the most glowing accounts. They thought that they had really beaten Russia. But what they had won were costly battles. When the terms of the peace were published—the best peace Japan could get—there was serious rioting in Tokyo against making peace; over 600 civilians were killed in the suppression of these riots. But the "unsatisfactory" peace was proof that winning a series of battles was not winning a war.

During the World War Japan was, as you recall, on the side of the Allies. But only a person who believes that babies come in baskets would say that Japan defeated Germany or contributed in any substantial way to Germany's defeat. Japan merely gathered some loot for herself. And since 1937 she has been trying to bring China to her knees. We all know how this has turned out so far.

THE TRAINING OF OFFICERS

The Japanese officer personnel has until now been mentioned only in passing. In a country where the armed forces play such a major part in the actual government of the nation itself, the caliber of its officer personnel becomes especially important.

Japan has two schools for the training of officers besides military preparatory schools: The Junior Military Academy and the Military Academy proper. The Junior Academy trains *two classes* of students: so-called *junior students*, who are either graduates of military preparatory schools, N.C.O.'s on the active list who are less than twenty-five years old, privates under twenty-two, and applicants at large who have a high school education; and another class, called *senior students*, who are selected from warrant officer and advanced N.C.O. grades by competitive examination. These latter older students attend for one year; they cannot rise above the grade of captain, and they must retire at forty-nine years of age.

The Junior Military Academy course normally takes two years, although the course has been shortened for the present. But at this point there is a striking difference from the American way of selecting officers. The graduate of the Junior Academy must serve eight months as a private first class, a corporal, or a sergeant *after* graduation. If he looks like good material, he then goes to the Senior Academy. The course there takes eighteen months, but on graduation he is not directly commissioned. He must do a four-months' tour of troop duty as a sergeant major or probational officer, and then he is commissioned only by *vote of the field officers* of his regiment.

This all seems at first glance a pretty good way and a fair one to obtain officers. The evil in the process is that the Japanese Army carries on a program of infusing the candidate's mind with only the things in which it wants him to believe. He is not permitted to read newspapers or to broaden his mind in any way. And the final approval necessary within the regiment itself will keep out not only anyone who might show any liberal thought, but anyone who does not see exactly eye to eye, *not only in military matters but in all other matters*, with those in high authority in the Army. In short, the system is the essence of single-minded militarism and military caste.

This infusing of the individual's mind with all manner of pickled thought goes on throughout the officer's career. The mess is not a place to relax; meals are accompanied by a form of school not only in professional but political, social, and governmental matters, all from the rigidly militarist point of view. The officer is constantly drilled in the idea that the Army is not a servant of the nation but is independent of anything but the Emperor, that it holds the true destiny of the Island Empire in its capable hands.

It must be admitted that such a system does breed excellent professional soldiers up to a point; but it also creates a clan of men pretty close to the lunatic fringe of life. Remember that one powerful cabinet member must be a general, another an admiral. Other high members of the government may be military personages also. With minds so narrowed by a lack of business, intellectual, and other civilian contacts, it is no wonder the Japanese military leaders demonstrate such abysmal ignorance concerning the realities of both domestic and foreign affairs. When preparedness, lust for power, pride of race, and the mythology of superiority are abetted by such ignorance, the tinder is set and ready for the spark to be applied for a war such as Japan launched upon the United States last December, a desperate gamble for domination over half the world at the risk of utter destruction.

Such is our enemy in the Pacific—his strength, which is considerable, and his weaknesses that will be breached and exploited only by the striking power of force and might. The "good little man" will awake one day in defeat and agony from his delusions of grandeur, but the "good big man" will know that he has been in a fight.

CHAPTER XXXIV

THE GERMAN ARMY: PERSONNEL AND LEADERSHIP

PRE-INDUCTION TRAINING

The German Army of today is a highly indoctrinated militarists' army. It is not only professionally trained, but its personnel are imbued with zeal for conquest and an avenging spirit. Its successes may have lessened its bitter spirit of revenge, but unless its ardor has been seriously dampened by winter reverses in Russia, its zeal for conquest remains a force to be reckoned with.

In considering armies such as Japan's and Germany's, it is necessary for the plain "garden variety" American, with his good common sense and individualism, to drop his preconceived ideas. There are fundamentals in human nature that are alike or strongly similar in all Western peoples, but human nature can be most considerably changed, warped, bent, and guided into controlled channels. The German Army is largely composed of young men whose human nature has been subjected to a long period of suggestion, direction, and control. The State may not have created the minds of these young men, but it has formed their mental processes. And the German State does not wait until a youth is clothed in an army uniform before it gets to work on the child. Its pre-induction training begins with the earliest training.

It is important to remember that every element of propaganda, including the schools, was brought to bear upon the German people after the first World War to convince them not only that they were never "fairly" defeated on the fields of battle, but that they were outrageously treated by the terms of peace.

It is not necessary for us to discuss the terms of peace. Suffice it to say that if they had been rigorously enforced, the world would be at peace today and the return of militarism to Germany would have been prevented. The misfortunes of Germany after the war, real, fancied, self-inflicted, or caused as a result of the war, have been briefly discussed in another chapter. The fact remains that Germany did suffer, that large numbers of the German people refused to make an adjustment to the peace, and that German youth was brought up in an embittered and revengeful atmosphere that was exploited by the militarists and that gave the Nazi Party its opportunity to rise to power.

While Hitler did not officially seize power until 1933, his party's influence had been growing for more than ten years. His book, *Mein Kampf*, had attained a phenomenal circulation. His storm troopers had become a leading and also an intimidating influence in every city and village in Germany. The influence of his party leaders had reached into all the schools. Coeducation does not exist in Germany as it does in the United States. Boys' schools are dominated by men teachers. A large proportion of the school instructors in Germany had been won over to the Nazi movement or driven into that movement during the 1920's. Nazi thought and principles, therefore, dominated educational institutions for years before Hitler was made Chancellor of the Reich—and the youth of the nation, year by year, came increasingly under the mental and moral control of Nazi Party leadership.

Children and youths were indoctrinated with the theory of race superiority and with the zest for revenge against those who had broken the might of the Germany of the first World War.

They were led to despise the French as an "inferior and degraded" people, the Poles as a Slavic race fit only to be the servants of the superior German race, the Slavs of other countries as brutal, bestial peoples unfit to control the rich and vital areas that Hitler looked upon with envious eyes as fit *Lebensraum* for a German race that in his dreams attained a future population of 250,000,000 souls. The Jews were made the scapegoats for Germany's misfortunes, and a brutal attitude towards Jews and towards so-called "inferior races" was assiduously cultivated in the youth of Germany.

It was held out to German youth that they had no future in a world that was left by the Versailles Treaty, that they had no outlook for a better and brighter life unless they would overthrow the "injustices of the peace" and assume their leadership as the superior race among the peoples of the world. A constant stream of propaganda and so-called education was brought to bear on every element of the population of Germany. By these methods and by this indoctrination of youth an army of fanatical soldiers was being prepared.

To the children of Germany, Hitler is a superman who alone can save Germany from her wicked enemies. At the age of six the German child begins his acquaintanceship with the Nazi uniform, black shoes, black shorts, a brown shirt, a trench cap, and a swastika armband. He is given a number and an efficiency record book. In that record book is kept an account of his physical development, military life, and home, school, and Party activities. After the boy's school day ends, he begins his Party day—runs errands for Party officials, does guard duty at Party headquarters, and makes himself generally useful to the Party. On week-ends these little boys frequently participate in tactical exercises.

The next division in training is the *Jungvolk*, including children aged ten to fourteen years. The training of this group is more intense. These youngsters are given harder physical work, more strenuous competitive games, more thorough ideological teachings; and they participate in special ceremonies that stimulate their fervor and mass fanaticism.

The division just before the age of military conscription is of greatest importance in pre-induction training. This division comprises the Hitler Youth, which is composed of the age group from fourteen to eighteen. The Hitler Youth maintains its own schools and camps, wears uniforms similar to those of storm troopers, has flying instructors, planes, and gliders; is equipped with motor trucks, motorcycles, pistols, and rifles; and maintains shops to keep its equipment in a state of repair. No army has ever known such extensive pre-induction training of the youth of its country.

Throughout Germany there are numerous youth hostels which are used by the Hitler Youth. A youth hostel is a very simple form of lodging house where bicycling or hiking groups may spend one or more nights en route from one place to another at a minimum cost. This cost is figured in pennies. At these youth hostels simple food may be obtained, or facilities for cooking the food that the youths carry with them. Marching is emphatically stressed for the

Hitler Youth, and some of the daily hikes between youth hostels cover twenty-five miles and more.

Military maneuvers and tactical exercises occupy a major portion of the week-ends of these boys. These activities are not merely squad drills or military movements but general tactical exercises.

It is necessary to understand that the German child, unlike the American, is raised from the cradle on military tradition. In every home there are the pictures in uniform of fathers, and often grandfathers and great-grandfathers as well, who served in previous wars. An Iron Cross awarded to a member of the family in a past war is usually to be seen in a frame mounted on a velvet background. There are the pictures of youths in uniform in the present war, of the uniformed *Jungvolk* and *Hitler Jugend* (Hitler Youth); in fact, the dominating photographs in German homes are photographs of uniformed men. The most frequently seen pictures of German leaders of the past are pictures of Frederick the Great, Bismarck, Hindenburg, and other military men. Battle scenes are often the pictorial ornament on the walls even of humble homes; and the photographs of Hitler and his satellite Nazi leaders are everywhere. The German child, from the earliest time, therefore, is raised on a military tradition. To this is added his indoctrination as a Nazi. To summarize: At the age of ten he begins the period of organized training in uniform, and at fourteen compulsory military training in uniform; at eighteen the boys enter the Labor Service for six months, after which they begin the regulation two years of military service.

Because of the regimentation of youth in Germany, the inculcation of obedience to authority, the goose-step, and other evidences of controlled thinking and acting, Americans assume that German youth have been moulded into military automatons and that these young men have been deprived of enterprise and initiative and are effective as soldiers only under orders that regulate their every activity. That assumption is a serious mistake. Perhaps the most skillful training of German soldiers is the emphasis that German military leaders place on self-reliance, aggressiveness, initiative, and quick thinking. Independent action is encouraged, and great latitude is given to youthful leaders. Skill and versatility are demanded in the application of tactics. In no army have these qualities been sought and developed to a greater extent than in the German Army of today.

Here is a typical situation as presented to a group of about fifty youths by their leader, a boy of fifteen or sixteen: "The enemy is reported advancing south to north through this forest. At 7 o'clock A.M. it was reported to be entering Blank village. My mission is to determine at once and report to headquarters the position, disposition and activity of its advance units. My sector is between Red town and Blue town."

This young leader, after giving a preliminary estimate of the situation, issues to his subordinates orders that would do credit to an experienced soldier; and yet this sixteen-year-old youth is still two years removed from service as a private in the army. In carrying out his mission, he issues a series of quick orders in a decisive manner, evidencing complete control of his group. Messengers carry reports back to him from his advance elements, and he in turn sends frequent messages to subordinates. He is completely in charge. There is no outside interference. Any who show lack of attention to his instructions are immediately and sternly rebuked. The various missions that he assigns are carried out, perhaps well, perhaps poorly; but before the group is dismissed, the performances of the patrols are criticized by the leader.

After the *Hitler Jugend* have completed their training, they enter the Labor Services. During this period they are physically hardened in strenuous and useful outdoor work. They also acquire further experience in living in the open, in cooking their own food in the field, and in undergoing long periods of hard physical labor. After six months of this Labor Service, all physically fit youths enter the armed forces.

THE TRAINING OF THE GERMAN RECRUIT

The first four months of service of the German recruit are devoted to individual training, despite the considerable pre-induction experience and training he has already received. He undergoes another period of physical hardening. His units make long, fatiguing marches. The limit of his endurance is tested. He spends a great deal of time studying and handling his weapons and his equipment and

learning the rudiments of soldiering. He is trained in the use of
several of the weapons of the infantry arm. By the end of this first
period he has been instructed in platoon and company tactics, and
two months later he has engaged in battalion and regimental problems. Up to this time he has received no combined training; that is,
training with different units of an arm or service other than his own.
It is not until he has received six months of basic training that he
participates in exercises with other units. These exercises progress
from regimental training up through division and corps exercises
and maneuvers.

There is no competition or jealousy between the arms and services of the German Army. Such attitudes are strenuously discouraged, and the utmost in coöperation and understanding is demanded. A sense of common team-play and coördination is thereby
thoroughly developed in the soldiers. Each arm and service recog-
nizes the others as indispensable for its success and knows that it is
indispensable for the others' success.

The military education of the German soldier is accompanied by
a continuation of his political education. Not only is he given confidence in his weapons and the teamwork of all arms of the service,
but the theory (or myth, if you will) of race superiority is employed to add to his confidence in his associates in arms, in the
home front, in his leaders, and in the Nazi Party as the vehicle that
coördinates all Germans for the welfare and future glory, responsibility, and prosperity of the German *Volk* as the super-race destined
to rule the world.

This political education is continuous. While troops are in training and in rest sectors, the propaganda campaign uses all media of
expression to improve morale, self-confidence, and the conviction
of inevitable success. Motion pictures are extensively employed.
Geopolitics is painstakingly explained from the German point of
view. The "weaknesses" of other peoples and other systems of government are thoroughly exploited, and such "weaknesses" are invented at will. The military practices, capabilities, tactical methods,
and habits of thought of other peoples are also explained. The
theories of the German "warrior race" are fully developed in the
minds of the simple soldiery. There is cultivated an impatience with
all "ignorant," "obstinate," or "Jewish-controlled" peoples that

"pig-headedly" refuse to accept the virtues and benefits of the "new world order."

Remember, most of these soldiers never read a book that hadn't passed the censorship of Herr Goebbels's ministry, nor a magazine nor a newspaper in which free expression was permitted.

The result, in the German soldier, is a soldier whose mind is saturated with propaganda, whose vision is entirely limited to the horizons that have been kept before him by his instructors from early youth on, whose notions of the outside world are warped and inflamed, whose zeal for Nazism approaches fanaticism. His mind has the answers to all questions—Herr Goebbels's answers. He has no doubts.

The process of scientific military training, combined with mental distortion, extreme hero-worship, and fanaticism, has created a soldier skilled in his craft, capable of extraordinary feats of endurance, and prepared to give his life for his fuehrer in aggressive offense or stubborn defense. It is natural that these qualities should be particularly demonstrated where resistance to German arms has been the most formidable. It has been noteworthy during the Russian winter, when the Russian armies went on the offensive. In the face of the biting, bitter Russian winter and the pressure of Russian Army bayonets and guerrillas in a winter campaign that has never ceased, the German defense of strong points and important centers of distribution has evidenced the highest qualities of determination, morale, and skill as well as of organization and leadership.

In Libya also, the hardened German troops have demonstrated against their tough and vigorous adversaries their capacity to give back punishment after being seriously tested on the receiving end.

Pictures of captured German troops (of whom there have been comparatively few) show doggedly sullen faces, the faces of men not only thoroughly maddened at being captured but ashamed of being in the enemy's hands. Reports from British sources about German prisoners indicate the recalcitrant attitude of these men for days and weeks after they have been taken prisoners, their resentment at fate and at their captors, their unwillingness to make the best of the situation or to coöperate with their captors even for their own welfare.

This marks a great change that has taken place in the German since the last World War. During that war, captured Germans proved to be tractable, highly coöperative, readily adjusted to their situation, and, except in rare instances, as friendly to their former enemies as the latter were to them. But the forced feeding of Nazi doctrines of hatred and contempt of other peoples, of race superiority over all others, and of disgust for everything that is not of Nazi origin has had its effect. To these Germans there is no sin except failure, no virtue except their own success. And to fail, ever, is to disgrace their fuehrer.

ARMY LEADERSHIP

The German Army has evolved a new leadership also since the last World War. When the Kaiser loosed his forces over the Belgian frontier in 1914, the German Army was officered by an "officers' class." Nearly all the higher commanders and the majority of the rest of the officers were of the "Junker" element of Germany. They were largely Prussians and those who had drawn from the Prussian tradition. They represented the landed aristocracy, not wealth; and although many of them were of wealthy families, many were of families of a "poor but proud" aristocracy, but an aristocracy none the less. The Army was their career.

There were few Junkers indeed in the Hitler Nazi movement in its early days, although opportunists among the aristocracy joined up later. When Hitler first came to power, he balanced the still-important influence of the Junker officers in the German Army against the more radical element among the Nazis. One of the motives behind the "blood purge" of 1934 was the destruction of the radical Nazi leaders, but Hitler was not yet in full control of the army, and at the time of the purge his troopers murdered General Von Schleicher, former Chancellor and himself a Junker, and Von Schleicher's wife as well. The purge was, however, believed to have had as its purpose, in part at least, a compromise with the officers of the Reichswehr, as was indicated by the official report that Von Schleicher "resisted arrest," while the radical Nazis were slaughtered in their beds.

As time went on, Hitler extended the Nazi influence into the German Army and new Nazi blood was infused into the officer ranks. When the time was right (from Hitler's point of view), there was another purge—this time of aristocrats among the officers of the Army, who had looked with disfavor upon the "upstart" Austrian, his brutal storm troopers, his concentration camps, and his National Socialism.

Today there is little remaining, compared with former times, of the Junker class among the officers of the Army; Nazism has taken over Prussianism and with it complete control of the German armed forces.

The German Army today is officered by men of all classes, selected on the basis of leadership capacity and Nazi Party loyalty alone. The remaining Junkers in its high places are either opportunists or converts to the Nazi faith. And while discipline is still strong in the German Army, its forms have changed and the former chasm between the soldiers and most of their officers no longer exists, even though the monocle may still be seen over the eyes of some officers.

Despite the purpose of the Nazi movement and the objective of the Nazi Army, the fact remains that Hitler introduced a form of democracy into the Army, in that every soldier with ability, leadership qualifications, ideas, and sufficient education may become an officer. Moreover, the German officer of today, like the American, must not only be the instructor and leader of his unit but also the servant of his men.

Officer leadership is discussed briefly in this volume in Chapter XXIX, "Duties from Private through General." What is said there about the ideal of leadership for American units may be said in German words of the same or similar meaning about the German officer of today.

However, the German officer has an added duty that is not required of the American officer. In the German Army the officer is a purveyor of Nazi ideas of culture and politics. His work includes the job of continuing the indoctrination of the German soldier in the principles of the Nazi Party. Hitler is his chief and idol to an extent that no normal American would accept for the relation of himself to any other man in mystic hero-worship. Any failure of the officer to exhibit complete Party loyalty would result in his dismissal; any least example of disloyalty to the Party would mean a concentration camp. And among his men are those fervent Party followers who are observant of the least blunder an officer might make in this respect.

The Junker officers that led the German Army at the beginning of the first World War were magnificent soldiers and fine professional leaders. The officers of the present German Army are all of that and, in addition, are much closer to their men. Highly schooled in Nazi ideology, they faithfully employ their closer relations with their troops to make stronger another common bond—the bond that binds them together in one political concept as well as in an army's normal purpose to destroy its enemy. Certainly also, the more democratic and natural relationship of officers and men in the German Army has improved the morale of that army and substituted a more intelligent discipline for the rigid, sometimes brutal form that once was the Germans' pride and boast.

THE GERMAN SOLDIER AS A FOE

An army fights more than terrain, equipment, and the plans of opposing commanders. It fights men.

Those may be good, poor, or indifferent soldiers, or a mixture of all three types. Their morale may vary from time to time. Their stamina may be influenced by many considerations—idleness or over-strain, the elation of victory or the fatigue of defeat.

The German Army is a formidable foe because, among other things, its capably led and well-equipped personnel is made up of thoroughly trained, thoroughly conditioned men indoctrinated with zeal for their cause and with fanatical hero-worship of the leader who has directed them to so many victories.

But this great army of expert and confident soldiers failed in 1941 to accomplish its mission in Russia, which was to destroy the Russian armies and winter in the cities of Leningrad, Moscow, and Rostov. With the advantage of the initiative and surprise attack in its hands, it did achieve several great victories in the summer and autumn of 1941. It killed and captured great numbers of men, destroyed and seized great quantities of equipment and supplies, overran thousands of square miles of territory—and yet it failed in its mission.

It failed because the Russian soldiers, whom the Germans describe as of an "inferior race," refused to quit after defeat. Although Russian initial tactical dispositions and methods did not break off the German spear-heads and methods of defense had to be changed during the flux of the campaign, Russian resistance stiffened, guerrilla soldiers and civilians carried on behind the German lines, and finally, as winter set in, the Russians counter-attacked. In Russia there was no "fifth column" to aid and abet the invaders.

The ability to make a counter-attack after long retreats and several major lost battles indicated the high morale, training, and fighting qualities of the Russian troops. While winter was hard on the Germans, Russians are people, too; and a Russian body will freeze as quickly as a German one. What the Germans had done in other campaigns they failed to do in Russia—they failed to break the fighting spirit of a fighting army and its leaders. In all history there never was an army, so badly mauled, that turned more vigorously against its attacker.

The myth of German superiority met and failed before one test in Russia, no matter what the final result may later be if German superior weight in air force, mechanized equipment, and heavily armed troops is thrown against the Russians in the much-heralded summer drive of 1942.

The final test of the myths of German youth will be given by American troops, who will know they are fighting for their world of free men against Hitler's world of concentration camps, firing squads, Gestapo police, and death penalties for listening to foreign broadcasts. It is then that the victims of the mythology of indoctrination will have their eyes opened wide, but until the bludgeoning of war beats them to their knees and knocks some plain common sense into heads stuffed with nonsense, they will fight hard, skillfully, and stubbornly. Their fathers remember with misgivings, doubt, and fear the Yanks of 1917 and 1918, and just so the sons will learn on the field of battle about the bigger, quicker, better-trained Yanks of 1942 and 1943.

The new education of German youth is soon to take place. It is a great misfortune to the world that the Germans must learn the hard way.

CHAPTER XXXV

THE GERMAN ARMY: ORGANIZATION AND TACTICS

PRINCIPLES OF ORGANIZATION

The demand for versatility in the soldier is paralleled by the German principle of versatility in organization. In the German Army there is nothing sacred about tables of organization. They vary the size and composition of regiments, divisions, armies, and air forces as the need arises and as the mission requires. However, all German organizations are based on certain principles which have a direct bearing on German tactical doctrines.

The Einheit (One Unit) Principle

A standard unit group with standard organization, standard training, and standard equipment is used as the basic unit in all organizations *where its use is practical.*

For example, a standard rifle group, consisting of a rifle team, a light machine-gun, and a light mortar team, is the basic unit in all organizations where the tactical employment is based on fire and movement, such as a rifle company (*Schutzen* company), motorcycle rifle company (*Kradschutzen* company), etc. This standard rifle group corresponds to an enlarged United States Army squad.

In communications units the group is one or more basic radio or telephone groups whose equipment, organization, and training are identical regardless of principle, size, or the organization to which they belong.

By adding or subtracting these basic units, the composition and size of organizations can be changed readily without disrupting those organizations.

476

The Principle of Tactical Self-Sufficiency

Each combat unit, from the *Einheit* up to a complete division, is so organized, armed, and equipped as to be actually self-sufficient to accomplish its *local combat mission*. Each combat unit contains organically the weapons necessary to accomplish its local mission. For instance, supporting artillery is included as a part of the infantry regiment. Distribution of supporting weapons is based on the answer to the question: "What type unit will habitually require this weapon as an organic weapon in accomplishing its mission, and how many such weapons will each unit require?"

The Principle of Administrative Self-Sufficiency

This principle requires that each tactical unit responsible for administration be organized so as to be independent, as to personnel and transportation, of the next higher unit. The administrative units are armies, divisions, and battalions. All other tactical units are attached to one of these for administration. With the administrative self-sufficiency of the battalion, an unlimited number of battalions can be attached to the regiment without impairment of administrative efficiency.

The detailed organization of German units is similar to that of other world powers, except that there is no hesitancy in combining arms and services for the accomplishment of a specific task or mission. Until recently the Germans had shown greater versatility in the development of task forces, especially talented for their objective, than any other army. Every major engagement or battle of the war up to this time has demonstrated the ability of the German Army to meet changed situations and prepare especially for them.

The German high command gambled on an inactive Western Front (although the actual situation was much better than a gamble) when it undertook the campaign to destroy the Polish Army and dismember Poland. In that campaign, the first actual fighting of the present World War, primary reliance was placed on the air force. Almost the entire Luftwaffe participated in the brief Polish campaign. It assumed the role generally taken by infantry or armored forces—that of shock troops, or the striking force. Its primary objective was the destruction of the Polish air force, an objective accomplished in two days. Its secondary objective was the destruction of troops and communications and the perfection of liaison with the ground troops.

Despite journalistic and popular conceptions to the contrary, the backbone of the German Army remains the infantry and its supporting artillery; and a study of German Army organization can most simply be effected by a brief analysis of the German infantry division.

The standard infantry division consists of three infantry regiments, three light artillery battalions, one medium artillery battalion, *an artillery observation battalion*, an engineer battalion, an anti-tank battalion, a signal battalion, medical personnel, and *a cavalry reconnaissance battalion*. At first glance there seems to be no major difference between the organization of the German division and that of our own. The important differences appear in the lower units; for example, each regiment has an organic unit—an infantry howitzer company. This supporting artillery is directly under the command of the regimental commander. There are six 75-mm. light infantry and two 150-mm. heavy infantry howitzers that can be employed by the regimental commander with minimum delay.

Another difference between German and American divisions is in the cavalry reconnaissance battalion in each infantry division. This is composed of a horse troop, a bicycle company, and a heavy weapons company. In the heavy weapons company again we find heavy artillery—two 75-mm. infantry howitzers.

Each infantry division also contains an anti-tank battalion.

It has been a general assumption in America that the German Army was fully and exclusively equipped with the most modern devices of war and that therefore the horse had been relegated to limbo. However, the outstanding difference between American and German divisions lies in the large number of horses in the German organization and the comparatively small number of motors. Moreover, the German infantry is a marching infantry, hardened to the task of covering long distances on foot with full equipment. It is obvious that Germany either cannot fully equip her army with motors or else places more trust in the foot soldier and in the use of horses for many reconnaissance missions. The ability of the foot soldier to keep up with the armored and motorized forces during the various German campaigns indicates the strenuous conditioning of the infantry as well as the great reliance placed on the marching soldier. While motorized troops have predominated in some actions and campaigns, in all of them marching infantry played a highly important part.

THREE GERMAN CAMPAIGNS

The campaign in Holland brought a change in the organization of task forces and differed greatly from the Polish campaign. Again Germany selected and trained troops for a specific operation against a specific foe at a specific time and a specific place. The seizures of The Hague and Amsterdam were demonstrations of the versatile methods the German command was prepared to employ.

The attack on The Hague was carried out by parachute troops and an air-borne division, the first air-borne division to be employed in warfare. This division was stripped of all equipment that was not strictly necessary for its task, and it was composed of carefully selected men. While the ordinary infantry division consisted of approximately 15,000 men, this air-borne division was cut to 8,000. In general, only those men were selected who were absolutely essential to the success of the first phase. Cooks were left behind, as were supply personnel, administrative personnel, and those elements of the military police that were not necessary for this operation.

The formation of this division, according to reliable sources, was as follows:

- 1 detachment Military Police for prevention of traffic jams
- 1 detachment Signal Troops
- 1 detachment Reconnaissance Troops
- 1 battalion Pioneer (Engineer) Troops
- 2 regiments Infantry (each 2800 men)
- 2 battalions Light Artillery (pack artillery because easily broken down for shipment)
- 1 Anti-Tank battalion
- 2 battalions Parachute Troops

Other infantry divisions in this campaign remained the same in organization as those employed in the Polish blitzkrieg, except for the addition of more pioneer (engineer) units, for attacks on fortifications.

Again in the campaigns in the Balkans and against Greece the German theory of adaptability to terrain, to enemy opposition, and to the mission was graphically demonstrated. The importance of the use of infantry in this period has not been sufficiently recognized.

Because of the mountainous country in which the operations were to take place, several mountain divisions (infantry) and a great number of pioneer (engineer) troops were used. The mountain divisions differed from the standard infantry divisions chiefly in the elimination of unnecessary impedimenta and in the fact that they were composed largely of soldiers from the mountain regions of Germany and Austria. Equipment which could be carried by men was used as much as possible, rather than equipment requiring motor or horse transportation. It was the skillful employment of this hardy mountain infantry that time and again enabled the stalled tanks to get past strong points in the passes that held them up. Terrain that would have been impregnable against the attack of tanks was encircled by the infantry, which destroyed the opposition, permitting the armored forces to move on.

In the battle of Crete, a parachute division was employed for the first time. While this battle was a great air victory and represents the first time in history that an air-borne army has seized a complete objective, it must be remembered that these air-borne troops were expert and highly trained infantry organizations, rifle regiments supported by mountain howitzers and anti-tank companies. The weapons of the mountain howitzer companies were not dropped by parachute but were brought to the field of action by the air-borne division.

The campaign in Libya is another demonstration of organization again changed to meet the conditions and the enemy in a set of circumstances altogether different from any that prevailed in previous campaigns. In Libya, because of the extended distances involved in battle and the great maneuver areas in the desert, the troops used were motorized and mechanized. The armored divisions were cut down from their former large size in order to make them more self-sustaining for operations at a distance from their base of supply, and the anti-aircraft defense was greatly strengthened, this augmented anti-air defense being made an integral part of the division.

A typical armored division in Libya is made up of the following elements, according to reports from usually reliable sources:

    1 Tank regiment, consisting of 2 battalions of tanks
    1 Motorized Infantry brigade, consisting of:
        2 regiments Infantry
        1 battalion Motorcycle Troops
    1 Artillery regiment
    1 Engineer battalion
    2 Anti-Air battalions
    1 Reconnaissance battalion
    1 Signal battalion
    1 Anti-Tank battalion
    1 Reconnaissance Aviation squadron
    Miscellaneous supply troops and repair companies

Let it be noted here that because of the German theory of versatility in operations, the rough "tables" of organization mentioned in this chapter are susceptible to further changes, and none should be considered fixed or, except from a broad point of view, standard.

GERMAN TACTICS AND OPERATIONS

It is not the purpose of this chapter to give a comprehensive study of applied German tactics nor to rehearse the details of tactical practices. Readers of the files of that admirable service magazine, the *Infantry Journal,* may discover there many pertinent articles analyzing military engagements of the present World War and demonstrating how theories were put into practice. Nor are German tactical theories unique. However, their successive demonstrations of applied tactics and their versatility in application have accomplished a series of successes that may properly be called unique in modern military history.

German tactics, like those of any modern army, are based on speed and surprise; on the importance of using all available means —moral, physical, and material—at a decisive point at a decisive time; and on a ruthless exploitation of success, whether that success

comes from a planned operation or from opportunism that a commander may suddenly seize and develop. The German theory of
war is not founded on winning battles but on complete annihilation
of the enemy.

The Germans teach that victory must be absolute, that the enemy
must be destroyed morally and physically. Therefore they wage
war ruthlessly on everyone who might encourage the will to fight
in the enemy. This includes not only soldiers but women, children,
aged people, factory workers, and all who might make any contribution to the war effort either spiritually or physically. This
explains in part the humiliations forced upon conquered peoples
by their German task-masters. Not only physical defeat but moral
breakdown is sought.

In order to make the most effective use of the theory of tactics,
German leaders of all ranks are impressed with the necessity for
boldness and decision. This applies to noncommissioned officers as
well as to higher commanders. The emphasis is drilled home by
constant training and exercises to develop the following factors:

1. Keep the initiative.
2. Remember your objective.
3. Keep your plan simple to insure speed of execution.
4. Maximum power into main effort, minimum power in
   secondary effort.
5. Preserve and renew fighting power of your troops.
6. Immediately recognize favorable situations and utilize to
   your advantage.
7. Consider tactical doctrines and methods of enemy.
8. If two equally reasonable courses of action exist, *always
   adopt the bolder.*
9. The offensive will always win.

While there is nothing unique in these points, the Germans
practice them down to the smallest units and have *put them into
practice* with confidence, enterprise, and initiative to an unusual
degree. This boldness has surprised and disconcerted their opponents and has repeatedly led to German successes, small and big—
the small successes contributing to the big ones.

From the German point of view, the squad or group can, should, and must be an *enterprising unit*. In the rapid movement and flux of modern battle, the small units have a higher importance in the scheme of battle than ever before. Companies and battalions exploit opportunities with extreme boldness and thereby create opportunities for the higher command to develop and exploit. German units have frequently overcome larger forces by the practical application *on the ground* of the teachings to "keep the initiative," "immediately recognize favorable situations," and always adopt the bolder of "equally reasonable courses."

The campaign in the Balkans illustrated German tenacity, quick support by other arms, and coördination of all arms.

In this campaign German panzer units were confined within comparatively narrow limits by the character of the terrain that extended along the few vital roads to southern Greece.

The German commanding officer would advance with the first team, the panzer troops, as the spear-head. When these units met determined resistance and were stalled, no desperate attempt was made to break through, but the second team, mountain troops, was quickly sent around and through the mountains to penetrate to a point in the rear, from which they could then threaten the defending force. Since no continuous line was held, this method was usually feasible. Therefore the defenders were constantly outflanked just as the British were in the defense of the Malay Peninsula.

If the mountain troops also met stiff resistance, the third team was brought into play—the Stukas. The Stuka bombers were employed as a reinforcement for either the first or the second team. This type of maneuver was followed throughout the campaign, and it accounts for the comparatively light losses suffered by the German elements.

During the retreat of the British forces, the air force team had the added mission of attacking along the roads. Bombs accurately placed on both sides of the roads were effective in destroying or disrupting transport and troop columns without serious damage to the roads over which the German panzer and motorized units were to advance. This effective close-range bombing was, of course, possible only because of the British deficiency both in anti-air defense weapons and in combat planes.

It is noteworthy that the German troops fought the Balkan campaign *without field kitchens or trains*. They refused to encumber themselves with impedimenta not strictly necessary to smash through into Greece. The first supply train arrived in Athens April 28—after the capitulation. Troops depended upon supplies dropped from the air, supplementing captured supplies. It is true that this method imposed tremendous physical demands upon the troops. But it kept the highways cleared of everything not immediately contributing to military success, thereby speeding up the campaign, adding to the element of surprise, and producing victory at a lesser cost in deaths and wounds than otherwise could have been attained. The "sacrifice" was worth it, not only from the point of view of military victory but in actual saving of German lives.

(The resulting scarcity of food in an operation of this sort, together with the great physical demands placed upon the troops, had an interesting later effect. When the assault troops were sent to rest camps after the capitulation of Athens, they suffered from insomnia and from an inability to keep cooked food on their stomachs. In some instances two weeks were required to bring these soldiers back to normal mental and physical condition.)

The fact that German troops were able to operate without their trains in the Balkan campaign is proof of an exceptionally high state of training and discipline.

DEFEATING THE GERMAN MACHINE

It is impossible in a brief chapter to give a series of illustrations of German tactical applications. They may be found in articles in service publications and in at least one important book on that subject recently published. But the principles enumerated here apply throughout; and the emphasis that needs to be placed here is on the fact of the *application* of tactical principles that are living only when applied and that are dead so long as they remain in service manuals and are not practised in exercises and finally on the field of battle by noncommissioned officers, company officers, and higher commanders, each according to his mission and the fire-power and tactical capabilities of his command.

The German Army is a formidable machine for warfare, but its mind is not machine-like. On the contrary, its mind indulges in extensive poetic license— according to its measure of its opponents' capacities and its opponents' mental reactions. All that is daring and bold, that "throws away the book" when *opportunity* is discovered is a form of military poetic license. Rigidity of form, organization, and method has been abolished by the Germans. Individual enterprise has not only been liberated in the German Army, it has been encouraged by awards, promotions, and success itself.

This enterprise and this boldness have been accompanied by meticulous planning and organization. The physical details conform to the ever-fluid patterns of changing methods and bold thinking.

It may reasonably be expected that German defensive methods, once the German Army has reeled back from the blows of equally or more greatly determined and enterprising powerful enemies, will be ingenious as well as stubborn. The so-called "hedge-hog" defense of German strong points in Russia, with fortified "quills" extending considerable distances from the center, has proved exceedingly tough for the Russians to deal with, despite the latters' expertness as night and snow fighters. The Germans, who probed the weakness of static defense, may not be expected to adopt the methods that crumbled before their blows. The American soldier and American military leaders will do no wishful thinking in this respect. Nor will they do wishful thinking about a breakdown in German morale, nor anticipate a victory won the easy way by vast armadas of bombers dropping explosives on German cities.

The war will be won when the German armies are decisively defeated on battlefields by the armies of the Allies augmented by vast manpower from the United States, hard-hitting with a plentitude of American implements of war and striking home with American zest to come to close grips with the foe.

The German soldier is a skillful killer of men. But he is just another man. He has hitherto benefited enormously by being able to surprise far less well-prepared opponents. He has benefited tremendously also by the operations of "fifth columns" in the countries of his victims. He has hitherto had everything on his side in the way of superior equipment in vast quantities and, in all campaigns up to now, control of the air. Moreover, he benefited by the propaganda build-up, that showed him as an irresistible force, to the terror of many of his European opponents. And that's something that won't work on Americans.

The German soldier will never have that combination of advantages again—and as American manpower and equipment reach the field of battle he will know it, just as he will know, when American bayonets flash, that the German is no superman, no matter what his story-books have told him.

But the American soldier has plenty to learn. Fortunately he has been given more time to learn about this enemy than was given to those who learned too late, after they had been struck. Most of all, the American must learn skill as a soldier and how to think quickly in terms of tactics. The place and time to learn the fundamentals and their application, to practise enterprise and initiative in leading men and meeting situations, is here in their training centers and NOW without waste of time. This requires more than study and instruction. It requires, among officers and enlisted men, a passion for self-improvement as soldiers.

In the words of the Commanding General of the Second Army, "Fighters will win!" *Skilled* fighters will win more quickly, at less cost in lives.

CHAPTER XXXVI

PROPAGANDA—TOOL OF PEACE AND WEAPON OF WAR

Like the air we breathe, propaganda has become a part of our daily experience. In its encouraging, in its educational, or in its malevolent or subversive forms, it flows constantly around us— carried to our eyes by the printed word, to our ears by radio and even by conversation.

This is not a new thing. Propaganda—the effort to influence one's thinking, one's attitudes, one's objectives—is as old as the first argument, the first debate, the first effort to persuade a person. But its intensification to the point where it is a continuing daily or hourly influence is as new as the developments of science and mechanics that have speeded up its flow and broadened its audience. A world reacts to propaganda today.

In war, propaganda is particularly, peculiarly intense—intensive and extensive. In this second modern World War most of all. Not only has the power of radio been added since the last war, not only are more millions of people able to read; but governments have applied propaganda as a science of persuasion and coercion on a scale never dreamed of in previous generations. And its capacity as a weapon of war has been developed to the degree where it is accepted as one of the most important weapons; on occasions, *the most important*, because it has been able to win victories without the direct use of military force.

We must seek to understand it and its capabilities in order that we may employ this weapon most effectively against our enemies, in favor of our friends, and as an influence upon those that might otherwise waver in the direction of the enemies' camps. And we must seek to understand it, so that we may intelligently combat its employment as a weapon aimed at us.

Bombs, shells, bullets, flame-throwers are used to destroy the human body and property. Their destructive work may clearly be

487

seen. Unlike such weapons, propaganda launches its attack on the minds of men and women and children. It works upon their human nature. It may have an effect before the effect is actually noticeable.

Our minds are marvelously complicated mechanisms. They store hopes and fears, prejudices and dislikes, ambitions and desires, love and hatred, and multitudes of habits that influence our actions and decisions. Physical victories may more easily be won if the weapon of propaganda is successfully used to attack the mind, develop the weaknesses of human nature.

It is of vital importance for soldiers and civilians alike to understand this weapon and how it is being used. The fundamental rules are not complicated. The best armament against it is *understanding*. Whoever understands propaganda is able to build up immunity to it. And there is no need to be afraid of it. We Americans are particularly skilled in its use. We have used it constructively in building up our civilization—in selling our products—in improving our standard of living. We used it with telling effect in World War No. 1.

More than any other people, we Americans have employed propaganda skillfully for good purposes. Our chambers of commerce are experienced in using propaganda to boost their communities. Our tourist centers have used it on a tremendous scale to build the tourist trade. When we undertake a drive for funds to combat infantile paralysis and choose the President's birthday as an annual occasion for that drive, we indulge in constructive propaganda for a noble purpose. That is also true of our fund-raising activities for community chests, the Red Cross, the anti-tuberculosis campaigns. With our newspapers and radio stations, speakers and civic clubs, we set forth to propagandize the public on the need and desirability to support these worthy efforts. We "sell" our neighbors the desire to be generous, to "give until it hurts," to do these acts of good will.

Therefore, do not be afraid of propaganda. It is an agency for good as well as a weapon for war. So is electricity; so is the automobile; so is the printing press.

Our purpose now is to seek a simple, clear understanding of it and learn to evaluate, to measure, to exercise our power of selection and choice. We will study the fundamentals of propaganda and then the methods that Hitler developed to create fear, confusion, dismay, division, and sometimes hopelessness among those that he would strike. By this understanding we will make useless this weapon in the enemies' hands.

PROPAGANDA IN THE FIRST WORLD WAR

German military leaders have claimed that the first World War was won by propaganda. We know that is not true, although we were skillful in using it as a means to undermine German resistance. Propaganda is not a magic wand that may be waved over the enemies' fortifications with the same success that greeted Joshua when he caused the trumpets to be blown at the walls of Jericho, whereupon the walls crumbled and fell.

But Allied and particularly American propaganda in the first World War did indeed *help* to win the war, did indeed bring that war to an earlier conclusion. Its success, however, was considerable only after Germany had failed in the final effort for a breakthrough on the Western Front, only after Allied military successes sent the German armies reeling back.

There was no radio in the first World War. No loud-speakers blared messages to the troops in the trenches. No short-wave radio carried propaganda to the homes of the people. Therefore propaganda in that war was to an important extent a dissemination of news, opinion, and persuasion through the printed word—through pamphlets, leaflets, proposals that were even printed in enemy newspapers, Wilson's Fourteen Points for instance.

More than 65,000,000 pieces of printed material were distributed behind the German lines. Airplanes were used for this distribution; small balloons that carried a few pounds of printed matter over the lines with the prevailing westerly wind; small waterproof sacks of pamphlets that were floated down the Rhine. Every practical means to distribute literature to German troops and their people behind the lines were used.

How much did this propaganda discourage our enemies' war efforts and help to break their resistance? That we don't know. But the German military leaders dreaded it and felt—rightly or wrongly —that Allied "paper bullets" had a decisive effect. At any rate that was *their* propaganda to save their military faces and try to convince German youth that they were never "honestly" conquered on the field of battle.

As early as July, 1917, there were bitter complaints by high German officers, the Chief of the General Staff of a field army on the Western Front reporting that leaflets were causing "a feeling of profound depression at home." [1] Early in 1918 there was this statement in a German Army journal: "In the sphere of leaflet propaganda the enemy has defeated us." [2] And after the weight of American forces was being considerably felt, later in 1918, a German magazine complained: "The majority of the German people place greater trust in Woodrow Wilson than in their own leaders." [3]

Finally Ludendorff, who would never, never admit military defeat, requested the German government in October to ask for an armistice, declaring that the country had been "hypnotized by the enemy propaganda as a rabbit is by a snake." [4]

What did the Allies say in these leaflets, that affected the Germans so considerably and made General Ludendorff despondent?

They said plenty of things that were entirely true—for instance, the news of the growing might of the American Army that was assembling in France.

One of them read: "1,500,000 American soldiers are in France, more than twice the number is being trained in America." [5] That was perfectly true. It was news to the Germans, who had been told by their government that American aid to the Allies would not be effective. It was very bad news to the German Army and to the German people.

There was a critical shortage of food in Germany. Allied propaganda made the most of that fact. Leaflets distributed in the vicinity of German trenches emphasized the suffering and deprivations of the people at home. One leaflet said: "After the revolt of the German people, the Allies, who have no hate for them, will supply them with food and clothing even as they are supplying the war prisoners now. But these provisions will be withheld until the military authority in Germany collapses." [6]

It was advertised to German soldiers that if they surrendered they would have good treatment and very good food indeed. That would not have appealed to well-fed German soldiers, but when these leaflets were scattered the German soldier was feeling the pinch of tiresome and short rations. The Americans told them that as prisoners they would be served beef, white bread, potatoes, beans, prunes, coffee, butter, tobacco. This propaganda increased the desertions of discouraged men. Moreover, German prisoners did fatten on American food.

Greatest blame for their breakdown has been attributed by the Germans to Woodrow Wilson, President of the United States. His was a powerful voice, and his Fourteen Points appealed directly to the people of Germany over the heads of their rulers. President Wilson's principles would not have rung the bell in Germany if the German armies had been marching triumphantly on. But those once great armies had been stopped, stopped cold. They had suffered immense losses. The dead and the maimed had become a legion of millions. The pressure of the Allied forces was becoming greater. The fresh and confident American troops had become a factor to be reckoned with. The Allies had won great victories in the Near East. Turkey was knocked out. Austria-Hungary was crumbling. What did Woodrow Wilson proclaim? Among other things, he heralded a League of Nations; he promised freedom of the seas and open diplomacy; he said there would be no discrimination between victors and vanquished in the final settlement. However, the Fourteen Points also declared for "self-determination" on the part of minorities—the Poles and the Czechs for instance. The Germans looked on the Fourteen Points from their disconsolate position of hunger and military defeat and found them brighter than any other expectations.

"Why fight any longer?" the Allies asked. By that time the war-weary Germans were echoing that question. They had lost faith that their resistance could bring them greater benefits. When they fully realized that, the war they had made was over.

What had the Germans done with propaganda as *their* weapon in the first World War? Not much.

They had, of course, blamed the war on the Russians and the French and on "perfidious Albion." For England they had a "Hymn of Hate." Their propaganda, which was fairly noisy before the United States entered the war, was a crude, blunt weapon and had little influence in America. The accusations and charges of conspiracy had been more than offset by the brutal invasion of Belgium, the sinking of the *Lusitania*, the torpedoing of merchant vessels without warning, the shooting of Edith Cavell by a firing squad, and the sabotage they undertook in the United States before this country entered the war. There were, of course, the "atrocity" stories, which in the light of later evidence were proved unfounded in fact. But it was the arrogant and brutal violation of treaties and principles of war that gave credibility to such stories; and no atrocity story had the effect upon public opinion of the German declaration that the treaty with Belgium was nothing more than "a scrap of paper."

After the United States entered the war, there was a vigorous propaganda campaign on our home front, directed by the Committee on Public Information, the head of which was an experienced and nationally known journalist, George Creel.

All the enterprise and talent of the American newspaper and advertising field were employed in a program to energize the spirit of the American people in a mighty war effort. There was a steady stream of posters, cartoons, syndicated news stories, special feature stories, movies, advertisements, and material for speakers. The "nation-wide hookup" of 1917 and 1918 was composed of some 75,000 speakers who made brief speeches (usually four minutes) in theaters and motion picture houses, in ball parks and before civic clubs and school assemblies—all according to plan. These speakers preceded the beginning of radio networks by six years.

Of course, the Creel committee was severely criticized by many newspapers and by other critics of the ways and methods of propaganda, especially after the war. The years following the struggle formed a period in which Americans indulged in very considerable self-criticism, a post-war wave of disillusionment with ourselves and with our former allies. We are prone to this tendency to self-criticism because we are, on the whole, a conscientious and idealistic people. (This condition among Americans Hitler tries to exploit in his propaganda, as we will later show.) And so, Mr. Creel and his associates were thoroughly lambasted for having issued some propaganda that wasn't based on facts or true conditions—"unfair," therefore, to our enemies. Our enemies, meanwhile, made the most of our tendency to criticize ourselves and very nearly succeeded in bringing us to tears over our "wickedness" in using propaganda successfully to aid in their defeat.

But despite the criticism, American propaganda was based essentially on fact and evidence. Never in the Committee's most excited moments did it put up a performance comparable even to the mildest of Herr Goebbels's "Ministry of Propaganda and Enlightenment." While it dealt occasionally with fiction or exaggeration, it chiefly stuck to the facts in influencing the American people to increase their war effort. It was the biggest and certainly the most skillful job of promotion at home and attack abroad that had ever been undertaken with words, pictures, and ideas.

DEVELOPMENT OF GERMAN PROPAGANDA
UNDER HITLER

It is not uncommon that the losing side in a war subsequently studies and takes over the successful weapons of the victor and develops them further. The Germans did that in the case of the tank and its employment. And they took up the weapon of propaganda —with which they had been so clumsy—in order to mould it into a tool of aggression for the next war that they began almost immediately to plan.

Moreover, the German people preferred to think that they were not "fairly" defeated by armies in the field. A warlike people fostering the myth of racial superiority cannot afford to entertain such thoughts. It was less hurtful to their pride to blame their collapse upon Allied propaganda. Having *felt* some of the dire effects of propaganda, they explored the possibilities of making it a truly mighty weapon.

No one held such convictions more fanatically than an obscure, insignificant character named Adolf Hitler. This little, unknown man had taken the defeat of Germany as a rankling sore into his Austrian heart. A moody and excitable person, he permitted this thought to depress him unspeakably. He thought of nothing but the humiliation of Germany. He dreamed of nothing but revenge. He put all other things out of his mind. This insignificant man sought to achieve the control of a nation.

In *Mein Kampf*, Hitler complains that German propaganda during the war was very poor. He said he "learned infinitely much more from the Allied propaganda" which worked (in his words) with "unheard-of skill and ingenious deliberation" and was "psychologically right."

He shrewdly understood that to carry out his amazing dreams to seize power over the German people and lead them to revenge and to world domination by the German race, he would have to become the master of all the tools of propaganda. Every trick would have to be learned. Every experiment would be attempted. Hitler himself says of the road to power: "The road cannot be cleared by dagger or poison or pistol, but by conquering the man in the street." [7] Of course, the Nazis never hesitated to use the dagger, poison, or pistol when the end justified the means. But they also learned to stab with words, poison with phrases, shoot with speeches.

Hitler did indeed scramble to the top of the heap of the other crack-pots that refused to make any adjustment in the post-war period. He did indeed employ every tool and method of propaganda to win his way to control over the German people. For the first time in history, all the malevolence and evil that are potential in propaganda were employed and diabolically devised in preparation for world conquest. Day and night, never-ending, this weapon of war is being exercised all over the world against America and our Allies—in scores of languages, over the air and in print, by every conceivable method of transmission.

THE RULES OF PROPAGANDA

How dangerous will it prove to be to us? The answer to this question depends, as we have stated before, on the strength of our own propaganda defenses and on our good native common sense. If we understand first the elements of propaganda, and then the strategy Hitler has built up on the basis of those elements, we certainly should not be vulnerable to its attacks upon our minds. Because that is the only place where it can attack us.

Therefore we will consider, in this course of immunizing ourselves, six simple but highly important rules. Moreover, these rules were not laid down by Hitler. He found them already in use, nowhere in more skillful use than in America. They are fundamentals of American advertising and salesmanship. No other country has ever developed the arts of journalism, press agenting, public relations, SELLING as highly as we have. According to Dr. Gordon W. Allport, Professor of Psychology at Harvard University, there are six basic psychological rules. Let us examine and discuss them.

Rule 1

If you want to sell a product or sell an idea, connect it up with something people already like or believe in.

Does that not explain to you why so many healthy, pretty, alluring girls appear in our advertisements, no matter whether the advertised product is a loaf of bread, an automobile from the dear, dim past, a recruiting poster, or perhaps even a piston ring? Girls of that sort are something people already like—and men believe in them, too.

An advertisement reads: "Keep your hands soft for caressing; buy Smoothskin Rubber Gloves."

On the back of Smith's Bakery truck is the kindly and welcome advice: "Look out for the kiddies." It warms the heart to Mr. Smith. Perhaps the next time you order bread, you unconsciously think of Smith's bread and decide to "try it."

How often the picture of a fine matronly-looking woman in her fifties or sixties, with good lines of strength and humor in her face, accompanies advertisements. It is the American mother, the good housewife who cooks and sews and looks forward to her grandchildren. Thousands of times we have seen her in advertisements, influencing us to purchase this or that product. Perhaps on "Mother's Day" throughout the country we *are* a little exploited by florists, candy stores, perfume sales places, and others that promote ideas for "Mother's Day." But we are happy, too, to be urged to remember Mother—and we approve of that propaganda in advertising. So, probably, does Mother.

Why is it that subversive organizations nearly always masquerade as patriotic groups. Why did the Communist Party in America, a few years ago, use the slogan, "Communism is twentieth-century Americanism"? Obviously because of the appeal of the word *Americanism*. Why do certain organizations that the F.B.I., for instance, distrusts use the word *democracy* in their titles? Obviously because we, the American people, have faith in democracy.

Many of us are shy, are easily embarrassed. We would like to carry things off more gaily, at least more easily. And so a well-known cigarette manufacturer advertises, "Be nonchalant. Smoke Murads."

Remember the rule: If you want to sell a product or an idea, connect it up with something people already like or believe in. Perhaps with what people would LIKE TO BE.

This rule works conversely, too. You can apply it in just the opposite way: *If you want to arouse fear or hatred for something, connect it up with something people already fear or hate.*

There is a famous soap that enlarges its sales prodigiously by advertising its efficacy in eliminating "B.O." It is B.O., remember, that keeps John Doe from being popular with the girls or that makes Jane Roe a wall-flower at dances when otherwise she might be the belle of the ball.

Falling hair may result in baldness long before your time. It is not popular to have dandruff on your collar. Such things may queer our social success, might stand in the way of our selling an order, perhaps might irritate the boss. We grow fearful and rush to buy the products that will prevent such disasters. And quite possibly the products will help us, too. At least they will give us more courage.

Also coming under this rule is the common trick of name-calling. In America we can damn a person by calling him a fascist or a communist, a fifth columnist or a fellow-traveler. People don't always stop to think whether these names really apply. Sometimes they do, sometimes they don't. But the names themselves tend to discredit the person they are attached to.

No one has ever used this trick as often, as steadily, as loudly as Hitler. He used it to climb to power. He has used it ever since. Every person that Hitler wanted to destroy in Germany, no matter how noble or illustrious the past of that person, he called a "betrayer" of Germany and of the German *Volk*. A terrible word— "betrayer."

Why does Hitler, of all people, call his enemies "war-mongers," and "would-be dictators"? Extraordinary, isn't it? He called poor

Beneš of Czecho-Slovakia (that *was*) a "war-monger." And finally he called Chamberlain a "war-monger." And Churchill. And Roosevelt. And everybody that doesn't bow the neck to Hitlerism. We heard that expression quite a lot in our own country, too— before Pearl Harbor.

The rule gives the answer. If you want to arouse fear or hatred for some person, connect him up with something people already fear or hate.

Rule 2

The second basic rule of propaganda is brief: *Avoid argument.* Do not admit that there is any other side to the question.

A politician running for office does not advertise his competitor's radio program or meetings, nor does he tell truthfully his opponent's side of the story and ask you to make a comparison. An advertiser does not invite you to try his competitor's product first so that you can then make an unbiased judgment.

Where there is free and full argument, people are able to make up their minds for themselves. Where there is biased argument constantly dinned at people, a large proportion of them tend to accept the one argument they hear. The propagandist does not want his listeners or readers to come to their own conclusions. He employs tactics designed exclusively to make them come to his conclusions—or the conclusions he desires to make them accept.

The Nazis in their rise to power and in the years following, became extremely adept in hammering home one side of the question —their side. They hammered it home as *the* fact, *the* opinions worthy of the German race to hold. All tricks were used to avoid any argument or any discussion. The final trick, of course, was the brown-shirt troopers who took into their own hands the business of dealing with any person who even tried to start an argument. No heckling was permitted at Nazi meetings. But tough Nazis were present to heckle speakers at other meetings. Here are some of the Hitler tricks used when Nazis were to speak (they are still used):

Violent clanging of church bells when the fuehrer arrived in the city where he was to speak

Lavish use of colored lights playing upon the background of the platform and spotlights upon the speaker

Loud marching songs before and after speeches, organized cheering, but carefully organized by troopers mingling with the crowds

The wide use of decorations and swastikas, enormous flags and banners, making for elaborate pageantry

Vigorous marching, goose-stepping, parading, giving the rhythmic beat of thousands of hobnailed boots upon the pavements

All of this created a form of hypnotism, which was developed in the frenzy of the crowds. Even experienced American newspapermen attending such meetings, many of which were of immense size and therefore exploited to the utmost the mob instinct, said that only with great difficulty could they avoid being carried away by the emotion, the hypnotic frenzy of those around them.

Of course, once Hitler attained power, he put an end to all free speech, free press, and free assembly. His system could permit no other to bid as a potential rival. Just as it avoided argument in its rise to power, it abolished all chance for argument after power had been achieved.

This was and is extreme propaganda. It is the antithesis of education. Education ideally presents various sides and issues, even though it may place some emphasis on one side. Propaganda has one side only.

Of course, in a democracy, there is a constant flow of counter-propaganda. You see that in the advertising pages of magazines and newspapers and in the competitive announcements made over the air by the sponsors of radio programs. No seller of products is enabled to monopolize your attention for his products.

Similarly in our politics. If there is propaganda on the part of one party, there is counter-propaganda on the part of another. The Democrats have their say, and forthwith the Republicans have theirs. The New Dealer may advocate one proposition, the anti-New Dealer then takes up the cudgels against him. The public is relatively free to decide who or which is right. The public in a democracy receives impressions from various points of view. It may compare the claims.

Rule 3

Every word has a meaning of its own; choose each one carefully. Propagandists, like poets and good prose-writers, are experts in selecting their words. They know how to choose each word according to the impression they wish to give and the color they wish to employ.

So do all good advertisers. You seldom see a butcher's advertisement for the sale of mutton or hen. On the contrary, it specifies lamb or chicken, even though they may be very adult.

Corsets are homely and not very attractive objects. They have not, for instance, been the subjects of any beautiful poems. The manufacturers select their words carefully when they name and advertise their products as "Freeflex," "Youthlastic," "Flexees," "Silkskin," "Lasteze," or "Super-Control." And the radio informs us that "Van Svelte" is "unsurpassed in modifying the rear profile."

We can pick up our magazines and newspapers at any time and there examine the skill with which American ad-writers select their words.

The Nazis have made a careful study of word-selection.

Hitler, like most of his tribe, speaks of *"Lebensraum,"* which means "living space." That sounds very decent. Everyone wants living space. Most of us think the other fellow is entitled to it. But with this attractive phrase, Hitler disguises his ruthless and aggressive invasions of thickly populated countries such as Holland, Denmark, Belgium, and the Russian Ukraine, where he intends to deny living space to others. He says he is preparing for the time when there will be 250,000,000 Germans in Europe. Obviously, the living space of a lot of people will have to be sacrificed to provide such *Lebensraum* for Germans.

Hitler speaks of the Germans as the German *"Volk"* and as the master race of the world, declaring that all constructive good in this world was originated by this master race or its antecedents. When the Japanese became his allies, his propagandists even had a trick for that odd alliance of the boastful Nazi Aryans and the yellow aggressors. They simply announced that the Japanese were "Yellow Aryans" and that they worshiped a god who was practically a brother of Wotan's.

A great deal of word magic has been employed by Hitler and his Nazi propagandists. Consider the constant repetition in speeches, press dispatches, and other forms of propaganda of such terms as *Destiny, Fate. It is inevitable. It will come to pass, Annihilation.*

~~The point is, they want to give the impression to their own people~~
and to the outside world, especially those they intend to victimize,
that Nazi victory over mankind is just a matter of time. Opposition,
therefore, is fruitless; it results in that very terrific thing called
Annihilation. It may be remembered how many times in 1941 the
Russian armies were "annihilated."

Rule 4

Make your statements brief and clear.

Hitler himself is a very wordy man and does not speak very
pure German diction. His average public address appears to take
about one hour and fifty-two minutes. However, few of the Nazi
propaganda brain trust indulge in the fuehrer's privilege of wordi-
ness. They go in for statements, slogans, cartoons, pictures, and
posters that "pack a punch."

Pictures are used on a lavish scale, and they are always taken of
exceptionally stalwart, healthy-looking people. The kneeling pos-
ture for taking pictures is very broadly used by German camera-
men when they photograph army units in action. Pictures taken
that way make their subjects look larger and more powerful. The
art of making the subject matter appear more deadly, more violent,
and more purposeful than it really is in life is an art these camera-
men carefully follow.

Similarly, they pose other pictures that show that everything the
Hitler forces do when not fighting is all sweetness and light.

It was a Chinese philosopher who said, "One picture tells as
much as 10,000 words." That may be entirely true. The first thing
we read is a picture book. The baby will be interested in pictures
before he learns how to hold them right side up. And it is a toss-up
today whether more business men than children read the comics.

The selection and sale of slogans is also one of the highest objectives of skilled propagandists. There should always be an economy
of words in creating a slogan. The shorter it is to pack its punch
the better. There has never been a shorter or more expressive slogan
than the simple letter "V," which people even in occupied countries can use. Even there, with a pencil or walking stick they can tap
out dot-dot-dot-dash.

Today we have new slogans arising, one of these being "Remember Pearl Harbor." That can mean several things to the soldier. To everybody it means remember the dastardly attack made upon our concentrated forces there when Japanese diplomats in Washington were still bowing and scraping as they talked of peace. But to the soldier, it also means "Remember to be eternally vigilant." It means "Remember the price that is paid when your vigilance falters even for a moment."

We have also the slogan "The Arsenal of Democracy."

The Second Army has had its slogan ever since August, 1941, when the Army Commander gave to the Second Army a three-word motto: "Fit to Fight."

There will be more as the war continues.

Hitler, too, has his slogans, which appear to have a great appeal among the German people, strange though they sound to our ears. *Blut und Boden* is a very stirring phrase to German multitudes. It means "blood and soil." It would be difficult to conceive of the average American going into ecstasies over a speaker clamoring from the platform about blood and soil. Another German slogan is even stranger to our ears: "Du bist nichts; dein Volk ist Alles," which means, "You are nothing; your people is everything." Imagine individualistic Americans, with their heritage, accepting the principle that they are nothing. It sounds screwy to us, but that doesn't mean it isn't forceful in Germany.

Rule 5

Keep talking and printing ceaselessly. Propaganda isn't something you dole out in occasional homeopathic does, but it is something that is constantly poured on. It costs a lot of money, whether it is done by the Anti-Saloon League in order to put over Prohibition, or by the opponents of Prohibition in order to have it repealed, or by the Nazis to keep their policies sold to the German people or to keep selling their ideas to their agents in other countries.

We know how our great advertisers repeat and repeat their messages in order to make them stick in people's minds. The message may be a slogan or it may be a picture, or it may be a combination of a picture and a slogan. When you see in front of a certain store the plaster figure of a somewhat stout fox terrier with his head cocked a little to the side, you do not have to be reminded that the slogan that goes with that figure is "His Master's Voice." You see pictures of that dog in magazines and newspapers, and we have become accustomed to his acceptable figure for a generation. He has helped to sell on phonograph discs the finest music produced in the world—and quite a lot of jazz to boot.

In the last war a veritable flood of propaganda was poured over the German soldiers and civilians, constantly repeating that they could not win, constantly repeating that America with all its mighty resources was bound to crush the Central Powers.

In the present war RAF pilots are dropping American leaflets over portions of occupied France, repeating over and over again that America is a loyal friend of France and that America will produce the overwhelming might that will save France from the Nazis.

The German people are drenched with one-sided Nazi propaganda from morning till night, year after year. It is a method of incessant pounding that appears finally to break down resistance on the part of all who are not the stoutest individuals.

The Communists also have kept their people soaked with propaganda for more than twenty years, showing all virtue on their side, all evil on the side of the capitalistic countries; and there is no room for any other side to the picture in their press or on their air, in classrooms or in conversation. However, it is now being recognized that America and Britain have some virtues after all.

But, remember, in Germany every agency of expression is busy carrying out Rule 5: "Keep talking and printing ceaselessly."

Rule 6

Finally: *For long-run effects aim at children.*

Our most impressionable years are the years of our childhood. What is learned then is remembered best. Psychologists claim that the attitudes of a lifetime can be fixed between the years of five and fourteen. Some claim it can be done in an even shorter time.

Rule 6 is a psychological rule that is well known to parents, educators, clergymen, and even to advertisers. You will note how often the appeal of the advertiser is made to the child, even though adults also may enjoy "Jack Armstrong, the All-American Boy."

In a political sense, democratic countries do not endeavor greatly

to influence the minds of their children. It is not considered sport-
ing. If a child grows up to be a Democrat or a Republican, it is
very unlikely that he became inclined to one or the other of these
political alignments in school. It is much more probable that it was
a contagion resulting from hearing his father's opinions voiced at
the dinner table.

But in Nazi Germany, Fascist Italy, and Communist Russia, it is
a scientific political business to make ardent Nazis, Fascists, and
Communists out of children. They start even before the child can
recognize the emblem of that faith, whether it is the swastika, a
bundle of fasces, or the hammer and sickle. It is a thorough business; and it pretty well eliminates the possibility of opposition in
the rising generation.

The child in Germany is brought up to be a ruthless member of
a master race that looks upon all other races as inferior. From every
side it is dinned into the child that only the Germans are fit to rule
the world, that all others are rascals and have secured the best
places by fraud, and that they always have proved themselves unworthy. They are indoctrinated with the conviction that non-
German races are inferior peoples, most of them—especially the
Slavs—sheer vermin to be exterminated as the right and duty of the
German master race. In one of his addresses broadcast to all German troops on the Eastern Front, Hitler himself described the Russians as "beasts" and told his troops that they were not to consider
the Russians as human beings like themselves.

Strength and ruthlessness are glorified to the child. Here is, in
translation, a typical nursery rhyme to be heard in German kinder-
gartens:

> "Please," begged the victim, "let me go
> For I am such a little foe."
> "No," said the victor, "not at all,
> For I am big and you are small." [8]

A marching song that is popular with the youthful element in
the army and throughout the schools of Germany has the following stanza with its horrible implications:

> Though the whole world lie ruined around us after the day of war,
> What the devil do we care, we don't give a hoot any more,
> We will go marching forward, though everything fall away,
> For the world will be ours tomorrow, as Germany is today. [9]

Hitler's influence over the children became considerable before he took over the control of the German Reich. Thousands of the school-teachers became Nazis during Hitler's rise to power. They were particularly solicited by the storm troopers—and you must remember that even before Hitler the great majority of all the teachers in Germany were men. After Hitler seized power he immediately seized all the schools. He has now had nine years of uninterrupted and intensive propaganda work on German youth. It is sad to think what their distorted minds must be like.

It is small wonder, therefore, that this long period of indoctrination has filled the young German soldier with fanaticism, with fierce hatreds, with a ruthless attitude toward the conquered, with a "passion for death." This "passion for death" is symbolized in a sense by the hero-worship which is devoted to the fuehrer. "What *der Fuehrer* wishes" is all that youth requires to know.

The fairy tales about racial supremacy and Germanic superiority together with the other nonsense and sacrilegious conceptions that have filled the minds of these soldiers we are to meet in battle will not be easily undermined by counter-propaganda. Hitler caught them too young. This dangerous rubbish can only be knocked out of their heads first by military reverses. That at least will loosen and make room for counter-propaganda.

Similar fairy tales exist in the minds of the Japanese. Why Japanese soldiers think as they do is covered in another lecture in this educational program.

CONCLUSION

In conclusion, we give you once more the six simple rules which are the ABC's of propaganda as enumerated by Dr. Gordon W. Allport of Harvard University:

1. Connect up your proposition with preexisting likes and dislikes.
2. Avoid argument.
3. Choose each word carefully.
4. Make your statement brief and clear.
5. Keep talking and printing ceaselessly.
6. For long-run effects, aim at children.

However, do not look upon these rules alone as the basic principles for propaganda that is an element of Axis warfare and therefore a weapon aimed to do us injury.

We, too, will use these rules in our way, according to our principles and our conceptions, to work upon the Germans and their allies and to spread our messages and carry our convictions to our friends. They will be the basis of our propaganda at home to encourage the war effort of all civilians.

Propaganda itself is not necessarily evil. It is, in fact, everywhere. It is found on all sides of every major question. It is used to advocate city-manager government, and to oppose city-manager government; to argue in favor of public ownership of utilities and to argue against public ownership of utilities; it helped us to win the last war earlier than otherwise we would have won it. We employ it to raise funds for charitable institutions and for the U. S. O. Its good or its evil depends on how it is used—for what cause—for what end in life—for what good to be attained.

Propaganda is a constructive tool on the one hand, a sharp weapon on the other hand. A great deal depends upon the character of the men and the society that use it. The element that founded the Nazi Party by bludgeoning, by assassinations, and even by blood purges among themselves might well be expected to use propaganda according to the instincts of men of that stripe. There is a criminal note and sadism in German propaganda. Men of honor employ propaganda very differently, just as their objectives are different.

And now, let us feel no sense of inferiority in this battle of propaganda. We Americans are great propagandists. We first developed the art, and we have carried it further for constructive uses than any other people. Our advertisers, film-makers, journalists, chambers of commerce, town boosters, cartoonists, and public relations experts are second to none. They may be depended upon to launch an appealing and mighty propaganda for democracy that will strike powerful blows for our cause.

Americans have never used propaganda with Hitler's satanic purpose, for so completely destructive an objective. His method is to confuse, terrify, and paralyze an enemy. He has made propaganda a major psychological strategy in modern warfare. What he has done and how we can fight it will be discussed in our next lecture.

REFERENCE NOTES

[1] G. G. Bruntz, *Allied Propaganda and the Collapse of the German Empire in 1918* (Stanford University Press), p. 188.

[2] Same, p. 201.

[3] Same, p. 189.

[4] Same, p. 216.

[5] Same, p. 93.

[6] Same, p. 162.

[7] Adolf Hitler, *My Battle* (Houghton Mifflin Company, Boston, 1933).

[8] G. Ziemer, *Education for Death* (Oxford University Press, New York).

[9] Erika Mann, *School for Barbarians* (Modern Age Books, Inc., New York).

CHAPTER XXXVII

THE PLACE OF PROPAGANDA IN TOTAL WAR

It has been pointed out that the German military leaders accredited Allied propaganda with notable effect upon the German people in the first World War. Strongly influenced by this belief was the insignificant Austrian Hitler, the brooding, unadjusted, bitter character who plotted and schemed in his obscurity what would have appeared to any disinterested observer to have been a madman's dream.

Hitler was not alone in his studies of the effects of persuasion over the minds of men. Ludendorff in his book, *Total War*, wrote: "In the total war propaganda must speak in the language which is understood by the people to whom it is addressed. Propaganda proper must be preceded by a careful study of the currents of opinion which exist in the enemy nation, of its hopes and duties, the attitude toward its government and the war."

It is difficult for Americans, with their good-humored, natural, and easy approach to life and their generous nature, to understand the concentrated bitterness and hatred that enveloped the lives of so many people in Germany, who had refused to accept defeat, refused utterly to adjust themselves to the thought that Germany could win back an eminent position in the world "short of war." To them there was no compromise. Their sole aim was to prepare for the next war. Since they recognized in propaganda a sharp weapon that had been successfully used against them—and that they had clumsily and ineffectively used against and among their enemies—they studied, planned, and experimented to make of that instrument of warfare a mighty, pervasive, and diabolical force. And their guinea-pigs for experimentation were the German people.

Hitler and his intimates were thorough men. Their master plan called first for the conquest of the German people. They intimately studied and plotted every characteristic of their fellow-countrymen. They probed every avenue of approach to influence their human nature. They were not inhibited by any scruples, since in their minds the end justified the means.

Of propaganda Hitler wrote: "In two years I was master of this craft." In *Mein Kampf* he frankly told his readers, "The German has not the slightest notion of how a people must be misled if the adherence of the masses is to be sought." [1]

The power of the deliberate lie was fully exploited by this man and his associates, and he wrote with enthusiasm: "The greater the lie, the more effective it is as a weapon." Moreover, it was easy to get away with lies because "The great masses' receptive ability is only very limited, their understanding is small, but their forgetfulness is great." [2] Hitler obviously had a certain contempt for his "master race."

Moreover, Hitler readily learned that propaganda could be planned and used to confuse and frighten people. Here again he experimented on human nature. He would employ propaganda along such lines to bewilder and strike fear among his enemies at home. He would later use it as a barrage to soften other nations before he attacked them. It was a form of artillery preparation hammering at the mind.

The story of how Hitler accomplished his purpose to dominate and finally control the minds of the German people may be read in the files of German newspapers in the 1920's and early 1930's, in the journals of the Nazi Party, in the tactics employed by his followers in the Reichstag, in the almost air-tight direction of their thoughts, hopes, fears, desires today. He convinced the German people, especially the children and young people who were to make up his armies, that they were indeed a "master race." He blotted out the insecure hold of democracy upon the Germans and substituted for it the worship of the state exemplified in hero-worship of himself. Where words were insufficient, the strong-arm methods of the storm troopers were applied. The brown-shirts became an army of occupation within Germany. The concentration camps became the bitter schools of those who dared to oppose.

While Hitler himself was the master persuader, Joseph Goebbels was selected by the fuehrer to be the directing genius of the Nazi propaganda machine; and Goebbels was given unlimited authority and funds to be used to direct the minds and attentions of the German people—and further staggering sums to construct propaganda machinery throughout the world. In every country where men could read and where radio could carry messages, this machinery ground out the program designated to spread the Nazi influence, to confuse or weaken opposition, and, in the words of Dale Carnegie, "to make friends and influence people." Goebbels's Ministry of Propaganda and Enlightenment extended its tentacles throughout the world.

There is a certain refreshing frankness to Herr Goebbels's statement of principles. He himself says his propaganda has only one goal: ". . . the conquest of the masses. Every means which can help to achieve this goal—is good. Anything which does not hit the target—is bad. Success is its only criterion."

In other words, the chief of Nazi propaganda coldly states that no holds are barred and that the end—success—justifies any means. No consideration of truth, decency, or humanity is a limitation.

It is in this manner that the Nazis brought total propaganda into their plans of total war, that three-dimensional war that is waged by enlisting military power, economic power, and psychological power for the purpose of overwhelming the enemy. In some instances the Nazis have demonstrated that economic and psychological attack are enough to bring home the bacon. At any rate they come first on the timetable. Military action is reserved until after economic power has been built up and until after "applied psychology" has been used. A Nazi professor of military science assists us in our investigation by describing "applied psychology" as follows:

Applied psychology as a weapon of war means propaganda intended to influence the mental attitudes of nations toward war. . . . It is essential to attack the enemy nation in its weak spots (and what nation has not its weak spots?), to undermine and break down its resistance, and to convince it that it is being deceived, misled and brought to destruction by its own government. Thus the people will lose confidence in the justice of its cause so that political opposition in those nations (and what nation is without one?) will raise its head and become a more powerful trouble maker. The enemy nation's originally solid, powerful and well-knit fabric must be gradually disintegrated, broken down, rotted, so that it falls apart like a fungus treaded upon in a forest.[3]

This method—to bring about decay in the will and purpose of the

intended victim before the fighting starts, is an outstanding feature
of Nazi propaganda and had never been practised before as a
method of warfare. The purpose is to confuse and smash the fighting will of civilians and of the combat services before the air fleets
unloose their bombs and the armies march.

NAZI PROPAGANDA STRATEGIES

We have witnessed the terrible pattern of this method of preparation for conquest in the period of "appeasement," of the so-called
"sitzkrieg," and of the collapse of one victim after another. That
now is a part of the history of the past several years. It no longer
has any secrets. What it *can* do we understand. How it can be
fought we also understand. We can take it apart and look at it just
as a student can dissect a frog in order to see what makes it tick.

The strategies of Nazi propaganda have been analyzed by students of propaganda. We will select the following analysis made
by Professor Gordon W. Allport of the Department of Psychology
of Harvard University. He describes six strategies as follows:

1. *Wedge-Driving*

One of the cleverest and most important of Nazi strategies is to
set people to quarreling among themselves. This propaganda
strategy is connected with the military principle of "divide and
rule." The Nazis set one country against another country and then
pick off the quarreling parties one at a time. Having used Hungary and Poland to help carve up Czechoslovakia, Germany then
gobbled up all three. Having provoked violent quarrels between
Bulgaria and Rumania, indeed between nearly every Balkan state
and every other, the Nazis swallowed them all.

In the propaganda field the strategy is the same. People who fight
among themselves fall easy victims to the Nazis. Often the propaganda attack upon other countries starts as it did in Germany with
an attempt first to set non-Jews against Jews. This is a strategy that
must be understood and must be defeated.

Hitler calls everything he doesn't like Jewish. About what is
Jewish and what is not Jewish he is not at all clear. But it doesn't
matter to him. He finds it convenient to have some scapegoat, some

one whom he can blame for everything, and some small minority of the population whose property he can steal.

But the main reason for the propaganda attack on the Jews is not so much to harm the Jew as to get all the other people to quarreling among themselves over the so-called Jewish question. Why? Because the Jewish race is widely scattered throughout the world. Therefore this poisonous propaganda potentially can take hold in many places and create much division.

The point is that some will fall for his anti-Semitic propaganda, and some will not; but both will begin to argue about the matter and will become bitter and intolerant, and lose their unity of purpose. On top of the anti-Semitism that is planted, Hitler's agents can then build further elements of the Nazi edifice of anti-democratic ideas.

But wedge-driving does not stop with anti-Semitism. If you have listened to the Berlin radio in recent years you have heard how it tries to drive wedges wherever it can: between Americans and Canadians; between Irish-Americans and British; between German-Americans and other Americans; between political factions; between the people and their elected leaders; between people and the newspapers they read. In recent months the most frantic attacks on the radio were made against the President, with the hope that a wedge could be driven between his leadership and the people of the United States. And unceasingly German propaganda is endeavoring to drive wedges between the Latin American republics and the United States.

You may say, "But not many people listen to the Berlin radio." That is true enough, but we must remember that the purpose of these broadcasts is not to reach the American population directly so much as it is to give the Nazi party-line to agents in this country, who after listening to it can, through subversive speeches, pamphlets, foreign language newspapers, or by rumor, put across the same dissolvent propaganda that Berlin has suggested.

2. *Accusation*

The strategy of accusation is a particularly poisonous form of propaganda. As practised by the Nazis against this country, the form it takes is to make Americans feel guilty and ashamed. Prolonging the war, they said, was America's fault. It was America's fault if her ships on peaceful trading trips were sunk. It is America's fault that the Treaty of Versailles was unjust. America is to blame for interfering with the affairs of Europe. America is imperialistic and wants to control all of Latin America.

These propaganda blows are below the belt, for people who have a sense of decency and justice are likely to examine their own consciences and admit that they do make mistakes. And we are a most conscientious people and are readily made critical of ourselves. Certainly we feel a bit humiliated that we did not in the last war really follow through on our own to make the world safe for democracy. But this propaganda of accusation, by encouraging us to take the blame on ourselves, is intended to weaken our will to fight the Axis. We can be certain that *Hitler's* conscience is not troubled by *his* breaking of every treaty and every promise, by his using torture on helpless prisoners in concentration camps, by his looting of Denmark, Holland, Belgium, France, and Greece, by his bringing war and famine to all Europe and to much of the world.

To try to make sensitive and decent people in a democracy feel guilt while the Nazi leaders feel none has been one of the constant aims of German propaganda.

3. *Rumor*

In wartime there are conditions that make fertile soil for rumor. In the first place we can never know all the important things that are going on. The theater of war is too big, the industrial life of our nation is too vast, the government is too complex. We cannot know all the facts, and when we don't know the facts we are likely to fall victims of rumor.

This is especially true when emotions of fear and desire come into play. We spread stories that reflect our fears, and we spread stories that reflect our wishes. Both classes of stories are likely to be false. Many times since war began we have had rumors of coming air raids in our cities—an expression of our fear. Many times we have heard false stories of revolts among the German or Italian people, of the exhaustion of Hitler's oil reserves, or of Hitler's sickness and death—all expressions of our wishes. Our fears and our wishes both give wings to rumor. Enemy agents exploit and constantly originate all manner of rumors. One great difficulty in fighting rumor propaganda is that it is difficult to trace the source.

Most dangerous to America at present are rumors that create doubt regarding the soundness of our military, naval, and air forces; that cast suspicion on the honesty or health of our leaders in government; that promote a feeling of helplessness before the Axis strength; that bring about disaffection in the armed services; or that try to put the blame for the war or the war's difficulties on our allies, upon our own government, or upon some group within our own nation.

4. Terror

To terrify the opponent and to break his will to resist is an important part of German psychological warfare.

The autumn before the attack on France the Nazis dropped pamphlets shaped like leaves from a tree, that said, "Next spring when the offensive comes you will fall as the autumn leaves are falling now, and for what?"

"Another tract was shaped like a coffin, and simply said, 'Frenchmen, prepare your coffins,'" according to Edmond Taylor.[4]

In the Battle of France, according to Taylor, the Nazis developed a peculiarly terrifying technique.

Spies with the French forces used small radio transmitters to send information to the Germans. Within a few minutes from German loudspeakers the soldiers heard all about themselves, their number, where they had come from, the names and records of their officers, and much more detail that showed how much the Nazis knew about them. It was a frightening and demoralizing experience.[5]

In the Polish campaign, Taylor reports this strategy of terror was developed in an especially devilish way:

German radio stations broadcast on Polish wave lengths. At first they gave out all kinds of false news, telling about Polish successes and about the entrance of Italy into the war on the side of Britain, and about the arrival of hundreds of British planes in Poland. The Nazis did this because the quickest way to shatter Polish morale was to arouse extravagant hopes which events would serve to destroy within a few hours.[6]

Nothing is so hard on morale as hopes raised high and then dashed. That is why Churchill spoke of "blood, sweat and tears."

He was not going to raise high hopes when grim months were
ahead. That phrase was magnificent counter-propaganda.

The strategy of terror includes also frightening deeds as well as
words. To bombs are sometimes attached sirens that give off un-
earthly shrieks as they fall to earth. Garish flare lights dropped
during an attack make a frightening scene through which scream-
ing Stukas dive toward the earth. It is a violent emotional attack,
the object being to make one's nerves give out even if one is never
struck by a shell. Emotional violence of this sort exhausts people,
confuses them, disrupts the will to fight, and creates panic in which
the Nazi gains an advantage. At least this is the purpose of terror-
istic propaganda. Sometimes it works, but sometimes it meets its
match in the stiffened moral fiber of its intended victims. Terror
bombing did not break morale in Britain. It strengthened it.

5. *Informing*

We must not make the mistake of thinking that all propaganda
is based on lies. Straight news, given out at the right time and in
the right amount, can have a powerful propaganda effect.

When the Nazis told the French through loudspeakers just what
regiment was present and where it came from; when they told certain groups at mess just what they were eating and just who were
present; when they told a certain village they were going to drop
bombs on it at 2 o'clock—and did so—all this information was true.
It was so perfectly true that it was terrifying.

But news, for the most part, does not interpret itself. In America
we have developed the radio commentator who helps us to understand the significance of the news. Berlin too has its commentators.
It is interesting to note how they slant the news differently for different groups to whom they broadcast it:

For example, when in 1940 America exchanged 50 over-age destroyers for leases of British territory to use as naval bases, the Nazis
gave the story at least three different slants. To the Germans, the propaganda ministry explained that this deal was a sign of England's great
weakness since she was giving up valuable territory for a few pieces of
scrap iron. To neutral European countries the Nazis explained that
the deal was worthless because the destroyers would never reach England; the Nazis' submarines would sink them all. To people in South

America the explanation went that the United States was trying to encircle them with more bases from which to attack Latin American countries.[7]

The point is that German news in wartime, though it may be true, is pointed for a propaganda effect, and is usually slanted to mean what the Nazis want it to mean in certain directions. It is therefore interpreted by them in diverse ways. We can be certain that seldom, if ever, do they let news go out that does not in some way help them.

6. Muddling

One of the chief aims of Nazi propaganda strategy is to muddle all the issues in order to create confusion and doubt in the minds of both neutral and enemy countries. Confusion is the best soil for Nazi advances whether made by the army or by fifth columnists.

While preparing to attack Holland the Nazi propagandists were working hard to make believe that Germany's plan was to invade the Balkans. Confused by this propaganda suggesting an attack on the Balkans, the Dutch felt a false security and lessened their preparations to meet the invasion. From time to time the Germans would bluff the Dutch by massing troops on the frontier and then withdrawing them.

For years the Nazis have attempted to cause confusion in the United States. Here are a few of the tricks employed:

First, there is the strategy of the "whopping lie." Berlin claimed that the British themselves sank the British steamship *Athenia* on which many American lives were lost. It claimed that England was preparing to invade Norway, Holland, and Yugoslavia. These lies were not intended to be believed so much as to create doubts as to whether Germany's attacks were entirely unprovoked aggression. But since it takes many people to make a world, many people believe lies.

The Nazis somehow contrive to call every act of aggression an act of defense. Confusion in some minds is likely to result.

Again, the Nazis make the most of the fifth-column scare to divert attention from themselves. One Berlin radio commentator said, "There is much talk of fifth-column activity in the United

States. Well, it would seem that such activities are being carried on; and if the investigators look carefully they'll probably find that the hatbands of the columnists have London labels." [8]

We have already noted the Nazi attempt to put the blame for their deeds upon Britain, the President, the Jews—on anyone at all in order to confuse the issue. And we recall Hitler's many promises that he would not make war, and that after the Czechoslovakian affair that he had no more territorial claims in Europe. Many people, to their sorrow, believed his promises.

A prize bit of confusion is the recent Nazi claim saying that Germany has the greatest democracy, the true government of the people.

The daring of all these lies startles us. We scarcely believe our ears. Who's crazy now, we ask? It's all so confusing. And that's precisely what the Nazi propagandist wants. He wants us to be muddled so that our fighting spirit will be weakened. He wants to befuddle our common sense. He doesn't want us to simplify our minds and our purpose.

7. *Exhausting*

From start to finish this whole propaganda barrage is intended to make us so weary, so exhausted that we are ready to give in.

The Nazis turn on their propaganda by degrees. Starting with cheap anti-Semitism, they go to sow confusion and doubt; then make threats of war; then hold out hopes of peace; then step it all up with new demands, new threats, whopping lies; then add terror, military attack, and propaganda to increase panic. When people are utterly exhausted, the propagandist still goes on with his alarms and suggestions of defeat. Britain and America, he says, must collapse. Germany is destined to play the dominant role in the world. The New Order is coming. Why not give in now? Give in and you will escape all this torment. It is inevitable. It is destiny—and so forth.

Even before the war began, Germany was giving these suggestions of hopelessness to the American people: A film widely shown in the country was called *Blitzkrieg in the West*. It was a long newsreel, a documentary film, showing the collapse of Belgium,

Holland, and France. "Its whole purpose was to show the invincible strength of the German Armed Forces, and to make people feel the futility of trying to resist them." [9]

But of course, this film didn't tell the whole story. It didn't tell what British, Norwegian, and Russian soldiers have told, namely that the German soldier is far from invincible. He can be defeated if met with equal equipment. The soldiers who have met the Nazi face to face are not impressed with his supposedly invincible qualities. It is propaganda that makes him look so irresistible.

These seven strategies of German propaganda warfare run like a web through their entire battle program of words and ideas. They are directed from Berlin, but they are employed by fifth columnists and German agents everywhere. Sometimes they are unwittingly used by muddle-headed persons who have no use for the Nazis.

In reviewing these strategies and fixing them in mind, Professor Allport suggests that their initial letters taken together spell a word.

W   for the strategy of Wedge-driving
A   for the strategy of Accusing
R   for the strategy of Rumor
T   for the strategy of Terror
I   for the strategy of Informing
M   for the strategy of Muddling
E   for the strategy of Exhausting

Together they spell WARTIME, and represent major propaganda strategies in the Nazis' conduct of a total war.

DEFEATING AXIS PROPAGANDA STRATEGY

In thinking of a defense against these strategies, it is well to think offensively also. The Germans do not control this field alone. Where they use propaganda in "total war" much as they might use poison gas, so can we, too, employ the genius of the American people for propaganda to take the offensive into all areas in which the Germans operate and into Germany itself.

The talents of American advertising men, journalists, radio experts, psychologists, and public relations counsels are already being combined in an aggressive organization to carry this phase of war around the world. Already our organization is operating. There will be many confused Nazis and Nazi sympathizers as a result. On our part we can bewilder and paralyze those who are committed to the Nazi idea; we can rescue and encourage those who have been trapped by it. And there are plenty of weak spots in the German armor.

Were not the Germans promised a blitzkrieg, a short war? Where is that "short war" now?

Were not the Germans once promised freedom from air raids on their great cities? How long did that freedom last—and what may they expect in the future?

What happened to Germany after the United States entered the first World War? What are Germans to expect when the inexhaustible might and productivity of the United States, and its vast man-power, are thrown into the final balance of the present conflict?

Do the German people know of the rising tide of hatred for Germany throughout the world, that is becoming greater with every threat, every extortion, and every word of their Nazi leaders?

What has become of Germany's one-time importance in the world of literature, music, and art? What great works of culture have been produced under Hitlerism?

What poison has been given the children of Germany, that they now have a "passion for death" and are taught to worship the strange god Wotan in place of Christ?

What does the word of a German mean now, after Hitler has broken every treaty he has ever made, all of his promises, has soiled German honor, and has behaved shamefully to the Dutch and Norwegians who did so much to care for German children after the last war?

Do the decent people of Germany, the kind the world remembers with friendship, know what Hitler has done to the wretched victims of his looting in Greece?

Who knows whose turn is next in a country where the Gestapo mark the disabled and the "too sick" for killing? Whose turn will come next when he or she is "too old" or "too sick" to be productive for the Moloch state?

Will there ever be sufficient "living room" for a country whose masters drive its women to excessive child-bearing, so that there will be more soldiers for more conquests?

These tactics—and there are scores of soul-searching questions that may be asked and answered—are based on essential truths. They will be brought home more and more greatly to the German people as they realize that no matter how many battles they have won, the fruits of victory are as distant as ever—more distant than ever. Already they question themselves whether THEY will ever enjoy the fruits of victory. They are becoming more and more acquainted with the fruits of death, of disgust, of hatred. When the tide begins to turn against them on the battlefields, there will be a terrific back-log of frustration on which American propaganda will work.

Allied propaganda may be depended upon to play upon the minds of other peoples by a method different from Hitler's. There is more direct talking, more truthful news. Effort will be made to clarify the difference between the propaganda of lies and dishonor and that based on evidence and the hope of a fairer world to come that may be rebuilt for the good of all. It will have its constructive side as well as point the accusing finger. Nor does it have to resort to invention to point that finger at the criminal acts of the Nazi ruling clique. The mass executions announced by the German authorities themselves are the true atrocity stories of this war. The cold and brutal starvation of the Greek people, after the draining of their foodstuffs and reserves from the country, is a tragedy that cannot be overemphasized.

Our propaganda does not have to be inconsistent with our ideals and principles. Certainly at home the American people would not tolerate the violent or lying type of propaganda. We are glad enough to have good radio programs dramatizing the Bill of Rights, arousing to a high degree our love of freedom, and reasserting the famous American vow by Thomas Jefferson: "I have sworn upon the altar of God eternal hostility to every form of tyranny over the mind of man." But beyond reaffirmations of our basic beliefs and traditional convictions, we Americans want the news, straight news, whether it be good or bad. And that is what our government and news agencies have promised us; the undoctored release of all news provided it has been checked as to accuracy and provided it cannot be of aid to the enemy.

There may be some question as to the extent to which this same policy should be used with the Axis populations. It is said that the novelty of it, the simplicity and decency of it, would win them over quicker than would a pounding with sledge-hammer propaganda.

Certainly we cannot afford to lose the whole ideal of our democracy in deceitful, lying, inhuman propaganda attacks filled as is Hitler's propaganda with promises that he intends to break. On the other hand, we cannot hope to defeat the Nazis by waving an olive branch and speaking sweet words of reason. We may have confidence that our own propaganda agencies will work out the right combination. There will be clever publicity, American style, with plenty of "oomph," appealing and persuasive. Yet it will not be contradictory to the long-range interests of democracy. Propagandists on our side have the advantage. They can easily show that the freedom of all peoples and the ideal of democracy are linked together; they can finally convince the common man in Germany that the American is just as interested as he is in seeing to it that when tyrants are destroyed a just and lasting peace shall be established, that we intend to win not only the war but also the peace . . . and to make of this peace an achievement for the betterment of the human race.

But this question of the strategy of counter-propaganda is not primarily the responsibility of the soldier. We have our own jobs to do. It is encouraging for us to know, however, that the agency of propaganda in our country is in competent, honorable, and trustworthy hands. And the greater its success, the sooner our work will be done.

But there are some things we as soldiers can do to defeat Nazi propaganda here and now wherever we encounter it in Army or civilian life.

For example, regarding rumors: we can and should make it a rule to question every statement that might damage morale. Unless news comes from authoritative sources we should neither believe it nor spread it. When a rumor-spreader passes on to us a damaging or confusing bit of gossip, we can and should give him to understand that he is, perhaps unintentionally, harming the nation's interest. Don't pass it up. If he is simply a thoughtless but loyal citizen, he will stop spreading his rumor; if he is disloyal, he will probably shut up because we have startled him by calling his hand. If he repeats, report him.

Men in service frequently meet with strangers, including strange women. It sometimes happens that these individuals deliberately put themselves in the way of service men and gladly provide some sort of entertainment. Note the conversation. Is it disloyal; is it anti-democratic? If so, make yourself a committee of one to silence it—in some law-abiding way. Get all the information you can about such a person and report him—or her.

We have, of course, trained government agents constantly tracking down spies and saboteurs. But every citizen—without becoming too hysterical or overly suspicious—should be on the watch. The tricks are clever. Efforts to divide your allegiance to our cause, to make you suspicious of our allies, to arouse your self-pity, or to cause you to have less confidence in our government and the leaders of our armed forces are all tricks that enemy agents or sympathizers may try to play upon you.

We Americans are so used to the fresh air of free speech that we are unguarded in what we say. We do not realize that carelessness on our part may make the task of winning this war more difficult. We tell things we should not tell and pass along information that might help the enemy if it reached him. We spread stories of fear or wishful thinking and we make complaints that, without our knowing it, may harm the morale of others.

Take the matter of complaints. We hold it our inalienable right to "crab." We criticize the government; we crab about our superiors; we crab about our work. We feel that it does us good to crab. Maybe it does, but suppose we ask ourselves one question. Suppose we ask ourselves what would happen if everyone crabbed as much as we do? What would be the psychological effect? Would it not be gloomy, depressing, discouraging, and defeatist?

Criticism is free in a democracy; but so too is appreciation. If everyone spoke as many words of appreciation for the good things he has in a democracy (compared with what the goose-stepping Germans, the humiliated Italians, and the poverty-stricken Japanese have) all morale would be lifted. In fact, we'd raise up our heads and sing.

When we are careless in our talk about fellow-Americans of other racial origins than ourselves, we are driving wedges of intolerance. When we are destructive or bitter in our criticism of the efforts of our elected government, we drive wedges that weaken our national unity. When we spread war gossip and war rumors that probably aren't true, we are creating confusion and perhaps fear. When we do all these things, we are doing the Nazi propagandist's job for him.

For so long have we Americans lived in the fresh air of free speech that we have almost no disciplined control of our tongues. We say what we please, when we please, and pretty much where we please. In wartime this habit can make trouble. As one of our Supreme Court justices said, "The right of free speech does not confer the right to cry 'Fire!' in a crowded theater." In a dangerous war we must watch our tongues. We have—and we will fight our enemies to preserve—the right to criticize. But if we use this right in a way that harms national morale we shall be doing the work of Nazi agents.

CONCLUSIONS

In the previous chapter it was emphasized that an essential defense against propaganda is our own understanding of what it is and how it works.

These two discussions have made it clear that there is no magic about propaganda. Its ABC's are simple, and even the new and violent strategies developed by Hitler for use in his "total war" are not hard to understand. We see now why it is that "applied psychology"—Nazi style—has taken its place in modern war along with ships, guns, and planes.

Understanding the nature of propaganda we can better resist it.

There is no reason to become upset and alarmed at the very word *propaganda*. In itself propaganda is nothing more than a communication intended to influence people's opinions. As we have shown, it may be used for good purposes: to raise money for charities, to get people to buy defense bonds, to arouse our loyalty to our own country. It can be used to strengthen the "war will" of the civilian population, to give a lift to enterprise, teamwork, and determination.

The connection between propaganda and morale is close. Our morale depends on the extent to which we can unify our purposes and consecrate our bodies and spirits to the task ahead. In building up this morale we need good, honest propagandists for democracy. We *want* our wills strengthened. We want to simplify our minds and keep our eyes focused on a common purpose. We welcome propaganda for national unity, that makes for courage and patriotism of the truly American type, that will help us in our soldiers' mission to destroy the enemy.

As a rule we shall have no trouble distinguishing between propaganda for democracy and the enemy propaganda that reaches us. Sometimes, however, we must be on our guard, for—*please note this warning well*—sometimes the propaganda for Fascism and Nazism in this country hides behind a patriotic mask. Nazi groups will *pretend* to stand for Americanism, and Fascists will speak of "liberty" and of "justice." Communists have done the same sort of thing for years. Not everything wrapped in an American flag is made in America.

Against subversive propaganda, in whatever form it comes to us, by far the greatest defense that we have is our own clear-eyed certainty as to what we ourselves believe and stand for.

Do we believe that a single party should take over the power of the state and with cruelty and violence stamp out every dissenting opinion? Or do we not?

Do we believe that the teachings of Christ and of the great moral leaders of civilization should be swept aside for a religion of nationalism in which the figure of a man is deified and glorified?

Do we believe that free speech, free press, freedom of assembly, and the right of a man to call his home his castle should be swept aside—and that the great books of free science, free history and a free spirit for men should be burned and denied us?

Do we believe that the state is so holy a thing that the group that runs it can plan and commit any crime in its name? Do we wish to rear our children in the belief that everything the state does is right? What is such a state other than the tool of an arrogant, dictatorial group of men using its power to magnify their own power? Do we believe in such insanity, such degradation of the human being, such violation of every principle on which this nation was founded—or do we not?

Let every man and woman ask himself or herself: Do we believe these things or do we not? If we do not, and if we are determined to die if necessary to bar this horror from our country and to defend ourselves against the poison that would rot the fabric of our democracy; if we are determined on a fight to the finish to stamp these degrading and inhuman ideas out of the world, then we need have little fear of totalitarian propaganda.

Understanding Hitler's tactics and strategy gives us protection from his psychological attack upon us. But hatred for his tyranny and ruthlessness and his abhorrent doctrines sharpens our battle weapons and our readiness to hurl them at the enemy. It is not enough to defend. With words and ideas as well as planes, tanks, and guns, we go forth to attack.

REFERENCE NOTES

1 A. Hitler, *My Battle* (Houghton Mifflin Company, Boston, 1933), p. 197.

2 A. Hitler, *Mein Kampf* (Reynal & Hitchcock, Inc., New York, 1939), p. 234. Reprinted by permission of Houghton Mifflin Company, owners of the copyright.

3 L. Farago, *German Psychological Warfare* (Committee for National Morale, 285 Madison Avenue, New York, 1941), p. 56.

4 Edmond Taylor, *The Strategy of Terror* (Houghton Mifflin Company, Boston, 1940), p. 207.

5 Same, p. 202.

6 Same, p. 203.

7 Reprinted by permission from *The Psychology of Social Movements* by Cantril, published by John Wiley & Sons, Inc.

8 J. S. Bruner, "The Dimensions of Propaganda: German Shortwave Broadcasts to America," *Journal of Abnormal and Social Psychology*, Vol. 36 (1941), p. 316.

9 J. S. Bruner, and G. Fowler, "The Strategy of Terror: Audience Response to 'Blitzkrieg im Westen,'" *Journal of Abnormal and Social Psychology*, Vol. 36 (1941), p. 561.

Conclusion

CHAPTER XXXVIII

CONCLUSION

In the chapters on Geography and World Trade, the stakes of war and of empire were briefly covered. These have to do with material things of life—for instance, the American standard of living and the "full dinner pail"—and with the responsibilities and relationships of world powers.

The portion of the book devoted to American history told of another phase of men's lives involved in the war. Here a free people came into being and, by dint of a war against the mother country, earned the right to determine by their exclusive will and judgment the way of life they wished to live. They moulded the Constitution to set up the machinery for a state of free men, and they added the Bill of Rights to protect and guard the individual liberties of a people. In those chapters are revealed the ideals and aspirations, the things of the spirit, for which men are fighting and dying today.

All of this has been challenged—challenged with bloody blows struck by the desperate and unprincipled forces that seek not only to loot the riches of the world, to exploit wealth and resources for military ends and for tyrannical control over civilization, but to hang upon free men the shackles of servitude and enslave the multitudes in the service of "superior races," white and yellow.

Old, hard-won conceptions of honor, heritages of the struggles for freedom in past ages; the ideals and philosophies of the pure in heart of past generations; the religion of humanity, of kindness, of mercy and of brotherly love—at these, too, the brutal blows are being ruthlessly struck in the cold, demonic fury of scheming, plotting gangsters who have taken advantage as never before of humankind's civilized and nurtured instinct not to believe such an attack was possible. Surely not that kind of war! Surely not a war upon the things of the spirit! Surely not such treatment of helpless conquered peoples! Surely not such objectives!

But surely it has happened.

527

The brief and general course of study prepared as the Second Army Educational Program is indeed a modest and unpretentious treatment of the subjects it has hurriedly covered, in order that American soldiers, who are a cross-section of American life, might better comprehend the large picture of the destiny in which they are involved, might go on from here with further studies or at least a clearer appreciation of the meaning and relationship of the current events that pass before their eyes in newspapers and magazines.

Their children's standard of living is being decided in this war. More completely their children's vistas of a free way of life are to be held open or allowed to close upon darkness. Nothing that victory can bring will add to America's material welfare, although incredibly much would be lost by defeat. No greater freedom and individual liberty can result from victory; but all that has been held dear to free men can be lost if victory is not won, whatever its cost.

Practically all the chapters in this volume were written before Pearl Harbor. They required little change, other than to indicate that Pearl Harbor had happened. What was involved in this conflict was clear before the first Japanese bomb caused American blood to flow.

The following remarks were made in an address by the Commanding General of the Second Army to the Economic Club of Detroit, on Army Day, April 6, 1942. Addressed to the civilian component, they form a fitting conclusion to this volume of lectures that were prepared for soldiers:

"How are we preparing these young men of yours? We are training them to be fit to fight; and we are constantly adding to the pressure of that training.

"There are few rules of honor for us to expect from our enemies in this war. We are preparing our men to meet foes that are strong, ruthless, tenacious, experienced, and infected—many of them—with the obsession that has been described as a 'passion for death.' Bluntly speaking, we are training your men efficiently and professionally to bring death to the enemy—and to do so at the least cost to themselves.

"This is no field for the amateur. From the infantry to the air force, this is a war that calls for professional skill, the closest teamwork, the sternest self-discipline, the most rigorous development of physical powers, and the highest degree of individual initiative, enterprise, and daring. It calls for leaders and instructors that are hard taskmasters; for the hard taskmasters are, in truth, the soldiers' best friends.

"And so, as you visualize their task, do not call these soldiers 'our boys.' It will take men, hardened men, to bring us victory and peace. Do not be sorry and soft over the youths in training. Your sympathy will not strengthen their muscles and their resolve. Your premature tears will not add to their manly stature. If they are worked hard and long, and their endurance developed by testing its limits, be thankful that their powers of stamina are being strengthened, that they are learning what physical and moral resources are within them, that they are being made fit to fight and kill their enemies.

"Demand the most of these young men of yours. Expect the most of them. Let them know it. Give your cheers to those that go forth for combat duty to preserve the Republic. They are the flower of our youth, the salt of the earth—these combat soldiers—and well may they be the proudest men of the land and the sons of the proudest fathers and mothers.

"Save your tears for the unfit—for whose unfitness you may in some measure have been responsible. It is they who are denied the honor of fighting for their country. . . .

"We are to pay dearly for the many years since 1918 when we had eyes but did not see, ears but did not hear; when we comforted ourselves with wishful thinking and listened to . . . the voices of propagandists and men of little faith spreading false doctrines as they deluded our people and demoralized the convictions and faith of impressionable youth.

"Today the guns of our warships thunder, and into their sides crash enemy shells. Our seamen of the merchant marine go down in their blazing ships. Our airmen battle against fearful odds as they come to grips with the enemy. Our combat teams and divisions go forth to meet the foe on battlegrounds determined by the enemy's successes. We are in a war like none we have ever experienced. We are in an endurance contest that will test our every resource of vitality, integrity, ruggedness, unselfishness, valor and stamina. This is the greatest war in history; and our destruction and reduc-

~~tion to impotence the greatest objective of the combined enemies~~
of free men.

"Gone from the minds of reasoning men is the futile and tragic conception of the static defense of the western hemisphere, as preached only a few months ago by the isolationists—the false, distorted theory that this land of free men can survive by taking those measures that have resulted in defeat wherever the aggressors have been given the initiative to make war on their own timing and according to their own plans.

"Today we know that all the world is our battleground, and that our troops must go forth through all perils to carry the attack to the enemy—that ours must be an aggressive war, bold, venturesome, loaded with the risks of daring action and distant objectives, a war in which *fighters will win*.

"Today we know that we must concentrate vast armadas of air and sea power, not to defend, but to advance our land forces against the enemy, to secure their beach-heads for attack, to aid them in pounding their war forward into enemy territory. Today we know that sea and air forces will not be our shield but our spear, that they will not save us from employing vast land armies but must prepare the way for those armies to come to grips with the land power of our enemies and destroy the evil at its source.

"There will be no escape from this reality, the alternative to which is defeat, humiliation and untold misery for humanity. We will enjoy the benefits of no tricks of military legerdemain, no ready collapse of enemy resistance, no secret weapons, no machine-made victory, no substitution of gasoline for the blood of heroes.

"For such a struggle—long, bitter and bloody—we are preparing our young men in the Army. Can *you* take it?

"For such a struggle, they look to you never to fail them, *not even for an hour;* never to fumble, never to falter, never to look backward, never to compromise with the evil that they fight. . . .

"One often reads and hears it said that food will win the war; or that planes, clouds of them, will win the war; or that machines and equipment, all kinds of equipment, will win the war.

"Let me tell you simply and emphatically—fighting men will win the war. And the greatest cost we will pay will be in the blood of the finest of our youth.

"Precious and valuable and necessary for victory as the machines and equipment are, man is the master machine in war. It is the right of the soldier and sailor as they face death to expect of you the *utmost* in production of the tools of war that, because of their stout hearts, will carry the conflict to the enemy and keep it from these shores.

"Whatever your sacrifices in treasure and labor, you will fare well at your table; you will live safely and securely in your homes; you will wear warm clothes and send your healthy children to school; you will have most of the pleasures and recreations to which you are accustomed; and you will live in your familiar circle, with your loved ones around you—except for those on the far-flung fronts of the Republic.

"It is those young men—the ones we have already sent to return the blows of the enemy, the ones we are now training to be made fit to fight, the greater numbers that are yet to be called to the colors—it is those men who will become acquainted with hunger and thirst, with oppressive heat and bitter cold, with endless fatigue and dreary days and nights. They will suffer in desert wastes and jungle thickets; and they will traverse treacherous seas in order to face even more treacherous enemies. They will see the ugly sights of war and feel its furies. They will bind the wounds of comrades and take last messages from dying friends. They will fight lost battles, some of them; and yet go on fighting to the end. Toil, exertion, danger, death and boredom will be their acquaintances; and over thousands of miles of distance they will ever be thinking of home.

"These are your men—our soldiers and sailors—the men who will keep war away from our homes, so that you may never hear in this fair and hallowed land the ominous, terrible tramp of enemy boots or see the horrible sight of local traitors elevated to positions over you. *You cannot do too much for these men.* . . .

"Let us moreover remember that we only have one leader, that we *can* only have one leader; and that he is the commander-in-chief of the Army and the Navy, the President of the United States. There is a world of difference between honest criticism, which is pertinent criticism, and that type that seeks to bury the fangs of poison in the spirit of the people. If there is one place for public intolerance, it is for intolerance of every attitude, every expression, every act that fathers and promotes disunity and creates distrust and confusion. . . .

"There is nothing more fundamental to our success than loyalty —the loyalty of the soldier to his commanders and to his comrades, of the people to their soldiers, of the nation to its leader in this time of peril. An Army without loyalty is without a fighting heart. A nation without loyalty is bereft of its soul. There is one common ground today on which only free men in this country can meet— the ground of a common loyalty, untouched by greed, untainted by jealousy and suspicion, and free of prejudice against any but the common enemy and those that do his work.

"We have one goal for the American soldier: that no soldier shall rest until he has advanced to grips with the enemy. There must be but one goal for those that labor at home: that none shall rest until he is doing his full share, to the utmost limit of his ability, to back up our fighting men. May our loyalty be complete and unswerving, no matter how heavy our losses, nor how mighty the bludgeonings of misfortune, nor how long and dreary the days before the tide of battle has turned. For then will come peace, the peace that will be earned no other way, the rich fruit of victory fertilized by the blood of countless men, the finest of our breed. If you do your share, *nothing is too much to ask of those men.* For none of us, no one of us will ever repay the debt we owe this land that is the one high beacon of hope in the world today, its promise of light tomorrow."

GENERAL REFERENCES

CHAPTER II, "THE GEOGRAPHIC FOUNDATION OF WORLD TRADE"

Klimm, L., Starkey, O., and Hall, N., *Introductory Economic Geography* (Harcourt Brace and Company, New York, 1940).

Stamp, L. Dudley, *The World: A General Geography*, 10th ed. rev. (Longmans, Green & Co., London, 1939).

Whitbeck, R., and Thomas, O., *The Geographic Factor* (The Century Co., New York, 1932).*

Huntington, E., Williams, F., and VanValkenburg, S., *Economic and Social Geography* (John Wiley and Sons, Inc., New York, 1933).

CHAPTER III, "THE MINERAL PROBLEM OF THE UNITED STATES"

Roush, G. A., *Strategic Mineral Supplies* (McGraw-Hill Book Company, Inc., New York, 1939).

Leith, C. K., *World Minerals and World Politics* (Whittlesey House, New York, 1931).

Zimmerman, E., *World Resources and Industries* (Harper & Brothers, New York, 1933).

Bain, H. F., and Read, T. T., *Ores and Industry in South America* (Harper & Brothers, New York, 1934).

Emeny, Brooks, *The Strategy of Raw Materials* (The Macmillan Company, New York, 1937).

CHAPTER IV, "THE RAW MATERIAL PROBLEM"

Chisholm, G. G., *Handbook of Commercial Geography* (Longmans, Green & Co., London, 1928).

Yearbook of Agriculture (1938), *Soils and Men* (U. S. Government Printing Office, Washington, 1938).

Kranhold, H., *The International Distribution of Raw Materials* (George Routledge and Sons, Ltd., London, 1938).

Lippincott, I., *Economic Resources and Industries of the World* (D. Appleton and Company, New York, 1929).*

* Now published by D. Appleton-Century Company, Inc., New York.

CHAPTER V, "THE STRATEGIC GEOGRAPHY OF 'LIFELINES' "

Spykman, N., *America's Strategy in World Politics* (Harcourt, Brace and Company, New York, 1942).

MacLiesh, F., and Reynolds C., *Strategy of the Americas* (Duell, Sloan & Pearce, New York, 1941).

Brodie, B., *Sea Power in the Machine Age* (Princeton University Press, Princeton, New Jersey, 1941).

Bacon, R., and McMurtrie, F., *Modern Naval Strategy* (Fred. Muller, Ltd., London, 1940).

Eliot, G. F., *The Ramparts We Watch* (Reynal & Hitchcock, Inc., New York, 1938).

CHAPTER VI, "THE NAZI–AMERICAN CONFLICT"

Farago, L. (ed.), *Axis Grand Strategy* (Farrar & Rinehart, New York, 1942).

Dietrich, E. B., *World Trade* (Henry Holt and Company, New York, 1939).

Spykman, N., *America's Strategy in World Politics* (Harcourt, Brace and Company, New York, 1942).

Condliffe, J. B., *The Reconstruction of World Trade* (W. W. Norton and Company, New York, 1940).

Laski, H., *The Strategy of Freedom* (Harper & Brothers, New York, 1941).

PART II, "THE WORLD CRISIS"

Millis, Walter, *Why Europe Fights* (William Morrow and Company, New York, 1940).

Orton, Wm., *20 Years Armistice (1918-1938)* (Farrar & Rinehart, New York, 1938).

The Treaties of Peace, 1919-1923 (Carnegie Endowment for International Peace, 1924).

Putnam, G. P., *Dictionary of Events* (Grosset & Dunlap, New York, 1936).

Hayes, C. J. H., *A Political and Cultural History of Modern Europe* (The Macmillan Company, New York, 1939).

New York Times, *Days of Decision* (Doubleday Doran & Co., Inc., New York, 1939-1941).

Birdsall, Paul, *Versailles, 20 Years After* (Reynal & Hitchcock, Inc., New York, 1941).

Churchill, Winston, *Step by Step* (G. P. Putnam's Sons, New York, 1939).

Harsch, J. C., *Pattern of Conquest* (Doubleday Doran & Co., Inc., New York, 1941).

Herring, P., *The Impact of War* (Farrar & Rinehart, New York, 1941).

De Wilde, J. C., *Handbook of the War* (Popper-Clark, New York, 1939).

Price, W., *Children of the Rising Sun* (Reynal & Hitchcock, Inc., New York, 1939).

Chakotin, S., *The Rape of the Masses* (Alliance Book Corp., New York, 1940).

Shepherd, W., *Atlas of Medieval and Modern History* (Henry Holt and Company, New York, 1932).

Watts, A. P., *A History of Western Civilization* (Prentice-Hall, Inc., New York, 1940).

Fisher, H. A., *A History of Europe* (Houghton Mifflin Company, Boston, 1939).

Hall, W. P., and Davis, W. S., *The Course of Europe Since Waterloo* (D. Appleton-Century Company, Inc., New York, 1941).

Sharp, W. R., and Kirk, G., *Contemporary International Politics* (Farrar & Rinehart, New York, 1940).

Brown, F. J., Hodges, Charles, and Roucek, J. S. (eds.), *Contemporary World Politics* (John Wiley & Sons, Inc., New York, 1939).

Benns, F. L., *Europe Since 1914* (F. S. Crofts & Co., New York, 1941).

Smith, R. A., *Your Foreign Policy, How, What and Why* (The Viking Press, New York, 1941).

Latané, J. H., *A History of American Foreign Policy* (Doubleday Doran & Co., Inc., New York, 1929).

Beard, C. A., *American Government and Politics* (The Macmillan Company, New York, 1939).

Maxey, C. C., *The American Problem of Government* (F. S. Crofts & Co., New York, 1939).

Baldwin, H. W., *United We Stand* (Whittlesey House, New York, 1941).

Shephardson, W. H., and Scroggs, W. O., *The United States in World Affairs* (Harper & Brothers, New York, 1940).

Selected articles from the following periodicals: *Current History, The Nation, Fortune, The Forum, Newsweek*, September, 1939 to January, 1942.

CHAPTER XXVII, "ORGANIZATION OF AN ARMY AND BRANCHES OF THE SERVICE"

Reserve Officers Training Corps Manual, Basic (Military Service Publishing Company, Harrisburg, Pennsylvania, 1939).

War Department, *The New Army of the United States* (Government Printing Office, Washington, D. C., 1941).

War Department, *Field Service Regulations, Administration,* (FM 100-10) (Government Printing Office, Washington, D. C., 1941).

War Department, *Field Service Regulations, Operations,* (FM 100-5) (Government Printing Office, Washington, D. C., 1941).

War Department, *Staff Officers Field Manual, Organizational, Technical and Logistical Data,* (FM 101-10) (Government Printing Office, Washington, D. C., 1941).

Baumer, W. H., *You're in the Army Now* (Robert M. McBride, New York, 1941).

Dodge, T. A., *Gustavus Adolphus* (Houghton Mifflin Company, Cambridge, Massachusetts, 1895).

Ewert, E. C., *The United States Army* (Little, Brown & Co., Boston, 1941).

Farrow, Edward S., *A Dictionary of Military Terms* (Thomas Y. Crowell Co., New York, 1918).

Phillips, T. R., *Roots of Strategy* (Military Service Publishing Company, Harrisburg, Pennsylvania, 1940).

Oman, Sir Charles, *A History of the Art of War,* Vol. II (G. P. Putnam's Sons, New York, 1898).

Oman, Sir Charles, *A History of the Art of War in the Sixteenth Century* (E. P. Dutton & Co., Inc., New York, 1937).

Weygand, General M., *Histoire de l'Armee Francaise* (Flammarion, Paris, 1938).

Ramnes, O. A., "History of the Development of Field Artillery Material," *The Ordnance Sergeant,* May, June, and July, 1941.

CHAPTER XXVIII, "THE SERVICES"

War Department, *Field Service Regulations. Operations* (FM 100-5) (Government Printing Office, Washington, D. C., 1941).

War Department, *Field Service Regulations. Administration* (FM 100-10) (Government Printing Office, Washington, D. C., 1940).

War Department, *Staff Officer's Field Manual* (FM 101-10) (Government Printing Office, Washington, D. C., 1941).

War Department, *The New Army of the United States* (Washington, D. C., 1941).

The Infantry Journal (Washington, D. C.), August, 1941.
Ewert, Earl C., *The United States Army* (Little, Brown & Co., Boston, 1941).
Phillips, Thomas R., *Roots of Strategy* (The Military Service Publishing Co., Harrisburg, Pennsylvania, 1940).

CHAPTER XXIX, "DUTIES FROM PRIVATE THROUGH GENERAL"

The Cavalry Journal (Washington, D. C.), November-December, 1941.
The Infantry Journal (Washington, D. C.), December, 1941.
War Department, Soldier's Handbook (FM 21-100) (Government Printing Office, Washington, D. C., 1941).
The Officer's Guide (The Military Service Publishing Co., Harrisburg, Pennsylvania, 1941).
The Infantry School Mailing List, *Men of War* (The Infantry School, Fort Benning, Georgia), Vol. XVII, 1939.
War Department, *Staff Officer's Field Manual* (FM 101-5) (Government Printing Office, Washington, D. C., 1940).
Complete Tactics: Infantry Rifle Battalion (The Infantry Journal, Washington, D. C., 1940 (Incl. FM 7-5).

CHAPTER XXXIII, "THE JAPANESE ARMY"

Bisson, T. A., *Japan in China* (The Macmillan Company, New York, 1938).
Colegrove, K., *Militarism in Japan* (World Peace Foundation, Boston, 1936).
Chamberlin, W. H., *Japan Over Asia* (Little, Brown & Co., Boston, 1938).
Layerle, Vice-Admiral J., *La Restauration Imperiale au Japon* (Armand Colin, Paris, 1893).
McLaren, W. W., *A Political History of Japan during the Meiji Era*, Charles Scribner's Sons, New York, 1916).
Naudeau, L., *Le Japon Moderne* (Flammarion, Paris, 1909).
Takeuchi, T., *War and Diplomacy in the Japanese Empire* (Doubleday Doran & Co., Inc., New York, 1935).
Young, A. M., *Imperial Japan* (William Morrow and Company, New York, 1938).
Young, A. M., *Japan under Taisho Tenno, 1912-1926* (Allen and Unwin, London, 1928).
Japan Year Book, 1921-22.
Japan Year Book, 1939-40.
Japan Weekly Chronicle and *Transpacific*, 1936 to 1940.
Fortune Magazine, February, 1942.

INDEX

Communism, 76
Communist Party, 75, 495
Concord (Mass.), 162
Condé, 355
Confederacy. *See* Confederate States of America
Confederate States of America, 244, 245, 247, 248, 249, 250, 251, 254, 255, 270
Confederation, the, 158, 184-190
Confiance (frigate), 228, 229, 230
Congress of Industrial Organizations, 276
Congress of the Confederation, 184, 185, 186, 187, 188, 189, 190, 194, 196, 207, 236
Congress (U.S.), and foreign affairs, 109-110; legislation during Depression, 312-313; meeting of first, 204; power challenged by Supreme Court, 239; Reconstruction policy, 269-270; *see also* Constitution
Connecticut, 154, 180, 184, 189, 227, 240
Connecticut valley, 146
Conscription, in Civil War, 247; in France, 330, 334; in Germany, 467; in Japan, 446
Conservation of natural resources (U.S.), 316-317
Constitutional Convention, 190, 191, 192, 193-204
Constitutionalism, 142, 144, 445
Constitutional rights of Englishmen, 142, 143-144, 157, 159, 163, 164
Constitution (frigate), 225, 226
Constitution (U.S.), amendments to, 202, 270-271, 278; changes demanded by New England, 232; checks and balances, 200f; distribution of power, 194, 204, 219; Federal courts, 198f; and foreign affairs, 108-110; framing of, 193-201; interpretation in 1930's, 313; Marshall's interpretation of, 235-237; powers of central government, 195f; powers of Congress under, 197-201 *passim*, 239; powers of President, 196-198, 238,

250; power of the States, 194, 195; protection against tyranny, 196, 197, 201, 203; is supreme law, 199f.
Continental Army, 171, 173, 174, 175, 186
Continental Congress, 161, 164, 172-177 *passim*
Convoys, 440-441
Cooper, James Fenimore, 250
Copper, 44
Cornwallis, Lord, 167, 169, 170, 186, 187, 236
Corporal, 380, 392, 393
Corps, 360, 412
Cortés, Hernando, 133, 134
Costa Rica, 29, 31, 45, 46
Cotton Kingdom, 254
Courts martial, 373
Covenant of the League of Nations, 68, 303, 307, 308
Coventry, 94
Crécy, Battle of, 328
Creel, George, 492
Crete, 97, 99, 100, 347, 407, 417-419, 480
Crimea, 104, 401
Croats, 75
Cruisers, 338, 343f, 437-439 *passim*
Cuba, 19, 46, 286, 287, 290, 301
Czechoslovakia, 54, 58, 72, 74, 79, 81-83, 87, 88, 89, 311, 497, 510

Dakar, 8, 38, 48, 50, 96, 347, 348
Dakota, 272
Daladier, 82, 83
Danube R., 8
Darlan, Admiral, 96, 97
Davis, Jefferson, 249
Dawes Plan (1924), 70
Declaration of Independence, 141, 164, 165, 180, 181, 182-183, 257, 271
Declaration of Rights (Mass.), 181
Declaratory Act, 158
Delaware, 185
Delaware R., 167, 341
De Lesseps Company, 286
Democracy, 51, 196, 527; in American Army, 176; American experi-

UNIFORM INSIGNIA—

* GUNNER'S MATE

* TORPEDOMAN

WARRANT OFFICER	CHIEF WARRANT OFFICER	ENSIGN	LIEUTENANT JUNIOR GRADE	LIEUTENANT

* TURRET CAPTAIN

* FIRE CONTROLMAN

OFFICERS' CORPS DISTINGUISHING INSIGNIA

LINE

BOATSWAIN

MEDICAL

* SIGNALMAN

RADIOMAN

MACHINIST

DENTAL

GUNNER

RADIO ELECTRICIAN

* QUARTERMASTER

* BOATSWAIN'S MATE COXSWAIN

COMMISSIONED AND WARRANT OFFICERS

The rank of an officer is indicated by the number and width of stripes on his sleeve and shoulder marks. In addition to the insignia of rank, officers of the several corps and warrant officers wear corps devices one quarter inch above the stripes.

CHIEF PETTY PETTY

The rating badges, con and specialty mark, of chie officers first, second and sleeve midway between the officers of the seaman bran the right arm, other petty left arm.

MASTER DIVER

DIVER FIRST CLASS

TORPEDOMAN THIRD CLASS

TORPEDOMAN SECOND CLASS

EXPERT RIFLEMAN

SHARP SHOOTER

SEAMAN BRANCH (NON-RATED)

OFFICER'S STEWARD OFFICER'S COOK THIRD CLASS

SEAMAN GUNNER

PARACHUTE MAN

GUN POINTER SECOND CLASS

SERVICE STRIPES ONE FOR EACH 4 YEARS SERVICE

GUN CAPTAIN

SUBMARIN

GUN POINTER FIRST CLASS

* INDICATES SEAMAN BRANCH

AVIATION MACHINIST'S MATE

AVIATION ORDNANCEMAN

AVIATION UTILITY